A NATURAL
HISTORY OF
TREES

of Eastern and Central North America

WITH AN INTRODUCTION
BY ROBERT FINCH

———————

ILLUSTRATED BY
PAUL LANDACRE

HOUGHTON MIFFLIN COMPANY
BOSTON

A NATURAL HISTORY OF TREES

of Eastern and Central North America

BY

DONALD CULROSS PEATTIE

Companion to this volume

A Natural History of Western Trees

Library of Congress Cataloging in Publication Data
Peattie, Donald Culross, 1898–1964.
A natural history of trees of eastern and central North America /
by Donald Culross Peattie : illustrated by Paul Landacre.
p. cm.
Includes index.
ISBN 0-395-58174-5 (pbk.)
1. Trees — East (U.S.) 2. Trees — Middle West. 3. Trees — Canada,
Eastern. I. Title.
QK115.P35 1991 91-2432
582. 160975 — dc20 CIP

Printed in the United States of America

FFG 10 9 8 7 6

The illustrations on pages 216 and 455 were
prepared by William Barss.
Parts of this book have appeared in *The Atlantic Monthly,*
Natural History, and *Scientific American.*

CONTENTS

INTRODUCTION *by Robert Finch*   vii

FOREWORD   xi

NOTES ON NOMENCLATURE AND DISTRIBUTION   xiii

ACKNOWLEDGMENTS   xvi

THE TREES OF NORTHEASTERN NORTH AMERICA   1

KEYS TO SPECIES AND GENERA   574

GLOSSARY   591

INDEX OF SCIENTIFIC NAMES   597

INDEX OF ENGLISH NAMES   603

INTRODUCTION

by Robert Finch

Like most children in the Eastern United States, I grew up thinking that trees grew everywhere. This despite my school geography lessons and all the Westerns and Biblical desert movies I watched, for everywhere *I* went I saw trees.

I grew up in northeastern New Jersey, nobody's idea of a sylvan paradise. But even along the cracked sidewalks of my town, trees were always at hand, not just as shady presences but literally, and somewhat illicitly, *at hand.* Each spring my friends and I sought out the crooked-branched, black-plated trees that seemed to grow in almost every backyard, playground, or park. Climbing their rough trunks, we stripped the fruiting branches of their small hard green berries, perfect ammunition for the peashooters that appeared each spring in our corner store. It was decades before I learned that these "pea trees" were actually Wild Black Cherries.

No less useful were the stunted thorny trees we found in vacant lots. Their sprouts, shooting up among junk and trash, made superb bows for our Cowboy and Indian games, and their weird fruit — large, warty, globular green spheres filled with acrid-smelling milky pulp — were superb for summer snowball fights. We might have taken more pride in our archery had we known that this tree was highly valued as bow wood by the Osage Indians of Arkansas and Missouri, after whom it was named — the Osage Orange.

And there was the fall ritual of helping our fathers rake the nameless, numberless leaves into piles in the street and setting them ablaze in the crisp early darkness of October evenings — a memory that even now seems not just environmentally innocent but curiously and powerfully primitive.

Like adults, trees were presences we children were ready enough to use but did not bother to know personally. It was only when I began to recognize that they were not a universal phenomenon, that the temperate zone woodlands of my childhood were something of a global aberration that I began to be interested in trees as distinct individuals. When I did, Donald Culross Peattie's *A Natural History of Trees* was among my earliest discoveries. I was initially attracted to it more for its vigorous narrative, sensuous descriptions, and contagious affection for its subject than as a source of factual information or as a field guide. Though *A Natural History of Trees* and *A Natural History of Western Trees* are excellent references, that is not their main strength nor the author's primary intention. As Peattie says in his Foreword: "A name is only a door open to knowledge; beyond lie the green ways of growing and, too, all that makes a tree most interesting and important to man. . . . To tell a little of these things is the main purpose of this book."

These volumes are above all collections of superbly wrought stories about trees; taken together, they tell one of the great environmental sagas in American history. In fact, these works might more accurately have been titled *A Natural and Human History of Trees,* for it is the long and intimate record of human and sylvan interaction on this continent that forms the focus of Peattie's great achievement. As Peattie says, "Nowhere else in the world . . . have trees so profoundly influenced the migrations, the destinies and the lives of human beings." We are a druidic race, both by heritage and by experience, and Peattie is one of our finest chroniclers. One can only regret that his plans for a third book, on the Southern Trees, never materialized; conspicuous by their absence in these two volumes are such magnificent species as the Southern Live Oak, the Southern Yellow Pine, the Bald Cypress, and the Catalpa.

Here one finds compendiums of colorful local names for trees; stirring accounts of our first encounters and relationships with hundreds of native species; stories of the historical, literary, and mythic significance of the great wilderness forests and of individual trees; and impressive, often appalling, narratives of the rise and fall of the great lumber industries. These books are a vibrant human document; through their pages flows a rich sap of heroes and villains, characters and comics, tragedy and romance.

Rereading these essays now, however, it seems to me that their most impressive quality is Peattie's ability to enter into an almost personal relationship with every tree he portrays. Though the two volumes describe more than four hundred species, there is not a single perfunctory account. His trees come across, not as abstract scientific flora, but as individuals, often gently imbued with an anthropomorphic will. The Hemlock, for instance, does not simply grow in rocky places, it "loves rocks; it likes to straddle them with its ruddy roots, to crack them with its growing, to rub its knees against a great boulder." Such descriptions do not sentimentalize trees; rather, they reflect the connection that we feel with them and the human responses they call up in us, as when, in the presence of the great Redwood groves, "you draw yourself up achingly, trying to find some undiscovered worth in yourself to add a cubit to mere manhood." Peattie *salutes* every species that he encounters, if not for its importance to human culture or its inherent aesthetic appeal, then, as in the case of the Pitch Pine, for the very fact that it "disdains even to be useful to man." He describes many remarkable individual trees (what botanists call "specimen trees," though he never uses the term) that have a special hold on the human imagination. Several species serve as springboards for what amount to sociological essays on American life. Peattie possessed an eye and an ear as fine as John Muir's for the religious and mystical feelings that certain trees evoke; he describes, for instance, the play of light and shade from an American Elm as "music without sound, a dance without dancers." In a two-page essay on the Balsam Fir he can, first, inspire admiration for the tree's remarkable resin, which makes a nearly perfect fixative for microscope slides, and then evoke a sense of nostalgia for its role as a Christmas tree, arriving "like a shining child at your door, breathing of all out of doors and cupping healthy North Woods cold between its boughs."

Nothing about trees seems beyond Peattie's interest or notice. Where else can you find a description of how a Saguaro cactus *sounds?* Or come on such wonderful throwaway lines as his comment that "several hundred pounds [of Mesquite gum] are exported annually to Australia, *for what purpose is unknown*"? Or find, along with descriptions of modern sawmills and paper-making processes, the assertion that "of all western Pines [the Ponderosa] seems to the beholder most full of light"?

It is in his treatment of the major tree species that Peattie's talents as a writer are given full expression. In the Eastern and Central North American volume his essays on White Pine, White Oak, Black Walnut, White Birch, American Beech, Sugar Maple, and dozens of others are rich, full-length portraits, skillful mixtures of geographic vistas, poignant elegies, botanical and cultural history, folklore, sylvaculture, ecology, humorous and sometimes bizarre anecdotes, and myth debunking (the famous Washington Elm in Cambridge, Massachusetts, was apparently only a slim sapling in 1775 when the general purportedly took command of the Colonial troops beneath its shade).

But it is with the Western trees that Peattie attains his loftiest achievements, particularly in the essays on the evergreen giants, which make up nearly half of that volume. The great Western monarchs — the Sequoias and Redwoods, the Sugar and Ponderosa Pines, the Sitka Spruces, Douglas Firs, and Western Red Cedars — compelled not only a greater and more dramatic scale of human enterprise than the Eastern trees, but also a new, and to some degree alien, set of emotional and psychological responses from Americans, including the sense that "such holy presences as these must be preserved." It was in the West, after all, that the great forest preservation efforts of this century were born.

At an environmentally enlightened distance of four decades, it is easy to criticize Peattie for what often seems a naive belief in American technology and "the greatest scientifically managed forests in the world." Though he is unflinching in his indictment of the lumber industry's exploitation of North America's irreplaceable wilderness forests, he also conveys the sense that we have learned from our mistakes, reflecting the nearly universal belief of the Eisenhower era (still alive and kicking today) that "properly managed" forests can accommodate *all* the needs of industry, recreation, wildlife, and broader environmental concerns.

Mistaken such faith may have been; naive it was not. While he may have believed in sustainable sylvaculture, he also recognized that it remained, in his day, an ideal rather than a reality. He delivers stern warnings to the forest industry and the Forest Service, and reminds us that not even the trees in our National Parks are necessarily forever safe. The conservation ethic Peattie espoused may not have been as radical as that of his contemporaries Aldo Leopold and Rachel Carson, but like them he knew that any enduring change in human environmental behavior must take place in individual sensibilities.

And it is in the celebratory spirit of books such as these, showing our affinity with our natural surroundings, that the basis for such change can be found. Rarely has American nature had a celebrant as broadly knowledgeable and as infectiously enthusiastic as Donald Culross Peattie. Though I have acquired several more up-to-date texts on trees, I still return to Peattie, not primarily to identify trees but to learn to identify *with* them — how they look and feel, how they have insinuated themselves into our consciousness as well as our lives. I open these pages, with their wonderfully evocative woodcuts by Paul Landacre, not to find "environmentally correct" attitudes, but to draw from their inexhaustible well of curiosity and affection.

Brewster, Massachusetts
February 27, 1991

FOREWORD

THE NORTH AMERICA SYLVA — our tree flora — is the grandest in the temperate zones of the earth, and in some ways the grandest anywhere. It has the tallest and the mightiest trees; it boasts so many kinds that there is no one who can say that he has seen them all in the life, and could name them every one on sight. It has still the densest stands of merchantable timber in the world; when the first Europeans came to our shores, our virgin forests, stretching from ocean to ocean and from arctic strand to tropic, staggered the belief.

Not in historic times have a great people and a great forest met in so tense a drama. That drama had the elements of the Greek tragedies, for it was the inevitable collision of destined forces. To each, the other force represented fate. The forests of America brought out in us, as fate will do, both our best and worst; they molded and they exposed us. We, in our human way, have brought out of the trees not best and worst — since trees are beyond moral judgment — but ever new qualities. First the trees were barriers and ambushes, then they became blockhouses and cabins, gunstocks and cradles, wagon wheels and railway ties. Now they are airplanes and newsprint, plastics and pre-fabrications. They remain our greatest renewable resource, and as every month brings forth fresh and more spectacular discoveries in wood technology, they may claim to be the most versatile of all crops. Always they have been, and will be, beauty and peace. They are the best we have left of wilderness, and the witnesses of our finest moments; trees still standing could tell us how Boone and Lincoln, Lewis and Clark, Washington and Penn took shelter beneath them or laid a hand on the bole while speaking.

This is planned as the first volume in a series on the trees of North America, north of Mexico. The present book deals only with the native species, and does not include hybrids. Its circumscription, or geographical inclusion, is most easily understood from the maps on the end-papers of this book. The western and southern boundaries are confessed artifacts, but they tend to include a sylva which has an inherent unity and to exclude almost completely the entirely distinct western trees, and — much less satisfactorily and with more inevitable overlapping — the southern trees. The subsequent volumes will deal with the western and southern sylvas, and with the cultivated trees of exotic origins.

Wherever you live, wherever you tramp or travel, the trees of our country are wondrously companionable, if you have a speaking acquaintance with them. When you have learned their names, they say them back to you, as you encounter them — and very much more, for they speak of your own past experience among them, and of our nation's forest life. So this book is intended, in part, as an aid to identification. The reader, unless botanically trained, may prefer to search first for a picture which resembles the specimen in hand. This is not an unsound method, if one will remember that leaves, in particular, are most variable on the same tree. The pictures represent leaves from mature, flower-bearing, or fruit-bearing branches. Those from seedling trees, and sucker shoots, and vigorous young branches may be widely different. When identification by picture seems reassuring, one should verify by the formalized description, which employs a minimum of terms not found in ordinary vocabulary; these are explained in the glossary. For the botanically inclined, field keys for identification will be found in the back of the book.

But a name is only a door open to knowledge; beyond lie the green ways of growing and, too, all that makes a tree most interesting and important to man. Almost every tree in our sylva has made history, or witnessed it, or entered into our folkways, or usefully become a part of our daily life. To tell a little of these things is the main purpose of this book. There will be those who will wish the author had told more about lumbering, for instance, and those who will wish that he had said less; more about furniture, or less; more about the ethnobotany of the American Indian and his trees, or less. He has told, simply, what has interested him most, stopping short (he trusts) of boring others. This book is designed to be neither brief as possible nor encyclopedic; it is an invitation to explore the woods for yourself.

NOTES ON NOMENCLATURE
AND DISTRIBUTION

THE ENGLISH NAMES of trees exhibit endless duplication and synonymy. Almost every tree has two or three names, and some have fifteen or twenty. Many names of trees are homonyms — one name for two or more discrete entities. Thus Yellow Pine may mean any one of a dozen species in the United States. To which species, one might wish to know, is it rightly applied? To this there is no pat answer, for lumbermen may call a tree one thing, while the same species is called by a different name by foresters. Who knows best — foresters or lumbermen? The answer would be subjective, and a matter of opinion. Farmers and nurserymen, landscape architects and North Woods guides, have each their own terminology for trees. Further, dwellers in one part of the same state may call a tree by quite a different name from that used in another section.

Attempts have sometimes been made to set up official names for trees — each botanical species to be assigned a single, supposedly correct common name which is not to be applied to any other species. But one and the same tree is Sweet Gum to the nurseryman, Red Gum to the lumberman, and its exudate is officially liquid-amber to the pharmacist. All three names are in old and good standing and if, in addition, we learn for this tree the picturesque name of Alligatorwood, we have but enriched ourselves. So it has seemed best, in the present work, to give a generous, though not necessarily complete, list of the synonyms of English tree names even when they are also homonyms. In choosing a single title to head the list, preference is usually given to the one used by foresters, in the full consciousness that other names might have equally valid claims.

The Latin names of trees, as given in this work, are those which, it is believed, should be employed by application of the Rules of the

International Code, in the judgment of the present author. Except in a few cases he has employed the nomenclature as given in the 1944 *Check List of the Native Trees of the United States,* published by the Forest Service of the United States Department of Agriculture. Yet after the rules have been applied as conscientiously as one knows how, there remains a large field where taste and judgment must play their subjective rôles. This is especially true of genera. Thus it is a matter of opinion whether the genus *Pyrus* is a large and inclusive one, embracing the Pears, Apples, Rowantrees and still other species, or whether it should be confined to the Pears alone, and the Apples should be considered to belong to the genus *Malus* and the Rowantrees to the genus *Sorbus.*

It is also only a question of judgment whether a given group of specimens represents in fact a validly separate species, whether it should be classed as a variety of another species, or whether it is a mere synonym of an older species interpreted in the wide sense. In general, in this work, the many varieties of species that have been described by botanists for North American trees have been passed by because they could be of slight interest to readers other than botanists. Most varieties based on presence or absence or kind of pubescence and glandularity and on variations in leaf shape would, if all enumerated here, lengthen the book while merely detracting from its easy comprehensibility. Rather have the descriptions of species been made wide or general enough to include most of these varieties.

The extensive synonymy that has grown up through the centuries, owing to changing views on nomenclatural principles, has not been given space in the body of the text, since it is of slight interest to most persons, but a selection of the most important synonyms has been included in the index. Thus a person who knows a certain tree as *Pyrus coronaria* will find it in the index where he is referred to *Malus coronaria,* the name under which it is treated here.

The task of stating correctly the ranges or distribution of our trees has been a difficult one in which the author and Dr. Norman Fassett of the University of Wisconsin have labored together. Paradoxically, it is growing harder and harder to state the ranges of trees! That is to say that botanists, and the entire public which has any interest in our native trees from any point of view, are constantly requiring a more detailed statement for the ranges of all plants.

Even as late as 1908, one of our finest botanical manuals was content to state the range of so common a tree as the Black Willow thus: "New Brunswick to Ontario, Dakota [sic] and southward." Today such a description of the range of this tree would probably not be classed as scientific information at all, for it would leave the limits of this Willow's distribution vague at all points of the compass, and students in thirty states would scarcely know whether the above statement was meant to include their home states or not. Nor is it sufficient, any more, to assert that a tree occurs in a given state. Every state in the Union can boast of more than one natural botanical province within its borders, and many states include ten, or even twenty. So that unless a tree occurs almost throughout a state it is usually requisite now that one specify which portions of the state are included or excluded.

The task of determining the range of a species must rest on three things — a wide field knowledge of plant distribution, access to a large herbarium or preferably many herbaria, and a close study of the published records of county and state floras, especially those of recent date. All three of these methods have their pitfalls and their irrefutable advantages. No one is sufficient, and the sum of all three is still never quite satisfactory. In consequence, the more conscientious the student the more tentative is his statement, and in that spirit Dr. Fassett and the present writer offer the range descriptions in this book — as true to the best of their present knowledge and belief. Much of the merit that may be found in the following statements of distribution is Dr. Fassett's. If there are any persistent errors of commission or omission, the present writer must bear the greater share in responsibility for them.

ACKNOWLEDGMENTS

THE AUTHOR is indebted to Francis H. Allen, the distinguished naturalist, for making numberless suggestions, editorial and dendrological; to Professor John W. Thomson of the University of Wisconsin for many valuable botanical and general criticisms; to Mr. Stanley F. Horn, editor of *The Southern Lumberman* for his most careful reading of the text with respect to lumbering and commercial uses of trees; to Mr. Ernest Palmer, formerly of the Arnold Arboretum, for his criticism of the treatment of the Hawthorns, and to Dr. C. H. Muller of the University of California for his revisions of the key to the Oaks.

Especial acknowledgment is due to Dr. Norman C. Fassett of the Department of Botany at the University of Wisconsin for his careful reading of the entire manuscript, above all with reference to the ranges of the trees. A nationally recognized authority in the fields of taxonomy and the geography of plants in eastern North America, Dr. Fassett undertook one of the most exacting and thankless of all tasks in revising for this book the statement of the ranges of the tree species included within it.

Much of the material of this book was first published in *The Atlantic Monthly, Scientific American, Science Counselor, Audubon Magazine* and *Natural History;* permission to utilize this material was kindly granted by the editors of these distinguished periodicals.

The author thanks the following publishers, and authors (when living), for permission to quote from the following books and articles: *The Flora of Indiana* by Charles C. Deam (Indiana Department of Conservation); *The Herbalist* by Joseph Meyers (privately printed at Hammond, Indiana); *Autocrat of the Breakfast Table* by Oliver Wendell Holmes (*The Atlantic Monthly*); *Some American Trees* by William B. Werthner (Macmillan); *William Byrd's Natural History of Virginia*, edited by Richard Croom Beatty and William J. Mulloy (Dietz Press); *Trees and Shrubs of Mexico* by Paul Standley (Chicago Museum of Natural History); *American Forest Trees* by Henry H.

Gibson, edited by Hu Maxwell (*The Hardwood Record*); *The Uses of Commercial Woods in the United States* by William Hall and Hu Maxwell (U.S. Department of Agriculture); *Travels of William Bartram* edited by Mark Van Doren (Dover Publications); *Relation of Alvar Núñez Cabeza de Vaca,* translated by Buckingham Smith (Grabhorn Press); *Growing Up with Southern Illinois* by Daniel Harmon Brush (Lakeside Press, R. R. Donnelly & Sons); *Pioneer Life in Kentucky, a series of reminiscential letters from Daniel Drake,* edited by Charles C. Drake (R. Clarke & Co.); *Pioneer Life in Dayton and Vicinity* by John F. Edgar (O. W. Shuey); *Edible Wild Plants of Eastern North America* by Merritt Lyndon Fernald and Alfred Charles Kinsey (Idlewild Press); *Travels to the West of the Alleghenies* by André and François Michaux, in Thwaites's *Early Western Travels* (The Arthur H. Clark Co.); *Travels in North America* by Prince Maximilian of Wied Neuwied in Thwaites's *Early Western Travels;* *The English Prairie* by John Woods in Thwaites's *Early Western Travels; Trees in Britain* by Alexander L. Howard (Collins); "Wild Plants in Cookery" by Milton Hopkins (New York Botanical Garden *Journal*); *The Katherine Petit Book of Vegetable Dyes* by W. S. and H. E. S. Viner (privately printed at Saluda, North Carolina); *History of Louisiana* by Le Page du Pratz (J. S. W. Harmanson); *The Maine Woods* by Henry D. Thoreau (Houghton Mifflin); *Joyfull Newes Out of the New Founde World* by Nicolas Monardes, edited by Stephen Gaselee (Constable & Co.).

In addition, a large debt is acknowledged to that classic work, Charles Sprague Sargent's *Silva of North America,* a monumental undertaking on which everyone who writes of native trees must draw heavily for information of many sorts, particularly as to the earliest discoveries and notices of our trees, by the first colonists and explorers. To the *Silva* the author owes a further debt for the extensive studies it contains of the weights of woods. It would be impracticable for the general student to assay for himself the weights of our many species of woods, and in the present work Sargent's statistics have been frankly embodied unless later analyses have revised his figures. It should be understood that such weights are, in general, mere averages or approximations of the weights of absolutely dry woods. They do not in the least represent the specific gravity of green lumber, and might not accord exactly with the weights of every specimen of dry wood that might be tested. If taken as general indications, and not as final and precise truth, they have their value.

THE PINES

(*Pinus*)

Pines are recognized by their resinous wood and their needle-like leaves which are found in bundles of 2 to 5 and enclosed at base in a papery sheath which may be, sooner or later, deciduous.

The male flower is a long catkin, usually grouped with several others on a terminal twig. Each cluster of stamens is surrounded at base by 3 to 6 scales. When ripe, the anthers are bright yellow with abundant, buoyant pollen. The female flowers, found on last year's shoots, form short, thick catkins with papery bracts, which soon disappear, and larger persistent fleshy scales become the woody scales in the mature cone. At flowering time the scales of the female conelet open wide and receive the wind-borne pollen. The sperm cells reach the egg cells and thus effect fertilization. The conelet, which till now has been small, begins to enlarge rapidly. When fertilized, the cones close again until the seed is ripe, or in some cases, often until years afterwards. The exposed tip of each cone scale is usually more or less thickened and shows the apex of the first season's growth in a scar or protuberance which is frequently provided with a prickle and transversely ridged with a keel.

WHITE PINE

Pinus Strobus Linnæus

OTHER NAMES: Soft, Sapling, Pumpkin, or Weymouth Pine.

RANGE: From Newfoundland to Manitoba and south to Iowa, northern Illinois, central Indiana, eastern Ohio, and Pennsylvania, thence south on the Appalachians to Georgia.

DESCRIPTION: *Needles* 5 or rarely 4 to a bundle, thin, soft, 3 to 5 inches long, bluish green, the lower side with 2 white lines, the papery sheath at the base of the bundle early deciduous. *Flowers* — male yellow, female bright pink with purple-rimmed scales. *Cones* on stalks ½ inch long, drooping, 4 to 8 inches long, light reddish brown when ripe, with thin, flexible scales without prickles. *Seeds* reddish brown mottled with black, ¼ inch long, their wings 4 times as long. *Bark* on young trees smooth, green, and shining, becoming purplish on older boughs and still smooth; finally furrowed on old trunks. *Wood* very soft, close-grained, very light (25 pounds to the cubic foot, dry weight) with white sapwood and reddish heartwood.

For three hundred years, till well after the turn of the present century, White Pine was unrivaled as a timber-producing tree. Perhaps no other tree in the world has had so momentous a career. Certainly no other has played so great a rôle in the life and history of the American people. Fleets were built to its great stands, and railroads bent to them. It created mushroom fortunes, mushroom cities. Earlier it was a torch in the hands of American liberty. Though now it has fallen dramatically from its high estate to a modest place among the other conifers, its saga is a tale worth recalling.

The hero of this saga may be distinguished at a glance, almost as far as it can be seen, by its pagoda-like outline and habit of growth. The whorled branches grow in well-separated tiers, as if they formed successive platforms of a tower. This structure is as clearly marked (where the trees have room to attain natural development) in very young specimens as in the oldest, though this characteristic outline is less obvious in dense groves where the older, lower branches have died and the congested crowns are deprived of full development.

The White Pine is a northern tree; in the aboriginal American forest it was perhaps the most abundant species almost throughout its range. Over vast areas it formed pure or nearly pure stands, or with only Red Pine for an intimate associate, according to the testimony of early "land lookers" (timber cruisers, as we would say now). The fact that today in those same localities it is intermixed with Spruce, Balsam, Aspen, Hemlock, Canoe Birch, Jack Pine, and many other North Woods species, only means that the kingdom which White Pine once held as its own has been invaded, since the days of the sawmills, by an influx of trees that once were its humble subjects. Much of Pennsylvania and almost all of New York outside the Adirondacks — so it has been asserted — was one vast White Pine forest. Pioneers used to say that a squirrel could travel a squirrel's lifetime without ever coming down out of the White Pines, and save for the intersection of rivers this may have been but slight hyperbole. When the male flowers bloomed in these illimitable pineries, thousands of miles of forest aisle were swept with the golden smoke of this reckless fertility, and great storms of pollen were swept from the primeval shores far out to sea and to the superstitious sailor seemed to be "raining brimstone" on the deck.

Nor can one easily conceive, from the second growth that is almost all that is left to us, of the toppling height of the virgin White Pines. Trees 150 feet tall astounded the first settlers and explorers; eighty feet or more of the trunk of such a specimen might be free of branches, marvelously straight and thick. On the present site of Dartmouth College, a specimen 240 feet in height was measured. This would surpass anything in the eastern United States and would do credit to Douglas Fir of the West, and even the Redwood. Similar heights were recorded from Maine, Quebec, and both eastern and western New York, in pioneering times. How many others were felled unmeasured

or unrecorded, we cannot know. It was possible for the old "land lookers" or "timber hunters" or "spotters," as they were variously called, to climb some lofty Spruce and from its top sight these mighty groves miles away on the horizon — "clumps," they called them, or "veins of Pine" running like sighing rivers through the primeval forest. A branch was thrown down on the ground, to point the direction of the groves, and the way was then found through the trackless wilderness by compass.

The first account of this tree in English appeared in John Josselyn's *Account of Two Voyages to New England* (1674): "The Pine-tree is a very large Tree, very tall and sometimes two or three fadom about; of the body the English make large Canows of 20 foot long, and two and a half foot over, hollowing them with an Adds and shaping of the outside like a boat." But White Pine had undoubtedly been carried to Europe by the earliest navigators in Canadian waters. Before the middle of the sixteenth century it was growing at Fontainebleau, and was mentioned then by the French naturalist Belon.

In 1605, Captain George Weymouth of the British Royal Navy sailed his vessels up one of the Maine rivers and, first of Englishmen perhaps, he got more than a coasting sailor's look at the White Pine. Away with him he took specimen logs of mastwood, and seeds of young trees. These were planted at "Longleat," estate of Thomas, Viscount Weymouth, second Marquis of Bath, since when the English have called our tree the Weymouth Pine. But it has never proved adaptable to the English climate. Only in its own country was White Pine destined to a great rôle.

Certainly it was the first gold that the New England settlers struck. The exploitation began immediately, and was so intensive that it was soon necessary to pass our first forest conservation laws. Not that anyone then could have envisaged the day when the virgin stands would all be gone, so vast and dense was White Pine's empire, but the wastefulness in the mills began with the first one, built about 1623, at York, Maine, and was never to cease while the virgin timber lasted.

It was not the wood needs of the puny colonies which threatened this great resource, but the fact that, aside from fish and fur, timber was the only great export of early New England. Within thirty years she was selling her White Pine not only to England but to Portugal, Spain, Africa, the West Indies, and ultimately even densely forested Madagascar.

How one could sell trees to jungle countries can only be explained by recalling that most tropical timbers are heavy and hard; they lack the very qualities of lightness and softness in which the White Pine excels. It is the softest of all the Pines of eastern America, yet in proportion to its weight it is strong. In proportion to its strength, it could be had in solid "sticks" of prodigious lengths for masts, such as no other known part of the world was then producing.

Certainly no wood light enough and strong enough for masting was grown in Europe in such lengths. And England, mistress of the seas and forever at war with the other navies of the world, had no mastwood at all. She pieced together her proudest masts out of Riga Fir (Scots Pine — *Pinus sylvestris*) but Prussia, Russia, and Sweden held monopolies in it on which England was dependent, to her own great discomfort. The Danes had only to close the Sound to cut off her supply entirely. So that the arrival of the first White Pine masts created a sensation in the Navy Board. Contracts were let at once to American agents like the Wentworth family of New Hampshire, and, with great mast sticks selling at £100 apiece, it is no wonder that the Wentworths grew rich and occupied a position of political power commensurate with their wealth.

In the meantime other colonists were growing rich. A great three-cornered trade was set up when, in all-Oak ships of their own building, the New England merchants exported White Pine to the Guinea coast of Africa, shipped on a load of human ebony, sold it into bondage in the West Indies, loaded up with sugar and rum, and raised sail for Portsmouth, Boston, Newburyport, or Salem. Of White Pine boards, and of the wealth that came from this trade, were built the quiet mansions of the seaport cities, the dignified doors, the exquisite fanlights. As tastes grew more sumptuous, an exchange might be made direct with the West Indies — light, utilitarian Pine for heavy Santo Domingo Mahogany to be made into the most elegant of early American furniture.

More and more the New England sailing ships came to be decorated by the famous American wood carvers with figureheads of a very special sort of White Pine, so smooth and soft of grain that it could be cut with almost equal ease in any direction. The woodsmen called it Pumpkin Pine, and they contrasted it with the coarser-grained Sapling Pine. To the lumberman, as to the wood carver, the distinction was profound. They asserted that Sapling Pine had more sapwood and that its trunk tapered more from base to crown, while the Pumpkin grew on uplands, and "held its contour better." Botanists and foresters today believe that the difference was a matter of age; they point out that in our day of second-growth Pine, Pumpkin is almost unobtainable; it was a product of centuries of undisturbed virgin timber growth.

Few historians mention it now, but White Pine was one of the chief economic and psychological factors in the gathering storm of the American Revolution, at least in New Hampshire and Maine. The trouble began in the reign of William and Mary, when by decree those monarchs began to reserve the grandest specimens for the use of the Royal Navy. In her desperate timber shortage, and her endless wars to keep the seas, the Mother Country naturally looked on aghast when pioneers, advancing far beyond the land grants, into the "Crown Lands" or royal domain, chopped down, or even burned down the finest trees along with the least, simply to farm the land. It seemed to the British that they were fighting the Empire's battles for the colonists as well as the home country; they could not understand what looked to them like the greed and short-sightedness and refractory spirit of the American pioneers.

To the colonists the same facts looked entirely otherwise. What the Crown called Crown Lands, reserved to His Britannic Majesty for sale, perhaps, to London land speculators, appeared to the Americans then (as the wilderness was to do for centuries) as Indian country, theirs for the taking. Unexploited, it was at once an impregnable fortress for cruel savages, and wealth, vast wealth, desperately needed by a struggling people. The man who could find his way fifty miles beyond the nearest settlement, into the primeval forest, cut down gigantic Pines, work them with boom and tackle to the river, ride and pole them down the whirlpools, rocks, and falls, to a secret market, perhaps in another colony, was (whatever else you called him) a man indeed. And as for masts for the wars of the English, the colonists had their own wars — with the Indians — and felt capable of winning them, if not called on to help fight Spain and Holland and France.

So one law, proclamation, or royal instruction after another was passed to restrain the colonists from what was called timber stealing on one side of the Atlantic, and on the other was practically considered the Lord's work. John Wentworth, baron of the New Hampshire pineries, later to become the last royal governor of that colony, was made Surveyor General of His Majesty's Woods in America, with authority to mark for the Navy Board every great Pine with a resented blaze known as the King's Broad Arrow. Tactful, cultivated, genial, he was a conscientious servant of his king. But well though he was personally liked by his fellow Americans, the King's Broad Arrow infuriated the pioneer, as the Stamp and Townshend acts infuriated the merchants, as the tax on tea the city dwellers. Not for this did the woodsman fight his way into the wilderness to make himself a home — only to find that his trees, as he thought of them, were branded with that hateful symbol of royal privilege. No wonder that he chopped them down, obliterated the blaze, sawed the giants into smaller lengths, and floated them down the Connecticut River to New London or some other Sound port for sale and export, perhaps, to England's enemies.

The Crown retaliated. In 1761 it instructed the royal governor that in all future land grants a clause was "to be inserted to reserve all white or other Sort of Pine Trees fit for Masts, of the growth of 24 Inches Diameter and upwards at 12 inches from the Earth, to Us our Heirs & Successors, for the Masting our Royal Navy, and that no such Trees shall be cut — without our Licence — on Penalty of the Forfeiture of such Grant, & of the Land so granted reverting to the Crown; & all other Pains and Penalties as are or shall be enjoined or inflicted by any Act or Acts of Parliament passed in the Kingdom of Great Britain."

More, a spy system was set up against those who cut trees in violation of these instructions, the spy to receive the land grant of the lawbreaker. In retaliation, the pioneers disguised themselves as Indians and did their cutting at night. A law decreeing that all who cut trees in disguise should be flogged had no known deterrent effects. American officers would not arrest other Americans for breaking British forest laws made in Britain for the sake of Britons, nor would juries convict them, or judges impose sentences. British agents drove the loggers from their homes and burned their sawmills, but the loggers had their own law — "swamp law" they called it, and it was not healthy for agents unaccompanied by troops.

When the storm of the Revolution broke, the Americans foresaw that their own White Pines might come back to them as the masts of armed ships bringing armed men. In 1774 Congress stopped the export of everything, mastwood included, to Britain. In April, 1775, after

Lexington had been fought, the lumbermen were patriots, to a man.
A British agent and his mastwrights were captured on the Kennebec,
with several masts. When the armed ship *Canceau* sailed into Falmouth to protect a Tory rigging and fitting the mast ship *Minerva*,
Maine men drove her off. Putting to sea, the men of Machias overtook
the armed ship *Margaretta*, boarded and captured her, and fitted her
out as a privateer. In revenge, the British flattened Falmouth to earth
with shot. Down at Portsmouth, the patriots seized the great masting
pools on Strawberry Bank. The last cargo of American White Pine
reached England shortly after Bunker Hill. From then on, the British
fought on sea with heavy, jointed masts of Riga Fir, while coasting
within sight of Pines that would have enabled them to meet the French
on equal terms.

The first flag of our Revolutionary forces bore for its emblem a
White Pine tree. But out of Portsmouth, November 1, 1777, sailed
the *Ranger*, Captain John Paul Jones, fitted with three of the tallest
White Pine masts that ever went to sea, and from the mainmast
fluttered a new flag, the Stars and Stripes, to carry the war to Britain's
shores.

Independence won, the New Englanders turned to their pineries as
the richest natural resource they had. This is not the place to tell the
story of White Pine lumbering, the greatest chapter in the history of
any nation's forests. There is a wide literature of the American
lumberjack, the old-style lumber baron, the whirlwind exploitation,
romanticized in such classics as John S. Springer's *Forest Life and
Forest Trees* (1851), bemoaned by Thoreau in our most beautiful
forest idyll, *The Maine Woods,* detailed in some twelve hundred pages
in Deffebaugh's unfinished monument, *The History of the Lumber
Industry in America,* recounted with gusto for the Rabelaisian details
in Stewart Holbrook's *Holy Old Mackinaw,* keened as a wake in his
Burning an Empire, and exposed in all its grime of ruthless waste,
greedy exploitation, bribery, corruption, labor wars, and timber thefts
in *The Great Forest* by Richard G. Lillard. To sum up a mighty epic
in a few poor lines — it was under the boughs of the White Pine that
there evolved the greatest woodsman the world has ever seen, the
American lumberjack (though much of the time he was a Finn, Dane,
Swede, Norwegian, or Russian by birth), an embodiment in himself
of the Paul Bunyan legend, a hero of courage and skill amidst toppling
giants and river jams, a demon of accelerating destruction. The in-

dustry built fortune after fortune acquired by ruthless exploitation, spent, in many a case, with the highest benevolence, evolving ever new methods, ever higher efficiency, including efficiency at lobbying and holding the forces of conservation at bay until the end of the northern pineries was reached.

In the days of its greatest utility and exploitation, White Pine gained its importance from factors partly environmental, partly inherent in the special properties of the wood. Most of the White Pine grew in a region of heavy snowfall, so that the logs could be, at low cost, sledded with oxen power to the river. The abundance of rivers made transportation to the mill inexpensive. Add to this that the extreme lightness of White Pine greatly aids it in flotation; heavy logs like White Oak or Black Locust would be floated with much less success. The great abundance of the forest, the continuity of its stands, made it possible to develop a concentrated industry, with mass production and mass marketing, and correspondingly cheap rates to the consumer. Then, too, the old-time lumberman was able to operate, in successive localities, on virgin timber. This yielded a much finer grade of wood — longer, smoother, free of defect and knot, and more easily worked than second growth can easily boast.

In the three hundred years of its exploitation, White Pine, more than any other tree in the country, built this nation, literally and figuratively. It would be impossible, in the scope of these pages, even to list all the uses of White Pine, the most generally useful wood our country has ever possessed. They range from the paneling of fine old colonial interiors to the famed bobsleds of New England, from hobby horses to the 72,000,000 board feet of this now precious wood which was still being split into matches in the year 1912. (Western White Pine has now taken over the burden of matchwood.) Of White Pine were built, according to François Michaux, speaking of the period around 1805, half a million American homes, those frame houses that are the most typical form of dwelling, save in great cities, from Maine to Florida, and west as far as White Pine was ever shipped on the treeless plains — houses viewed with amazement by foreigners, accepted complacently by natives. No other wood served so well for window-sash material, for it could be moved at a touch of the hand, yet did not warp. No other furnished such great clear boards for doors and interior finish. In every sort of millwork White Pine reigned supreme while it lasted. It was the favorite material for heddles of looms, since the weaver must lift or lower the heddle for every thread that goes into the woof. Because it is so light, smooth, easily planed and polished, untold amounts of cheap furniture have been made of it. It takes paint and gilt better than almost any rival.

The amount of shingles made of this Pine for the roofs of American homes is beyond calculation. In twenty-four years Michigan, Wisconsin, and Minnesota produced 85,000,000,000 of them. For two centuries they were hand-rived with a frow. An expert (and he was indeed an artist at his profession) could rive 500 a day and earn a dollar doing it. He professed to know when a given specimen in the forest would rive well, but if he had any doubt he whacked out a big block from the standing tree to test its splitting qualities. If they were unsatisfactory, he simply left the tree to bleed its resin from the cut, providing thereby a wick that would ignite the tree to its crown in the next woods fire. "The pioneer custom in Kentucky of killing buffaloes for their tongues was little more wasteful than the primitive white pine shingle maker's procedure. He used only the choicest parts of pine trees. The sap-wood, the knots, much of the heart, and practically the whole trunk above the first 20 feet were left in the woods to rot. It was not un-usual to sacrifice a 3000-foot tree to get 1000 shingles — throwing away about fourteen-fifteenths and using one-fifteenth. The introduction of shingle-making machinery put a stop to that enormous waste, for the saws could make shingles of knots, slabs, tops, cross grains, and all else, from stump to crown. The old-style method of shingle-making died hard, for the shavers opposed the introduction of machines, and declared the ruination of the country would follow so radical a revo-lution in a widespread industry." [1]

The famed covered bridges of America were built of White Pine in preference to almost any other wood, because of its long-lasting qualities and its lightness in proportion to its strength. Of this wood was built the bridge over the Charles, connecting Boston and Cambridge, the same on which Roger Taney passed his momentous decision in the Charles River Bridge case, dealing a blow at monopoly. The Delaware River Bridge at Trenton (where Washington had crossed through ice floes) and the aqueduct for the State Canal over

[1] William Hall and Hu Maxwell "Uses of Commercial Woods of the United States. II. Pines." Forest Service *Bulletin* 99. 1911.

the Allegheny River at Pittsburgh were White Pine structures. This aqueduct, considered a miracle of its day, was 16 feet wide, 1020 feet long; with seven spans, it carried one water-course, and the commerce borne upon it, over another.

"Many of the bridges in the interior of Pennsylvania and West Virginia, by which the old pikes crossed the numerous streams, were built of white pine," say Hall and Maxwell, "and it is said of some of them that no man had lived long enough to witness their building and their failure through decay. Some of these structures were marvels of efficiency. Extra-large timbers were unnecessary, and though slight in appearance, they carried every load that came during periods often exceeding half a century. They were roofed — usually with white pine shingles — and were weatherboarded with white pine or yellow poplar, and though painted only once or twice in a generation, they stood almost immune from decay."

In each state the White Pine brought sudden wealth; all the great rivers of northeastern America, except the Hudson with its alternating tides, were choked at one time or another with tremendous rafts of logs, each bearing its owner's mark or brand, like cattle going to market. The longest haul was from the pineries of Pennsylvania, 200 miles above Pittsburgh, to New Orleans, 2000 distant by the windings of the streams. One raft that passed Cincinnati covered three acres, and contained a million and a half feet of Pine, valued at $5 a thousand in Pittsburgh, at $40 a thousand in the Creole capital. When the timber was gone, the farmer followed, at a temporal distance of about twenty-five years.

Or he did so in the most rosy pictures of exploitation. Actually much of the land could never be profitably farmed. Between the millions of stumps it was acid or rocky; in place of the forest giants of yesterday spring up the Aspen and Spruce, the brambles and the fireweed. Too often the end came in fire and smoke. Forest fires in northern Michigan in the eighteen-nineties sent palls of smoke 200 miles up Lake Michigan to Chicago. The Peshtigo fire in Wisconsin killed more people than the Great Fire of Chicago that began on the same day. The story of what happened to Hinckley, Minnesota, is an almost unreadable record of human agony. The end was miles of ashes, like a landscape of hell, or ghost towns, or sawdust piles.

By 1900 there was nowhere to turn for virgin White Pine except the the southern Appalachians. And certainly there were some dense stands of White Pine in the high coves. Trees 150 feet tall were then known there. At Shady Valley, Virginia, the yield reached an all-time record, for the South, of 100,000 board feet of White Pine to the acre. So here the industry turned for a last skid to the mills. Not that many of the old-time lumberjacks of Bangor or Alpena came this way — they followed the lumber barons and the saws to the "big sticks" of Oregon. In the Appalachians, the industry developed with local resident labor; no great lumber camps ever evolved. Everything that had given the North Woods lumbering its characteristics was lacking in North Carolina; there was no snow, there were no rivers capable of carrying big logs, no great central mills. Instead steep inclines, narrow-gauge railroads, migratory mills, and stationary labor created a pattern far less picturesque, though not lacking in effectiveness.

The wood, too, was different. Appalachian White Pine is heavier and coarser than the northern grades, with a somewhat reddish color. In consequence it has never commanded the high price of the best northern Pine. The Southern boom in White Pines lasted from 1900 to 1915. Today the stand of White Pine is in the neighborhood of 14,000,000,000 board feet in the United States and 8,700,000,000 in Canada. Maine, which was one of the first states to lose its paramount position in White Pine production, is once again the leading region in the United States. This is because the second growth has, after nearly a century, reached maturity.

The glory and tragedy of the White Pine epic had its lessons, and its lasting results. The boom was, in the nature of historical factors and economic and social pressures, inevitable. The "bust," by dramatizing the situation as in the case of no other American tree, roused public opinion to the support of the conservationists who had fought for twenty years without allies. Though public opinion came too late to save the virgin White Pine, it made itself felt just in time to save the great forests of the Western States, to back Theodore Roosevelt and the Forest Service and National Parks in their battle for timber conservation.

RED PINE

Pinus resinosa Aiton

OTHER NAMES: Norway or Hard Pine.

RANGE: Newfoundland and the Maritime Provinces, southern Quebec, west to southeastern Manitoba, south to northeastern Minnesota, south-central Wisconsin, southwestern and central Michigan, southern Ontario, central New York, northwestern Connecticut and eastern Massachusetts; south on the mountains in Pennsylvania and West Virginia.

DESCRIPTION: *Needles* 2 to a bundle, 5 to 6 inches long, slender, soft, flexible, dark green, and lustrous. *Flowers* — male flowers dark purple, in dense spikes; female flowers short-stalked, terminal on the twig, and scarlet. *Cones* symmetrical, scarcely stalked, 2 to 2½ inches long, with thin, flexible scales and no prickles; when ripe, light chestnut-brown. *Seeds* mottled and chestnut-brown, ⅛ inch long, the wings ¾ inch long. *Bark* with narrow furrows and broad ridges, with red-brown, thin, loose scales. *Wood* with pale red heartwood and thin pale yellow sapwood, very close-grained, medium-soft, medium-light (33 pounds to the cubic foot, dry weight).

From aboriginal times to the present, the Red Pine has been the companion of the graceful White Pine, that queen of the forest. Like a consort to a queen, seldom mentioned, the rugged Red Pine has shared much of its fate. Red it is called for its colorful bark of armor-like plates. The name of Hard Pine was used only by the old North

Woods lumbermen, in contrast with the soft wood of the White Pine. The name Norway may be traced, according to François Michaux, in his *Sylva*, to a misapprehension among early English explorers who knew of the Norway Spruce — a vital wood of British import from Scandinavia — yet knew it not by sight. Widely held, in New England, is the erroneous belief that the name of Norway Pine derives from the town of Norway, Maine. The facts are that this justly proud and heroic town was not incorporated and named until 1797, yet in 1790 the name of Norway Pine was already in use.[1] "Norway" remains the commonest, and most misleading, name of this tree; lumbermen still maintain it with the stubbornness that only mistakes seem to inspire.

Red Pine's real empire lies around the north shores of the Great Lakes. There this tree attains its greatest height and girth. There it is the most beautiful tree in the forest. Sigurd F. Olson, in his fine book, *Listening Point*, about Nature in the Quetico-Superior region, has many references to the spell cast by the Red or Norway Pine. Here are two of them, quoted by permission of Mr. Olson and Alfred A. Knopf, publisher:

"Not long ago, walking in a stand of climax pine, I was thinking of the meaning of those old trees with reference to those that had gone. Among them was no levity or laughter, but instead the somberness and gravity that goes with life that has been long and a goal attained. Looking up at the great black boles of the White pine and the reddish trunks of the Norways, listening to the soft whisper of the wind in the high branches, the nasal twang of the nuthatches among them, I sensed the benevolence that comes only with age.

"Young before the American Revolution, these trees had seen the voyageurs and were tall and straight long before discovery. Two to three hundred years of age, they now had reached the end of their growth."

"A hundred years ago great pines and cedars rimmed the bay and the crash of combers during storms and the whispering of its sands when they were through were part of the music of Listening Point."

---

[1] See Castiglioni, *Viaggie negli Stati Uniti*, vol. II, p. 313: *"Pinus sylvistris, Norvegica,* Norway-Pine nel Massachuset."

Throughout its history a large part of the cut of Red Pine has gone to market as White Pine. The two trees were found growing together, fulfilled scores of similar uses, were cut and sold together — under White Pine's more aristocratic reputation. Serving more or less anonymously under the other tree's banner, Red Pine went to glory with it — to fame, and almost to extinction as a commercial tree.

JACK PINE

Pinus Banksiana Lambert

OTHER NAMES: Gray, Black, Black Jack, Scrub, Princess, or Banksian Pine.

RANGE: Local in Nova Scotia and New Brunswick, northward in Ungava almost to James Bay, and northwestward to the Yukon, south to northern and eastern Minnesota, locally on sterile soils to south-central Wisconsin, northeastern Illinois and northwestern Indiana, southern peninsula of Michigan, southern Ontario, and southeastern Quebec; rare in northern Vermont and northern New Hampshire, and locally plentiful in Maine.

DESCRIPTION: *Needles* sparse and scrubby, 2 to a bundle, flat on the inner face, short (¾ to 1½ inches long), thick, stiff, twisted and dull dark green. *Flowers* — male flowers yellow, in short crowded clusters; female dark purple, clustered. *Cones* dull green or purple, finally becoming shiny light yellow, 1½ to 2 inches long, remaining closed for years, the scales thick and armed with a delicate prickle which is usually deciduous.

Seeds black, triangular, minute (¹⁄₁₂ inch long). *Bark* thin, on old trunks with irregularly branched and braided ridges bearing thick dark brown scales. *Wood* — heartwood pale brown, sapwood thick and white, weak, soft, and very light (29 pounds to the cubic foot, dry weight).

The great North Woods of Canada and the northern United States boast three Pines, the stately White, once the most valuable of all their timber trees, the Red, hard and strong and noble of aspect, and the present species, the Jack Pine, a mere runt as to height and grace, a weed in the opinion of the lumberman, fit for nothing but pulpwood.

The French Canadian woodsman has — or used to have — his own opinion of Jack Pine. He believed that a woman who passed within ten feet of its boughs would become sterile, her womb closed — an analogy suggested perhaps by the way the cones remain on the tree for years, obstinately unopened, never seeming to shed their seeds. Jack Pine was supposed to poison the very soil where it grew, a superstition easy to understand since this tree is driven by its tall competitors to seek the most sandy or sterile soils, granitic rocks of the glaciated regions, and acid bogs. Cattle browsing near it might droop and die, it was thought. Almost any misfortune that befell a man's ox or his ass or his wife could be blamed on the nearest Jack Pine, and the only thing to do was to get rid of it. Yet so powerful are the spirits of perversity supposed to inhabit this ill-omened tree that no one who valued his life would cut it down. So wood was heaped around it, and the owner then set fire to the kindling. If in its turn it set the tree ablaze, the powers of evil could not blame the man!

Jack Pine constitutes the Pine barrens of central Michigan, famous for their infertility. In Minnesota it covers a wilderness 20,000 miles in extent, or about the combined areas of Massachusetts, New Hampshire, and Connecticut with, however, some large enclaves of Spruce forest in the boggiest parts. This area is, of course, not bounded by the International line but extends over a glacier-scoured, granitic and lacustrine area, north of Lakes Superior and Huron, and west to the Lake-of-the-Woods.

Fossil cones of Jack Pine from the Glacial Period have been found as far south as Spartanburg County, South Carolina, washed out, no doubt, from the Blue Ridge mountains, where this Pine must have grown in a cold epoch that brought a Canadian flora far down into Dixie. If in historic times the Jack Pine has not changed its boundaries, it has not suffered such loss of territory as have some of its betters. For the old-time lumberman left the knotty, stunted Jack Pine contemptuously alone. As for the forest fires, the strange cones that remain closed for so many years upon the tree will sometimes open only if fire has forced them! In consequence, Jack Pine does better in burned-over land than its aristocratic kin.

If it is a low tree, sometimes only 25 feet tall, never over 70, its twisted stocky form is not uprooted by great winds as are taller and more slender trees. If its wood is weak, soft, and light, its lack of worth has had a negative survival value. Complain as one may of its misshapen form, Jack Pine covers thousands of square miles of cold, sterile, wind-swept ground which might otherwise be bleak as the tundras that lie beyond the northern limit of its distribution.

Reckoned as a nurse tree, too, as foresters say, Jack Pine takes possession of lumbered or burned ground, able as it is to endure wind and heat and light and drought, growing rapidly at first, and thus it forms a shelter for the tenderer Red Pine seedlings. But the Red Pine is even faster-growing. After fifteen or twenty years it outstrips its nurse, and can live without its protection.

When growing well in the open, Jack Pine is likely to have a crooked trunk; only under conditions of forest competition does it grow straight enough, in its search for light, to produce saw logs. The cones have a humpbacked look in maturity. They may cling on the tree almost indefinitely before they drop their seeds with pale lustrous wings that bear them, insect-like, upon the northland's winds. Of all the features of the tree that enable one to identify it, these crops of curved-back, stubbornly unopening cones are the most visible at a distance.

Now that he has cut the great virgin stands of White and Red Pine to ribbons, the lumberman has come to have a belated respect for Jack Pine. It is cut for bed slats, staves for nail kegs, plasterer's lath, keg headings for slack cooperage, posts, fences, and boxes. Out of the largest and straightest trees a certain number of dimension timbers can be sawed. It was valued once as frames for the Canadian Indians' canoes; it is useful today for railway ties. Above all it is an inexpensive firewood, and with its resinous content it burns readily. Today pulp mills are chewing up Jack Pine where sawmills whined once for the flesh of White Pine. Thus Jack Pine carries the burden of many plebeian uses for which, otherwise, finer woods would be taxed.

A Jack Pine which is 60 years old is fast approaching its last days. At an age when the White Pine is in all the charm of youth, the plebeian Jack Pine is already an old crone of a tree which has not, in all likelihood, grown an inch for twenty or thirty years, but has merely clung on to life in the hard-bitten environment where it is forced to live. After its death the winter winds soon whip away its branches; then the bark falls off, leaving a naked stick of a tree to stand a few more desolate years.

PITCH PINE

Pinus rigida Miller

OTHER NAMES: Black, Torch, or Sap Pine.

RANGE: Rare in western New Brunswick; southern Maine, across New Hampshire, Vermont, and at low altitudes in New York to the Thousand Islands in Ontario, west to southeastern Ohio and western Kentucky, south at low altitudes to New Jersey and Delaware, and in the mountains to Georgia.

DESCRIPTION: *Needles* 3 to a bundle, 3 to 8 inches long, stout, rigid, twisted, dark green and shining, triangular in cross-section. *Flowers* — male yellow, in short crowded spikes; female light green flushed with pink, clustered on short stalks. *Cones* often clustered, almost without stalks, 1 to 3½ inches long, light brown, the flat, thin scales armed with a stout recurved prickle. *Seeds* mottled, dark brown, triangular, ¼ inch long, the wing 3 times as long. *Bark* dark red-brown tinged with purple, thick and deeply divided on old trunks into broad, irregular, connecting ridges. *Wood* brittle, weak, but durable, medium-light (35 pounds to the cubic foot, dry weight) with brown or reddish heartwood and white or yellowish sapwood.

Almost black against the sky, the tufts of the Pitch Pine's dark green and shining foliage stand out upon the twigs nearly at right angles. Usually the tree has a short thick trunk, more so than any of our other pines, with whorled, contorted and often pendulous branches that form a thick, round-topped crown. Where sea winds or mountain winds torture the tree, the crown may be flat-topped or lopsided or picturesquely broken and irregular. The cones tend to persist on the tree, not as living unopened cones, as in the Jack and Pocosin Pines, but dead and black, as if hundreds of black birds were clustered on the boughs. Or, after long weathering, they turn gray like the color of an unpainted, abandoned house down in the Jersey Pine barrens, while at a distance the trunk seems to be black.

The Pitch Pine is *the* Pine of Cape Cod and of storm-swept Montauk Point on extreme eastern Long Island. It is the most important Pine of rocky ledges in the Pennsylvania mountains. Above all, it predominates in the famous Pine barrens of New Jersey. This is a lozenge-shaped area, lying west of the great coastal marshes, on the average 80 miles long and 30 miles broad, corresponding almost exactly with what the geologists call the Beacon Hill formation, a nearly flat, shield-shaped area composed of alluvial deposits when this region was under the sea in Miocene times, nineteen million years ago. Since then other parts of New Jersey have been under the sea, leaving the Beacon Hill formation as an island; it has never been submerged again, nor glaciated. When the white man first entered this region, he found it one vast forest of Pitch Pine and Southern White Cedar, with more or less Shortleaf and Virginia Scrub Pine on its perimeter.

It was a region of sterile sands and bogs, and in the bogs was found abundant bog iron ore — some of the first iron available to the early colonists. In the era before the use of coal, iron was smelted by charcoal, and the Pitch Pine, right at hand, was an ideal wood for the purpose. Tar, pitch, and turpentine were extracted by crude distillation from the intensely resinous knots.

Down at Cape May a large boat-building industry grew up, and the Pitch Pine, though not a durable naval construction material, was heavily cut for it. Pitch Pine went also into barn floors, bridges, inexpensive houses. So began the intensive exploitation of the great Pine barren resources. During the Revolutionary War, and the War of 1812, the Pitch Pine charcoal and the bog iron ore at Batsto forged weapons for our armies, and there was made the steam cylinder for John Fitch's *Perseverance*. Today the hundreds of small forest forges of the Pine barrens are but picturesque ruins, if they survive at all; the weed-grown circular hearths of the charcoal burners are still discernible, to those who penetrate the sandy wood roads.

But a century of exploitation and of terrific, unchecked forest fires among these pitchy trees which become living torches have destroyed all the virgin timber. The Pine barrens are now invaded by the worthless scrub Oaks, and the Pines themselves are stunted, never growing 50 and 60 feet tall as once they did, and sometimes, when repeatedly fire-swept, ceasing growth altogether at knee height. Agriculture, however, has not been able to replace the vanished forest on such sterile soils, and today the Pine barrens remain a wilderness some 2400 square miles in extent yet only one hour by motor from Philadelphia, two from New York.

Dwelling in these Pine barrens is an isolated people known to the outside world as the "Pineys." Some, at least, of their ancestors were deserting Redcoats, others were hunted Tories, others still escapists from religious intolerance in the days of stocks and pillories and whipping posts. To these were added the "Pine Robbers" whose "cruelty and lust" were dreaded by every man and woman within their reach. The first sociological report on these people, cut off by the Pitch Pine wilderness from law, medicine, education, and commerce, was made by Elizabeth S. Kite of the Vineland Training School, who shocked the country with her article in *The Survey* for April, 1913.

Conditions have probably changed much since the black picture she drew of the Pineys' lives. Today they cut lumber, gather sphagnum moss for the florist trade, and raise cranberries in their bogs. Those who have known them best have not found them violent. A tale is related by a detective who came among them to discover the body of a murdered man. He enlisted the aid of the men who knew their wilderness best. As he tracked the woods with them he was amazed to find that they watched the tops of the Pitch Pines instead of the ground. At a certain point they stopped, and exhumed the body. The reason, they said, was that where the roots have been disturbed, the needles turn yellow.

The Pitch Pine's wood today enjoys no better reputation than the Piney's worst fame. It is full of knots, coarse-grained, hard to work. It holds nails and bolts so poorly that ships built of it have been known to pull apart at sea. Yet its resistance to water decay made it invaluable for ships' pumps and the old water wheels of primitive American mills. A barn floor laid in this wood in Pike County, Pennsylvania, was found so good, after 160 years of use, that it was taken up and relaid in a new house.

Pitch Pine knots, which weaken and disfigure the wood for carpenters' use, yet are so filled with resin that they resist decay long after the stump has rotted away, and in regions where the tree was abundant, they used to cover the forest floor. Pioneer children were kept at work, stooping and gathering these, day after day. The knots were then tied to a Hickory withe. Burning for hours, such torches lighted the pioneer for miles through the forest at night. These flambeaux made ideal lights, too, for "shining" deer — their eyes fascinated and illumined by the flame while the hunter drew his bead upon them.

The tar obtained from Pitch Pine was considered the best axle grease for wagons, and no wagon in the old days but had its tar bucket and paddle swung from the rear axle. Though today it is still employed for wharf piles, mine timbers, and above all for cheap crate material, the great days of Pitch Pine in the domestic economy of Americans are over. But as long as our forests stand, as long as trees march down to the sea or climb the wind-swept ridges of the Alleghenies, its dark plumy crown, its grand, rugged trunks, the strong, sweet, pitchy odor of its groves and the heavy chant of the wind in them will stand for something that is wild and untamable, and disdains even to be useful to man.

POCOSIN PINE

Pinus serotina A. Michaux

OTHER NAMES: Pond, Marsh, or Meadow Pine.

RANGE: Central and western Florida north on the coastal plain to Cape May, New Jersey.

DESCRIPTION: *Needles* in bundles of 3 or 4, triangular in cross-section, flexible, dark green and shining, 6 to 8 inches long. *Flowers* — male dark orange, in crowded spikes; female in pairs or clustered, on stout stalks. *Cones* heavy, very tardy in opening, almost without stalks, often densely clustered, light yellow-brown when ripe, armed with slender, incurved, deciduous prickles. *Seeds* black, triangular, ⅛ inch long *Bark* dark red-brown and thick, divided into irregular little flat plates. *Wood* medium-heavy (38 pounds per cubic foot, dry weight) and pitchy, brittle, coarse-grained, and soft, with dark orange heartwood and pale yellow sapwood.

Pocosin, in the language of the Delaware Indians and other Algonquin tongues, means a small but deep pond or bog, and that is the place to look for this curiously aquatic Pine. Only sometimes does it come far enough out of water to grow in marshy flats. Its black twigs stand somber against the sky; its dusky red-brown trunks grow spindling in dense stands 70 or 80 feet tall. But in the open the tree takes on a round-topped head and a short thick stem, with contorted branches often drooping at the extremities.

Printed on the sky or reflected in the water, the outline of this strange tree is never forgotten by those who know the lonely places where it grows; but of practical use it is little, save to burn fiercely on your hearth as it surrenders its stored resin.

LOBLOLLY PINE

Pinus Tæda Linnæus

OTHER NAMES: Rosemary, Old-field, Bull, Indian, or Longstraw Pine.

RANGE: Eastern Texas and southern Arkansas to central Florida, and north on the piedmont and coastal plain through the Carolinas to tidewater Virginia, the Delaware peninsula, and Cape May, New Jersey. It reaches the foot of the Blue Ridge in Georgia and South Carolina but is lacking from the Delta country of Louisiana.

DESCRIPTION: *Needles* in bundles of 3, pale green with a slight bloom on them, stiff, slender, and slightly twisted, 6 to 9 inches long. *Flowers* — male yellow, crowded in short spikes; female yellow, solitary or clustered. *Cones* 2 to 6 inches long, almost without a stalk, light reddish brown, with stout short prickles. *Seeds* blotched dark brown, 1 inch long, rhomboidal. *Bark* of the trunk of broad, flat, bright red-brown plates. *Wood* light brown to orange, coarse-grained, decaying readily, weak and brittle or sometimes hard and tough, medium-light (38 pounds per cubic foot, dry weight) with very broad, nearly white sapwood.

The dictionary tells us that a loblolly is a lout or clownish fellow, a thick gruel, or a mud puddle. Down in eastern North Carolina a loblolly is a natural pocket or depression, and in such situations grows the Loblolly Pine. But it is not confined to such areas. It takes over abandoned, worked-out, cut-over, or burned fields on the coastal plain, whence its name of Old-field Pine. The name Rosemary refers no doubt to the incense of its resinous boughs and foliage, and Bull to its great trunks sometimes 5 feet in diameter and 80 to 100 feet high.

Too southerly a tree to claim in this book the tributes that would be due it down South, Loblolly is used there on a wide scale for lumber. Inferior to Shortleaf Pine in hardness, it is yet one of the most important of American timber trees, and once it ranked close to the top in amounts cut. This was due not to the excellence of the wood but to the abundance of the tree, and to the size of the virgin timber and the broad boards that could be sawed out of it.

Plebeian as lumber Loblolly may be, but in the southern landscape it is second only to Longleaf in beauty — grand in its trunks like marshaled columns, colorful in its bark. So Loblolly gives to the vast, somewhat mournful coastal plains that loftiness, that movement and singing, which one longs for there, and seems to people with noble lives the sun-bitten stretches where so often no people live.

SHORTLEAF PINE

Pinus echinata Miller

OTHER NAME: North Carolina Pine.

RANGE: From northern Florida through the Gulf States to Texas and Arkansas, and north on the piedmont and coastal plain from Georgia to Virginia, and on the Delaware peninsula; on the coastal plain only, in New Jersey and on Staten Island.

DESCRIPTION: *Needles* in clusters of 2 or 3, flexible and slender, dark blue-green, 3 to 5 inches long. *Flowers* — male pale purple, in crowded short clusters; female pale rose, in clusters of 2 or 3 on stout erect stalks. *Cones* 1½ to 2½ inches long, dull brown, with flat thin scales and short, usually deciduous prickles. *Seeds* pale brown mottled with black, ⅛ inch long, triangular. *Bark* broken into big irregular plates covered with cinnamon-red scales. *Wood* yellow-brown or orange, with white sapwood, coarse-grained, hard, strong, and heavy for a softwood (38 pounds to the cubic foot, dry weight).

The greatest beauty of this Pine is its heavy armor of rosy-orange plates of bark. Under forest conditions it has a tall straight trunk, massive and even noble of aspect; true that its crown may then be rather thin and high, but this gives a lofty appearance to its groves, as if the tree disdained to put much effort into the gracile parts, and were devoted to growing clean straight saw timber. Given room in the open, the Shortleaf Pine may keep its lower boughs, that sweep grandly toward the ground, and a house beside such a specimen, humble though it may be, borrows some of the great tree's dignity.

Typical of the red clay hills of Virginia, Shortleaf Pine covers with its strong columns untold miles of such terrain. The pyramidal crown is outlined against any such southern sky; the thin high whisper is not stilled even on the hottest days; the warm resinous aroma is baked out eternally by the sun, or tinctures the very raindrops dripping from the needles.

For the first hundred years, this pine grows about a foot a year and as the tree seeds freely and bears heavily every two or three years, it bids fair to keep pace with the mills that eat it. From the early days of colonization began the export of this tree to the West Indies as general lumber, and it was used in the domestic markets, especially for masts, spars, yards, beams, decks, cabins, and interior finishing in marine architecture. The wood of the Delaware peninsula was considered the best in the virgin forest. It is often used as furniture core for veneering with another wood; it is also responsive to wax and oil and polishes, and so makes good flooring and interior house trim. The fuel value is high, and the firewood burns with a hot yellow flame. Very resinous splinters of the heartwood are known to everyone who has ever had a southern home, and a black boy to start the bedroom fire, as "fat Pine" or "lightwood" — a sweeter kindling for green or wet logs than any smelly Cape Cod lighter ever sold to the unwary tourist in New England.

VIRGINIA SCRUB PINE

Pinus virginiana Miller

OTHER NAMES: Jersey, Nigger, or River Pine.

RANGE: From upland Georgia and northern Alabama to southern and west-central New Jersey and from the hills of northeastern Mississippi through eastern and middle Tennessee to western Kentucky, southern Ohio, and the "knobs" of southern Indiana. Also on Staten Island, New York.

DESCRIPTION: *Needles* 2 in a bundle, stout, gray-green, 1½ to 3 inches long. *Flowers* — male orange-brown in crowded clusters; female pale green with rose-tipped scales, on opposite stalks. *Cones* abundant, only

1½ to 2½ inches long, often bent backward on the twig, shiny and dark red-brown, with thin flat scales armed with persistent prickles. *Seeds* ¼ inch long, oval, their wings short. *Bark* smooth, with flat, plate-like reddish brown scales. *Wood* weak, brittle, coarse-grained, light orange with thick, nearly white sapwood, durable in contact with the soil, and medium-light (33 pounds to the cubic foot, dry weight).

In abandoned fields, by small streams, on the rolling red clay hills of the piedmont, this Pine is abundant, forming in youth thickets with, presently, many dead branches. Few plants can tolerate association with a dense young growth of Scrub Pine except catbriars and Japanese honeysuckle. Then, as these sapling thickets grow up and thin themselves out by elimination, other plants enter into association with them. Thus, when Scrub Pine takes over an abandoned field, its seedlings begin to appear about the fifth to tenth year, succeeding broom sedge. After 25 to 50 years Redbud and Dogwood find a place here, and later more valuable and taller trees finally overtop and crowd Scrub Pine out. As the wood is almost useless except for fuel, the greatest value of Scrub Pine thus is that it swiftly takes over abandoned lands and holds them for seventy-five years or so until better types of forest can, in the cycle of succession, assume control. No other tree in its range does this more effectively.

At first one may be inclined to despise this tree, with its spindling trunks and its bark neither blocked out in great plates like the Short-leaf's nor smooth as the White Pine's, its needles in scrubby tufts, with none of the flashing beauty of the Longleaf's, and its inelegant crop of weathered cones. Yet an old high grove of Scrub Pine has its own odd, temple-like nobility, it is so full of its own music and incense. The crowns stand dark against the sky; the outlined branches are at once unsymmetrical and fine of line, when compared with the more ponderous outlines of its frequent companion, the Loblolly. A Chinese landscape painter would not despise the silhouette of these trees, marching over the crest of some hill or etched against the slanting lines of Virginia's winter rains.

Indeed, the Scrub Pine in Virginia is characteristic of all the piedmont country, sometimes forming pure groves. Many of the Civil War battlefields had then, and still have, this Pine for their commonest forest tree, and to one who visits them its somber shapes, its elegiac sighing become fixed in the mind with these mournful places of glory.

BUR PINE

Pinus pungens Lambert

OTHER NAMES: Table Mountain, Southern Mountain, Prickly, or Hickory Pine.

RANGE: In the Appalachians from Georgia to southern Pennsylvania, with isolated localities on the piedmont of Virginia and Maryland, and in the mountainous region of New Jersey.

DESCRIPTION: *Needles* 2 to a bundle, 1¼ to 2½ inches long, twisted, dark blue-green, rigid and crowded. *Flowers* — male yellow, in long loose spikes; female long-stalked and clustered. *Cones* seated directly and inclined backward on the twig, light brown and shining, unsymmetrical, very tardy in opening, often whorled in dense clusters, with thick scales armed with short thick fierce prickles. *Seeds* ¼ inch long, triangular, roughened and light brown. *Bark* thick and broken into irregularly shaped reddish plates. *Wood* soft, weak, brittle, coarse-grained, with pale brown heartwood and thick white sapwood, and medium-light (30 pounds to the cubic foot, dry weight).

Sooner or later he who rides or climbs in the southern Appalachians finds himself on some wind-swept, sun-bitten rocky ledge where a grove of the strange Bur Pine suddenly surrounds him. It may reach 60 feet, up there in the Great Smokies, with stout vigorous branches that sweep to tne ground, in trees growing in the open, while the upper branches curve upward toward its rather flattened top. Its big cones encircle the twigs in dense clusters, each knob of the cone armed with a horrendous hooked prickle, as if to guard the harsh fruit through to its slow maturity. For the cones cling on the tree till ripe, yet ripeness may not come for 20 years. And the tree allows no one without an axe to bear off these mace-like trophies; elastic though the branches are, they are unbreakable by human muscle.

This intransigent Pine has no business future, nor will it — slow-growing, stingy of shade, without one concession to grace — ever find a rôle in horticulture. Its place is high on mountain ridges, where it looks down on the soaring buzzards, where the wildcat lives and the rattler suns his coils.

THE LARCHES
(*Larix*)

THE LARCHES have central trunks that run up straight through the tree like masts, and tier upon tier of whorled branches with frequently pendulous branchlets that are studded with knob-like short-shoots (spurs). On these the slender, flat, keeled foliage is borne in spreading clusters of many needles of different length; or on fast-growing, leading shoots the needles are single, sparsely spiraling around the twig. Distinct rings of old leaf scars mark each season's growth on the short-shoots, while the long shoots are grooved and channeled by the scars of old leaf bases.

The blood-red buds on the tips of the short-shoots produce not only the leaves but the flowers, which appear in earliest spring before the foliage. The male flowers are composed of numerous stamens, arranged in catkins, while the female come in conelets, with vivid scales. The small cones, which ripen the first year, are erect on the twig, with leathery, woody scales each one of which is accompanied by a papery, bright-colored, extruded scale. After the winged seeds have fallen, the dead, blackened cones cling for years on the twigs, adding to the somber aspect of these northerly trees.

TAMARACK

Larix laricina (Du Roi) K. Koch

OTHER NAMES: American, Black, or Red Larch. Hackmatack.

RANGE: Almost throughout interior Labrador, Newfoundland, Quebec, the Maritime Provinces of Canada, and Ontario, and all the way across Canada between the prairies and the tundra, to the shores of the arctic in Mackenzie, and down the Yukon River to its mouth. South through Minnesota and Wisconsin to northern parts of Illinois, Indiana, and Ohio, northernmost West Virginia, Pennsylvania except the southeastern parts, extreme northwestern New Jersey, throughout New York State except Long Island and Staten Island. Absent from eastern Connecticut, from Rhode Island, Cape Cod and southeastern Massachusetts.

DESCRIPTION: *Needles* numerous, in bundles, on short spur-like shoots, or solitary and spiraling around the stem on long shoots, triangular in cross-section, with the upper side rounded, the lower sides keeled, ½ to 1 inch long, bright light green. *Flowers* — male bright yellow, nearly spherical, seated directly on the twig, female oblong, the scarlet scales extended with long green tips. *Cones* ½ to ¾ inch long, with about 20 thin bright chestnut-brown scales. *Seeds* ⅛ inch long, with long chestnut-brown wings. *Bark* thin, bright reddish brown, scaly. *Wood* heavy for a Conifer (38 pounds to the cubic foot, dry weight), hard, very strong, close-grained, and long durable.

The Tamarack goes further north than any other tree in North America and at the farthest limits of its distribution it grows in summer by the light of the midnight sun. At that season it is one of the most tenderly beautiful of all native trees, with its pale green needles like a rime of life and light.

But in winter it is the deadest-looking vegetation on the globe. Many a tenderfoot has been horrified, coming upon a Tamarack swamp, to see miles of these trees that he concludes have been swept by fire the bark seemingly scorched to its rusty hue, the twigs apparently seared to stumps, and the corpse-like forms still standing rooted in the muck.

Then when spring comes to the North Woods, with that apologetic rush and will to please which well become the tardy, these same trees that one thought were but "crisps" begin, soon after the wild geese have gone over and the ice in the beaver ponds is melted, to put forth an unexpected, subtle bloom. The flowers are followed in a few weeks by the renewing foliage, for the Larches are the only Conifers (except the Bald Cypress of the South) which drop their needles in autumn and renew them again each spring. And there is no more delicate charm in the North Woods than the moment when the soft, pale-green needles first begin to clothe the military sternness of the Larch. So fine is that foliage, and so oddly clustered in sparse tufts, that Tamarack has the distinction among our trees of giving the least shade. The northern sunlight reaches right to the bottom of a Tamarack grove.

Tamarack may grow on high land, and in the far northern Rockies even tries to climb their bases, but over most of its vast range it loves boggy land; it delights in old, silted-up beaver ponds while the soil is still quaky with water, where one can neither paddle a canoe nor walk, nor even touch solid bottom with a ten-foot pole. It is especially abundant in the interior of Labrador, where it constitutes itself the chief tree inhabitant, but reaches its finest dimensions north of Lake Winnipeg. There, and in Maine and New Brunswick, people often call it "Juniper" and, absurd and misleading though such a name is, the traveler must accept local names as facts, in the district where they are used.

Long before the white man came, the Indians used the roots of Tamarack for sewing the strips of Birch bark in their beautiful canoes. The best roots came from trees in beaver ponds, for they were especially tough, pliant, slender, and elongated. When the white man began to build his own boats, he sought out Tamarack roots for a very different purpose. He used them for "instep crooks" or ship's knees —

that is, a solid piece of durable wood with a natural angle or bend. Such bends were found in the roots of Tamaracks which grew in shallow mud underlain by a hardpan clay that deflected the growing roots at a sharp angle. However, only small knees are ever made by Tamarack; the great knees of the sailing ships were got out of Southern Live Oak and Eastern White Oak. But because it is so durable in contact with water, Tamarack is still used by builders of small boats for knees, stringers, keels, and floors.

Durable too in contact with the soil, Tamarack was ideal for railroad ties before creosoting rendered almost any hard wood suitable, and the mast-like trunks had only to be lopped of their branches to make telegraph poles. Yet it is not the axe that has decimated the great northern stands of Tamarack, but an insect pest, the sawfly, which a few years ago swept them like a plague, leaving the great trees skeleton. New growth is fortunately coming in.

It must have been the Indians who showed the first New England settlers hidden virtue in the Tamarack. Good old John Josselyn, first naturalist-historian of the Bay Colony, recorded: "The Turpentine that issueth from the Larch Tree is singularly good to heal wounds, and to draw out the malice . . . of any Ach rubbing the place therewith." As long as woodsmen know their woods, the Tamarack can prove their friend in time of need, for its curative powers are genuine.

THE HEMLOCKS
(*Tsuga*)

HEMLOCKS are soft-wooded, densely pyramidal trees, usually with gracefully nodding tips. The branches bear alternate twigs, mostly all in one plane. The evergreen, dark, and glittering foliage is usually whitened beneath by glaucous lines of stomata; not collected in bundles, the needles, jointed on very short stalks to cushion-like woody bases, are borne singly but densely on the twigs, in 2 or 4 ranks, and are flat or angular and blunt-tipped. The solitary male flowers grow in the axils of last year's leaves, and consist in numerous spherical anthers; the female stand erect on the tips of shoots, with numerous nearly circular scales. The small reddish brown cones droop under the boughs, and have only few, thin, flexible, roundish, and concave scales. After the seeds have fallen, the scales persist on the axis of the cone which falls without breaking. The seeds, furnished with resin vesicles, are flattened and much shorter than the membranous wing that surrounds them.

EASTERN HEMLOCK

Tsuga canadensis (Linnæus) Carrière

OTHER NAMES: Canadian Hemlock. Spruce or Hemlock Pine. Hemlock Spruce. Suga.

RANGE: Nova Scotia to the north shore of Lake Huron and the south shore of Lake Superior to Minnesota (where rare) and soutnwestern Wisconsin; almost throughout Michigan, Pennsylvania, West Virginia, New York, and New England except the high mountains, in New Jersey away from the coastal plain, in Maryland away from tidewater, in southern and eastern Ohio, in northern and eastern Kentucky, and south on the mountains at intermediate altitudes to Georgia and Alabama. It occurs in a few scattered counties in central and southeastern Indiana.

DESCRIPTION: *Needles* borne apparently all in one plane, flat, dark green and shining above, whitened beneath, ⅓ to ⅔ inch long. *Flowers* — male yellow, female pale green. *Cones* on slender stalks, ruddy brown, ½ to ¾ inch long with thin scales that soon open. *Seeds* half as long (1⁄16 inch) as their wings. *Bark* thin, cinnamon-red to purplish, divided by narrow fissures into long rough plates. *Wood* light brown tinged with red, or nearly white, not very strong in proportion to its very light weight (26 pounds to the cubic foot, dry weight), not durable, difficult to work, brittle and coarse-grained.

In the grand, high places of the southern mountains Hemlock soars above the rest of the forest, rising like a church spire — like numberless spires as far as the eye can see — through the blue haze that is the natural atmosphere of those ranges. Sometimes even its branches reach out like arms above the crowns of other trees. But though the Hemlock's top may rejoice in the boldest sun and brave any storm, the tree unfailingly has its roots down in deep, cool, perpetually moist earth. And no more light and heat than a glancing sunbeam ever penetrates through the somber shade of its boughs to the forest floor.

The very opposite of a pioneer species, with its light-sensitive, drought-fearing seedlings, Hemlock must wait until other trees have created a forest. When the ground has become strewn with centuries of leaf mold, and the shade so dense that other trees' own seedlings cannot compete with their parents, the Hemlock moves in. Conditions on the forest floor are then more favorable for it than for any other tree. Painfully slow though the Hemlock's growth is, it will inevitably make its way above its neighbors. One by one they are eliminated, until at last only the shade-loving Beech can keep company with Hemlock. They associate together gladly, shaggy bole contrasted with paper-smooth one; somber, motionless needles with light and flickering blades; strength with grace. The hemlock has then reached what ecologists call the climax stage — that is, a vegetational group which cannot be invaded or displaced by others unless axe or fire violently intervene, or an actual change of climate in the course of geologic ages.

Besides shade, the Hemlock loves rocks; it likes to straddle them with its ruddy roots, to crack them with its growing, to rub its knees against a great boulder. The north sides of hills, the sides of mountains facing the rain-bearing winds, exactly suit it. Unlike the Tamarack, it seems never to grow on level land if it can find an incline. It loves to lave its roots in white water — rushing streams and waterfalls; it despises slow water, warm and muddy, and so avoids the Mississippi valley and all its works.

But where it grows, it has long served the mountain people. They learned from the Indians long ago that the high tannin content of the bark made it a valuable curative for burns and sores. More, the earliest settlers were quick to find that its bark could be used for tanning leather, and for two hundred years and more they stripped the trees in the most wasteful manner; only the broad thick bark of the lower trunks was taken, the rest unutilized. The peeled logs were left in the forest to decay, though the old-time lumbermen sometimes had a use for "Hemlock peelers" in driving Pine logs down river to the mill, since the slippery naked logs helped to ease along the Pine. Still in the southern Appalachians the bark is used as a brown dye for wool, but to leather it gives a red tone, and serves in immense quantities for tanning. Today, however, its chief use is for the making of pulp, especially in Michigan and Wisconsin.

But not in newsprint and cheap wrapping paper does Hemlock serve us best, but rather rooted in its tranquil, age-old stations. Approaching such a noble tree, you think it dark, almost black, because the needles on the upper side are indeed a lustrous deep blue-green. Yet when you lunch on the rock that is almost sure to be found at its feet, or settle your back into the buttresses of the bole and look up under the boughs, their shade seems silvery, since the under side of each needle is whitened by two lines. Soon even talk of the tree itself is silenced by it, and you fall to listening. When the wind lifts up the Hemlock's voice, it is no roaring like the Pine's, no keening like the Spruce's. The Hemlock whistles softly to itself. It raises its long, limber boughs and lets them drop again with a sigh, not sorrowful, but letting fall tranquillity upon us.

CAROLINA HEMLOCK

Tsuga caroliniana Engelmann

RANGE: Irregularly distributed between 2500 and 3000 feet altitude from southwestern Virginia to northern Georgia, chiefly in the Blue Ridge.

DESCRIPTION: *Needles* bristling around the twig in all directions, the tip often notched, ⅓ to ¾ inch long, dark green above, paler beneath. *Flowers* — male purple-tinged; female purple. *Cones* 1 to 1½ inches long on short stout stalks, their pale scales spreading. *Seeds* ⅙ inch long, the pale shining wings 4 times as long. *Bark* thick, red brown; with connecting ridges and deep furrows. *Wood* very light, weak, brittle, and coarse-grained.

Unlike the preceding species, the Carolina Hemlock never seeks deep ravines, the neighborhood of streams, or ancient forests. Rather it elects to grow on the southern and eastern slopes of mountains, on the edge of dry rocky ledges and cliffs. Even from the valleys it is distinguishable there, by its dark foliage, as a band of vegetation.

Usually only 40 to 50 feet tall, Carolina Hemlock is in its prime a beautifully symmetrical tree. In old age, when twisted by the elements on its exposed crags, it is apt to form a broad, flat, and more or less broken and picturesque crown. Its dogged growth is slow; a specimen only 14½ inches in diameter, inside the bark, was found to be 170 years old.

Inaccessible as the trees are on their crags, they will — one hopes — never go to the tan vat or the pulp mill, but will endure forever, secretive, contorted, stubborn in tenacity, singing their heavy chant in the mountain wind, that has been heard only by those who love the southern mountains and have climbed to the Hemlock groves and rested on the bed of their needles.

THE SPRUCES

(*Picea*)

Pʀᴏᴅᴜᴄɪɴɢ soft white or reddish wood and straight, mast-like trunks
with scaly rather than furrowed bark, the Spruces are pyramidal trees
with regular whorls of narrow, horizontal branches. Their aromatic
needles are usually 4-sided and tipped with a pungent prickle. Borne
separately, not in bundles, they crowd densely on the twig and, disposed in several spiral ranks, they bristle out in all directions, or if by
curvature they bunch toward the top of the twig they do not, at any
rate, form flat sprays of foliage as in Hemlock and Fir. They are not
jointed by a stalk to the twigs but seated directly on minute woody
knobs which remain, after leaf fall, as spiral roughenings on the
branchlet. Rows of white stomata mark the uppersides of the leaves.

The male flowers, found in the leaf axils, consist in many spirally
arranged stamens to form a catkin. The short female catkins grow
terminally on the twig, and are brightened at flowering time by numerous rounded or pointed scales. Always pendant under the bough,
the cones have thin, leathery, persistent scales with still thinner papery
scales between them, which, however, are not longer than the woody
ones. Maturity comes to the cones the first year; they soon open their
scales and drop their small winged seeds. When the cone falls, it falls
with its scales intact; they do not break away separately from the
central axis as do the cone scales of Firs.

WHITE SPRUCE

Picea glauca (Moench) Voss

OTHER NAMES: Skunk, Cat, or Single Spruce.

RANGE: Newfoundland and Labrador to Alaska, south on the Alberta Rockies to Montana, Minnesota, Wisconsin, northern Michigan, northern New York, Vermont, New Hampshire, and Maine. Also on the Black Hills of South Dakota.

DESCRIPTION: *Needles* erect and crowded, bristling, twisted to the upper side of the twig, incurved, blue-green or pale blue with a bloom, 4-sided, 1/3–3/4 inch long, narrowed to the sharp tip. *Flowers* — male pale red under the yellow dust of pollen; female oblong-cylindric with red or pale green scales. *Cones* 2 inches long, pale green tinged with red, and shining, the scales thin and flexible and not ragged. *Seeds* 1/8 inch long, pale brown, with slender wings. *Bark* thin, with brown-tinged gray scales, not furrowed. *Wood* very light (25 pounds to the cubic foot, dry weight), light yellow, soft, weak, and straight-grained.

The most beautiful approach to the North American continent from Europe is up the St. Lawrence to Quebec. The grandeur of this estuary, the greatest, save the Amazon's, in all the world, the storm of gannets from the bird rocks, the white cliffs of the Gaspé peninsula, would be enough to make it incomparable. But most impressive of all is the vast coniferous forest, so dark a green that it looks almost black, stretching from the north shore away and away to the horizon and beyond, for hundreds of impenetrable miles, to the arctic limit of trees. In this forest are set the little villages of French Canada, the inevitable white steeple and gold cross gleaming bright against the evergreens and the raw, elemental blue of the sky. Each of these villages seems, from the deck of the ship, a collection of toy houses and churches pressed closely by Christmas trees. And of all the Conifers there, the fairest is the White Spruce, the beauty of its family.

It was in the basin of the St. Lawrence, indeed, that the White Spruce was first seen by Jacques Cartier when in the autumn of 1535 he sailed up the Saguenay River. "From the day of the 18th to the 28th of this month we have sailed up this river without losing an hour nor a day, during which time we have seen and found as beautiful a country and lands and views as one could wish for, level as aforementioned, and the finest trees in the world, to wit Oaks, elms, walnuts, cedars, spruces, ash trees, willows and wild vines."

In youth the White Spruce forms a fine spire-like top, with a central stem straight as a mast, ending at the acute symmetrical tip; the lowest arms sweep benignantly down almost to earth, then turn up at the twig, like fingers lifted, in a gesture of easy grace. The foliage tends to curl, no matter from what side of the branch it may spring, toward the top of the twig, and so appears combed up and out. When crushed, it gives out a pungent, almost skunky odor.

Banks of streams and lakes, and borders of swamps, are the habitat of this fine tree; it seeks out ocean cliffs along the coast of Maine, where the salt spray of the Atlantic burns the needles on the windward side, and the sea winds sculpture it into fantastic forms. On the eastern slopes of the Canadian Rockies it attains its greatest height — sometimes 150 feet, with a trunk 3 or 4 feet thick. It reaches almost to the Arctic sea in scattered groves, and every one of the rivers of the Mackenzie and Yukon provinces is choked with the naturally fallen logs of White Spruce, while its driftwood is piled, whitening, on their banks and shoals.

In Canada, especially the western provinces, White Spruce is often a fine lumber tree, used for interior finish. Its greatest use, though, is in

the making of paper pulp; the least hymned of all forest industries, pulping is, since the disappearance of the great stands of virgin White and Red Pines, the most important forest industry of eastern Canada. For pulp manufacture is requisite a very abundant tree with very soft fibers. White Spruce answers exactly to this description, and so tremendous has become the drain on our pulp woods that many great newspapers in the United States own their own Spruce forests in Canada, and by operating on successive tracts over a sufficiently great area they hope that this fast-growing Spruce will furnish them a self-renewing crop to perpetuity. In vain have American pulp manufacturers sought to raise a tariff wall against Canadian Spruce; for once the pulp interests have met their equals in the press, and Canadian pulp still comes in duty-free as a needed raw material just like rubber, silk and coffee.

In the making of pulp, the fiber is torn apart by great grindstones kept cool by water, till the once proud log is reduced to a dirty slush, or else the pure cellulose is freed by dissolving out the gummy lignins with sulphite or soda. To this sludge are added all the fillers, such as rosin, alum, and gelatine for sizing, and clays to give body and polish to coated papers, and dyes for colored papers. Then the pulp is drained and mechanically dried, in principle as one dries clothes with wringer or mangle, but by a series of machines that are a marvel of inventive skill. There emerges at last a continuous flowing sheet of paper which in the great mills never stops, year in year out, unless the paper breaks. To produce a ton of newsprint requires one cord of wood, 2800 tons of water, nearly 2000 kilowatt hours of electrical energy or 100 horsepower for twenty-four hours, and a capital up to $50,000 per ton of daily output. And thus it is we get, each morning, our bad news and our comics.

BLACK SPRUCE

Picea mariana (Miller) Britton, Sterns and Poggenberg

OTHER NAMES: Bog, Swamp, or Double Spruce. Lash-horn.

RANGE: Newfoundland to Labrador, Mackenzie, and Alaska, south to
northern Minnesota, Wisconsin, Michigan, the Adirondacks, northern
New England, the mountains of the Virginias and coastal swamps of
New Jersey. Rare in the Great Smokies of Tennessee.

DESCRIPTION: *Needles* appearing brushed forward, ¼ to ¾ inch long,
incurved above the middle, abruptly tipped with a sharp point, pale
green and hoary above, shining below, 4-sided. *Flowers* — male dark
red; female with purple scales, oblong-cylindric. *Cones* ½ to 1½ inches
long, on strongly recurved stalks, dull gray-brown, the scales with irregular margins. *Seeds* ⅛ inch long, oblong, very dark brown with pale
brown membranous wings. *Bark* not furrowed, thin, with innumerable
gray-brown scales. *Wood* heavy for a conifer (33 pounds to the cubic
foot, dry weight), soft, close-grained and weak, with reddish-tinged heartwood and pale sapwood.

In Minnesota the Black Spruce is a dominant tree over a vast area
which you can locate at once on the map by the fact that there are
almost no towns, no roads, no railroads. In many places the forest is
so dense that there exists no clearing large enough to afford a landing
field for an ordinary plane, and the most satisfactory ingress is by sea-
plane, where a landing can be made upon the lakes. There the Black
Spruce's dark spear-like points are repeated a thousand thousand times
on every sky; there the loon laughs and the grebe dives, and the wild
geese and ducks find refuge.

Of all the habitats of the Black Spruce the strangest is the muskegs,
the lakes and ponds of this ill-drained, highly glaciated region, which
are gradually being invaded by sedges and sphagnum moss. The
detritus of the life and death of these aquatic plants has formed floating islands, and on them Spruce has grown without contact with

mineral soil. These muskeg trees often bear cones when only two or three feet in height; however, two or three feet of growth may represent a long life. In such cases the cone-bearing branches are almost the only ones and become "densely crowded near the top of the tree, while the trunk below is often destitute of living branches, although unshaded and growing far from other trees. These dense tufts of dark branches like plumes upon poles present a strange spectacle to the traveler who for the first time crosses the larger muskegs, especially at twilight, for he seems to be looking over a weird procession, stretching often mile after mile until lost in the distance. . . . "[1]

Probably no American tree takes on more curious forms, sculptured by every sort of natural force, so that it would be hard to say what is its normal form, since it were arbitrary to state which of all its strenuous habitats is its true home. On well-drained bottom-lands and low stony hills of Manitoba and Saskatchewan it reaches its greatest height — sometimes 100 feet. It is then a spire-like, narrowly pyramidal tree with spindling trunk and high crown, and stiff branches. Where it grows in open groves on the Canadian prairies, the branches are pendulous and the old ones clothe the tree to the base. At timberline on Mount Ktaadn it is dwarfed to ten, five, even two or three feet in height, no matter how old, and has such intricate and such stiff and strong branches that the mountaineer can walk upon the top of these groves. On the high Adirondacks, a semi-prostrate form is found. On the mountains of Virginia, where it is called Lash-horn, it forms absolutely impenetrable thickets. Yet it is all the same tree, endlessly adaptive, secure only by its very knottiness, its contortion, its cretin stature or inaccessible refuge in cold bogs, from destruction by man. As soon as it becomes a fair-featured tree, we cut it down for paper pulp.

A thing of the past now is the gathering of Spruce gum, by gummers on snowshoes, carrying long poles fitted with chisels to knock off the resinous exudations. In the old lumber camps, Spruce gum was the chewing-gum; today it is replaced by tropical *chicle*. But Spruce beer has never quite gone out of fashion. In *The Maine Woods* Thoreau puts the taste of it on your tongue. "Instead of water we got here a draught of beer," he writes, "which, it was allowed, would be better; clear and thin, but strong and stringent as the cedar-sap. It was as if

[1] Ayres, "The Muskeg Spruce" in *Garden and Forest,* vol. 7.

we sucked at the very teats of Nature's pine-clad bosom in these parts, — the sap of all Millinocket botany commingled, — the topmost, most fantastic, and spiciest sprays of the primitive wood, and whatever invigorating and stringent gum or essence it afforded steeped and dissolved in it — a lumberer's drink, which would acclimate and naturalize a man at once, — which would make him see green, and, if he slept, dream that he heard the wind sough among the pines."

RED SPRUCE

Picea rubens Sargent

OTHER NAMES: Yellow Spruce. He-Balsam.

RANGE: Nova Scotia to southern Quebec, and south throughout Maine, New Hampshire, and Vermont to Cape Ann, Massachusetts and the Berkshires, Catskills, Adirondacks, and Hudson valley, south on the higher mountains of New Jersey, the high ridges of the Alleghenies in Pennsylvania, above 3500 feet in the Virginias, and above 4500 in the Tennessee and North Carolina mountains.

DESCRIPTION: *Needles* bristling around the stem in all directions, incurved above the middle, ½ to ⅝ inch long, 4-sided, dark green tinged with yellow and shining. *Flowers* — male bright red, scarcely stalked; female oblong-cylindric, reddish-green, their scales reflexed. *Cones* ¼ to 2 inches long on very short stalks, red and shining, the scales with intact, curved margins. *Seeds* ⅛ inch long, dark brown, with short broad wings.

Bark moderately thick, scaly and not furrowed, dark reddish brown washed with gray. *Wood* light (28 pounds to the cubic foot, dry weight), soft, easily worked, elastic and strong in proportion to its weight.

Seldom is the Red Spruce seen save in the company of its constant companion the Fir tree, or Balsam. The southern mountaineers, indeed, call both Spruce and Fir "Balsam"; they speak of a certain type of mountain as a balsam — meaning one conspicuously crowned with these two trees, for their evergreen, very dark and pointed tops contrast in the sharpest way with the paler green and broad crowns of the deciduous forest zones beneath them. The southern Appalachians have no true timber line and no snowcaps; usually trees march to the very summits of the highest peaks. All the highest, save some of the grass or heath "balds," are crowned with these black caps of Spruce and Fir, and from them the Black Mountains, culminating in Mount Mitchell itself, take their name.

The mountain people recognize the intimate association of the Spruce and Fir by calling them respectively the He-Balsam and the She-Balsam. Observing that the Fir has swollen blisters of resin under the bark, they fancifully compared them to breasts filled with milk; hence the She-Balsam. And supposing perhaps that a mate must be found for the She-Balsam and noting that its companion tree had no resin blisters, they named it the He-Balsam.

To tell the "He" from the "She," when you find yourself among these two companion trees, crush the needles in your fingers and discover the two distinct odors — the orange-rind aroma of the Spruce, and the balsam-pillow smell of the Fir. Yet in these high groves there is only a delicious commingled fragrance, reminding you of Christmas morning even though it may be a day in July when, panting in the thinner air after a 6000-foot climb, you rest beneath the intense shade of these trees, on the deep bed of mosses.

The Red Spruce is much the commonest Spruce of the White Mountains of New Hampshire, and as one climbs Mount Washington it is soon met with, amidst the Birch, Beech, and Maple of the lower forests. But, companioned by the Balsam Fir, it leaves the other trees behind, and for a while we climb easily in fine groves of these two trees; though their canopy is close, and the shade is perpetual — cool and damp — the forest room in which we seem to be walking has a high ceiling, and there is a striking lack of understory trees and shrubs.

But at about 5000 feet above sea level, we find ourselves looking out over the tops of the Spruce and Fir, for they have shrunk to breast height and, intricately branched, the branches thick and tough with years, they make a thicket through which it would be impossible to force one's way. Only the trail, hacked out by axe, makes any going easy here, though one may try walking on top of the dwarf trees. When the Spruce is down to ankle height, no taller than the Labrador-tea bushes, you are at timber line.

As a saw-log tree, Red Spruce is all that the softwood lumberman could ask, with fine straight stems, the knots sound, the wood strong in proportion to its weight, and elastic. So heavy cutting and fires have, in the short time between the end of the age of the White Pine, when lumber companies first deigned to look at Spruce, and the present, done execution on this valuable timber resource. On the high southern Appalachians the virgin Spruce-Fir forests do not, when removed, replace themselves. A hardwood forest, when cut over, sprouts from the stumps, but the Redwood is the only conifer that shows any regular ability to reproduce by sprouting. A cut-over Spruce growth must reproduce from seed, and if lumbering is followed by slash fires, the deep bed of humus, the kindly protection of mosses, are destroyed. Or the Spruce seedlings die soon after germination in the sun-bitten, wind-scorched desert left after fire. Instead, the brambles move in, then Fire Cherry and Trembling Aspen.

To the pulpmill goes Red Spruce whenever the paper manufacturer catches a stand of it not included in a National Park or Forest. The wood has a long list of other uses; to enumerate them would be almost a repetition of White Pine's versatility, and indeed if ever eastern forests are managed by the government, as Swedish forests are, with controlled cutting and a long-term policy of planting for sustained yield, Red Spruce will be a great natural resource.

Red Spruce has one precious quality for which it is cut in small but choice amounts, and this is its resonance. Musical resonance in any wood is superior to that of the resonance of metal because it enriches and softens the tone and also damps it off quickly; metals make it hard and prolong it, and heighten the pitch. The wood selected for musical instruments is chosen with exquisite care. It must have an absolutely uniform texture and be free from all defects and irregularities of grain. Spruce measures up to these qualifications in the highest degree

— at least the best quality does so — being a wood with fairly narrow growth rings of uniform width. So it is preferred for guitars, mandolins, organ pipes, piano sounding boards, and violin bellies. For the latter Spruce is considered by the best makers to have no substitutes.

It is often asserted that the old violin makers had secrets, in the selection of wood, in design, in the nature of the varnish or the way it was dried, that made their instruments better. But the serious historians of the violin all doubt this; modern techniques and materials are certainly the equals of the old ones. There is, however, an undeniable difference between a violin that has been used for many years, and a "green" one that is not "broken in." Here the wood technologists step in, to tell us that the wood cells become more and more elastic with constant vibration; old violins are, as it were, aged in music. But the finest of instruments, if neglected, stiffen up again. The fiddle of Paganini, after lying in the museum of his native Genoa, was found in fifty years to be a ruin, so far as tone was concerned. At the Library of Congress in Washington the historic instruments are, on the contrary, taken out and played regularly to keep them in condition.

THE FIRS
(*Abies*)

THESE TREES of superb form, with their lance-sharp tips and regular tiers of whorled branches, have trunks which go up through the tree, from root to tip, straight as a pole. On young shoots the foliage bristles out in all directions, but on older branches it generally twists up to the top so that in appearance all the needles are borne on the upper side of the twig; or else the foliage lies flat in one plane, like that of Hemlock. Again, like Hemlock needles, Fir needles are usually flattened, not squarish, and blunt, not prickle-tipped, and they are whitened beneath by two pallid lines. The upper surface is deep green and lustrous.

From large bud scales appear the flowers in the axils of last year's leaves. The male flowers cluster abundantly on the lower sides of branches above the middle of the tree, showing scarlet or yellow anthers; the female are always borne on the upper sides of twigs. Consequently the cones are borne erect. The thin leathery scales are closely overlapping and broadly rounded at tip but narrowed at base to a claw. Often the papery scales between them are longer and hence extruded. Finally the scales drop one by one, leaving the axis of the cone erect on the twig, like a spike. The winged seeds are furnished with conspicuous resin vessels.

NORTHERN BALSAM

Abies balsamea (Linnæus) Miller

OTHER NAMES: Balsam or Balm-of-Gilead Fir. Blister, Fir, or Silver Pine.

RANGE: Newfoundland to the Yukon Territory and northeastern British Columbia, south to northern and eastern parts of Minnesota and Wisconsin, northern Michigan, throughout northern New England, the Berkshires, eastern New York, and south on the mountains to southwestern Virginia. Absent from the south shore of Lake Ontario, and both shores of Lake Erie. Rare in northwestern Connecticut and northeastern Iowa.

DESCRIPTION: *Needles* on cone-bearing twigs appearing brushed up to the top of the twigs and only ½ inch long, but twice as long on young shoots and then lying all in one plane; shining dark green above, silvery below, blunt or acute but never prickle-tipped. *Flowers* — male yellow or purple; female pale yellow-green. *Cones* dark rich purple, 2 to 4 inches long. *Seeds* ¼ inch long; the light brown wings a little longer. *Bark* thick, smooth or thinly scaly, rich brown, with many resin blisters. *Wood* very light (26 pounds to the cubic foot, dry weight), soft, weak, coarse-grained, and swiftly decaying, the heartwood pale brown, the sapwood thick and yellowish white.

Except with the old-time logger, who had no use for Balsam save to make himself a natural sweet-smelling mattress laid on a springy frame of Spruce boughs, this is the most generally popular of all the trees of the great North Woods. To anyone whose childhood summers were luckily spent there, the delicious spicy fragrance of Balsam needles is the dearest odor in all of Nature. Merely to remember it is to raise before the eyes lake waters, or the soft high swell of the northern Appalachians, or the grandeur of the St. Lawrence gulf. It brings back the smell of wild raspberries in the sunlit clearing, the piercing sweetness of the white-throated sparrow's song, the bird-like flight of the canoe from the gurgling paddle stroke. For Balsam loves the rocky soil close to water, where its familiar is often the Paper Birch. At the edge of any sparkling lake, in the great glaciated province of eastern Canada and the northern United States, these two grow in the happiest of contrasts, the Balsam with its darkly gleaming but motionless evergreen foliage and its militarily straight stem and precise whorls of branches, and the white-barked, leaning, and gracile Birch, with its showers of pale green, restless, and talkative foliage.

For success in the eternal forest battle for survival, Balsam depends upon its adaptability, the speed of its growth, its fertility. The seeds, which fly through the woods on trim bright wings, are many and highly viable, but the grouse and the red squirrels and the pine mice eat them, just as moose and deer browse on the foliage. Balsam is, too, a danger to itself because of the resin blisters under the bark, which, in case of forest fire, ignite so that the whole tree is soon a blazing torch.

These resin blisters yield what is called Canada balsam, a sort of turpentine employed in the manufacture of varnish. It is familiar to all advanced students in the biological sciences as a transparent fixative for mounting and preserving specimens for the microscope. It not only seals the cover glass to the glass slide, but as a matrix for the specimen holds and preserves it from drying and decay. More, balsam has the fortunate property of refracting light to exactly the same extent that glass does so that the balsam matrix, the cover glass, and the microscope lenses become one optical system with the same refractive index.

One of the odd things about the lovely aroma of Balsam branches is that many of those who live with it constantly can no longer smell it. The city child has the sharpest pleasure in it. If he collects the needles to make a balsam pillow to sleep on, he dreams of the North Woods for the time that he can smell the pillow. But presently he may fail to do so, though the smell is there for others, and may not do so again until the fresh Christmas tree is brought into his house. Balsams are the ideal Christmas trees — fragrant beyond all others, with long lower branches and thick, spire-like tops. The needles do not drop like those of the Spruce, even after a month without water, nor do they stab the hand when one is decorating the tree, since they are not tipped with prickles.

The Christmas tree industry is now a big, though a seasonal, business. On forest land the proper selection of little trees will merely result in betterment of the stand. On farms and estates the raising of trees, from seedlings supplied free or at cost by state forestry nurseries, offers, on land not otherwise profitable, possibilities that were dramatized by the highly successful plantations at "Hyde Park" by President Roosevelt. Yet from time to time some overzealous moralist decides that we are depleting our forests by cutting millions of young Christmas trees every year for a momentary pleasure, thus robbing ourselves of tens of million of feet of lumber. But out of every ten young trees in the forest nine are destined to lose out and die. No harm, but only good, can follow from the proper cutting of young Christmas trees. And the destiny of Balsam, loveliest of them all, would otherwise too often be excelsior, or boards for packing cases, or newsprint bringing horror on its face into your home. Far better that the little tree should arrive, like a shining child at your door, breathing of all out of doors and cupping healthy North Woods cold between its boughs, to bring delight to human children.

SOUTHERN BALSAM

Abies Fraseri (Pursh) Poiret

OTHER NAMES: She-Balsam. Fraser Fir.

RANGE: High mountains of North Carolina, Tennessee, and the Virginias.

DESCRIPTION: *Needles* ½ to 1 inch long, appearing as if brushed upward on the cone-bearing shoots, dark green and lustrous above, whitish beneath. *Flowers* — male reddish yellow, female with pale yellow-green scales. *Cones* 2½ inches long, the woody scales dark purple and half as long as the papery, pale yellow-green scales whose tips are handsomely reflexed on the outside of the cone. *Seeds* ⅛ inch long with dark shining wings. *Bark* thin with close-pressed cinnamon-red scales which weather to grayish. *Wood* pale brown, with nearly white sapwood, coarse-grained, very light, weak and soft.

Like many another Scot, John Fraser, for whom this tree was named, came to London, in 1750, to get rich. In Paradise Row he set up a linen draper's establishment; but a visit to Chelsea Botanical Garden

gave him a taste for botany. Forsaking calicoes and dimities, he sailed
in 1784 for the then young United States, landing at Charleston, and
set off for the southern Appalachians. He was indeed the first plantsman who ever explored their highest peaks, in the days when they
were still wild and largely trackless country.

On his wanderings he fell in with a rival — the celebrated André
Michaux, and for a while they traveled together. But in spite of the
identity of their interests, or perhaps because of them, they did not
get on well. Michaux believed Fraser was dogging his footsteps perhaps to be sure to discover for the British any new flower or tree that
Michaux sent back to Louis XVI. So, offering as an excuse that his
horses had strayed and he must catch them, Michaux let Fraser go on
ahead. And that is how it happens that John Fraser was the first —
by his nose perhaps — to discover this deliciously aromatic tree, which
grows right to the top of Mount Mitchell, Clingman's Dome, and all
the most famous peaks of North Carolina and Tennessee.

After four visits to America, Fraser entered into the service of
Catherine the Great, and subsequently of Czar Paul. So he revisited
the New World as a Russian official, but after expending large sums in
collecting our finest Conifers, azaleas, rhododendrons, and Magnolias,
he was not reimbursed by the new Czar, Alexander, and his previous
appointment was not recognized. However, he had a little nursery
business of his own in Chelsea, and, returning once more to America,
he brought back from the sweet-smelling high groves of our southern
mountains the first living specimens of the Southern Balsam that
England had seen.

But this tree has never done well in cultivation, and to see it in its

perfection you too must take the climb up from the blazing heat of the
Carolina piedmont, under Tuliptree and Magnolia, up through Maple,
Beech, and Oak, through the thickets of purple rhododendron, to the
groves of Red Spruce and Southern Balsam. True that you can motor
close to some of the summits in half an hour, but if you do you will
never know the sense of contrast, or of conquest, as you find yourself
at last in the damp and fragrant climax forest.

The depth of the perpetual shade in these woods is due in part to
the darkness of the foliage itself, to its density upon the boughs, and
to the interlocking of the crowns above your head. And a large part
of the year these groves are swept by mists and clouds; in winter they
are deep in snow. As a result, the ground is covered with a carpet of
lichens and mosses, hepatics and ferns. Especially on the trunks and
logs of the Balsam do the lichens delight to grow, and usnea moss
drips from the dead lower boughs like waving beards upon old
prophets. So everything conspires to give these trees, which are really
not long-lived, a look of hoary age. A child would call the Balsam
groves a fairy-tale wood, and it is doubtful if the ecologists, with all
their synthetic terminology, could more aptly characterize this woodland type.

THE ARBOR–VITÆS
(*Thuja*)

THESE ARE resinous and aromatic trees, with massive and buttressed trunks, thin branches, and heavy crowns, living to a great age and with correspondingly durable wood. The branchlets incline to be gracefully pendulous and to lie all in one plane, making flat sprays of foliage. Completely clothing the twigs in 4 ranks, the leaves are scale-like and closely overlapping. The sexes occur on different branches of the same tree, the flowers solitary and terminal on the twig. The few-scaled cones are leathery and erect and mature the first season. The thin-coated seeds are winged.

ARBOR–VITÆ

Thuja occidentalis Linnæus

OTHER NAMES: Vitæ. Northern White Cedar. Cedar.

RANGE: Nova Scotia to Manitoba and south through northeastern Minnesota and northern and eastern Wisconsin to northern Illinois, Ohio, New York, and Massachusetts; south on the limestone Alleghenies of the Virginias, rare in the mountains of Tennessee, and very rare in western North Carolina.

DESCRIPTION: Foliage with a tansy odor when crushed, scale-like, thick and very small, on mature branches completely clothing the flattened twig, the leaves on the upper and lower surface of the twig keeled and overlapping the 2 lateral ranks which are much flattened; on seedlings and vigorous young shoots the leaves concave-convex, sharp-pointed, oblique to the twig. *Flowers* — male egg-shaped, consisting of 4 to 6 stamens each with 2 to 4 pollen chambers; female oblong, with 8 to 12 acute scales in opposite pairs, each subtending a smaller ovule-bearing scale. *Cones* with the middle scales larger and seed-bearing. *Bark* thin, light red-brown, tough and stringy. *Wood* very durable, aromatic, pale yellow-brown, coarse-grained, soft and brittle, and very light (19 pounds to the cubic foot, dry weight).

Why is one kind of tree short-lived, like the Cottonwood which scarcely outlives a man, and another, like the Arbor-vitæ, sempiternal? This cannot be due to chance, and it tells us nothing we did not know to say that it is the tree's nature. Usually the explanation is found in the wood, but that of this tree is brittle, weak, and soft, and so subject to wind-shake that its annual rings are often found pulled apart even in the living tree. True, the resin in this wood may save it from decay, but many short-lived Pines are also resinous, while the Bigtrees of California are non-resinous. Perhaps freedom from insect pests and fungus would explain much in the longevity of a tree, and, still more, a heavy, nearly fireproof bark. All these the Arbor-vitæ has; more, its growth in constantly damp ground would further protect it from forest fires. Though these are but partial explanations, the fact remains that an Arbor-vitæ has a life expectancy of 200 or 300 years, and from that circumstance it takes its name of Arbor-vitæ, tree-of-life — a long life, and noble.

Yet in the lumber trade and to the inhabitants of the North Woods, its name is and probably always will be Cedar — a title claimed with equal or more justice by about twenty other American trees. If this one is Arbor-vitæ to the gardener, nurseryman, and botanist, the lumbermen are merely sorry for city folks who cannot recognize a Cedar when they see it. There is nothing for one to do, if one wishes to understand and be understood widely, but to learn both names for the tree, as one learns that an American elk is also a wapiti, a flicker likewise a high-holer.

Except in the Virginia mountains, where Arbor-vitæ clings to limestone ledges, this tree commonly inhabits swampy grounds; it forms impenetrably thick rings around Tamarack bogs, not venturing so deep into the watery, quaking muck as the Tamarack, but loving to grow in soggy, springy ground and the deep and ancient humus of decay where, as Thoreau said, "the woods are all mossy and *moosey.*" Arbor-vitæ, with Hemlock, finds a favorite habitat along all the rivers of the great North Woods, thrusting its long roots down through the rocks to the water, and seeming to like to find its lovely young proportions — one of the most perfectly conical of all our trees — reflected in the streams wherever they run quietly.

It cannot be said that Arbor-vitæ is a tall tree — 60 feet is considered a good height, and 100 feet is a thing of the forest's lost virginity. Yet Arbor-vitæ, both in the spire-like straightness of youth and the pendulous limbs of age, carries itself superbly. Where other conifers have mast-like stems going straight up through the tree, old Arbor-vitæ trunks are apt to fork, as if split by lightning. And the heavy buttressing of the trunk and the way it is likely to be twisted make one think time and the elements have racked but not broken the indomitable frame.

All the old lumber camps of the North Woods had "Cedar" (Arbor-vitæ) shingles because the wood resists decay forever. Otherwise the old-time lumberman had little use for this faulty wood when he could exploit virgin White Pine. Yet despite its many faults it has remarkable qualities. If it is weak as a beam, it is one of the toughest woods we have; a mere shaving from a carpenter's plane may be laid on an anvil, folded, and struck repeatedly with a hammer, yet not break. For this reason and because it withstands wear so well, it is unexcelled for the planking of small craft. If it is a soft wood, it also splits easily; the Indians of the North Woods used it for frames for their canoes. It was easy to work with their primitive tools, for the very reason that makes it so subject to wind-shake, for the red men could split it with a stone maul along the growth rings into very thin slats. More, it is the lightest wood in the northeastern states, and lightness in a canoe is a virtue second to nothing.

Even the bark served the traveling Indian well. Thoreau has well described this in *The Maine Woods:* "The Indian [guide] prepared his canoe for carrying in this wise. He took a cedar shingle or splint eighteen inches long and four or five wide, rounded at one end, so that the corners might not be in the way, and tied it with cedar-bark by two holes made midway, near the edge of each side, to the middle cross-bar of the canoe. When the canoe was lifted upon his head bottom up, this shingle, with its rounded end uppermost, distributed the weight over his shoulders and head, while a band of cedar-bark, tied to the cross-bar on each side of the shingle, passed round his breast, and another longer one, outside of the last, round his forehead. . . . A cedar-tree furnished all the gear in this case, as it had the woodwork of the canoe."

Arbor-vitæ was probably the first tree of North America (north of Mexico) to be introduced into cultivation in Europe, since it was cultivated in Paris before the middle of the sixteenth century. For it was brought back by Jacques Cartier, who encountered it on his voyage up the St. Lawrence in 1535–36, when the whole ship's company fell deathly sick of "Scorbute" — scurvy, the plague of the days of sailing vessels. As Cartier was walking on the ice he encountered Domagaia, an Indian whom he had expected, ten days before, to die, for he "had bene very sicke and had his knees swolne as bigge as a child of two years old, all his sinews shrunke together, his teeth spoyled, his gummes rotten, and stinking.

"Our Captaine seeing him whole and sound, was thereat marvelous glad, hoping to understand and know of him how he had healed himself, to the end that he might ease and help his men." Domagaia replied that he "had taken the juice and sappe of the leaves of a certaine Tree. . . . Then our Captaine asked of him if any were to be had thereabout, desiring him to shew him. . . . Domagaia straight sent two women to fetch some of it, which brought ten or twelve branches of it, and therewithall shewed the way how to use it, and that it is thus, to take the barke and leaves of the sayd tree, and boile them together, then to drinke of the sayd decoction every other day, and to put the dregs of it upon his legs that is sicke." Thus, though Cartier could not understand it then, his men were cured of scurvy by the vitamin C in the Arbor-vitæ sap.

THE FALSE CYPRESSES

(*Chamæcyparis*)

THE MEMBERS of this group are long-lived trees with aromatic, resinous foliage and wood, the trunks (in old specimens) swell-butted and fluted; they have nodding shoots, spreading branches and flattened and very slender branchlets that lie all in one plane, closely invested by the scale-like leaves, so that the foliage forms a flat spray. The leaves, closely overlapping, are like those of *Thuja* in occurring in alternate pairs — a flat pair on the upper and lower side of the twig almost enfolded by a keeled pair along the sides; leaves of seedlings are quite unlike those of mature shoots, since they are long, slender, sharp-pointed and spreading and occur in whorls of 3 or 4. When the foliage of a *Chamæcyparis* grows old (after 3 or 4 years) it turns rusty or brown and may persist more or less woody and seemingly a part of the twig, for some time. The minute flowers open in early spring from buds formed the previous autumn, with the sexes on separate branches of the same tree. The small spherical cones, erect on the twigs, consist in club-shaped scales, their broad end facing outward. The seeds are provided with wings but lack resin vesicles.

SOUTHERN WHITE CEDAR

Chamæcyparis thyoides (Linnæus) Britton, Sterns and Poggenberg

OTHER NAMES: Swamp or Post Cedar.

RANGE: Gulf coast from Mississippi and northeastern Florida, north on the coastal plain to southern Maine; absent from the Georgia coast except at Savannah; present in interior west central Georgia; rare in New England north of Boston.

DESCRIPTION: *Leaves* scaly, 1/16 to 1/8 inch long, keeled and dotted with resinous glands, on cone-bearing and old shoots flattened and closely overlapping on the forking twigs so that each branchlet appears like a flat, forked spray of leaves; on young plants and leading shoots the foliage bristles out from the twig. *Flowers* — male black at the tip, dark brown below, of 5 or 6 pairs of stamens; female roundish, with pale liver-colored scales and black ovules. *Cones* 1/4 inch thick, seated directly on the twig, pale green and covered with a bright bluish white bloom, when fully grown turning bluish purple and finally dark leather-color. *Seeds* 1/8 inch long, with dark ruddy wings. *Bark* dark reddish brown and divided into flat, slender, braided and twisted ridges. *Wood* light brown tinged with red, soft, weak, close-grained and very light (20 pounds to the cubic foot, dry weight).

In the heroic age of American lumbering, Southern White Cedar was one of the most versatile and important trees, but, far from the northern pineries, it never knew the gangs of lumbermen or the sensational river drives of White Pine. Quietly, steadily cut from early pioneer times, this odd amphibious tree, living on tenaciously from geologic yesterdays, has never had its due. Its timber goes to market with the preceding and the following species, all three lumped as Cedar (the lumberman has no use for botanical distinctions.) The living tree is (Linnæus forfend!) "Juniper" to many of the folks who live in the lonely swamp country where it grows.

And it grows, as the bittern lives, surprisingly close to our greatest seaboard cities, but unrecognized when seen, even as the bittern is mistaken for a dead stick. If sighted at all, the Cedar swamps are seen by most people from a flying train, or a car on an elevated super-highway designed to get you to Atlantic City or Philadelphia without seeing anything but the car ahead of you. And, speeding by, the traveler tosses them the idle thought that someone — Uncle Sam, or the Rockefellers — ought to drain those swamps and turn them into good farms.

Yet though the natives often kill out the Cedar by flooding the land for cranberry culture, and lumber companies ravage the stands to give us more telegraph poles to desecrate the landscape, the one thing you cannot have where White Cedar has grown is a good farm. For, over the thousands of years that it has been rooted in our coastal marshes, it has laid down a bed of intensely acid peat that will grow nothing readily but more White Cedar and its smaller companions, the poison-leaved Thunderwood, the little inkberry, and the sweet bay with its waxed and fragrant flowers.

Through the ages before the white man came, Swamp Cedar grew and died and fell and grew again, in the secret rhythm of its life, flowering in early spring, ripening its cones — very small for such a massive tree — its old leaves turning rusty, hardening like wood, clinging tenaciously to the twig, to give the boughs a strange, sorrowful look of standing fossilization, only denied by the bright green of the new spring growth. No trees in our range grow so densely. The dark, straight trunks, crowding one against another, the dense boughs, lacing overhead, screen away the sunlight; the roots are swathed in dank sphagnum moss. One of the finest of such grandly gloomy woods is at Green Bank State Forest, New Jersey, where a 900-acre Cedar swamp with giant trees still presents an impenetrable growth and the road through it is like an aisle in a darkened cathedral. The near-by town of Batsto, with its foaming dam and ruined forges, is still inhabited by Cedar cutters. In the American Revolution it was the fine black charcoal of the Cedars from this countryside that went into the making of patriot gunpowder. So White Cedar, no less than the White Pine that masted our infant navy, and Black Pine that was burned to smelt bog ore for Washington's cannon, helped to win our national independence.

Almost any swamp tree possesses the power, living or dead, or sawed into planks, of resisting water decay, but Southern White Cedar is excelled in this by none of the eastern woods. And so, easily worked and split along the grain, and very light, Cedar might have been designed by Nature for shingles, piers, piles, fence posts, barn floors, log cabins, small boats, and staves for water barrels, and, in our times, telegraph poles and trolley-line ties — any and all situations where endurance, without the protection of paint, is required. It did not take the early colonists long to perceive the value in such a tree, and the first sawmill soon began to eat into our supply of it.

The pioneers of southern New England and New Jersey laid the floors of their houses in this Cedar because it scoured so white. Most of the roofs of colonial Philadelphia were shingled with White Cedar, the lightest and the longest-lasting type of roof that could be had, and great quantities were exported to the West Indies. They had a beautiful resonance, too, those old Cedar shingles; listening to the sound of the raindrops pattering on shingles of different pitch, the German organ-builder Mittelberg, visiting in Philadelphia, decided to construct all his future organ pipes of Southern White Cedar.

In pioneering times whole logs were cut for cabins; the bark was allowed to slough off gradually, while the wood beneath lasted forever. By 1750, however, White Cedar was too scarce for that and houses were built of sawn planks. But already fears were justified for the approaching end of the supply. Not that anyone did anything about it — there was no federal forest policy, and the only effect of rising prices was to send the woodcutters on a quickening search for more timber. The slow creeks and old canals carried a busy traffic in lumber barges then, and the sawdust piles rose higher than the trees.

But Nature had in reserve one last source of Swamp Cedar. A hint of its presence was early known in New Jersey when from time to time an enormous tree would rise to the surface of the swamp, not waterlogged after untold centuries, from unsounded depths below. Some of these logs were 6 feet thick — a dimension never attained in our more meager times. So, about 150 years ago, lumbermen conceived of mining the swamps for Cedar, as the bog iron was mined from this same district. The digger locates his supply by a sharp-pointed iron rod, and an experienced log digger can tell from a mere chip of these sunken stores how good its state of preservation. The top trees lie near the surface, but the supply may run down 100 feet and more. Shingles made of this ancient wood last 60 or 70 years. At present the demand for mined Cedar is greatest in the shipbuilding industries.

These Cedar swamps had a now-forgotten virtue, in the lasting purity of their ale-colored water. Indeed, the old sailing ships out of

Chesapeake Bay made a special effort to obtain it. The sailing masters knew from experience that the clearest spring water will, on a long voyage, go bad, from multiplication and decay of micro-organisms. But the peat-tinctured water from the Cedar swamps kills all such. What it tasted like is known to anyone who ever drank rain water collected from Cedar-shingled roofs into barrels of Cedar staves — tannic and almost medicinal, but wondrously soft and pure. Early American cities laid their water systems in bored logs of White Cedar, not only because it never decays in contact with the soil, but in the not ill-founded belief that the water would be more healthful.

THE JUNIPERS

(*Juniperus*)

THESE ARE aromatic trees with durable, close-grained, soft wood and thin, shreddy bark. The scale-like leaves occur in pairs or threes on the twig; the minute flowers appear from buds formed the previous autumn, in small lateral catkins, the male with numerous stamens in pairs or threes, the female with 2 to 6 pairs of pointed scales each bearing on its inner face a minute ovule-bearing scale. The female flower scales fuse, in fruit, into a succulent pulp, surrounding the bony seeds and enclosed in a skin.

COMMON JUNIPER

Juniperus communis Linnæus

OTHER NAMES: Dwarf, or Ground, Juniper. Horse Savin. Hackmatack. Gorst. Fairy-circle.

RANGE: Greenland and Newfoundland, and across Canada to Alaska, south to Pennsylvania, thence southward on the Appalachians to South Carolina, and to the shores of the Great Lakes (as in northwestern Indiana) and in southern Illinois, and west to Nebraska; south on the Rockies to western Texas, the high peaks of Arizona, and in the Sierra Nevada to central California. In Asia, across Siberia and south to the Caucasus and Himalayas; in Europe throughout the northern countries south to the Maritime Alps, the Riviera and Portugal and the high mountains of southern Spain, and on the Italian peninsula (but not Sicily), and Greece.

DESCRIPTION: *Bark* thin, dark reddish brown and peeling into papery scales. *Twigs* smooth, shining, triangular between the nodes during their first and second years, in color at first light yellow tinged with red, gradually growing darker. *Winter buds* minute, acute, loosely covered with scale-like leaves. *Leaves* very narrow, ½ to ⅓ inch long, seated on the twig without stalks, in rather remote whorls of 3 and spreading at nearly right angles to the twigs, the upper surface concave and snowy-white with a band of stomata, the lower surface obscurely ridged and dark shining green, the base of the leaf swollen but the tip ending in a very sharp prickle. *Flowers* — male solitary, 1/16 inch long and cylindrical with yellow stamens in 5 or 6 whorls on the scaly central axis; female consisting of 3 slightly spreading ovules enlarged at the base, alternating with 3 subtending fleshy scales united at base and with the ovule and, in turn, subtending 5 or 6 alternate whorls of 3-forked leaf-scales. *Berry* ¼ inch thick and at maturity becoming oblong or spherical, with the dark blue or bluish black skin covered with a glaucous bloom, and tipped with the vestige of the enlarged points of the ovule, the flesh thick and resinous. *Seeds* usually 3 in number, about ⅛ inch long, flattened or angled, acute, penetrated by prominent resin glands, the bony outer coat enclosing a membranous, chestnut-brown inner coat. *Wood* close-grained, durable, hard, the heartwood light brown, the sapwood paler.

The Common Juniper has what is perhaps the widest natural range among all trees; certainly it is the only tree native both in North America and Europe. On the other side of the ocean it is commonly of tree size in the Mediterranean basin; in this country, as in northern Europe, it is usually only a shrub, sometimes with creeping stems, forming circular clumps which, as they expand, may die at the center — hence the old English name of Fairy-circle. Yet in the mountains of New England, in eastern Pennsylvania and, reportedly, sometimes on the high mountains of North Carolina, it grows up to 24 feet high. The trunk may be as much as a foot in diameter but is always short and eccentric and irregularly lobed or fluted. The erect branches form an open, irregular or broken crown. The spine-like tips of the bristling leaves make this a fiercely hostile thing; to thrust one's hand in among the branches and gather the handsome berries from the female tree is an act of courage!

The leaves have an agreeable fragrance when crushed; though technically evergreen, persisting about 3 years, they change in winter to a deep bronze color which again freshens in spring to the beautiful whiteness of the upper surface, the shiny green of the lower.

When the ovules are ripe for fecundation, they secrete a drop of clear stigmatic liquid at their enlarged and open apex. The fruit at first looks like a flower bud and does not enlarge much during its initial year, but when the flowers again bloom in early spring, the upper scales become consolidated around the ovules and by the commencement of the second winter the berry is about three-fourths grown and is then a light green, hard and globe-shaped, the seeds still soft and milky. In the following autumn (the third season since fertilization), the berries are mature and covered with a glaucous bloom over the dark blue skin. The flesh is fragrant, sweet, and resinous-tasting, and much devoured by birds. If not eaten, the berries may remain a year or two on the tree after ripening.

It is the flavor of the berries which imparts to gin its characteristic aroma and tang, for they are used in the preparation of this alcoholic drink which would otherwise be a nearly tasteless *eau-de-vie*. Indeed our word gin comes from the French *genièvre*, as gin is still called in Flanders and Belgium. And that, in turn, derives, of course, from the name of the tree in French, *genévrier*. Formerly the berries were in high repute medicinally and the oil is still sometimes used therapeutically in India and Europe.

Juniper wood is used in Europe for vine stakes because it is so durable in contact with the soil, and in India is burned as incense.

Back into ancient times stretches the cultivation of this tree for hedges. For topiary it is probably the favorite — if one likes to see trees trimmed to look like lions and pyramids balancing balls, and such. Forms with weeping branches or with golden foliage, and dozens of other horticultural sports are known in gardens but not in the wild.

EASTERN RED CEDAR

Juniperus virginiana Linnæus

OTHER NAMES: Pencil Cedar. Virginia Juniper.

RANGE: Southern Maine, across north-central New Hampshire and Vermont to southern Ontario and Hull, Quebec, westward through the southern half of the lower peninsula of Michigan, southern Wisconsin and Minnesota to the Badlands of South Dakota, and southward to eastern Texas and the Gulf states, but absent from the Gulf coast itself, and from the high Appalachians.

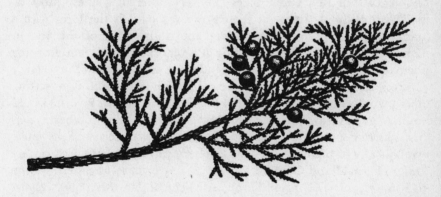

DESCRIPTION: *Foliage* of 2 sorts: (1) that on seedlings and vigorous shoots concave-convex, prickly-pointed and spreading on the stem, and (2) that on mature shoots thick, blunt, bearing a resin gland on the back, and so closely overlapping the twigs as to form a flat sprig of foliage. *Flowers* blooming in late winter, the sexes borne on separate trees, the male with 10 or 12 stamens each bearing 4 to 6 pollen chambers; female with spreading violet scales. *Berries* ¼ to ½ inch thick, at first pale green, becoming dark blue covered with a whitish bloom; the flesh sweetish resinous to the taste. *Seeds* ⅙ to ⅛ inch long. *Bark* thin, shreddy, fringed, ruddy brown. *Wood* medium-light (30 pounds to the cubic foot, dry weight), soft, easily worked, with fine smooth grain, the heartwood rich soft red, contrasting handsomely with the creamy white sapwood.

No stone-walled hilltop too bleak, no abandoned field too thin of soil but that the dark and resolute figure of the Red Cedar may take its stand there, enduring, with luck, perhaps three centuries. In aboriginal America the Cedar probably formed extensive groves, sometimes excluding almost all other trees, and remnants of such are still to be seen occasionally on the limestones of eastern Tennessee and Kentucky, where the tree reaches a height of 100 feet. As the country has been cleared of trees for farms and pastures, the Cedar has come out of the forest and invaded abandoned fields. It troops along the fence rows, where it is common with poison ivy, and along roadsides where its seeds have been dropped by birds sitting on telegraph wires. For the berries are eagerly devoured by a long list of birds, headed by the handsome cedar waxwing who takes his very name from his fondness for the fruit of this tree.

Our Eastern Red Cedar takes two very different shapes. Most familiar to millions living on the eastern seaboard is the form with a narrowly conical, spire-like outline, much like that of the Italian Cypress, with its branches ascending at a very sharp angle, and hugging the trunk to make a compact mass. Indeed it may be called the farmer's Cypress, for he is fond of lining the road to his house with it, or setting it as a windbreak along one side of the farmyard. It is a favorite in old country graveyards, where, to the imagination of our forebears, perhaps, its finger seemed to point to heaven; its evergreen boughs spoke symbolically of life eternal. This has been called, by botanists, variety *crebra*, Fernald and Griscom. It is common from southeastern Maine to Pennsylvania and in southernmost Michigan, northern and western Indiana, northeastern Illinois and southeastern Wisconsin and, occasionally, in eastern Missouri, southern Illinois, northwestern Tennessee, and the foothills of the southern Appalachians.

The other form of the tree is not at all spire-like; it takes on a

broadly conical form, with the branches widely spreading. The range of this form, which is considered to be the true species (or at least the first form to be discovered and described to science), is, on the whole, more southerly and westerly. It is the typical form of the Red Cedar from the piedmont of Maryland southward and from the western slopes of the Alleghenies westward (except in a wide zone around the southern end of Lake Michigan). There is considerable intermingling of the two forms, however, and there are many trees intermediate in form.

The earliest explorers of the Atlantic seaboard did not fail to mention so handsome, so fragrant a tree as this one — "the tallest and reddest Cedars in the world," wrote Arthur Barlowe and Philip Amadas in their opening sentences of description of the New World which they touched for the first time at Roanoke Island in 1564. The early colonists recognized the value of the Virginia Juniper from the start — for fences and shingles, benches and tables, coffins and the superstructures of boats. So easy was it to split with the frow and to smooth with the plane that it could be worked even by people as woefully ill-prepared for wilderness life as the theologian-tradesmen and overdressed gold hunters who first sought our shores. When the log cabin and the snake-rail fence appeared on the American scene, Red Cedar was a favorite because of its endurance when exposed to rain and soil.

The better craftsmen of colonial Virginia were soon producing in Cedar such complex types of furniture as bedsteads, secretaries, and virginals. The fragrance of the wood and the showy contrast in color between the red heartwood and the creamy sapwood compensated, to the tastes of those days, for the fragility of the material. In our times Red Cedar finds employment chiefly in the linings for mothproof chests and closets. How repellant the odor may be to moths is less certain than the psychological attraction it has for the careful housewife.

For over a century Red Cedar bore the brunt of the attack of pencil makers. It was a perfect wood for this purpose on account of its lightness and the ease with which it can be sharpened. However, only the very clearest knot-free heartwood was employed and pencil making wasted 70 per cent of the bulk and 90 per cent of the weight of every log cut for that purpose. As pencil manufacturers could afford to pay higher prices than anyone else, they consequently got all the best wood. For nearly a century our Cedars supplied the world with pencil wood. The famous Faber Company used them exclusively. Tennessee, in 1900, sent 3,000,000 feet of fine quality Cedar down the Cumberland River in great timber rafts. But only ten years later Cedar "cruisers" had searched out the last virgin stands, lumbermen were working over the stumps of their previous destruction, and buyers were snapping up log cabins, barn floors, and even rail fences that had stood exposed to the weather for fifty years.

Fortunately it does not pay the lumberman to cut down roadside, dooryard, and cemetery trees, or he would do to the friendly fence row and old-field Juniper what he does to the Black Walnut. The easterner is spared his Cedars only because the pencil industry has transferred its affections to the Incense Cedar of the West. So once more we have escaped the consequences of our economic sins — our wastefulness and lack of planning — by cheerily moving out West and finding a gold mine.

Cedars are often disfigured by the galls of a fungus disease (*Gymnosporangium Juniperus-virginianæ*), the cedar-apple rust. In dry weather these galls are small, hard, and relatively inconspicuous, but in wet weather in spring, long, yellow, gelatinous processes are extruded and render the disease obvious. Spores from these extrusions next infect the leaves of Apple trees, producing damaging yellow blotches. From these, again, spores may re-infect the Cedars. Different as the infections on Apple and Cedar may appear, they are the same disease, and the Red Cedar, which carries the rust as a chronic but not a fatal malady, thus becomes a reservoir of infection, in woods near orchards, for a harmful disease of Apples.

Pathologists pointed out that the easiest control of the disease was the destruction of all Cedar trees within a mile radius of the orchard. "Cedar eradication is the cheapest form of orchard insurance that you can buy. The cost on the average is less than the cost of a single spray application." So declared the *Annual Report* of the Virginia State Horticultural Society for the year 1918. Acting on this, the apple growers of Virginia, particularly in the famed orchards of the Shenandoah Valley, went to the legislature and got Cedar-eradication laws enacted. West Virginia did the same. These laws permitted the destruction of all Cedars in a large area, upon the certification of "ten freeholders," without any recompense to the owners of Cedars. In 1929 there was a short, sharp clash between them and the Apple orchardists, in which one Cedar owner at Shepherdstown, after exhausting every legal resource, attempted to prevent the destruction of her trees by clasping them, one after the other, as axemen sought to cut them, and only when she dropped with exhaustion could the trees be felled. Where they stood, their embattled owner planted 48 American flags, for the States.

That the legislation eradicating the Juniper is high-handed and one-sided seems obvious. If the slogan of the orchardists, "Cedar or Cider," were changed to "cider or pencils," the relative merits would be more truly set forth. And the statement that "Cedar eradication is the cheapest form of orchard insurance" might not certainly be true if the orchardists had to pay for the value of the destroyed Cedars. One wonders, too, what would happen if the orchardists of Tennessee should demand the felling of the sacrosanct Cedars set out at "The Hermitage" by the hand of General Andrew Jackson. Plainly there are cases in which it would be as reasonable to pass a law that all Apple trees must be cut down for a mile in the vicinity of valuable Cedars, as that any and all Cedars must fall for the sake of any and all orchards!

THE POPLARS

(*Populus*)

Poplars are fast-growing, short-lived, tall trees with bitter and astringent bark, light, weak wood, thick, brittle, pithy twigs, and restless foliage. Frequently the big, scaly, more or less gummy buds give off a marked aroma. Prominent leaf scars generally roughen the thick twigs. Long-stalked, alternate, and deciduous, the leaves are seldom more than twice as long as broad, and often broader than they are long.

Frequently appearing well before the leaves, the flowers are wind-pollinated and grouped in long catkins, with the sexes on separate trees. Each male floret consists in 8 to 30 or more stamens; the female floret is an ovary with two stigmas. From the flask-shaped, thin-walled seed pod escape the minute, short-lived, innumerable seeds, which are borne on the wind by their cottony down.

TREMBLING ASPEN

Populus tremuloides A. Michaux

OTHER NAMES: Quaking Aspen. Quaking or Aspen Poplar. Popple.

RANGE: Newfoundland and Labrador to Alaska. South on the Rockies to northwestern Mexico and the Sierra Nevada of California, throughout New England and the Great Lakes basin and upper Mississippi valley, south on the Appalachians to Kentucky; absent from the Atlantic coast south of New Jersey, from most of the prairie province of Canada and the United States and most of the Ohio valley.

DESCRIPTION: *Bark* thin, at first nearly white, and powdery and smooth, becoming on old specimens nearly black at base and roughened by horizontal bands of wart-like thickening. *Twigs* reddish brown or gray, shiny the first season, covered with scattered lenticels. *Winter buds* slightly resinous with smooth (not downy) red-brown scales. *Leaves* on laterally flattened stalks, the blades up to 4½ inches long, and wide or kidney-shaped, shining above and dull below, with meshed veinlets. *Flowers* in catkins 1½ to 2½ inches long, appearing in early spring about one month before the leaves. *Seed pods* ¼ inch long, pale green, maturing in early summer. *Wood* very light (25 pounds to the cubic foot, dry weight), soft, weak, and brittle, with light brown heartwood and very thick layers of greenish white sapwood.

Of all our trees, none is more talkative than this. A breeze that is barely felt on the cheek will set the foliage of the Trembling Aspen into a panic whispering. Almost all Aspens, Poplars, and Cottonwoods rustle somewhat, but the most restless foliage is that of those species of *Populus* which have the ribbon-like leafstalks longer than the blades themselves and flattened contrary to the general hang or plane of the leaf blades, with the result that the stalk acts like a pivot so that the blades cannot but turn in every breath of wind. The small leaves of the Trembling Aspen make a much softer sound, high and delicate, than the coarse Cottonwood's. And as they rustle they also twinkle, their lustrous upper surfaces forever catching the light like thousands of little mirrors flashed in mischievous fingers to dazzle the eyes.

Over its immense range this vivacious tree naturally occupies many habitats — in the Middle West old sloughs that have silted up, old beaver ponds in the Rockies, the zone of timber in Canada between the prairies and the tundra, the marge of high mountain lakes, and the depths of canyons down which rushes white water. Above all, terrain formerly under coniferous forest, but logged-off or swept by fire, is the favorite site of this quick-springing tree. Naturally the Aspen has many different tree companions in these various settings, but it shows to greatest advantage against a background of dark Spruces and Firs. With its Birch-like bark, its tremulous and lisping foliage, it finds the perfect foil in the unmoved, dark strength of the conifers.

Spring has come to the North Woods when the mouse-gray flower buds burst their shining chestnut scales. About a month later the leaves put forth, and from the first they are a cleanly brilliant green. In autumn the foliage turns clear gold, brilliant even on a dark day, but when the sunshine slants through the Aspens they blaze with yellow light. In Colorado people are so rich in Aspen gold they can forget how poor they are in all the other hues of the eastern forest. And this foliage lasts particularly late; in the Middle West, after the leaves of the Bur Oaks are shed, those of the Aspen are not only still upon the tree, but still green, still gossiping and dancing.

Naturally a tree so abundant, especially in the northern regions where hardwoods are less common, has entered into the lives and habits of all manner of men and creatures that therein dwell. In the days of open fireplaces at the posts of the Hudson's Bay Company the backlog of Aspen was kept burning the year around. The inner bark,

though bitter as quinine, is the favorite food of the beaver, and Aspen poles are the preferred structural material in his dams. The winter buds are devoured by grouse; snowshoe rabbits feed on bark and twigs, and through all seasons the moose finds browse in the tree.

In the evolution of the forest, in the crises that come to it through axe and fire, Trembling Aspen plays an indispensable rôle. Critics may call it a short-lived tree, prey to many diseases, with weak, soft wood, unworthy to succeed such noble predecessors as Pine and Oak. But its seedlings can take hold even in burned-out and denuded soil; tolerant of light and drought, wind and cold and heat, they spring up by the millions. Though the viability of the seed is of short duration, its tiny germs of life are produced in such numbers and carried so far on their downy wings over plains, over mountains, over barrens, that perpetually the Trembling Aspen is restocking the land that man has ruined. And in the shade of this nurse tree better and more permanent forest vegetation can arise.

Despised once as the veriest weed of a tree, Popple, as the lumberman prefers to call it, has in our age of paper come to the fore as a valuable pulp source, not, like Spruce, for newspapers, but for magazine stock. Deflated boom towns of the worked-out pineries are coming back where Popple grows. When it has been cut, it reproduces itself within 50 years by its unaided exertions and fertility. And so what seems like a shallow-rooted, frail vagabond of a tree may prove to have more value than many a species with a more solid reputation. All that — and charm as well!

BIGTOOTH ASPEN

Populus grandidentata A. Michaux

OTHER NAMES: Bigtooth or White Poplar. Popple.

RANGE: Nova Scotia to southern Minnesota, south to central Iowa, central Tennessee, Maryland and North Carolina, where rare.

DESCRIPTION: *Bark* of trunks smoke-gray tinged with green, thin and smooth; in old age dark brown and fissured into broad flat ridges. *Twigs*

dark orange, shiny, stout, with scattered orange lenticels. *Winter buds*
bright chestnut-brown, slightly resinous, downy. *Leaves* on laterally
flattened stalks, dark green above, pale beneath, 2 to 3 inches long, 2 to
2½ inches broad, thin and firm, hairless except for a white down on the
lower surface in spring. *Flowers* precocious, in downy catkins, 1½ to 2½
inches long; stamens 6 to 12, with light red pollen chambers; ovary
bright green. *Fruit* in elongated catkins, the seed-pods pale green, thin-
walled, downy. *Wood* close-grained, soft, and weak, medium-light (29
pounds to the cubic foot, dry weight).

The Bigtooth Aspen is a common companion of the Trembling
Aspen, though without nearly so wide a range, or such beautiful
bark, or twinkling, singing leaves. In the eastern states, however, it
grows taller than does the Trembling Aspen — 30 to 50 feet high and
sometimes as much as 70, with a long, clear, slender trunk and an irregular, rounded crown. In autumn the leaves turn a soft yellow, not
the equal of the translucent gold of the Trembling Aspen. Like its
relative, this tree comes up freely in burned-over ground and so is a
valuable nurse tree for subsequent forest growth. Going to the pulp
mill with other Aspens, it does an unhonored duty, and even in the
full vigor of its growth is passed over, by most persons, amidst the more
eye-taking splendors of the North Woods.

Yet this tree, of no great fame, only moderately beautiful, and plebeian in its uses, has its secrets. The very close-grained, soft, light wood is, uniquely in the tribe of Poplars, occasionally beautiful. The sapwood, velvety white, has a natural sheen of its own, yet the light tan of the heartwood is sometimes streaked with brown in a way that gives an effect like that of Olive wood. Sometimes it happens that fancy grains develop — feather-crotches, as the veneer salesman calls them — or a small block-mottled figure eagerly sought out. Though such logs are so rare that an entire carload of crotches (where stem and branch join) may yield but two or three with figured grain, the rare beauty when it is found is immediately moved up to the veneer saws. So are unrolled from the log what appear like sheets of living flame, which are especially popular for radio cabinets and bedroom suites. When finished in "natural" or in slightly brownish tones, paneling of feather-crotch Aspen wood is sought out by department stores as the perfect background for displaying fine feminine apparel.

EASTERN COTTONWOOD

Populus deltoides W. Bartram

OTHER NAMES: Big or Yellow Cottonwood. Carolina or Necklace Poplar. Cottontree. Whitewood.

RANGE: Throughout the Ohio valley to western Pennsylvania, the Mississippi valley (except northern Wisconsin and Minnesota), up the Missouri and its tributaries to about the 102nd meridian west, on the inner coastal plain and lower piedmont from Texas to Connecticut, up the Connecticut valley to Vermont and the shores of Lake Champlain, along the shores of southern Lakes Michigan and Erie, the north shore of Lake Ontario and the upper St. Lawrence. Absent from Florida, from the vicinity of the coast between Texas and Cape Hatteras, from eastern New England, and the Appalachian and Ozark highlands.

DESCRIPTION: *Bark* of trunks ashy gray and heavily furrowed with short, plate-like, irregular ridges. *Twigs* stout, marked by long, pale lenticels, light yellow tinged with green, becoming in their second year angular with thin but prominent wings extending along the angles and roughened by the big 3-lobed leaf scars. *Winter buds* lateral, brown, shiny, resinous and fragrant. *Leaves* thick and coarsely veined with a strong tannic and balsamic aroma, 3 to 7 inches long and often equally broad or broader, light bright green and lustrous above, paler below, with light yellow midrib; the stalks laterally flattened, reddish tinged, and furnished with small glands near the tip. *Flowers* in short-stalked, long, thick catkins. *Seed pods* thin-walled, ⅖ inch long. *Wood* soft, weak, brittle, the heartwood dark brown, the thick sapwood nearly white, very light (24 pounds to the cubic foot, dry weight).

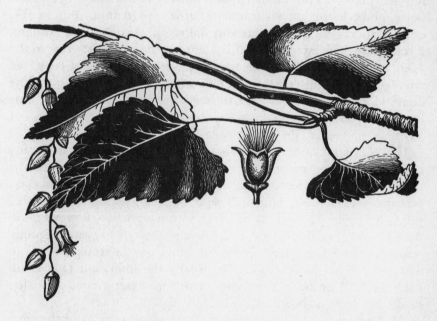

On the Atlantic seaboard the Cottonwood is just a tree among many trees, and few of the colonists, it would seem, held it in much honor. But as the pioneers of later times came out of the Oak openings of the Middle West and faced the heat of the prairies, the Cottonwood groves around the sloughs, so tall you could see them for miles across the waste, offered sweet shade, and even on the hottest, driest day reminded you, by the sound of their rustling leaves, of lake waters coolly lapping. On the other side of the Missouri, men found that the Cottonwood withstood the blizzard and drought. Poor though its wood might be, it gave the prairie pioneers their fences and corncribs, their cabins and stables, their ox yokes and saddletrees, and even their coffins. Though the wood checks and warps badly in seasoning, many a primitive church or first hotel or school was run up out of green Cottonwood.

Nor could the lumber industry despise a tree which might be 150 feet tall and 6 to 8 feet in diameter, with 50 or 60 feet of the bole clean of branches under the crown. The wood, for all its faults, is as stiff as White Oak, yet weighs no more than White Pine. For decades it was made into every kind of crate and box from packing for the heaviest pianos to the lining of cigar boxes. It was cut for excelsior, poles, posts, barrel staves, ironing boards, and trunks. But in this century its production has steadily fallen off, for the fine, straight, forest-grown trees have been felled. Left are the trees that grow in the open, by the banks of streams, on the shores of midwestern lakes, the muddy beaches and crumbling bluffs of the Missouri, the front-line dunes of Lake Michigan. Such trees usually fork from near the base into two to six trunks, making a crotch ideal for children's play, but anything save what the lumberman desires.

The life of a Cottonwood is short; at 75 years of age it is already old, the heartwood eaten away by decay, and the hollow becomes the home of the high-holder, the red-headed woodpecker, and the sapsucker, perhaps, too, of owls, bluebirds, and starlings. A Cottonwood 125 years old is probably exceptional. Yet, in compensation, it grows faster than any other of our trees — 4 or 5 feet a year. In 15 years a Cottonwood may be 60 feet high and in 50 years have a trunk 2 yards in diameter. A height of 125 feet is usually the limit, but only death halts the broadening of the crown, which may cast a pool of restless shade and light as broad as the tree is high.

The Cottonwood presents, through the seasons, a drama of changing appearance. In late winter the bark of the boughs and twigs begins to brighten and thus announces the rising of the sap. So the Cottonwoods shine across the prairie, serene and cheerful, just at the season when the snow is dingy, the vegetation sodden and colorless, the atmosphere heavy with damp.

Early in spring the catkins appear on the naked wood, and may drop, three weeks later, so heavily into the sloughs that they cover the water, the male bright yellow, the female a rich carmine. Cottonwoods shed immense amounts of pollen and cause hay fever in a few persons. Not until the flowers are falling do the leaves begin to shoot, coppery at first and strikingly handsome. Then in midspring the seed pods burst and the downy seeds are loosed in great quantities upon the wind, reminding one of thistle down and milkweed down in fall, so that the spring is touched with a wild autumnal quality wherever there are Cottonwood groves and in all the Middle Western towns where this tree is planted. And all summer long there is the constant motion of the leaves, heavier and coarser than the music of Aspen foliage, a sound like a sudden gush of water that as quickly stops, like the rustle of heavy skirts, like distant pattering applause.

About the last week in August, in the latitude of Chicago, the leaves on some individuals, particularly those in dry soil, begin to turn yellow, but leaf by leaf — not all at once — and to drop, leaving the tree naked in September. Around sloughs these trees stay green much longer. When the slough, too, goes dry in autumn, the leaves fall and the drying marl is found littered not only with the leaves but with quantities of punky twigs, for the Cottonwood is forever pruning itself of dead wood, and is, indeed, forever dying even while it continues its phenomenally rapid growth. Yet though so short-lived, so swift to decay, the Cottonwood, when cut back, sprouts with great vigor. So that, after all, though its years are numbered, youth may return to it over and over.

GREAT PLAINS COTTONWOOD

Populus Sargentii Dode

OTHER NAMES: Western Cottonwood. Sargent Poplar.

RANGE: New Mexico to Alberta, in the foothills of the Rockies, and east through the panhandles of Texas and Oklahoma, to eastern parts of Kansas and Nebraska (to the Missouri) and the Dakotas.

DESCRIPTION: *Bark* of the trunk thick and pale and deeply divided into broad, rounded ridges. *Twigs* stout, angular, light yellow. *Winter buds* downy, light orange-brown. *Leaves* on flattened stalks, furnished with one or two small glands where stalk and blade join, the blade 3 to 3½ inches long, and ½ inch broader than long, thick, heavy, pale green and very shiny. *Flowers* — male catkins 2 to 2½ inches long; female catkins becoming 4 to 8 inches long. *Seed pod* ⅖ of an inch long, thin-walled. *Wood* dark yellowish brown with thick, nearly white sapwood.

For many years this tree was not distinguished, even by botanists, from other Cottonwoods of the prairie states. It is now recognized as a smaller tree than the eastern Cottonwood, ordinarily ranging in height from 50 to 75 feet and rarely to ninety. Yet the trunks are often 4 to 6 feet thick. From such mighty boles were made the Missouri River pirogues, in the period from 1860 to 1870, according to the reminiscences of Frederick Chouteau.[1] Hollowed out with fire, these primitive river craft were often 4 feet through, and two of them placed side by side and solidly lashed together, could carry a burden of 10 to 15 tons.

This Cottonwood grows naturally in low moist ground, in the vicinity of streams, water holes, and old buffalo wallows. So in the days of prairie schooners immigrants sighted their way on the Santa Fe trail and the Oregon trail, from one grove of the Great Plains Cottonwoods to the next, sure that there they would find water, fuel, and shade in the burning day. Upon that shelterless sea of grass 400 miles wide, these Cottonwood groves were the wayside inn, the club, the church, the newspaper, and the fortress when the wagons drew up in a circle beneath the boughs. Whether the traveler "nooned it" or by night sent the sparks of Cottonwood logs flying to the stars, here he was sure to meet other travelers and with them exchange the vital news of the trail. And these trees, whispering among each other, must have heard the talk of the women, exchanging the immemorial secrets of their kind.

SWAMP COTTONWOOD

Populus heterophylla Linnæus

OTHER NAMES: Black, Swamp, or River Cottonwood. Cottontree.

RANGE: Western Louisiana to western Florida, north through southern Georgia, on the coastal plain to Long Island and Connecticut and in the Mississippi valley to southern Illinois, northern Indiana, central and northern Ohio.

[1] Kansas Historical Society *Collections* vol. 8, p. 428 (1904).

DESCRIPTION: *Bark* of trunks dirty brown, tinged with red, fissured into broad, flat ridges that in old age bear long, narrow plates attached only by the middle. *Twigs* of the season stout with small, pale lenticels, dark brown and shiny or ash-gray, smooth after dropping their early spring downiness, with orange pith. *Winter buds* slightly resinous and fragrant, with broad, bright, red-brown scales. *Leaves* on rounded stalks, dark green above, paler beneath, 4 to 7 inches long, 3 to 6 inches wide, thin and firm with conspicuous, meshed veinlets, and pale yellow midrib. *Flowers* — male catkins thick, becoming 2 to 2½ inches long, each floret with 12 to 20 stamens; female catkins slender, drooping, few-flowered, 1 to 2 inches long. *Seed pod* dark red-brown, thin-walled, long-stalked. *Wood* very light (25 pounds to the cubic foot, dry weight), soft, the heartwood dull brown with a thin band of pale brown sapwood.

In the rich bottom-lands of the lower Mississippi valley there grows a Cottonwood known to few but the natives. This tree reaches a height of 100 feet, with a clean, straight trunk, clear of branches for perhaps 50 or 60 feet; producing logs 4 and 5 feet in diameter, it is the most important commercial saw timber of all species of *Populus*. Yet even the lumber merchant, unless he happens to be located in that region, does not think of the Swamp Cottonwood as a separate entity; he buys and sells it simply as "Cottonwood" along with numerous other species. But this species, which gets least recognition of all, does at present most of the work in the family. It is said that 50 per cent of all excelsior now used in the United States comes from Swamp Cottonwood. And, indeed, as eastern Cottonwood is becoming exhausted as a commercial tree, Swamp Cottonwood is replacing it, in the utilitarian work of the lumber world, by furnishing cheap boxes and crates of all sorts. Commonplace such uses may be, but once far nobler trees were put to them; more fitting is it that a species like this, of value for nothing else and of no particular beauty, should serve in this rôle. One of the hopeful things about the future of this tree is that it grows so rapidly that in the lifetime of present lumber operators it has already replaced itself.

BALSAM POPLAR

Populus balsamifera Linnæus

OTHER NAMES: Tacamahac. Balm-of-Gilead. Bam. Rough-barked Poplar.

RANGE: Nova Scotia, Newfoundland and Labrador to Hudson Bay, the valley of the Mackenzie and Alaska, south to Idaho, Colorado, the Black Hills, the Turtle Mountains, northwestern Nebraska, Minnesota (except the corn belt), central parts of Wisconsin and Michigan, and to northern New England. Of scattered occurrence throughout New York State, rare in western Pennsylvania, in Iowa, northern Nevada, and British Columbia.

DESCRIPTION: *Bark* of trunks thin, light brown, smooth or warty, and in old age gray, furrowed, with broad, round ridges. *Winter buds* saturated in sticky, aromatic gum, the terminal bud large. *Twigs* of the season red-brown, becoming shiny the first winter, yellow-green the following spring, the lenticels bright orange. *Leaves* on rounded stalks, at first

gummy, becoming dark green and shiny above, but paler or rusty or whitened with a bloom on the lower surface, 3 to 5 inches long, ½ to 3 inches wide. *Flowers* in long-stalked catkins, the female becoming 4 or 5 inches long. *Seed pods* small, light brown. *Wood* soft, weak, very light (22 pounds to the cubic foot, dry weight), with pale brown heartwood and thick bands of white sapwood.

Those who have ventured beyond the great North Woods, out on the arctic prairies, where all the rivers fall into the polar sea or Hudson Bay, tell us of the surprising beauty of the isolated groves of Balsam Poplar there. How fair it must look then is something we can hardly realize when we encounter this species in the United States, for even when it is a fine tree, as in northern Michigan, it is still a forest tree, crowded upon by others, its best points rivaled by the similarities of its own close relatives the Aspens, and its claims to kingship contested by Birch and Maple, Beech and Pine. But up there, far to the north, the Balsam Poplar accompanies the lonely canoeman all the way, like a friend. In the endless monotony of horizontal scenery, it may tower up to heights of 100 feet, such as it never attains in the southern part of its range. And, forever twinkling its bright foliage and shaking it in the breeze, it makes music where otherwise all were silence. It gives fuel and shade where none could be expected. The foliage is like a cloak with a lining of another color, the upper leaf surface brilliant and cleanly, contrasted with the white or rusty lower surface. When the wind turns all the blades over, they flash silvery, and then, the breeze failing, the tree once more assumes its dark green and lustrous habit.

Balsam Poplar delights to grow upon low and repeatedly inundated bottom-lands — riverbanks and sand bars, borders of bogs and swamps. So streams like the Athabasca, the Peace, and the Mackenzie, as they eat at their banks or change their course in flood, are continually sweeping down great trunks of the Balsam Poplar on their turbulent floods, to bleach upon their estuaries and the unvisited shores of the arctic sea.

A fast-growing tree, whose trunk may attain 6 or 7 feet in diameter, this species, like so many other Poplars, acts as a nurse tree, preparing the way for the seedlings of Spruce. But as the Spruce grows tall it creates about itself and on the forest floor a dark, cold environment, completely hostile to the future seedlings of the sun-loving Balsam

Poplar. So it is driven away by the brood that it nurtured, and on its far-flying wings the seed must seek a new home.

The forester's name for this tree is Balsam Poplar, but to the pulp loggers of the North Woods it is Balm-of-Gilead (though the horticulturist means by that a variety mentioned below). Sometimes the loggers call it Balsam, which is confusing to say the least, or, again, they may designate it simply as Bam — a corruption, presumably, of Balm. Yet when it goes to market this wood usually loses identity in the general designation of Popple, and so the cut of this particular species cannot always be distinguished statistically on the ledgers of the wood-using industries.

A wood so quick-growing, so abundant on otherwise useless logged-over and burned-over lands and so soft amongst hardwoods, is nearly ideal for pulp, especially in the manufacture of magazine stock. Slim poles of young growth will do as well as large old trees, where pulp is the only consideration, and if the stand is cut over frequently it tends to keep on reproducing itself instead of giving way, at length, to Spruce.

The lumberman too has an interest in Balsam Poplar, but prefers large trees which yield broad clear planks. Though so soft and weak a wood, Balsam Poplar is remarkably tough in proportion to its light weight. This makes it valuable for boxes and crates, and for cutting into thin veneers for berry baskets. It is not even despised by the furniture manufacturers, as a core for costlier surfaces.

There is a variety of the Balsam Poplar, called by horticulturists the Balm-of-Gilead — botanists call it variety *candicans* (Aiton) A. Gray — which some think is a wild or natural hybrid between the Balsam Poplar and what other parent who can say? Nor does anyone seem to know where this offspring originated. Some say, or rather guess, it was in a European nursery, and others that Siberia is the birthplace of Balm-of-Gilead Poplar; they insist that it is never seen far from cultivation in this country and so it must be an exotic tree which has naturalized itself. But the distinguished horticulturist Liberty Hyde Bailey thought that it was native in early days in Michigan, where he grew up, and formed extensive groves which were felled in the whirlwind destruction of Michigan's forest resources. Balm-of-Gilead differs from Balsam Poplar in that the blades of the leaves are much darker on the upper surface — darkest of all Poplars' — and downy or hairy on the lower surface; also the leaf is broader and more heart-shaped, with coarser teeth. The leafstalks are downy, not smooth. And instead of forming a tall, more or less conical crown, Balm-of-Gilead has a much broader, more open head; so one may designate it as a broad shade tree, not a towering giant of the wilderness. It has the same general range as the true Balsam Poplar but is much more erratic in its occurrence.

An ointment is, or used to be, made of the clear gum of the buds, hence the name of the tree. Bees are said to smell this gum from afar, and to gather it on their thighs, later to employ it in sealing up the crevices of their hives. The name for the gum amongst the bee masters is "bee glue," and in consequence of its now widely recognized use in the honey business the tree is often planted near apiaries.

THE WILLOWS
(*Salix*)

WILLOWS are fast-growing trees, with bitter, astringent, aromatic bark, soft, light wood, with commonly a shrub-like habit of forking almost from the base. The vivid and limber twigs are frequently jointed near the base and so snap off easily. In our species the leaf-stalks are short and the alternate, deciduous leaves are narrow and long (more than twice as long as broad) and turn yellow in autumn. In falling, the leafstalk marks the twigs with prominent scars. The sexes occur on separate plants, in elongated catkins; the sex organs are set on disks, provided with nectar glands. Thus Willows are insect-pollinated, though probably also wind-pollinated. The stamens are few in number and the ovaries bear 2 recurved, short, 2-lobed stigmas. The fruit is a flask-shaped seed pod containing numerous seeds winged with silky down.

In no case, except Hawthorns, is it so difficult to distinguish between trees and shrubs as in the case of Willows. All the tree species are also frequently shrubby; many of the habitually shrubby species are occasionally 20 to 25 feet tall. In our circumscription only the following are regularly of tree size, but one may occasionally find that other species are too.

BLACK WILLOW

Salix nigra Marshall

OTHER NAME: Swamp Willow.

RANGE: New Brunswick to the region north of Lake Superior, and to southern North Dakota, southeastern South Dakota, Nebraska, Kansas, and Oklahoma; southward to Georgia and eastern and central Alabama and into the south-central states — Arkansas, Louisiana, and eastern Texas.

DESCRIPTION: *Bark* of trunks heavy, black or very dark brown, with deep, narrow cracks, and broad connecting ridges which are made up of freely peeling scales, becoming shaggy in old age. *Twigs* reddish olive to reddish brown, with tip bright orange or red. *Leaves* 3 to 6 inches long, 1/8 to 3/4 inch broad, sometimes rather curved, thin and light green. *Catkins* terminal on the twig, with yellowish scales. *Seed pod* only 1/8 inch long, light green. *Wood* very light (26 pounds to the cubic foot, dry weight), soft, and weak.

Our great Black Willow, perhaps the largest Willow in the world, occupies many habitats over its vast range, and takes on many forms. On the dunes of Cape Hatteras it is but a shrub; beside the brooks, streams, and smaller rivers of the eastern seaboard it is a moderately tall tree 40 to 50 feet high; in the deep muck of the bottom-lands of the

Middle South it may be a forest tree with a single straight bole fairly thick and very tall and clean of limbs a long way up. But beside the Father of Waters and its mighty tributaries, the Willow is a sprawling giant of a tree. In such sites Black Willow has usually several forks, beginning low down, each fork leaning somewhat outward; or trunks arising from the same root system seem to separate at the base. These leaning riverbank trees, when grown to large estate, have a sort of slouching picturesqueness, not unlike the lazy brown streams themselves.

Water-loving at all times, the Black Willow is especially fitted for its life as a riparian tree of the great slow rivers, for its twigs snap off easily at the base, as every American with a country childhood knows, and are capable of rooting if thrust in the ground. Most of us have known a native Willow, in some familiar dooryard, that was planted by this very means, and doubtless untold numbers of giant riverbank Willows were once floating twigs.

The bark of the root is intensely bitter and used to be an ingredient of spring tonics to "purge the blood." In Revolutionary and pioneer times Willow was much employed in the making of a fine charcoal for the black gunpowder of those days. As a wood compared with others, Willow would seem at first to have few good points. One of the lightest and probably the softest of all our eastern hardwoods, it is extremely weak in a structural sense; at least no one would think of building a bridge of Willow beams! Yet it has a strength of its own. When nails are driven into it, Black Willow does not readily split; on the contrary, its springy fibers hold a nail far better than most woods. Flexible, it serves for wickerwork furniture and baskets.

And though it has the worthless lazy look of some old riverbank loiterer, it plays, too, a heroic rôle. For where engineers have to face the problem of reinforcing levees, the Willow is unsurpassed for revetments. No other wood is so pliant yet tough, no other is so cheap, nor so ready at hand. Right on the banks of the Mississippi, the Ohio, and the Missouri, thrives the tree that can hold in check the fury of their powers in flood. Probably no other American tree is worth so much in property that, thanks to it, has not been destroyed; none, it may be, has saved so many human lives.

PEACH WILLOW

Salix amygdaloides Andersson

OTHER NAME: Almond Willow.

RANGE: Montreal to Winnipeg, along 50th degree north latitude to southeastern British Columbia, south to central Oregon, southeastern Washington, Nevada, Utah, Colorado, the panhandles of Oklahoma and Texas, Kansas, and central Missouri, southwestern Illinois, northern Indiana, along the southern shores of Lake Erie, and south to northern New York State.

DESCRIPTION: *Bark* thin, reddish brown, divided by irregular furrows into flat braided ridges with thick plate-like scales. *Twigs* dark orange or red-brown and shining, marked with scattered pale lenticels. *Winter buds* dark chestnut-brown, shiny, minute, and unsymmetrical. *Leaves* 2½ to 4 inches long, pale green and shining above, pale and whitened with a bloom below, with stout orange or yellow midrib and prominent veins and meshed veinlets. *Catkins* 2 to 3 inches long, with yellow scales. *Seed pod* light reddish yellow, ¼ inch long. *Wood* soft, close-grained, light (28 pounds to the cubic foot, dry weight) with light brown heartwood and thick, nearly white sapwood.

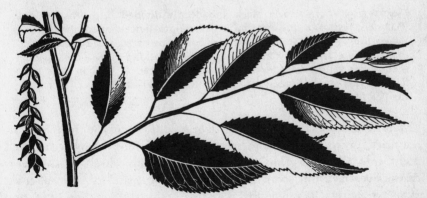

The Peach Willow, named for the shape of its handsome blades, so like the foliage of the Peach, grows 60 or 70 feet tall, with a fine single straight trunk up to 2 feet thick. and straight ascending branches. Not a frequent tree in the eastern states, it begins to be abundant around the mouth of the Ohio River, where it grows with its big sister species the Black Willow. But the further one goes toward the Rockies, the more Peach Willow tends to replace Black Willow along the Missouri and all the shallow braided streams tributary to it, and all the rivers that flow from the Rockies to the Gulf of Mexico.

With its gleaming leaves and general air of cleanliness and sprightliness, it is a vivid note in western river scenery wherever it occurs, and it holds innumerable banks from washing away. Lewis and Clark in their toilsome journey up the Missouri must have seen this glittering foliage around every bend. Still fresh, still shining in the western winds that blow it, it speaks to us softly of the heroes — uncouth, Homeric and immortal — who must have rested, panting, in its shade.

WARD WILLOW

Salix caroliniana Michaux

RANGE: Valley of the Potomac southwestward through northern parts of Kentucky and Tennessee to Arkansas and southeastern Kansas.

DESCRIPTION: *Bark* nearly black and deeply divided into broad ridges. *Twigs* red-brown or gray-brown. *Leaves* elliptic-lance-shaped, about 2 to 4 inches long, $\frac{1}{2}$ to $\frac{1}{3}$ inch wide, on hoary-downy stalks. *Flowers* terminal on leafy twigs, in narrowly cylindrical catkins 3 or 4 inches long, their scales yellow and densely pubescent; stamens 3 to 7 in each male floret. *Fruit* an oval green capsule abruptly contracted above the middle for $\frac{1}{4}$ of its length.

The Ward Willow, a slender tree about 20 or 30 feet high at maturity, grows on the borders of rivers and in swampy woods and melts into the background without proclaiming itself in any very distinctive way. But sooner or later the careful student of local trees, if he lives within its range, will note that beside the common Black and Peach Willows, there is another kind, resembling the Black Willow in its black and furrowed bark, but having a leaf much like that of the Peach Willow. It differs from it, however, in the fact that the twigs do not snap off when pulled, but cling with limber tenacity to the branch.

The Ward Willow is commonly seen around the city of Washington, in the low woods along the Potomac, and commemorates a Washingtonian whose importance was little realized when he lived. Lester Frank Ward was born in Illinois, grew up in Iowa, fought in the Civil War up to the battle of Chancellorsville when he was wounded and discharged, and in 1865 came to live in Washington, where his official title was that of geologist in the United States Geological Survey. But the wide ranging of his brilliant mind covered the fields of botany, anthropology, psychology and sociology — indeed, he was probably the first important sociologist in this country.

The verdict of his successors is that Ward was a genius working almost alone in his field. Because he lived before sociology had invented a peculiar jargon of its own, his meaning in such a classic as the *Psychic Factors of Civilization* is perfectly clear; the human mind can will the evolution of society; even a mediocre mind can be taught to double and treble its accomplishments; the highest function of government is social welfare.

But Lester Ward was also an excellent botanist, and in his long study of the flora of the District of Columbia the Willow later named in his honor came to his attention as something still undescribed. And as one tramps in earliest spring down in the river woods and sees the limber red-brown twigs putting forth their first pale green shoots, one will remember the springtime of this man's life. For in it he wrote one of the most charming diaries ever penned by an American, only recently discovered and published under the title of *Young Ward's Diary*, describing his passionate courtship of the girl who became his first wife. Some passages he put in French; others he left to the imagination which is summoned by asterisks. The diary of his ten years of first married bliss was burned, after his death, by his second wife.

SANDBAR WILLOW

Salix interior Rowlee

RANGE: From Lake St. John, Quebec, west to Manitoba and Wyoming, south to northern Virginia and in the Mississippi valley to the mouth of the river.

DESCRIPTION: *Bark* smooth, thin, dark brown slightly tinged with red and closely covered with close-pressed small scales. *Twigs* slender, light or dark orange or purplish red at first, growing darker after their first season. *Winter buds* acute, chestnut-brown, ⅛ inch long. *Leaves* 2 to 6 inches long, ⅛ to ⅓ inch wide, gradually narrowed to a long point, the margins with remote callous and glandular teeth, light yellow-green, the lower side paler and with a strong yellow midrib. *Flowers* appearing after the leaves, in cylindrical catkins, the male about 1 inch long and terminal and axillary, the female 2 or 3 inches long with light yellow-green scales; stamens 2 in each male floret. *Fruit* a light brown capsule about ¼ inch long. *Wood* soft, light (31 pounds per cubic foot, dry weight) the heartwood light brown tinged with red, the sapwood thin and pale brown.

Every stream, as soon as it loses the clear-eyed speed of its youth among the hills or mountains, begins to drop its load of silt as, with slackened velocity in the lowlands, it is no longer able to carry the burden of its particles. Thus sandbars or mud banks then begin to form upon the shores, or as islands in midstream. These would soon be swept away by the currents but for the swift growth of the Sandbar Willow, which binds the soil with its roots, and holds the ground until other trees can move in and take possession. Swiftly as Cottonwoods and Hackberries and Black Willows make their appearance, the Sandbar Willow is almost always prompter than they; it lands, like the Marines, as the first occupying force. And this is as true of the delta of the Mississippi as of the smallest river island of some stream just slackening speed after leaving the Appalachians.

The Sandbar Willow never grows to be much more than 20 feet high, and its trunk is always spindling — only a few inches in diameter

— but by underground stolons or creeping subterranean stems it sends up a whole thicket of slim trunks which are, properly considered, all part of the same tree. In its cryptic way, then, this is a very large tree — large enough at any rate to hold back even the mightiest rivers and turn them at last from their courses.

The catkins do not appear until the leaves have their full growth. It is by its leaves that you may most readily know the Sandbar Willow. No other Willow, indeed no tree of any sort in our sylva, has such extremely long leaves in proportion to their breadth — 16 to 18 times as long as broad. There is in consequence but little shade under a Sandbar Willow, if you should try fishing from the banks where it grows, but the bank is where you find it because of the pioneering, conquering spirit of this tree.

PUSSY WILLOW

Salix discolor Muhlenberg

OTHER NAME: Glaucous Willow.

RANGE: Nova Scotia to Manitoba, and south to Delaware, southern parts of Indiana and Illinois, southwestern Iowa and northeastern Minnesota. Also in the Black Hills.

DESCRIPTION: *Bark* of trunks thin, light brown tinged with red, on old trees divided by shallow fissures into thin, plate-like, oblong scales. Twigs stout, dark reddish purple and coated at first with pale deciduous hairs, becoming flecked with occasional orange-colored lenticels. *Winter buds* flattened and acute at the apex, ⅜ inch long, shiny and dark reddish purple. *Leaves* 3 to 5 inches long, remotely toothed, thick and firm, the upper surface bright green, the lower glaucous or silvery white, with conspicuously meshed veinlets. *Flowers* appearing before the leaves, in erect oblong-cylindric catkins terminal on the twigs, the catkins about 1 inch long, ⅔ inch thick, the male soft and silky in bud, and densely flowered; scales dark reddish brown toward the tip and covered on the back with silvery, silky hairs; stamens 2 in each male floret. *Fruit* a cylindric capsule more or less contracted above the middle to a long point, light brown coated with pale down.

Of all the native willows of the eastern United States, the Pussy Willow is the favorite. In earliest spring, or even in the last weeks of winter, the flower buds begin to burst their scales and the male catkins, still much shortened, peep out on the naked wood of the twigs, clothed in their silky soft hair. This constitutes the "pussy fur" known to everyone from childhood on. Even in florists' windows, in the city streets, pussy willows are displayed for sale and find purchasers who must, surely, be people with old memories of a country or a village past.

But you will enjoy them best if you go out in the country and cut your own Pussy Willow twigs. Take your galoshes, or whatever you choose for dry footing, for the Pussy Willow delights to grow around sloughs and swamps and riverbanks, and even when it takes up a position that in summer is comparatively dry, at this season the melting snows and high brimming of the streams will make your way an amphibious one. As you go sloshing into the mucky ground, you will hear the sweet piping of the first spring peepers and the swamp tree frogs and perhaps the old fence post you observed will suddenly pluck itself out of the marsh and go flapping away — for it was a bittern — with a raucous cry of *faugh!* It is a poor Pussy Willow that does not have a song sparrow perched on it at this season, his throat vibrating with the tumbled, jingling notes of his early love-song.

If you will keep the pussies in water after they have begun to turn into flowers, and wait a week for them to pass through an awkward age in which they have lost the charm of babyhood and not gained the splendor of maturity, you will be rewarded at last by the appearance of the beautiful golden stamens. Out in the woods these are sought by swarms of bees gathering pollen to make pollen-cakes for their young. It is doubtful, though, that they effect pollination, since there is little about the modest female catkins to attract them. Wind is the true pollinator. The Pussy Willow has therefore to produce enough pollen to satisfy the needs of the bees and to waste in unthinkable quantities upon the chill winds, for only a minute part will actually alight upon the female flowers. That is why the male flowers are so intensely laden with this golden dust that it drifts sometimes in swirls upon the cold waters of the woodland pool.

Leafing comes after the flowers, but in full leaf the Pussy Willow is in no way disappointing. The contrast of the dark green upper surface of the foliage with the bluish silvery undersides is lovely all season, and when fall comes the leaves turn a buttery yellow before dropping.

The leaves and twigs of Pussy Willow frequently become involved in a gall (*Rhabdophaga strobiloides*) which takes on the appearance of a pine cone or strobile and is sometimes mistaken for a fruit. It is so curious and handsome that it manages somehow not to be disfiguring like most of the galls.

BEBB WILLOW

Salix Bebbiana Sargent

OTHER NAME: Beak Willow.

RANGE: Southeastern Canada (valley of the St. Lawrence), south to New Jersey, northern parts of Ohio, Indiana, and Illinois and western Nebraska; west to the Rockies (as far south as Arizona) and northwest to Mackenzie and Alaska; south along the Coast Ranges in British Columbia.

DESCRIPTION: *Bark* thin, reddish or olive-green or gray tinged with red, and only slightly divided by shallow fissures into scaly plates. *Twigs* at first hoary-downy, varying from reddish purple to dark orange-brown and marked with scattered raised lenticels and roughened by elevated leaf scars; becoming light reddish brown in the second year. *Winter buds* oblong, bright chestnut-brown, gradually narrowed to a blunt point. *Leaves* 1 to 3 inches long, ½ to 1 inch wide, thick and firm, dull green above, silvery or bluish below, with conspicuous meshed veins. *Flowers* in catkins terminal on short leafy branchlets; male catkins short-cylindric, densely flowered, with 2 stamens in each floret; female catkins long and loosely flowered, with the ovary densely clothed in long silky white hairs. *Fruit* a long-cylindric capsule gradually narrowed into a long thin beak, and raised on a slender stalk sometimes ½ inch long.

The Bebb Willow, when conditions are easy, forms a luxuriant bushy growth up to 25 feet in height, with stout ascending branches that form a broad round head. But in the region west of Hudson's Bay it is a shrub with intricate twisted branches and reclining stems that creates impenetrable thickets over a vast and desolate domain. In Colorado it ascends the Rockies to 10,000 feet; it ranges into the arctic and yet is found as far south as Arizona. In the St. Lawrence valley and all the most thickly settled parts of the northeastern United States, it dwells as successfully with man as on the wild banks of the Mackenzie. One reason, it may be, is that the Bebb Willow is no timber tree. There is no reason why anyone, except an Indian making himself a wickiup, should ever cut it down. Absolute uselessness to man is one of the most valuable assets a tree can possess.

But the cottontail rabbit has a use for this Willow, as he has for so many others. In winter hunger he ekes out his hunted and timorous existence by gnawing on the bitter inner bark. If he girdles the tree, it will die. But Nature is apparently very fond of Willows, just as she is of rabbits, since she has made so many of them, and for every one that a rabbit kills, more, many more are forever springing up.

The easiest way to distinguish the Bebb Willow is by the undersides of the leaves. They are distinctly glaucous and their veins are intricately meshed and stand out so prominently that your fingers could identify the leaf even if your eyes were closed.

MISSOURI WILLOW

Salix missouriensis Bebb

RANGE: Along streams and lakes, North Dakota to Oklahoma, northeastern Kansas and the mouth of the Missouri, and eastern and western Iowa. Rare in southwestern Minnesota.

DESCRIPTION: *Bark* thin, smooth, light gray, slightly tinged with red, and covered with plate-like scales. *Twigs* slender, reddish-brown and downy, becoming brown tinged with green and hairless, with pale lenticels. *Buds* large (about 1 inch long), coated with hoary down, bright reddish, close-pressed to the twig. *Leaves* 4 to 6 inches long, 1 to 1½ inches broad, thin and firm, dark green and shining above, pale below and often silvery with a bloom, the midrib yellow, the forks of the veins uniting archwise within the margin of the blade. *Flowers* in elongate, erect, densely flowered catkins which appear before the leaves in earliest spring, the scales light green with silvery hairs. *Seed pod* light reddish brown. *Wood* dark reddish brown with thin pale sapwood.

The Missouri Willow is never a tall tree — 40 or 50 feet in height at the most — with a trunk 10 to 18 inches thick and slender branches which rise sharply up to make a narrow symmetrical head. Because its wood is durable in contact with the soil, Missouri Willow has been used for fence posts, but its greatest service to man is in the making of the land itself. For, with the Black Willow and the Sandbar Willow, the eastern and the Great Plains Cottonwoods, the Red Maple and the Green Ash, it is forever reclaiming sand bars, and holding banks in the ravenous shifting course of the Missouri.

The scientist who discovered this species was Prince Maximilian of Wied Neuwied, a little Rhenish principality. As an antidote to the patronizing or vicious pictures of America as we get them from early British travelers, his *Travels in the Interior of North America* (1832–34) [1] are a delight, showing this country as it looked to a man of cultivation and scientific objectivity, who traveled both in the cities and as far out upon the wilderness as the state of Indian warfare allowed. For with the blessing of General William Clark, partner in the great Lewis and Clark expedition and governor of Louisiana Territory, Maximilian and his party ascended the Missouri from St. Louis in the steamboat *Yellowstone,* and it was at Fort Osage that he first (April 15, 1833) collected this new tree species. Of his impressions he wrote:

"The drift wood on the sand bank, consisting of the trunks of large timber trees, forms a scene characteristic of the North American rivers; at least I saw nothing like it in Brazil, where most of the rivers rise in the primeval mountains, or flow through more solid ground. On the banks which we now passed, the drifted trunks of trees were in many places already covered with sand; a border of willows and poplars was before the forest, and it is among these willow bushes that the Indians usually lie in ambush, when they intend to attack those who tow their vessels up the river by long ropes."

And in his words, as from a window in a speeding train, we catch a glimpse of the wild scene of the Missouri as it looked in our heroic age, the days of Lewis and Clark, of Catlin, and of Audubon.

[1] Vols. XXII, XXIII, XXIV of Thwaites's *Early Western Travels.*

THE WALNUTS
(*Juglans*)

WALNUTS have strongly aromatic leaves, bark, and fruits, with thick, round twigs whose pith occurs in overlapping flakes (easily seen by splitting the twigs lengthwise). The terminal buds have two pairs of opposite and rather open scales, the inner conspicuous. In falling in autumn, the leafstalks mark the twig with 3-lobed elevated scars.

The alternate, deciduous leaves are compound and consist in numerous (11 to 23) leaflets; the veins near the margin tend to recurve and mesh. The flowers occur in separate catkins on the same tree, the thick, heavy male catkins drooping from the branch, with 8 to 40 stamens in each floret; the female catkins are few-flowered, each ovary with a finely feathered stigma.

The fruit consists in a leathery, woody husk enclosing the nut which is hard-shelled, the shell furrowed and sculptured and opening by two natural sutures; the oily seed or kernel is 2-lobed between the ruminations or inner wall of the nut and enclosed in a thin papery, veiny coat.

BUTTERNUT

Juglans cinerea Linnæus

OTHER NAME: White Walnut.

RANGE: New Brunswick to southern Minnesota, southeastern Nebraska, eastern Kansas, and Arkansas, and northernmost Mississippi, south on the Atlantic coast to Delaware, in the piedmont and mountains of Virginia (rarely tidewater), in North Carolina chiefly in the mountains, in South Carolina, Georgia, and Alabama, wholly so. Absent from the basin of Lake Superior.

DESCRIPTION: *Bark* of trunks light brown, smooth until old age, when rugged with deep cracks and broad, braided, scaly ridges. *Twigs* in their first year dark orange-brown, bright green and lustrous after they lose their rusty, sticky down; on older growth smoke-gray and roughened, conspicuously marked by the bud scars and the large U-shaped, hairy-fringed leaf scars. *Terminal buds* enclosed at first in two palely downy outer scales, the two inner large, somewhat flattened and obliquely truncate. *Leaves* 15 to 17 inches long, in over-all dimensions, the leaflets 11 to 17 in number, each 3 to 4 inches long and 1½ to 2 inches broad, hairy and sticky, the upper surface dull, yellow-green, the lower paler. *Flowers* — male catkins drooping, bright green, with 8 to 12 dark brown stamens in each floret, and rusty scales; female catkins on the ends of the twigs, erect, with bright red stigmas, the scales coated with sticky pink hairs. *Fruits* — husks clothed in sticky hairs, thin but hard and enclosing

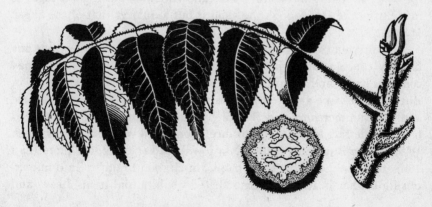

the thick-walled nut, which is deeply sculptured between the prominent four ribs and encloses the sweet, oily kernel in its papery, veiny coat. *Wood* very light (25 pounds to the cubic foot, dry weight), weak, soft, rather coarse-grained, easily worked, with a satiny surface capable of receiving high polish; light brown growing darker upon exposure to the air, with thin bands of pale sapwood.

When, all unwary, you pick up a Butternut's fruit where it has fallen on the ground after a windy autumn night, you learn your first botanical lesson about this tree, for the sticky, rusty hairs of the husk leave a brown stain upon the fingers. You try to wipe it off but find that you cannot, nor can you scrub it off; only time will cleanse your hand. For this is no ordinary stain; it is a genuine dye. Even the white inner bark yields a yellow or orange dye that has been used for a century and a half by the southern mountaineers in dyeing their homespuns. During the Civil War, the backwoods Confederate troops were sometimes dressed in homespun "uniforms" of butternut-dyed cloth, and they became known as "Butternuts." So the very name of this tree has become a synonym for tattered glory.

The kernel is agreeable when fresh — oily and sweet — but soon becomes rancid. Today one seldom sees in the markets these delicious nuts; walnuts and pecans have captured the popular fancy. Yet the Indians appreciated butternuts, for Roger Williams mentions that the Indians made of them an excellent "Oyle good especially for annoynting their heads. And of the chips of the Walnut-tree, the barke taken off, some English in the country make an excellent Beere both for taste, strength, and color." Few know it now, but a good sugar is made from the sap, though the yield is but a quarter that of the Sugar Maple.

A countryman's tree is the Butternut, known to the farm boy but not his city cousin. One who takes thoughtful walks in the woods may come to know and admire it for the grand old early American it is. But the landscape architect complains that the leaves are often sparse and by summertime may be dingy-looking, and that many dead branches detract from its appearance. Compared with the stately Black Walnut, the Butternut is usually a low, broad tree, seldom more than 40 feet tall, with a short thick trunk which soon branches into numerous limbs that in themselves may be very substantial stems, heavy and wide-spreading. In the forest it may tower up 100 feet and develop a fine unbranched trunk clear for half its total length.

Very light and soft and easily worked, the wood of Butternut has been largely employed as a cabinet wood and for interior finish. In the old days of carriage building, fine "shays" were often paneled in Butternut because of its beauty combined with lightness. Though soft-textured, the wood of Butternut is so lustrous and satiny as to be a favorite of the architect designing rooms of dignity and luxury. The paneling of the Chicago Board of Trade grill is veneered in perfectly matched half-panels, and used in conjunction with light brown pigskin it produces an air of sumptuousness. Age only mellows Butternut's surface, and like Black Walnut it "stays put," never warping or cracking. It is still a favorite of the wood carver, and many fine old American altars were made of carven Butternut. Alas, the demands upon this tree have been unremitting, and today "White Walnut" can seldom be procured in practical lengths. This uniquely American wood is rapidly becoming a scarce and precious hardwood, nor does the future promise better things, unless that day ever comes when the American people demand that their wooden resources be restored to them by a planned forestry.

BLACK WALNUT

Juglans nigra Linnæus

RANGE: Western Massachusetts and Connecticut to the coast of North Carolina, west through the upper districts of the Gulf states to central Texas and Oklahoma, and from southern Ontario to southern Minnesota and central Nebraska and Kansas.

DESCRIPTION: *Bark* of trunk deeply furrowed, thick, and broken into broad dark brown or reddish-tinged ridges with thick scales. *Twigs* stout, rigid, clothed at first with pale or rusty matted hairs, becoming orange or rusty, and marked by conspicuous orange lenticels and large pale leaf scars. *Winter buds* invested by a pale silky down, the terminal buds larger than the lateral ones which open, partially, during the winter. *Leaves* 1 to 2 feet long in over-all dimensions, leaflets 15 to 23 in number, not hairy and sticky, upper surface shining, and smooth, bright yellow-green, the lower softly downy especially on the veins, each leaflet about 3 inches long and 1 inch wide. *Flowers* — male catkins stout, drooping, 3 to 5 inches long; female flowers in 2- to 5-flowered little oval spikes, the stigmas yellow-green tinged with red. *Fruit* with clammy-hairy husks, 1 to 2 inches thick, light yellow-green, roughened by groups of pale short hairs; nut oval, slightly flat, dark brown and deeply divided into irregular ridges. *Wood* medium-strong and hard, medium-heavy (39 pounds to the cubic foot, dry weight) with rich, dark brown heartwood sharply contrasted with pale sapwood.

The home of the Black Walnut is the deep rich soil of bottom-lands and fertile hillsides; it grew abundantly throughout the primeval hardwood forests of America. There in their days of glory it used to reach heights of 150 feet, with the first 50 feet clear of branches, making a splendid saw log sometimes 6 feet in diameter. But the Black Walnut really prefers to stand well by itself in an open field; it dearly loves a dooryard where it will be watered and pruned and protected by the hands of its human friends. Then its limbs spread widely, the head becomes a great green dome, and the whole tree seems to luxuriate in space and deep soil and abundance of sunshine and rain. At all times its appearance suggests massive strength, the trunk solid and heavily furrowed, the compound leaves like big fronds, the catkins, which appear with the leaves in midspring, heavy and vivid, and the clusters of fruits in fall hard and solid on the tree.

Of all the native nut trees of America, the Black Walnut is the most valuable save only the Pecan, and in the traditions of pioneer life and rustic childhood it is even more famous. In a more innocent age nutting parties were the most highly prized of children's festivities in autumn, throughout the eastern forest belt, and though butternut and hickorynut, hazelnut, chestnut and chinquapin, and even beechnut and kingnut were gathered, walnut was the favorite. The charm of the nutting party, of course, did not depend solely on the subsequent pleasure of cracking the rough shell and extracting the delicious, oily sweet kernel from its intricate walls. It derived much from the tingling autumn airs, the flaming forest leaves, the wild telegraphing calls of the crows, and the shouts and games of the other children. Someone still gathers the nuts, for Walnut is a valuable confection in the market, and a favorite flavoring for ice cream.

Black Walnut provides the finest cabinet wood of North America. The colonists understood its utilization from the first — indeed were exporting it to England from Virginia as early as 1610 — without, however, being able to develop its beautiful figured grains as can be done now with veneers. On the contrary, they employed solid Walnut wood and often had so little appreciation of it as a grain beautiful in its own right that they painted its surface. Walnut was used in every sort of homemade furniture of the Colonial and Federal periods, but seldom in fine styles. By the time that appreciation of rare grains was born and the rage for Walnut really began (1830 to 1860), machine-made furniture, turning out Empire, Victorian, and Revival styles, ruined many a fine piece of wood. Then, as the final irony, when styles improved, Walnut had become comparatively rare.

There is so little Black Walnut in the forest now (except in the southern Appalachians) that it is sought by lumbermen in a door-to-door hunt throughout the countryside, where owners are sometimes tempted by a small price to sacrifice a magnificent shade tree worth in some cases, if they but knew it, more than their houses.

But in pioneer times these giants were so abundant in our earth that they were used for such humble things as snake-rail fences; probably many of the rails that Lincoln split were Walnut. Millions of railroad ties have, on account of its durability in contact with soil, been made of this now valuable wood. Cradles were almost exclusively made of Walnut in our heroic era. For gunstocks it was, and is, unsurpassed, since no other wood has less jar or recoil; it never warps or shrinks; it is light in proportion to its strength, never splinters and, no matter how long it is carried in the hand, will not irritate the palm, with its wonderful satiny surface. In every war, the United States

Government has made a fresh raid upon Black Walnut for gunstocks. Unfortunately, armies are always growing larger, and Walnut grows rarer. In our day some of the old heirlooms of solid Walnut furniture are being dragged out of garrets, barns, and cellars where they had been thrust in the first craze for Victorian elegance, and either refurbished by the cabinetmaker or sold to him to be sawed into veneer.

There is a significant difference between the solid Walnut furniture of the pioneers and the modern Walnut veneers. The old trees were mostly forest-grown, hence slow-growing; it took about 100 years to produce a Walnut of timber size under those conditions, and the boards show a straight grain and very dark heartwood. Thus the old-time Walnut furniture often has a somber, heavy look, lacking refinement either in grain or design. But there is an honesty about it that links us to our past. Perhaps the best example of the middle period of American Walnut furniture is the great secretary of President Jackson, to be seen at "The Hermitage" near Nashville, at which he wrote his sizzling and misspelled correspondence.

The wood of the dooryard trees that are being cut now is quite other. It is lighter in color and much more varied and handsome in grain. This beauty can be brought out by skillful cutting. The first veneers were sawed out ⅛ inch thick, but it is now possible to rotate the log against a knife and unroll, as a continuous band of paper may be unrolled, a sheet of wood only ½₈ inch thick. An old tree may thus yield up to 90,000 square feet of precious veneer, valued sometimes at $20,000 wholesale. This method also permits the nicest matching of mirror-image cuts of the same fancy grain, resulting in butterfly or even double-butterfly or diamond patterns that no art of man can touch for delicate intricacy and subtle shading. They simulate, too, feathers, flames, or bees' wings. In some cases the wood actually changes color, like changeable silk, when viewed and lighted first from one angle, then another, so that this once living stuff seems to keep still a secret life of its own.

THE HICKORIES

(*Carya*)

THE HARD, TOUGH TWIGS of these trees have solid pith; the bark is rough, scaly, or shaggy. The axillary buds are much smaller than the terminal but all are covered with more or less conspicuous scales. A heavy aroma pervades the foliage. The large leaves are compound, with 5 to 9 leaflets with toothed margins and unsymmetrical bases, the veins forked but running to the margins. Though the leaflets are opposite, the leaves themselves are alternate and deciduous. The leafstalks have large, cushion-like bases that partially clasp the twig; when they fall they leave on the twig a big, elevated, somewhat 3-lobed leaf scar.

The catkins of the male flowers are branched, solitary or clustered; each floret bears 3 to 10 stamens with bright red or yellow anthers. The female flowers are found in 2- to 10-flowered spikes. At maturity the hard husk of the roundish or egg-shaped or pear-shaped fruit splits naturally along four valves. Within is the nut with a hard shell that is 4-valved at base; it is not sculptured as in Walnuts but the seed within is variously grooved on the flat or concave lobes.

BROOM HICKORY

Carya glabra (Miller) Sweet

OTHER NAMES: Brown or Black Hickory. Pignut.

RANGE: Southern and western New England to southern Michigan, Illinois, and southeastern Iowa, southward from New Jersey to Georgia on the piedmont and lower mountain slopes, all of Tennessee except the Mississippi bottom-lands and south to east-central Mississippi.

DESCRIPTION: *Bark* light gray, close and firm, divided by small fissures into low ridges, but at times displaying plate-like scales. *Twigs* marked with pale oblong lenticels, slightly angled, light green, marked by small leaf scars. *Buds* shining, light orange-brown or dark reddish brown. *Leaves* in over-all dimensions 8 to 12 inches long, composed of 5 or rarely 3 or 7 leaflets with sharp, incurved teeth, texture firm and thick, the upper surface dark yellow-green, without hairs, the under surface paler and often furnished with tufts of pale hairs in the axils of the veins. *Flowers* — male catkins 3 to 7 inches long, bright yellow-green and fuzzy with light down; female flowers in 2- to 5-flowered spikes, hoary, about ½ inch long. *Fruit* — pear-shaped husk 1 inch long, ¾ inch wide, contracted to a stalk-like base, opening tardily by 2 sutures, nut of the same shape, compressed though without ridges, enclosing the kernel. *Wood* very strong, tough, very heavy (48 to 55 pounds to the cubic foot, dry weight) with light or dark brown heartwood and thick yellow or nearly white sapwood.

To turn from the preceding species, the native Walnut, prince of cabinet woods, to the incomparably tough, heavy, shock-resistant Hickory, is like turning from a polished nobleman to a sinewy, hard-bitten backwoodsman. And of all Hickories the Broom is, on the whole, the most rugged of a hardy breed. Its wood is the heaviest in our range, equaled only by Shagbark Hickory (from which this species is hardly distinguished in the lumber business). Tough yet flexible, and resistant to an impact load, it is in the highest demand for axe handles and every sort of striking tool. Because of its low conductivity of heat, it is prized for wagon parts, like the hub, where the heat of friction may be great, or others, like singletrees, that may endure a sudden strain. No wonder that the covered wagons of American history rolled westward on Hickory hubs and Hickory felloes, or that Hickory sulkies have made the American trotting race famous. The terrific vibration on the big picker sticks in textile looms can be sustained only by Hickory. Skis, too, must stand violent strains, so that American Hickory is the most prized wood of skiers the world over. For Hickory is stronger than steel, weight for weight, more elastic, less brittle, less heat-conductive. It is not possible to imagine another wood which could replace our Hickories if all of them were depleted — a situation now looming well above the horizon.

This species alone was cut — under the stimulus of increasing war needs — to the tune of 78,000,000 board feet annually. This is not a high figure compared with the cuts of some of our western softwoods, but it is high when other factors are considered, such as the extreme slowness of the growth of the tree under forest conditions (sometimes twice as slow as such a notoriously slow-growing species as White Oak). Add to this the tremendous toll taken by wood-boring insects, which in inconceivable numbers attack the living trees, while other species destroy the lumber just when it has been carefully seasoned for a year. And finally there is the wasteful way in which the wood is utilized, only the pale sapwood normally being accepted by buyers, because of an unfounded prejudice that the darker heartwood is weaker, although scientific tests do not bear this out in the least.

But Hickory fights back toward survival in its own stubborn way. Like backwoods children flourishing, the seedlings can come up through dense shade. So Hickory is a "pushing" species, able to succeed other hardwoods in the ecological course of events, even to succeed itself, generation after generation, on the same land. More, it will endure poorer soils and drier situations than many of our hard-woods. And, when released from intense forest competition, it can put on comparatively fast growth where, before, it had been the slowest of all.

Spring is late in coming to most of the Hickories, and well after other trees have flowered or leafed out this one stands forth, naked and massive, on the dry ridges and hillsides where it delights to grow. Thus bare, its thin, contorted branches give it an awkward look. But the winter gales may wrench at it as they will, for its very deep taproot — remarkable even for a Hickory — makes it one of the most windfirm of trees. And if the tree be closely examined in winter, it will be seen that the outer bud scales have already fallen and the next inner pair of scales, clothed in shining golden hairs, are ready to expand till they look like petals. Finally the innermost bud scales open, and with sustained warm weather they curl back almost like Magnolia flower parts, luminous as spring sunshine and with the downy look of young life. Very different are the bold spring leaves from the weather-worn foliage of autumn, turned a dull yellow. Often the leaflets fall off separately, leaving the leafstalks clinging, bare, to the twig, like so many yellow darning needles, while the hard little fruits come rattling down in the wind. The small kernel is insipid or bitter, not in the least in the class of the nuts of Shagbark and White Hickory and Kingnut and Pecan.

The name of Broom Hickory was given it by the early settlers because narrow strips were split from the wood and made into brooms — how, is well told by Doctor Daniel Drake in his memoirs of *Pioneer Life in Kentucky*:

"Till I went to Cincinnati to study medicine, I had never seen a scrubbing brush. We always used a split broom, in the manufacture of which I have worked many a rainy day and winter night. A small hickory sapling was the raw material. The 'splits' were stripped up for eight or ten inches with a jackknife pressed by the right thumb, bent back, and held down with the left hand. When the heart was reached and the wood became too brittle to strip, it was cut or sawed off, and the splits turned forward and tied with a tow string made for the purpose on the spot. It only remained then to reduce the pole above to the size of a handle. A lighter and genteeler work was making 'scrubs' for the buckeye bowls and the good old black walnut table (bless it!) with a crack in the middle, from end to end, occasioned by the shrinking of the boards. The 'scrub' was a short hand-broom made precisely like the scrubbing broom, but out of a smaller sapling."

That Age of Wood was a stouthearted age, and the Hickories, tattered old sentinels yielding reluctantly to the screaming saw and the silent enemies boring from within, stand as its rude but noble symbols.

SAND HICKORY

Carya pallida (Ashe) Englemann and Graebner

RANGE: Louisiana, north in the Mississippi valley to western Tennessee, and east to northern Florida and the piedmont of Georgia and Carolina, going up to 2200 feet in the southern Appalachians of North Carolina and eastern Tennessee, north on the coastal plain of Virginia and the Delaware peninsula to Cape May, New Jersey.

DESCRIPTION: *Bark* of trunks dark gray and deeply furrowed or even nearly black or sometimes pale and slightly ridged. *Twigs* red-brown, slender. *Winter buds* reddish brown covered with silvery scales. *Leaves* in over-all dimension 7 to 15 with 7 or rarely 9 leaflets, the terminal and largest one 4 to 6 inches long and 1 to 2 inches wide, all with very long drawn out tips, finely toothed margins, shining and pale green above, even paler below, resinous and fragrant. *Flowers* — male catkins covered with bunched hairs and silvery scales, 2½ to 5 inches long; female solitary, oblong, covered with yellow scales. *Fruit* ½ to 1½ inches long, the husk covered with yellow scales, splitting entirely to the base by 2 or 3 sutures and enclosing the compressed and prominently ridged white nut. *Wood* brown with nearly white sapwood.

When those not trained as botanists first begin to study trees they are usually content to learn that a given specimen is an Ash, an Oak, an Elm or a Hickory. But as they go about on their walks, noticing the forms of trees, the dates of leafing-out and flowering, and sampling the taste of nuts and berries — "out of compliment to nature," as Thoreau said — they begin to realize that almost every region has more than one kind of Ash, of Oak, of Elm, of Hickory. At this point the botanist, who may have been regarded as a hair-splitting old fuddy-duddy, is treated with a new respect. It is he who patiently follows out the line dividing one kind of tree from another, who describes the new species and gives them, whether we like it or not, their Latin names.

And the Sand Hickory is one of the botanists' species, not specifically distinguished by laymen, though it grows as much as 100 feet high with a trunk 3 or 4 feet in diameter, and bears sweet-tasting nuts; so for a couple of centuries it awaited recognition that was given it at last by Mr. William Ashe, of the Forest Service. The Sand Hickory has no illustrious history like so many of its close relatives; probably only squirrels, boys, and botanists are epicures of its nuts, and if its wood ever goes to the lumber yards it passes simply as Hickory. Yet in the economy of Nature it may have its place; in the future it may meet needs which today we wot not of.

SHAGBARK HICKORY

Carya ovata (Miller) K. Koch

OTHER NAMES: Shellbark or Scalybark Hickory.

RANGE: Southern Maine to Delaware, thence south on the piedmont to southern Georgia, west to southeastern Texas (but not the Gulf Coast) and from Ontario through southern Michigan to central Wisconsin and southeastern Minnesota, central and southwestern Iowa and extreme

southeastern Nebraska, eastern Kansas, and Oklahoma. Absent from
northern New Hampshire and northern Vermont.

DESCRIPTION: *Bark* smoke-gray and usually shaggy with very heavy long
strips connected with each other by their edges, rarely with close smooth
bark. *Twigs* slightly angled, at first bright reddish brown to light gray,
turning dark gray and marked with leaf scars. *Terminal buds* ½ to ¾
inch long, obtuse, and broadly egg-shaped, the outer pair nearly triangular, hairy, dark brown, falling in autumn. *Leaves* 8 to 14 inches long
in over-all dimensions, of 5 or rarely 7 leaflets, the three terminal leaflets
each 4 to 6 inches long, the others smaller, firm, dark yellow-green on the
upper surface, paler below. *Flowers* — male catkins 4 or 5 inches long,
fuzzy with glandular hairs, female borne in small, inconspicuous, 2- to
5-flowered spikes, clothed in rusty wool. *Fruits* in pairs or solitary, 1 to
2½ inches long, dark reddish brown to nearly black at maturity, the
husk flecked with pale lenticels, woody, ⅛ to ½ inch thick, splitting
freely at last nearly to the base, revealing the compressed, angled, nearly
white nut. *Seed* 2-lobed, divided nearly to the base by a thin partition,
covered with a thin, light brown, rather shiny papery coat. *Wood*
extremely hard, tough, close-grained, and flexible, very heavy (52
pounds to the cubic foot) with light brown heartwood and thin, nearly
white sapwood.

To everyone with a feeling for things American, and for American history, the Shagbark seems like a symbol of the pioneer age, with its hard sinewy limbs and rude, shaggy coat, like the pioneer himself in fringed deerskin hunting shirt. And the roaring heat of its fires, the tang of its nuts — that wild manna that every autumn it once cast lavishly before the feet — stand for the days of forest abundance.

"The fruit" wrote William Bartram in his *Travels in North America,* "is in great estimation with the Indians. The Creeks store [Shagbark Hickory nuts] in their towns. I have seen above an hundred bushels of these nuts belonging to one family. They pound them to pieces and then cast them into boiling water, which, after passing through fine strainers, preserves the most oily part of the liquid; this they call by a name which signifies hiccory milk; it is as sweet and rich as fresh cream, and is an ingredient in most of their cookery, especially homony and corn cakes."

When the Indians were gone and the white men came, "nut cracks" were a popular diversion of pioneer boys and girls. The tough hickory nuts, and black walnuts too, were cracked with hammers and flatirons and then shelled. As many were eaten at the time as young appetites could endure — which is a great deal — and the rest saved for sale and for future consumption. Quite as important as the nuts at these cracks seemed the kissing games played by the children and the courting that got done among the older boys and girls. Today it is to be feared that even on farms nut cracks are a thing of the past; the farm children get to the country store and buy packaged peanuts and pecans, like the rest of us.

A Shagbark can usually be distinguished as far as it can be seen by the smoke-gray bark which is forever warping away from the stem in great plates a foot long or more, and 6 or 8 inches wide. Frequently the strip is loose and curling at both ends, and is only more or less loosely attached by the middle while its edges usually touch those of another strip of bark, so that if one tries to pull it free from the trunk, it is so engaged on both sides that one soon gives up the task. True, there are other trees with exfoliating bark, but none in our sylva with such great segments, so long or so thick. This shagginess begins to develop in comparatively young trees. Around the feet of old speci-mens the forest floor may be quite littered with the cast-off heavy coat of armor. But the tree is not shedding its bark preparatory to some other condition, for normally new shagginess has simply thrust the old away. Occasionally a tree has close, not shaggy bark, and is called by lumbermen "Bastard Hickory."

In rich deep soil, Shagbark attains heights of 120 feet, and under forest conditions it may form a columnar trunk, free of branches for the first 50 or 60 feet. It tends to have a narrow crown, with short branches and heavy, yet graceful, drooping branchlets. Against the winter sky the outline of form and twigs is scraggly and uncouth.

But about the first week in April the inner bud scales begin to open, arching out and twisting at the same time but with their tips at first still adhering in a pointed arch. Shining and downy on the inner surface, and yellow-green richly tinged with red, they look like petals of some great Tulip or Magnolia as finally they part and curl back. The young leaves and catkins are then seen standing up in a twist, like a skein of green wool. The catkins now rush into growth simultaneously with but more swiftly than the delicate, pale, and lustrous young leaves.

Dark, heavy, and aromatic is the foliage all summer but if the season is a dry one the leaves may begin to turn a dull brown even in August and drop, leaving the tree prematurely naked. Yet if they last through, they join modestly in the autumn splendor of our Middle Western woods, with a soft dull gold, not without its luminous beauty when the sun of Indian summer shines through them. To all who know the Shagbark, such memories are linked with visions of the violet smoke of asters curling low through the drying grasses, with peeled October skies, with crow calls that signal your presence through the woods, and the shining of red haws, like little apples, on the thorn trees.

The fuel value of Shagbark is higher than that of any other American wood except Locust. A cord of Hickory is almost the equivalent in thermal units of a ton of anthracite, and even today costs less. In our times of scarcity, it is horrifying to think that untold millions of cords of this wood were chucked into the hearths and stoves of pioneers. The log cabins, notoriously drafty if not perfectly constructed, were kept warm by a roaring fire, day and night, a large part of the year, and Shagbark was the favorite wood to feed this Moloch.

Green wood of Hickory is considered by epicures the perfect fuel for the preparation of smoked hams. The pioneers found this out, and no one has ever discovered a finer source of coals or fumes for this purpose. The aroma of burning Hickory enters into the ultimate

taste of the smoke-cured ham as definitely as that of Spanish Cedar in cigar boxes blends with the taste of the finest Havanas. True that, weight for weight (not volume for volume), White Pine fuel has more thermal units, but for seasoning hams it would never have the long-lasting coals, or impart the subtle flavor, of Hickory.

The pioneers made boxes of the shaggy bark. They made ramrods for their guns of Hickory, and fenced in their grounds with Hickory rail fences, though it is one of the most difficult woods in the temperate zone to split, and decays swiftly when exposed to the elements. The early furniture makers discovered that seasoned rounds of Hickory in posts of green "sugar wood" (Maple) made unbreakable joinery, for as the green wood shrank it clasped the iron-hard Hickory dowels forever. Green Hickory splits made perfect hinges for the pioneers' cabin doors. Yellow dye from the inner bark tinctured the homespun of the cabin housewife. Hickory hoops encircled the ubiquitous pork barrel and are not surpassed in general utility by the metal hoops of today.

That Hickory was a symbol of strength in the pioneer mind is attested by the nickname of "Old Hickory" given General Andrew Jackson. It was accorded him when, a major general of militia, he received callous orders from the Secretary of War to discharge his troops, in the War of 1812, at Natchez, when they were 500 miles from home. Flatly refusing, he marched his men back along the Natchez Trace to Tennessee in order that they might be mustered out near their homes. Sharing their poor fare with them, sleeping with them on the hard ground, he wrung from the backwoodsmen their admiration. "He's tough," admitted the tough boys from the Hickory groves, "tough as Hickory." "Old Hickory" they dubbed him, and the name chanted him to the White House. Today he sleeps beneath six towering Shagbarks, in his grave in "The Hermitage" garden.

BIG SHELLBARK HICKORY

Carya laciniosa (F. Michaux) Loudon

OTHER NAMES: Bottom, Western, or Thick Shellbark. Kingnut.

RANGE: Western New York through southern Ontario to southeastern Michigan, west to southern and eastern Iowa, southeastern Nebraska, eastern parts of Kansas and Oklahoma, northern parts of Arkansas and Mississippi, and through the western Alleghenies to Tennessee and extreme northern Alabama. Known in outlying stations in southeastern Pennsylvania, central and eastern North Carolina, and northeastern Georgia. Absent from the basin of Lake Michigan.

DESCRIPTION: *Bark* of trunks dividing into thin, firm, long curved plates, shaggy. *Twigs* stout, dark brown, with long pale lenticels. *Terminal buds* ¾ inch long, blunt, egg-shaped, covered with 3 or 4 dark brown, loosely fitting, overlapping, hairy scales. *Leaves* 1 to 2 feet long in over-all dimensions, with usually 7 leaflets, these 5 to 9 inches long, 3 to 5 inches wide, the terminal broadest, dark green and shining above, the lower surface pale yellow-green and invested with velvety hairs. *Flowers* — the male in 3-branched catkins, 5 to 8 inches long, with yellow hairy anthers; female in 2- to 5-flowered spikes. *Fruit,* large, 1 to 2 inches long, thick, chestnut-brown to orange-brown, enclosing the light reddish-brown or yellowish-brown, 4- to 6-ribbed nut; seed sweet. *Wood* very heavy (50 pounds to the cubic foot, dry weight), very hard, very strong, very flexible, and close-grained, with dark brown heartwood, and only a thin band of pale sapwood.

When American pioneers first ventured into the Middle West they made for the "bottoms," or alluvial flood plains of the rivers, where the tall timber grew. They had come from a forested land, and prized the layer of humus left by centuries of forest leaves; they assumed that the prairies must be infertile, since they produced no trees. So the Sangamon Bottom, the Muskingum Bottom, the Tiwappaty Bottom, the Wabash Bottom, the Kaskaskia Bottom, and a hundred more, figure by name in the early history of midland America. None was more famous than the one where the Big Shellbark grew in such abundance — the American Bottom along the Mississippi from Kaskaskia to Alton, Illinois, so named because a large party of Americans settled there in 1781, though previously it was one of the oldest and best-settled French colonies in the United States.

Edwin James, the distinguished botanist and geologist of the Long Expedition to the Rockies, has told us what the vegetation of the American Bottom was in aboriginal state. He noted towering Tulip-trees and gigantic Sycamores that leaned across the streams, the inevitable Box Elders, Cottonwoods, and Black Willows of the banks, Soft Maple and wild Catalpa, and the river-loving Hackberry, and the finest grade of Black Walnut. Ironwood and Hop Hornbeam, Blue Ash and Green and White grew there, Pecans too, and above all the Bottom or Big Shellbark Hickory.

In those days it often soared up 100 feet, though today we seldom see a specimen more than 70 feet high, and its present trunk diameter of a foot and a half is but half that of the massive columns in the old bottoms. But it still has the largest leaves of all the grand old tribe of Hickory, and the biggest nuts. Much though it resembles the common Shagbark in general, you may know it apart by its bright orange twigs, unlike those of any other species. The bark is flaky, like the Shagbark's, but the flakes are smaller and close-fitting, and do not come loose in great, connected strips, so that, armored though the Big Shellbark is, its trunks are neater in appearance and not so rugged-seeming.

Everything that is finest in the other Hickories is rivaled or excelled by the Big Shellbark. Its wood is marvelously hard and strong and tough, enduring friction and impact in a way to make it useful for the highest grade of axe handle, wagon hub, or ski. Its nuts are flavored like the best of the Hickories'. No finer and more stalwart tree was there in the sylva of the old bottoms.

But today the bottoms are largely deforested, and where the tall trees grew beside the bayous and sloughs and oxbow bends, the corn stands high. One has to search far for a forested bottom comparable with that of other times when the sun never saw the forest floor, and the wild harvest of the Kingnuts, Walnuts, and Pecans sank into the deep soft litter. In consequence, the Big Shellbark Hickory is rare now, even in the experience of most Middle Westerners, while the upland-loving Shagbark of the groves is still known to every farm boy.

Tradition has forgotten the Bottom Hickory; the literature of our vanished midland frontier has passed it by; and only the operators of portable sawmills still search it out, with a knowing eye.

RED HICKORY

Carya ovalis (Wangenheim) Sargent

OTHER NAME: Oval Pignut.

RANGE: Southern New England to northern Indiana, central Illinois, central Missouri, northern Arkansas, northern Louisiana, and southward from the District of Columbia on the Appalachians to central Georgia and Alabama.

DESCRIPTION: *Bark* pale gray, usually separating into small plate-like scales, rarely close and smooth. *Twigs* shiny red-brown marked by pale lenticels. *Winter buds* with outer scales red-brown, shiny, the inner covered with close pale down. *Leaves* 6 to 10 inches in over-all dimensions with usually 7 leaflets, the upper one 6 or 7 inches long and 1½ to 2 inches wide, only the terminal stalked. *Flowers* — male in downy catkins 6 to 7 inches long, the stamens with yellow anthers thickly covered with pale hairs; female in 1- or 2-flowered spikes, thickly invested with yellow scales. *Fruit* very small, ½ to 1½ inches long with thin husk splitting freely to the base and pale, oblong, slightly flattened, 4-angled nut with a thin shell; seed small and sweet. *Wood* very heavy, very hard and tough, flexible, with light or dark brown heartwood and a thick paler sapwood.

In its shaggy bark this species much resembles the true Shagbark Hickory, though the plates are much smaller; in sweetness the kernel is the equal of the Shagbark's, but is very much smaller. Most people and certainly most lumbermen do not remark the Red Hickory as in any way different from several of the other kinds of Hickory, and it must be admitted that this is what we can only call a botanist's species. Yet it is valid and real, and sooner or later anyone who wishes to know all the trees he meets, and to greet them by name as friends, will come to know the Red Hickory. It is most abundant and generally distributed in Indiana and grows to a fine height, sometimes 100 feet, with a trunk almost 3 feet thick, keeping company with many kinds of Oaks and other Hickories on dry upland soil.

In fact the wood of this tree is in many respects the finest of all the hardy breed of Hickories. It goes to market, under the generic name of Hickory, as much as or more often than any other species. It fulfills all the uses enumerated for the other species as a heavy-duty lumber of incomparable strength, resistance to sudden shock, to impact, and sustained loads, the heat of friction, vibration, wear and tear.

Long ago the great virgin stands were culled out of the forest. Many lumber companies are now re-working their second growth, and even this is hardly allowed to reach satisfactory maturity. The finest Hickories are now found widely scattered in farmers' woodlots, where it is expensive to discover and remove them. In spite of this, Hickory still does not fetch a high price; there is much poor or damaged wood in every considerable cut, and the primary use for the wood demands only certain portions of the highest quality, wasting the rest.

More serious than any drain by man is the loss occasioned by beetles. It is odd that Hickory, one of the hardest of all temperate-zone woods, should be the especial prey of so many kinds and such untold billions of wood-destroying beetles. One sort attacks the living tree and kills it, others then destroy the standing timber in the dead trees. Even sound Hickory when stacked in the wood yard is subject to invasion by still further kinds which turn its mighty sinews to thin rivers of sawdust. The loss of Hickory was probably great even in primeval times, but injury from fire and over-browsing by cattle so weakened Hickory groves that their insect foes are forever quickening the pace of their destruction. Yet not even Ash is in all respects its equal and there is no substitute for Hickory to which we can turn.

WHITE HICKORY

Carya tomentosa Nuttall

OTHER NAMES: Whiteheart or Bigbud Hickory. Mockernut.

RANGE: From the shores of eastern Massachusetts south to Florida, west through southern Ontario and southern Michigan to southeastern Iowa and eastern Texas. Rare in eastern Oklahoma, eastern Kansas, and southeastern Nebraska. Absent from northern New England, New York State except the western and southern parts, and the Gulf coast.

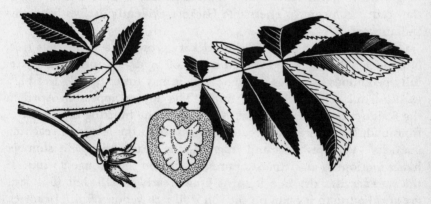

DESCRIPTION: *Bark* of trunks close, not shaggy, rather thin, shallowly ridged and furrowed in age. *Twigs* stout, marked by conspicuous pale lenticels, at first bright brown, later becoming light or dark gray and marked with pale leaf scars. *Terminal buds* very large, three times the size of the axillary buds, with 3 or 4 outer, dark reddish brown, thick and fuzzy bud scales which drop before winter; inner scales opening in mid-spring, pale green tinged inwardly with bright red and covered outwardly with soft silky down. *Flowers* — male catkins 4 or 5 inches long, pale yellow-green, thick and fuzzy with down and marked by bright red anthers; female crowded into small spikes, conspicuous by their dark red stigmas. *Leaves* 8 to 12 inches long in over-all dimensions, with 5 to 7 dark yellow-green and shining leaflets which are paler on the lower surface. *Fruit* with dark red-brown husk which splits to the middle or nearly to the base, releasing the light reddish brown, 4-angled nut with hard, thick shell enclosing a small, dark brown seed. *Wood* very hard, tough, strong, close-grained, very heavy (51 pounds to the cubic foot, dry weight), rich dark brown with thick, nearly white sapwood.

Because White Hickory grows abundantly on the coast of the Middle Atlantic states it seems to have been the first to have come to the notice of the colonists in Virginia. As early as 1640 it was being described by an English botanist, and though it is difficult sometimes in the accounts of the first settlers and explorers to distinguish between the kinds of Hickory, Strachey's *Historie of Travaile in Virginia Britannia* seems to be referring to this species when he says "exceeding hard shelled and hath a passing sweet karnell; this . . . the Indians beat into pieces with stones, and putting them, shells and all, into morters, mingling water with them, with long woodden pestells pound them so long togither untill they make a kind of mylke, or oylie liquor, which they call *pocohicora.*" The name Hickory evidently derives from this Indian word.

Given room to expand, White Hickory grows to a ponderous tree, often with a broad, round-topped crown of rigid and upright or gracefully pendulous branches. In the forest it may tower up 120 feet high with a trunk sometimes 3 feet thick. The flowers appear in April in the South, a month later in the North, with the bursting of the leaves from bud, but they make greater progress than the leaves in reaching maturity. Very resinous and fragrant, the heavy foliage in summer hangs motionless and almost oppressive save in the strongest wind. If the summer is a dry one it turns brown early in fall, but if it lasts green till autumn it takes on the soft dull rich yellow of all Hickories. In late summer the fruit ripens, but it is so hard-shelled that only a great lover of our wild harvests will go to the labor of cracking it for the sake of the small but sweet kernel.

The wood of this species is of the best amongst the Hickories. Some specimens that were tested by Forest Service showed that White Hickory had more strength in bending and in compression parallel to the grain (crushing strength) than any other of the Hickories and was also superior in stiffness. For this reason it has been much used in the making of Hickory splints and is sold along with other Hickory woods for the making of rustic furniture. The sapwood, which is the part of the wood preferred by buyers, is especially wide in this species.

BLACK HICKORY

Carya texana Buckley var. *villosa* (Sargent) Little

RANGE: Northern Arkansas and northeastern Oklahoma to southern Illinois and central Missouri.

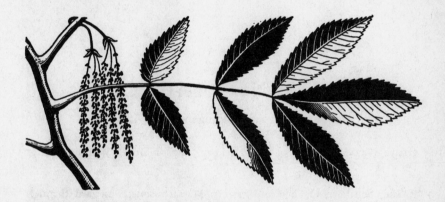

DESCRIPTION: *Bark* thick, furrowed, rough, dark, sometimes with close-pressed scales, but not shaggy. *Twigs* slender, light red-brown, flecked with pale lenticels, becoming dark brown. *Winter buds* with a rusty down mixed with yellow scales and often tufted near the tip with white hairs. *Leaves* 6 to 10 inches in over-all dimensions, with usually 7 leaflets, dark green above, pale and downy below. *Flowers* — male in catkins 4 to 8 inches long covered with clusters of hairs; female in 1- or 2-flowered spikes, and rusty-downy. *Fruit* rusty-downy, about 1 inch long, 3/4 inch thick, with thin husk splitting tardily to the base by 1 or 2 sutures or not at all, the nut reddish tinged, with thin shell; seed small and sweet. *Wood* hard, heavy (45 pounds per cubic foot, dry weight), not very strong, brittle, and close-grained, light brown tinged with red, with thin, lighter brown sapwood.

Growing on dry rocky hills, the Black Hickory forms a small tree only 30 or 40 feet high with a trunk of a foot or a foot and a half in diameter. The head of stout contorted branches is heavy and uncouth. Little is known of the wood; if it is ever cut, it goes to the lumber yards simply as Hickory. If the hogs of the Ozarks root for it, then the fruit is just one more pignut to the natives.

Growing with it in the Ozarks and in southern Illinois and southern Indiana is the closely related variety, the Arkansas Hickory, *Carya texana* var. *arkansana* (Sargent) Little, with larger leaflets, the terminal ones 4 to 6 inches long and 2 to 2¼ inches wide, the male flowers shorter — 2 to 3 inches long and rusty-downy. This, the common Hickory of the Ozark mountain region, is found on dry hillsides and rocky ridges to southern Indiana, southern Illinois, and northeastern Missouri, and south to Texas and western Louisiana.

BITTERNUT HICKORY

Carya cordiformis (Wangenheim) K. Koch

OTHER NAMES: Swamp or Pig Hickory. Pig or Bitter Walnut. Bitter Pecan Tree.

RANGE: Southern Quebec and eastern Massachusetts, westward through southern Ontario, central Wisconsin, to northern Minnesota, southeastern Nebraska, eastern parts of Kansas and Oklahoma, northeastern Texas, south to southern Georgia, and northern Louisiana, but absent from the coast from Virginia southward, absent from the basin of Lake Superior, northern Wisconsin, and the north shore of Lake Huron.

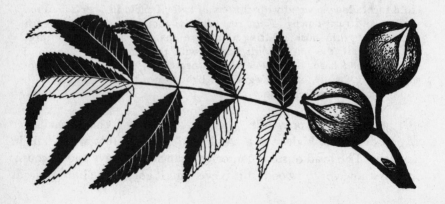

DESCRIPTION: *Bark* of trunk light brown tinged with red, rather thin, shallowly furrowed, with thin, braided ridges, never shaggy. *Twigs* slender, at first bright green, then pale gray, roughened by numerous pale, small, corky growths and small leaf scars. *Winter buds* bright yellow, the terminal large, 1/3 to 3/4 inch long, blunt and oblique, enclosed in two pairs of rough scales; lateral buds small, 4-angled, sharp-pointed, egg-shaped. *Leaves* 6 to 10 inches long in over-all dimensions, leaflets 4 to 6 inches long, 3/4 to 1 1/4 inch wide, dark yellow-green and shiny above, the under side paler and hairy. *Flowers* — male green, in catkins 3 or 4 inches long, hanging in clusters from a common stalk, borne on twigs of the preceding season; female 1 or 2 to a stalk, 1/2 inch long, invested with yellow wool, 4-angled. *Fruit* nearly round, suddenly contracted to a tip, with scaly, thin husk splitting by four sutures halfway down, the kernel reddish brown or gray. *Wood* very hard, very heavy (50 1/2 pounds per cubic foot, dry weight), strong, tough, close-grained, the heartwood dark brown, the sapwood thick and light brown or paler.

The Bitternut ranges farther north than any other kind of Hickory; it is *the* common Hickory of the Missouri valley in Nebraska, Kansas, and Iowa, and grows in the rich bottom-lands of the lower Ohio valley sometimes 100 feet tall with a fine straight trunk 2 or 3 feet thick and stout spreading or ascending branches that form a handsome dome-like head. Some specimens have almost the vase-shaped contour of the White Elm, and even when the tree stands bare, its numberless twigs, unusually fine and slender for a Hickory, etch a delicate pattern against the snow-filled winter skies of the Middle West. If its kernels were not inedible, the Bitternut would lack nothing to be a favorite door-yard tree. In spite of this acrid flavor, the early settlers used to express an oil from the nut, which they used as a remedy for rheumatism; they even burned the oil in their crude lamps. And, since this tree, like all its genus, has wood with resolutely shock-resistant qualities, they used it for striking tools and agricultural implements, for hoops and wagon parts. It burns, too, with an intense flame making but little ash.

This species has, for a Hickory, a short life — a little matter of 200 years. For a Hickory, it grows swiftly, but that is slow, by the rate of other trees. Its seeds are so unpalatable to most animals that they have a better than average chance of sprouting; its seedlings are able to endure dense shade for many years. As the older trees die or are cut down and the sunlight reaches the seedling Bitternuts, they will make a swift growth, and finally succeed in forming pure groves of their own kind. So this species, though the wood is considered inferior to that of most other Hickories, may come, when finer timber is exhausted, to figure more and more in that ceaseless demand for Hickory lumber which is ever in excess of the growth rate.

PECAN

Carya illinöensis (Wangenheim) K. Koch

RANGE: Texas from the Rio Grande valley north through the central and eastern parts of the state, central and eastern Oklahoma, eastern Kansas, Missouri except the northern part, up the Mississippi River valley to southeastern Iowa, central Illinois, up the Ohio to southern Indiana and western Kentucky and east to central Tennessee and west-central Alabama.

DESCRIPTION: *Bark* of trunks thickish, grayish brown or light brown, divided by irregular, flattened, interlacing ridges broken into small scaly surfaces. *Twigs* stoutish, reddish brown with conspicuous orange-brown lenticels. Terminal buds ½ inch long, pointed, yellowish brown. *Leaves* 10 to 20 inches long in over-all dimensions with 9 to 17 leaflets each 4 to 8 inches long and 1 to 2 inches wide, dark yellowish green and smooth above, paler below. *Flowers* — male in 3-branched catkins, 3 to 5 inches long, with yellow anthers; female yellow, hairy, borne in several-flowered spikes. *Fruit* in clusters of 3 to 12, the husk thin-skinned, 4-winged from top to bottom and enclosing the reddish brown, thin-shelled nut, which is 1½ to 2½ inches long; seed deeply 2-grooved, and sweet. *Wood* medium heavy (45 pounds to the cubic foot, dry weight), hard, brittle, not strong, the heartwood dark brown, the thin layer of sapwood nearly white.

Far in the heart of the North American continent, remote from any seaboard except the shores of the Gulf of Mexico, the Pecan might have stood long unknown to the white man save for its chance discovery in 1541 by the renowned Hernando DeSoto. On his wanderings, he crossed the Mississippi with his gold-seekers, who in their Castilian armor floundered through the swamps of eastern Arkansas until they emerged upon high, dry ground where the fields abounded with what DeSoto's chronicler called Walnut trees. But he describes the nut as thin-shelled, and thus can have meant only the Pecan tree. So here,

only fifty years after Columbus first sighted San Salvador, appears in history one of the most strictly interior trees of North America, its most famous nut tree, and the largest and kingliest of all species of *Carya*.

All the early chroniclers of French Louisiana mention the pecan, telling us that the Indians of many tribes in the lower Mississippi stored it, and that the Creoles soon came to appreciate it deeply, using it at least as early as 1762 in that heavenly confection known as the New Orleans praline.

Long before the American pioneers crossed the Alleghenies into the fertile wilderness of the Mississippi Valley, unknown traders and fur trappers brought the first pecan nuts over the mountains with their beaver skins. In consequence, pecans were first known in the east as "Mississippi nuts," or "Illinois nuts." Men curious about the wonders beyond the mountains turned them over in their palms, fingered and tasted and smelled them, and began to plant them.

So it was that Thomas Jefferson, himself a naturalist and great tree-planter and a man who always thought westward, following the explorers with his mind like an eagle who watched where they toiled, set out Pecan trees at "Monticello." Presently he dispatched pecans to George Washington. Ever on the watch for new and useful crops, the master of "Mount Vernon" planted them eagerly, and in his journal of May, 1786, he refers to a row of "Illinois nuts" which he had just planted. Today those Pecans, gift of Thomas Jefferson, are the oldest living trees at "Mount Vernon" where the visitor will find them towering above the southeast corner of the mansion.

Until almost the turn of the present century, pecans reached the market largely from wild trees. The harvesting methods in early times consisted in nothing less heroic and criminal than cutting down gigantic specimens — the bigger the better — and setting boys to gather the nuts from the branches of the fallen giants. It seemed to the pioneer then, as it did to every American, that the forests of this country were inexhaustible. Thus it came about that the wild Pecan tree had become rare before men began to realize how much was lost.

But already the farther-seeing had been at work on selection of fine varieties and their propagation. Slow-growing though the tree is in its native state, under cultivation and with plenty of fertilizer and deep soil, it reaches bearing in a few years. As with most crop trees, it does best when grafted on wild stock. The earliest successful graft was made by Antoine, the black slave gardener of Governor Telephore J. Roman, at famous "Oak Alley Plantation" in St. James Parish, Louisiana. That was in 1846, when 16 trees were trunk-grafted and the variety known as "Centennial" was produced. Today perhaps a hundred named horti-cultural varieties of the Pecan are known, and every form of grafting has been mastered. The culture of the Pecan — the only case where a native nut tree has been extensively grown in orchards — now extends to far-off California and Oregon. Georgia is the leading pecan-producing state.

The Pecan is the state tree of Texas, for there it reaches its grandest dimensions — sometimes 120 feet high with a trunk as much as 30 feet around, and a spread of enormous limbs which gives the crown a diameter of 100 feet. It is one of the surprises of your first trip to Texas (if you are a traveler who motors deep into the country and then walks into the woods) to come upon a centenarian grove of Pecans down in the bottom-lands. Even in winter, or perhaps especially then, the grandeur of the ancient trees stands forth; the trunks appear sometimes as if they had been stung by fabulously large insects, or to have grown to their elephantine shape as a result of pollarding, like the Burnham Beeches in England.

The first settlers of Texas, now well over a century ago, told of such gigantic and patriarchal trees under which they drove their wagons or pitched their camp, finding beneath the Pecans shade, fuel, lumber, and the food that fell in the wilderness like manna from heaven. If it is painful to think that it was such trees as these that the pioneers of the American bottom in Illinois destroyed for a single year's harvest of nuts upon them, it is good to think that here at least is one of America's noblest trees which is being extensively planted. True, Pecans in an orchard, planted in rows and methodically trimmed, do not have the venerable and picturesque appearance of the wild trees of the bottom-lands. Yet time may take care of that. In Southern Europe one sees Chestnuts and Olives planted by the Romans, which are now majestic monuments to the long-dead men who set them out. So the Pecan orchards of our time may take on the same august appearance, and future generations will astonish our shades by exclaiming how wise we were and how well we builded!

THE HORNBEAMS
(*Carpinus*)

THE HORNBEAMS are twisted and slim-stemmed little trees, often with several rather shrubby trunks, with smooth bark and no terminal buds; growth is only by axillary buds, which in winter display many pointed overlapping scales. The leaves are alternate, deciduous, thin, and light bright green. In falling, their stalks leave semi-oval, oblique small scars; numerous pale lenticels also fleck the twigs.

The inconspicuous flowers have the sexes borne in separate catkins on the same tree, the male catkins long and slender, each floret consisting in 3 to 20 crowded stamens, the female flowers in pairs at the base of a leafy deciduous scale, each floret subtended by smaller scales and enclosed in a toothed calyx. The egg-shaped nut, which is seated in, but not enclosed by, large green leafy scales, is acute, compressed, and conspicuously ribbed lengthwise.

AMERICAN HORNBEAM

Carpinus caroliniana Walter

OTHER NAMES: Smooth-barked Ironwood. Blue or Water Beech.

RANGE: Nova Scotia to northern Florida and westward to central Minnesota, eastern Iowa, eastern and southern Missouri, eastern Oklahoma, and eastern Texas. Also on the mountains of Mexico and Central America.

DESCRIPTION: *Bark* smooth, close, gray, and fluted both on stems and branches with low broad ridges. *Twigs* zigzag, at first pale green, becoming orange-brown on older wood, then dark red and shining during the first winter, finally dull gray tinged with red. *Winter buds* acute, egg-shaped, only about 1/8 inch long, with chestnut-brown scales margined with papery white. *Leaves* 2 to 4 inches long, thin, firm, the upper surface dull green, lower with tufts of white hairs in the axils of the prominent yellow midrib, with conspicuous cross-veinlets. *Flowers* — scales of the male catkins green below the middle and red above; female flowers with scarlet styles. *Fruit* — nuts only 1/3 inch long, subtended by leafy scales which are crowded on downy, red-brown stalks 5 to 6 inches long. *Wood* very hard and heavy (49 pounds per cubic foot, dry weight), the heartwood light brown with nearly white sapwood.

The first reward of tree study — but one that lasts you to the end of your days — is that as you walk abroad, follow a rushing stream, climb a hill, or sit on a rock to admire the view, the trees stand forth, proclaiming their names to you. Though at first you may fix their identity with more or less conscious effort, the easy-to-know species soon become like the faces of your friends, known without thought, and bringing each a host of associations.

Such is the Hornbeam, a tree recognizable on sight by its beautiful fluted stems and branches. Each trunk and bough is spiraled with low, rounded, broad ridges that look like twisted muscles. This is a trait which begins to develop almost from the first, while the tree is still in youth; the smooth bark seems to be corrugated with some sort of swelling or twisting inside the wood itself, as if the life within showed itself proudly, as a young man will flex his arm in the joy of its strength.

The name Hornbeam has reference to the extreme hardness of the wood — "horn" for toughness, and "beam," an old word for tree, comparable with the German *Baum*. "The Horne Bound tree," wrote William Wood in *New England's Prospects*, "is a tough kinde of Wood that requires much paines in riving as is almost incredible, being the best to make bolles and dishes, not subject to cracke or leake." Hornbeam has been utilized, too, for levers and handles of striking implements, but, as it cannot be obtained in large quantities from so small a tree, it is employed chiefly by local tool makers and does not figure as a wood of commerce. The hardwood lumberman thinks of this as a mere weed tree.

But the rest of us who know it deem the Hornbeam a very lovely companion of our wood walks. True, it is only an understory tree of the forest, seldom over 40 feet tall, usually only about 20 at maturity. The crooked, slender trunk is short and soon forks in a bushy way, with slightly zigzag, tough, but slender branches that towards the ends become pendulous. Late in March or early April, we see its slim catkins and dainty leaves appear together. In summer its foliage is like that of the Beech — the blades themselves thin and beautifully translucent but the foliage in the mass dense, giving a shade cool yet not dark. In late autumn the leaves turn deep scarlet and orange.

The Hornbeam plays second fiddle to the famous taller trees of our eastern forests wherever it occurs, and sometimes an officious landscape architect or forester will urge that it be destroyed to make way for more important species. But in the judgment of more mature authorities it is seldom wise practice, in the management of the mixed deciduous woodland, to try to grow just a few species of the highest economic value. Forest trees do best in a forest and under the most natural conditions. By that standard, Hornbeam is of value as a companion tree and a contributor to the total biota. Certainly with its picturesque trunks and rich autumn hues, Hornbeam should be spared, if not planted, whenever a natural landscape effect is desired.

THE HOP HORNBEAMS
(*Ostrya*)

THESE ARE Beech-like but small trees with simple alternate deciduous leaves. The male catkins in winter stand naked, without scales, each male floret composed of 3 to 14 crowded stamens. Each female flower has a closed calyx surrounded by united hairy scales which become enlarged, inflated, and bladdery, hence the resemblance to hops. The fruit is a nut which is flattened and obscurely ridged longitudinally and quite enclosed by the veiny, pale, thin, bladdery scales. These are clothed at base with sharp, rigid, stinging hairs. At maturity the cluster of fruits is suspended on a hairy stem.

EASTERN IRONWOOD

Ostrya virginiana (Miller) K. Koch

OTHER NAMES: American Hop Hornbeam. Rough-barked Ironwood.

RANGE: Cape Breton Island (Nova Scotia) through southern Quebec and southern Ontario, across the northern peninsula of Michigan to the Black Hills of South Dakota (but not north of Lake Superior), south to northern Florida (but not on the coastal plain of the south Atlantic states), thence west to eastern Texas (but not in the Delta country of Louisiana and not on the Gulf coast), and west to eastern parts of Oklahoma and Kansas.

DESCRIPTION: *Bark* thin, grayish brown, with numberless fine, flaky, plate-like little scales, often with a discernible twist. *Twigs* tough, slender, switch-like, at first light green becoming by midsummer smooth, shiny, and light orange; dull dark brown after the first winter. *Winter buds* light chestnut-brown. *Leaves* 3 to 5 inches long, dark, dull, yellow-green above, paler beneath, thin in texture but remarkably firm and tough. *Flowers* — male catkins becoming about 2 inches long at flowering time, their scales green with a red tinge; female catkins small, green tinged with red, hanging on very slender stalks. *Fruit* of very small nuts appearing as if enclosed in papery bags. *Wood* very heavy (almost 50 pounds to the cubic foot, dry weight), extremely hard, the heartwood light brown, the very thick sapwood white.

In our rich sylva a little tree like the Ironwood melts into the summer greenery, or the silver intricacy of naked twigs in the winter woods, in a way that makes it difficult to pick out and identify. Not that it lacks for distinctive features; it has two — the hop-like scales around the nut that make it look as though the fruit were enclosed in little papery bags, and the bark which somewhat resembles that of the Birches, but is more scurfy than papery.

Except for the Dogwood, this is the hardest wood in our northeastern sylva, harder than Oak or Ash, Hickory or Locust or Persimmon. In proportion to its great hardness and strength, its heaviness is not disadvantageous. This should make Ironwood ideal for use wherever great toughness is required, but only occasionally does this tree grow as much as 30 feet high, or produce a trunk a foot thick, nor does it occur abundantly enough to make it commercially profitable. So Ironwood is only locally used, when someone is searching for material for the handle of a mallet or an axe, or a lever to endure great strain. Even this presupposes a man who knows of the high qualities of the wood, and can recognize this rather undistinctive tree when he sees it.

For the beauty of Ironwood is subtle, with its dainty beechen leaves which turn a soft, dull gold in autumn, and in summer shut out all the heat of the sun but only a little of the light. A modest component in the mixed deciduous forest of our eastern sylva, it finds its place as a nurse tree and as a contributor to the rich and ancient mold of the forest floor. Being an understory species, it gives shade or, rather, redoubled shade, to the wild flowers and the mosses. Its tiny nuts, which no human would ever bother to dig out of their casing, feed the bobwhite and the deer, the pheasant and the rabbit. The unsensational color of the autumn foliage serves for what the gardener calls a "softener." Everything about this little tree is at once serviceable and self-effacing. Such members of any society are easily overlooked, but well worth knowing.

THE BIRCHES
(*Betula*)

BIRCHES have waxy smooth bark, marked by long narrow lenticels, which commonly peels in thin papery plates; on old trunks the bark becomes deeply furrowed at the base. The branches are slender and rather erect on young trees; on older ones they become pendulous. The twigs are switch-like, and very tough, and covered by the leaf scars of many previous years. Decidedly slender and elongated, the scaly winter buds are usually somewhat sticky when pressed between the fingers. Birch leaves are alternate, with more or less heart-shaped blades and sharp teeth along the margin.

The male catkins appear in bud in summer in the axils of the last leaves of a twig; during the following winter they stand erect and naked; in early spring they lengthen and droop, the scales becoming orange or yellow in the lower part, lustrous brown in the upper, and in midspring they flower. Each male floret consists in a 4-lobed membranous calyx as long as the 2 stamens. The female catkins are thicker, terminal on the spur-like lateral branchlets, each floret without calyx, but the scales overlapping, of light yellow hue often tinged with red, becoming brown and woody. In autumn the scales are deciduous with the nuts from the central axis of the cone-like fruiting head (strobile). The minute seeds are wind-borne by the wing-like margins on the outer coats of the shell inclosing the flattened nut.

PAPER BIRCH

Betula papyrifera Marshall

OTHER NAMES: Canoe, White or Silver Birch.

RANGE: Newfoundland and Labrador west to Hudson's Bay, eastern Manitoba, eastern Wyoming and central Colorado; south to Long Island, northern New Jersey, northern Pennsylvania, around the shores of the Great Lakes, and west through northern Illinois to Iowa and Minnesota; also on Mount Mitchell, North Carolina, above 5500 feet and in the Black Hills of South Dakota.

DESCRIPTION: *Bark* creamy white, or more rarely bronze color, dark brown or orange-brown, peeling into papery, thin layers and marked by raised lenticels; inner bark bright orange. *Twigs* at first green flecked with scattered orange lenticels, becoming dark orange-brown and shiny, with dark chestnut-brown winter buds 1/4 inch long. *Leaves* 2 to 5 inches long and 1 to 2 1/4 inches wide, thick and firm, dull dark green and smooth above, pale yellow-green below and flecked with black glandular dots, on stout yellow and glandular stalks 1/2 to 3/4 inch long. *Flowers* — male catkins 3 to 4 inches long, slender and brownish; female catkins 1 1/2 inches long, erect, slender, and greenish with bright red styles. *Fruit* in cone-like heads 1 1/2 inches long, bearing nuts 1/16 inch long with broad wings. *Wood* of medium weight (39 pounds to the cubic foot, dry weight), medium-hard, medium-strong, tough and close-grained, with light brown heartwood tinged with red, and thick, whitish sapwood.

Of all the sites this famous Birch may choose none is more dramatic than its stand on Goat Island, at the very head of Niagara Falls. Here where great clouds of mist, rising like battle smoke from the tumult below, perpetually assault the rocks with drenching spray, the Canoe Birch and the Arbor-vitæ flourish in abundance. They make a telling contrast, the filmy green of the Birch feminine beside the dark spires of the Arbor-vitæ, its slim whiteness gracile against the shaggy bark of the twisted and more ponderous tree. And while the sturdy evergreen appears unmoved by the winds that perpetually rush upward from the awful chasm, the Birch shivers and trembles even as must the human visitor, and the fronds of the little oak fern, too, and the pallid blooms of enchanter's nightshade and naked miterwort that cower, yet rejoice, beneath the trees.

Wherever it grows the Paper Birch delights in the company of Conifers and in the presence of water; it loves a white and rushing stream; it loves a cold clear lake where its white limbs are reflected. Sometimes it is found in swamps and boggy meadows, and, if it must leave the neighborhood of moisture, it likes deep, rocky woods with cool soil. Fortunately it is light-tolerant in youth, so comes up readily on cut-over land, and has replaced the White Pine and the Spruces over large parts of New England, eastern Canada, and the northern peninsula of Michigan.

Thus has Paper Birch gained ground, within historic times, and if there are fewer grand specimens than there were, time may take care of that. For the Birch, where it is found near habitations, is usually spared for its beauty. As a result it is now one of the best-loved trees of the New England landscape, and when we remember a scene there, we see Birches in it — gleaming white trunks, houses, and churches painted a cold, clean white, and pure country snow stretching white over dale and hill.

In its great range, the Paper Birch takes many forms; on the mountains of New England it is sometimes a dwarf and bushy plant, while in the rich forests it grows 60 feet high; in the virgin woods it probably attained twice that height, if old reports can be trusted. Though a botanist may quibble over differences in a leaf, all the botanical varieties add up to the same thing — a tree of incomparable grace and loveliness, identifiable at a glance by its shining, scaly bark. The only possible confusion would be with the much-cultivated European White Birch, which you will know by its pendulous "weeping" branches and by the bark that is much closer and tighter than the more readily peeling bark of our Paper Birch.

To any American of an older generation (now, alas, even canoes are being made of aluminum) there was no more blissful experience than the moment when on his first visit to the North Woods he stepped into a Birch bark canoe weighing perhaps no more than fifty pounds, but strong enough to carry twenty times as much. At the first stroke of the paddle it shot out over the lake water like a bird, so that one drew a breath of the purest ozone of happiness, for on all the waters of the world there floats no sweeter craft than this. The Indians taught our race how to strip the bark from the Birch and sew it with long slender roots of Tamarack for thread. The bark was then stretched and tied over the frame — commonly made of northern White Cedar or Arbor-vitæ — while the holes in the bark and the partings at the seams were caulked with resin of Pine or Balsam or Balm-of-Gilead. Other barks, and skins, were often used for canoes, but of them all Birch is the most renowned — the lightest and most beautiful, and yet so strong that the Indian trusted his life to it when he shot the rock-fanged rapids.

Birch wood furnished the Indians with snowshoe frames. The bark served him, sometimes, as a covering for the tepee or lodge; rolled into a spill, it constituted a taper or a punk-stick to keep away mosquitoes. It made good paper for kindling a fire started first in punkwood of rotten Yellow Birch. A moose-calling horn of Birch bark was carried by all the red hunters in the North Woods — a straight tube about fifteen inches long and three or four wide at the mouth, tied about with strips of more Birch bark.

The inner bark of Paper Birch is a favorite of the beaver, when Aspen fails. Deer and moose browse the twigs in winter; the buds are eaten by grouse. Sugar can be tapped from this Birch, as from the Maple. Thus to each inhabitant, man or beast, of the North Woods, Birch is life-sustaining. Though the lumbermen in the days of the White Pine had little use for the wood itself, they were glad enough to stuff Birch bark, as a waterproof inner lining, under the Cedar shingles of their bunk houses made of Yellow Birch logs.

And, to the delight of children, the peeling bark has long been a woodland paper. But pray do not strip it from the living trees, for once the beautiful outer bark is pulled away, it never grows again. Instead, ugly black rings — which you see all too often — take its place. There is always a fallen Birch log from which you can tear sheets. For the Birch is, despite its strength, not a long-lived tree; once it is dead, decay is swift, and the white form soon topples into the old forest loam. Then the mosses gather on its fallen limbs, a pale green halo that shows how life carries on, though its forms forever change.

GRAY BIRCH

Betula populifolia Marshall

OTHER NAMES: Poplar-leaved, Poverty, Wire or Small White Birch.

RANGE: Nova Scotia, Prince Edward Island and central Quebec, south to Delaware and Pennsylvania and in the uplands to Virginia, west to northern Ohio; rare and local in northern Indiana.

DESCRIPTION: *Bark* at first dark brown; later becoming dull grayish or chalky white, smooth and not peeling readily. *Twigs* slender, covered with warty glands, reddish brown. Lateral *buds* somewhat sticky, spindle-shaped; terminal buds lacking except on spur shoots. *Leaves* 2½ to 3 inches long, 1½ to 2 inches wide, thin and firm, dark green and shiny and somewhat roughened on the upper surface with small pale glands in the axils of the conspicuous criss-crossed veinlets. *Flowers* — male catkins solitary or in pairs, 2½ to 4 inches long; female catkins slender with pale green glandular scales. *Fruits* about ¾ inch long, ⅓ inch thick, drooping or spreading on slender stalks. *Wood* medium-light (35 pounds per cubic foot, dry weight), medium-soft, weak, close-grained, not durable, the heartwood light brown, the sapwood very thick and nearly white.

The traveler who enters New England for the first time sees from his train or his car window, in every abandoned field, on every dry and gravelly slope around the margins of swamps, and springing up beside the rambling stone walls, a little tree never over 30 feet tall and com-

monly only 15 to 20 feet, with a spindling stem and Aspen-like, flutter-ing foliage. Indeed, the newcomer is apt to mistake it for the Trembling Aspen, for like that tree it comes up in little groves; frequently a group of several stems, apparently rising from the same root, lean out from each other in a domed group of graceful sister trees that are pretty enough if no Paper Birches are at hand to put them in their places. In autumn, when the leaves turn a soft gold, the Aspen-like character of the tree seems confirmed. Yet this is no Aspen, or any of the Poplar sort, but a Birch and, though closely related to the princess Paper Birch, only a stunted sister of it, of no utility — unless it should prove useful for pulp by some of the new methods being evolved — except for barrel hoops and firewood.

The Blue Birch, (*Betula cærulea-grandis* Blachard) is a tree which has until recently been confused with the European White Birch. It is now known to be a native species ranging from the Gaspé Peninsula to eastern New York State and south to Nova Scotia and northern New England. It is a large tree with creamy- to pinkish-white and freely peeling bark, and shining bluish-green, triangular and long-pointed leaves 3 to 4 inches long, the fruiting catkins 1 to 2 inches long. A large tree, it occurs in dry woods, and flowers in May and early June.

YELLOW BIRCH

Betula lutea F. Michaux

OTHER NAMES: Bitter, Silver, or Gray Birch.

RANGE: Newfoundland to northern Maryland, thence south in the highlands to North Carolina, Tennessee, and southern Indiana and the northeastern corner of Ohio, westward in the general area of the Great Lakes across southern Ontario to northern Indiana, northern Illinois, eastern Iowa, Minnesota and Manitoba.

DESCRIPTION: *Bark* of old trunks reddish brown or sometimes dull yellowish brown, but on younger growth bright silvery gray or light orange, and lustrous. Twigs light orange-brown, covered with long hairs, gradually becoming hairless and light brown tinged with orange, slender, with faint aroma of wintergreen. *Leaves* 3 to 4½ inches long, dull dark green above, paler below. *Winter buds* somewhat sticky, becoming light chestnut-brown, small and sharp. *Flowers* — male catkins formed during the previous year becoming in spring 3 to 3½ inches long, ⅓ inch thick, with light chestnut-brown and shining scales; female catkins formed in spring, ⅔ inch long, the scales tipped with light red and clusters of white hairs. *Fruit* in erect cone-like, short-stalked heads, 1 to 1½ inches long, and ¾ inch thick. *Wood* medium-heavy (43 pounds to the cubic foot, dry weight), medium-hard, with light brown heartwood tinged with red, and nearly white sapwood.

In the early days of pioneering in the northeast, the "land-lookers" brought back tales of a tree of gigantic height, which grew in the wildest and remotest recesses of the great North Woods. It was a tree unknown to science for more than two hundred years, until in 1803 the French botanical explorer André Michaux described and named it. True that today it does not look to us so tall as the old tales of it, but there are still examples which tower up 100 feet — a height seldom equaled by any other tree in the North Woods save White Pine — and perhaps, indeed, there were specimens in the virgin forest loftier than any we have left today, just as no White Pine can be found to equal the grandest example of two centuries ago.

In the North Woods the Yellow Birch inhabits the upland; southward, in the Middle Atlantic states, it finds the cool habitat that it prefers in swampy ground; on the southern Appalachians it is a characteristic member of the cove hardwoods, usually at an altitude between 4000 and 5000 feet, where it grows on steep mountainsides with White Pine, Canada Hemlock, Cherry Birch, Ironwood, and Buckeye. But wherever it occurs, and tall as it may grow, it somehow manages to melt inconspicuously into the great forest mass; it does not shine forth like its relative the Paper Birch, save in autumn when it shows its rich, clear golden foliage.

Yet though so long unrecognized by science and never deemed worthy of cultivation, Yellow Birch is the hard-working member of the Birch tribe, for it is by all means the most valuable timber tree in it. Most Birch furniture is made of this species; the nearly white sapwood is customarily deepened to a pale gold by stains and varnishes, and beautiful roll and other fancy figures develop in some specimens. Formerly, at least, Yellow Birch was much sought by shipbuilders of Nova Scotia and Maine for the parts of vessels continually under water. It was used in the Maine lumber camps for ox yokes — because it was both light and strong — for the frames of the sledges that traveled over the snows, and, in the form of logs left with the bark still on them, for the walls of the old bunkhouses. Because it grips with unrelaxing strength, Yellow birch was a favorite for hubs; the spokes can never work loose and no normal strain can crack them. Today Yellow Birch is cut for interior finish, from floor to ceiling. Of the growing stand of 10,000,000,000 board feet in the United States, 145,000,000 are annually cut.

Fortunately, Yellow Birch produces great quantities of seed, and it travels miles, on the autumn winds, by its little winged nutlet coats. Whether it alights in an abandoned field, the soil exhausted by agriculture, or in a logged-over tract exposed to drying wind and sun, or in a deep dark moss-covered forest, it is content with conditions and germinates almost at once. If the lodgment of the seed is no more than the moss rime on an old rock, the sapling sends its roots straddling down the boulder till the soil is reached. A favorite forest site is an old log, which is straddled in the same way as the rock; when the log decays the Birch is left on stilts of its own roots.

Frequently when a Yellow Birch comes to the end of its life-span, it stands a long time, though decay is going on swiftly under the bark. Such a tree is then nothing but a skin of bark stuffed with punkwood. Even this had its use, to the Indians; they collected and dried it, and carried it with them as tinder in which to start a fire by friction.

CHERRY BIRCH

Betula lenta Linnæus

OTHER NAMES: Black, Sweet, or Mahogany Birch.

RANGE: Southern Maine to eastern Ohio and southward to the head of Delaware Bay, thence south on the Appalachians to Kentucky, Alabama, and Georgia, ascending to 4000 feet in the southern Appalachians.

DESCRIPTION: *Bark* very dark shiny red, nearly black, smooth, or eventually scaly plated, but not flaking off in thin papery scales. *Twigs* light green and slightly sticky and downy at first, soon turning dark orange-brown and lustrous, by the first winter bright red-brown, gradually darkening to dull brown tinged with red; inner bark with strong aroma of wintergreen. *Leaves* 2½ to 6 inches long, thin and filmy, dark dull green above, paler below. *Winter buds* with light chestnut-brown loosely overlapping scales. *Flowers* — male catkins 3 to 4 inches long at maturity in the spring with bright red-brown sharp-tipped scales; female catkins ¾ inch long with pale green scales rounded at the tip, light pink styles. *Fruit* erect, 1 to 1½ inches long. *Wood* medium heavy (46 pounds to the cubic foot, dry weight), medium hard, dark brown tinged with red, sapwood yellow or light brown.

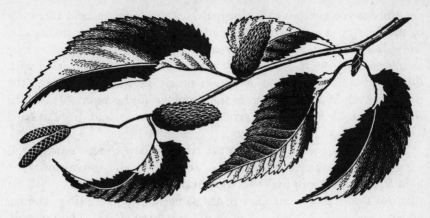

Two characteristics in combination easily identify this lovely tree. The first is the strong wintergreen aroma of the bark and the leaves (a trait which it shares with the slightly aromatic Yellow Birch) and the second is the close, lustrous, mahogany-red bark, a characteristic not in the least shared with any other Birch, but instead with the wild Black Cherry — whence the name of Cherry Birch. The Black Cherry, however, does not have the wintergreen odor.

The Cherry Birch is an inhabitant chiefly of the Appalachian forest, where it grows at the head of cool coves, as the mountaineer calls his ravines and steep-pitched valleys. For it loves the ancient forest loam; it likes to have lady fern and maidenhair around its feet; it is almost always found within sound of mountain streams. To come on it in one of these richly forested coves, to place one's hand upon the exquisitely smooth bark, to smell the delicious aroma of the twigs, is to make acquaintance — or renew an old love — with a dryad.

All the Birches of the United States emerge from the sawmill simply as Birch; in this generic sense Birch stands today fifth in amount cut, on the list of hardwoods. Probably Yellow Birch yields the most, but Cherry Birch undoubtedly is in second place, with a very heavy demand and a constantly diminishing supply. For it takes this tree about 150 years to grow large enough to interest the lumberman, and no second growth can now supply his wants.

Since this wood tends to warp and is hard in every way to season, it was not till the dry kilns of our time came into existence that the heavy cut of Cherry Birch began. But it has had from the beginning a property which has long tempted the furniture manufacturer, for on exposure to the air the wood slowly deepens in tone, and old furniture of this species, if well cared for, might pass in its color for mahogany. Indeed, it has been sold in the past as "Mountain Mahogany," a title which possibly the law would not now allow. A little doctoring with fillers and stains made the deception nearly perfect, but, though the purchaser might be cheated as to the name, he got his money's worth in quality. For Cherry Birch is actually stronger than, and quite as hard as, Mahogany and Black Cherry.

This tree has been a source of the commercial extract known as oil of wintergreen. In taste and odor and chemical composition it is identical with the original wintergreen obtained from the dainty little plant of that name, a member of the same family as trailing arbutus, which creeps through the woods in our northern states. The quantity that could be produced from the tree, however, was found to be so much greater that country folk no longer bothered with the true wintergreen. Whole families of Appalachian mountaineers went through the woods cutting down Cherry Birches and chopping them into chips. Young and sapling trees were the preferred source, and it took about one hundred such to produce a single quart of the oil that emerged from the crude mills. The country folk sold the oil by the quart to the storekeepers, who passed it on to the wholesale druggists, and these in turn refined it and used it to flavor drugs, medicines, and candy. Today, however, oil of wintergreen can be produced synthetically from wood alcohol and salicylic acid, so that this lovely tree may be spared from as wasteful a process of exploitation as any in our forest history.

But those who have drunk Birch beer hope that the manner of its making will not be forgotten in this sophisticated day. Here is one recipe: Tap the tree as the Sugar Maple is tapped, in spring when the sap is rising and the buds are just swelling; jug the sap and throw in a handful of shelled corn, and natural fermentation — so the mountaineers tell us — will finish the job for you.

RIVER BIRCH

Betula nigra Linnæus

OTHER NAMES: Red or Black Birch.

RANGE: From eastern Texas to Florida; northward in the valley of the Mississippi River to eastern Oklahoma, eastern Kansas, eastern Iowa, southeastern Minnesota, and central Wisconsin, southwestern and southern Indiana and southern Ohio; northward in the Atlantic States to southern New York; isolated in northern Indiana, and again along the lower Merrimac River in Massachusetts.

DESCRIPTION: *Bark* on old trunks thick, dark red-brown and deeply furrowed and broken into closely fitting, thick scales; on younger wood separating freely into large, thin, papery scales. *Twigs* dark red and shining, becoming in the second year dull red-brown, and thereafter beginning to produce thin, flaky, peeling gray bark. *Winter buds* small, shining, with bright chestnut-brown scales. *Leaves* 1½ to 3 inches long, thick, tough, deep green and shining above. *Flowers* — male catkins clustered, drooping; 2 to 3 inches long at maturity in the spring; female catkins ⅓ inch long with bright green scales. *Fruit* 1 to 1½ inches long, ½ inch thick.

Wood hard, strong, close-grained, medium-heavy (40 pounds to the cubic foot, dry weight), with light brown heartwood and clean, light, thick sapwood.

The River Birch ranges far south of all the other Birches; others may be found by rushing streams, by cold, clear lakes; this one alone avoids such spots and grows beside the larger, slower, more silt-laden rivers of the coastal plain and piedmont, and throughout much of the course of the Mississippi and its tributaries. There it is the Birch paramount, seldom or never seen in close company with its more aristocratic relatives.

Yet all Birches are graceful, and this species, like most riparian trees, is apt to have several forks from the base, each trunk leaning outward so that a sort of indolent charm may be claimed for it. When the trunk is straight and unbranched, it may soar 80 or 90 feet on the bottom-lands of the Gulf states, but northward it is usually not more than 40 or 50 feet tall. That it is a Birch is known from its thin, papery, scaly bark, which peels back after several years, to show the pink-brown tints of the inner layers. The foliage in the summer gives the typical refreshing shade of all the Birches, but in autumn the leaves of this one turn only a dull yellow before they drop, late in the season.

The wood of River Birch has never enjoyed much of a reputation with lumbermen; the stems are spindling, the lumber knotty, the trees themselves scattered along tens of thousands of linear miles of rivers, never forming merchantable stands. Yet the wood has been used for woodenware and furniture, and once upon a time for ox yokes and wooden shoes. The rice planters of the Carolina coast used to employ it for hoops for their rice casks, as a substitute for Hickory. But the rice-planting aristocracy is gone, gone as are the old wood-burning river boats, gone as beaver hats and Confederate money; today the River Birch is not called on to justify itself in terms of human gain.

Yet Nature must be well content with this tree, since she has produced it in quantity. For the seeds ripen in May and June, just when the water in the rivers is high, and are borne far on the currents, until they became stranded on some muddy shore. Mud is requisite to them and they germinate in it quickly. In a few weeks the first shoots are up and ready to give a good account of themselves. The River Birch holds the banks, prevents erosion and flood and, safe from the attentions of lumbermen, it has a survival value unequaled by its more salable sister species.

THE BEECHES
(*Fagus*)

The Beeches are noted for their smooth, smoke-gray or pale-gray bark, and their very slender, elongated buds with enlarging inner scales that leave a ring-like, persistent scar at the base of the twigs. The foliage is firm but deciduous; in falling, the leafstalks leave small, elevated, semi-oval scars.

The male catkins appear at the base of the shoots of the year or in the axils of their lowest leaves. Each floret consists in an almost bell-shaped, 4- to 5-lobed, minute calyx and 8 to 16 extruded stamens with green, oblong anthers. Subtending the female florets, which occur in the axils of the upper leaves of the year, are numerous awl-shaped hairy scales, the outer bright red and longer than the flowers and soon falling, the inner short, united into a cup that eventually becomes the half-woody, egg-shaped, thick-walled husk; this is 4-valved and covered with stout recurved prickles, and partially encloses the 3 nutlets. The calyx of the female floret is hairy, urn-shaped, its 3-angled tube adhering to the ovary, which is surmounted by 3 green styles.

The nut is unequally 3-angled and concave between the angles, shining and chestnut-brown, rusty-woolly, and thin-shelled. The dark chestnut-brown seeds are oily and sweet.

AMERICAN BEECH

Fagus grandifolia Ehrhart

RANGE: Throughout Nova Scotia, Prince Edward Island and New Brunswick to the north shore of Georgian Bay, south to northern and western Florida and eastern Texas, and west to eastern Wisconsin, eastern and southern Missouri, and extreme southeastern Oklahoma.

DESCRIPTION: *Bark* close-fitting, blue-gray, smooth, thin, and frequently mottled with dark bands and blotches. *Twigs* very numerous, whip-like, bright reddish brown on the new wood. *Winter buds* long and slender, shining, pale brown. *Leaves* thin, straight-veined, and a light, glossy blue-green (or thick, leathery, and dark blue-green in the variety *caroliniana* found in the southern states), the blades 3 to 5 inches long. *Flowers* in early spring, the male yellow-green, drooping on long stems; female catkins in pairs and covered with numerous pointed scales. *Fruit* ½ to ¾ inch long, in cross-section triangular, and enclosed in 4-cleft burs, the spines soft and weak. *Wood* medium-heavy (44 pounds to the cubic foot, dry weight), medium-hard, strong, close-grained, difficult to split. Heartwood light red, the sapwood thin and paler.

A Beech is, in almost any landscape where it appears, the finest tree to be seen. There are many taller trees, and many that attain to moments of showier glory, like the Sugar Maple in autumnal coloration, or a Dogwood starred with snowy blossoms. But, taken in all seasons and judged by all that makes a tree noble — strength combined with grace, balance, longevity, hardiness, health — the Beech is all that we want a tree to be. And more besides, for it is a tree deep-rooted in the history of our people, in this new world and the old one, and figures beloved to us both in fable and fact move under its ancient boughs.

Far down the aisles of the forest the Beech is identifiable by the gleam of its wondrously smooth bark, not furrowed even by extreme old age. Here it will be free of branches for full half its height, the sturdy boughs then gracefully down-sweeping. The gray bole has a further beauty in the way it flutes out at the base into strong feet, to the shallow, wide-spreading roots. And the luxuriant growth of mosses on the north side of such a tree, together with the mottling of lichens, add to the look it wears of wisdom and serenity.

The elegant clear gray of the bark extends from the trunk to the main mighty boughs, then to the hundreds of branches, and out to the thousands of branchlets. So that when the tree stands naked in winter it seems to shine through the forest, almost white in contrast with the dun colors all about it, or against the dark evergreen backgrounds of the Canadian Hemlock and White Pine with which it associates. In very early spring an unearthly pale pure green clothes the tree in a misty nimbus of light. As the foliage matures, it becomes a translucent blue-green through which the light, but not the heat, of the summer day comes clearly. And in autumn these delicate leaves, borne chiefly on the ends of the branchlets and largely in one plane, in broad flat sprays, turn a soft clear yellow. Then is the Beech translated. As the sun of Indian summer bathes the great tree, it stands in a profound autumnal calm, enveloped in a golden light that hallows all about it.

As the leaves fall, late in the season, the twigs are revealed wearing a tinge of reddish brown, and the little triangular nuts can be seen, that with the first frost begin to drop. Fruit is abundant, in general, only every third year on any one tree, and commonly a heavy or a light harvest of the nuts prevails over a whole region.

In the days of America's virgin grandeur, forests of this luminous and stately tree covered a large part of Ohio, Kentucky, Indiana, and central Michigan. But they bespoke their own destruction, for the pioneers soon learned that the Beech was a sign of good soil. It loves what the farmer loves — rich limestone overlain by deep, level, dark loams. So in the Ohio valley the axe soon felled the growth of centuries, followed swiftly by the plow. Today, speeding easily through that candid country, the Middle Westerner may marvel at a report, written from southern Indiana in June of 1833 by that princely traveler, Maximilian of Wied:

"We came to a tall, gloomy forest, consisting almost wholly of large Beech trees, which afforded a most refreshing shade. The forest continued without intermission . . . the lofty crowns of the trees shut out the sky from our view. They were the most splendid forests I had yet seen in America." He speaks of how the canals in Ohio ran through Beech forests, and even near Rochester, New York, finds them "wild and magnificent," adding with, perhaps, a homesick sigh, "The dense Beech forests constantly reminded us of the scenery of Germany."

For to the newcomer to this savage land the Beech tree had a kindly look of familiarity. Our species does not differ greatly from the Beech of Europe (*Fagus sylvatica*), which from time immemorial had already played a great rôle in human life. Beech nuts seem to have been a food of the New Stone Age man, just as they still are eaten by the peasants of central Europe. The most abundant tree in its wide range, Beech provided the principal fuel, both for keeping warm and for the charcoal used in the Old World's iron smelters. It supplied much dimension timber, a vast quantity of furniture wood, handles of agricultural tools, wooden shoes, and too many other uses to number. Indeed, it has long been the general utility hardwood of Europe.

And on the Beech was written, probably, the first page of European literature. For, it is said, the earliest Sanskrit characters were carved on strips of Beech bark; the custom of inscribing the temptingly smooth boles of Beeches came to Europe with the Indo-European people who entered the Continent from Asia. Indeed, our word *book* comes from the Anglo-Saxon *boc,* meaning a letter or character, which in turn derives from the Anglo-Saxon *beece,* for Beech. So if you find a big old Beech tree in the woods, hacked by some love-struck boy with the outline of a heart and his girl's initials in it, forgive him. He is but following a custom older than Shakespeare, who also records it:

> *O Rosalind! These trees shall be my books,*
> *And in their bark my thoughts I'll character;*
> *That every eye which in this forest looks*
> *Shall see thy virtue witness'd everywhere.*

And Virgil asks:

> *Or shall I rather the sad verse repeat*
> *Which on the beech's bark I lately writ?*

An epic line in pure American vein might have been read by all who passed that way, until about 1880, on a Beech tree on Carrol Creek, in Washington County, Tennessee, on the old stage road between Blountsville and Jonesboro.

> *D. Boone*
> *Cilled A Bar*
> *On Tree*
> *In Year 1760.*

This tree fell in 1916, the scars of the inscription, but not the exact wording, still visible. It was 28½ feet in girth, and 70 feet high, and its age was estimated by the Forest Service to be 365 years. So it began to grow in the year 1551, half a century before Orlando mooned about Rosalind in Arden, and was an ancient of two centuries when Daniel Boone inscribed his hunter's triumph on it.

For such glory, and for its own beauty, is the Beech tree justly famous, not for more mundane usefulness today. Though in Europe the Beech was utilized in every part, by a wood-hungry civilization, as the best of available hardwoods, in America the early settlers soon found twenty hardwood trees better than Beech. Here it has never been more than a second-rate tree for service, when compared with Walnut's beauty, Hickory's strength, White Pine's dimension timbers. Not as hard as Birch or Maple, it has the further disadvantage of being heavier than they. When green it is tough to split, yet it is all too apt to split when seasoned. It is knotty, and has but half the value of White Oak in resistance to atmospheric decay. So, though it has a long list of modern uses, including furniture and flooring, they are most of them trivial, such as for boxes and crates, barrels and crossties, down to picnic plates and spoons, culminating — for humility — in the lowly clothespin.

Let other trees do the work of the world. Let the Beech stand, where still it holds its ground, a monument to past glories. Of these, none is more wholly vanished than the passenger pigeon, to which the Beech played lavish host. It was upon the mast of Beech nuts that the great

flocks fed, and their seeming migration, Audubon writes, was more exactly a quest, by the million, for rich harvest of the Beech.

"As soon as the pigeons discover a sufficiency of food to entice them to alight, they fly around in circles, reviewing the country below. During their revolutions, on such occasions, the dense mass which they form exhibits a beautiful appearance, as it changes its direction, now displaying a glistening sheet of azure, when the backs of the birds come simultaneously into view, and anon, suddenly presenting a mass of rich deep purple. They then pass lower, over the woods, and for a moment are lost among the foliage, but again emerge and are seen gliding aloft. They now alight, but the next moment, as if suddenly alarmed, they take to wing, producing by the flapping of their wings a noise like the roar of distant thunder, and sweep through the forests to see if danger is near. Hunger, however, soon brings them to the ground. When alighted, they are seen industriously throwing up the withered leaves in quest of the fallen mast. . . ."

Speaking of the night roosts of the pigeons in the Beech forests of Kentucky, he goes on to write:

"It was . . . in a portion of the forest where the trees were of great magnitude, and where there was little underwood . . . I arrived there nearly two hours before sunset. Few pigeons were then to be seen, but a great number of persons, with horses and wagons, guns and ammunition, had already established encampments on the borders.

"Two farmers . . . had driven upward of three hundred hogs to be fattened on the pigeons which were to be slaughtered . . . Many trees two feet in diameter, I observed, were broken off at no great distance from the ground; and the branches of many of the largest and tallest had given way, as if the forest had been swept by a tornado. Everything proved to me that the number of birds resorting to this part of the forest must be immense beyond conception. . . . Suddenly there burst forth a general cry of 'Here they come!' The noise which they made, though yet distant, reminded me of a hard gale at sea, passing through the rigging of a close-reefed vessel. As the birds arrived and passed over me, I felt a current of air that surprised me. . . . The fires were lighted, and a magnificent as well as wonderful and almost terrifying sight presented itself. The pigeons, arriving by thousands, alighted everywhere, one above another, until solid masses as large as hogsheads were formed on the branches all round. Here and there the perches gave way under the weight with a crash and, falling to the ground destroyed hundreds of the birds beneath."

So together they fell, bird and tree, from their supreme place in the history of American Nature. For after the Beech forests were swept away by the man with axe and plow, the fate of the passenger pigeon, the most marvelous bird on the North American continent, perhaps in the world, was sealed. As much by the disappearance of Beech mast as by mass slaughter were the shining flocks driven to extinction.

When Audubon was young, in Kentucky, in love with his young wife Lucy, he painted his "Passenger Pigeon" — a pair of them — and to some of us it is his greatest picture. The curve of the soft necks, the lift of shining wings, are eloquent, unconsciously, of a tenderness and passion not all theirs. It is on a Beech bough that he has perched his pigeon pair, and two withered beechen leaves tell us that the season is autumn when the mast is ripe. An autumn that will not come again but lingers, immortal, in those leaves that cannot fall.

THE CHESTNUTS

(*Castanea*)

THE CHESTNUTS have deep, straight taproots and furrowed bark, and bear roundish twigs with axillary buds covered by two pairs of scales, the inner one enlarging and marking the base of the branch with narrow, ring-like scars. Deciduous and alternate, the leaves have straight veins running to the points of the teeth. In falling, the leaf-stalks leave a small, elevated, half-oval scar.

The male catkins stand erect, in 3- to 7-flowered clusters. Each male floret consists in 10 to 20 stamens with pale yellow anthers and a pale straw-colored, deeply 6-lobed calyx. The female flowers are solitary or in few-flowered globular heads in the axils of later leaves; each floret consists in an ovary with six slender, spreading, white styles, seated in an urn-shaped calyx and subtended by bright green little scales.

The fruit of 1 to 3 nuts is enclosed in a husk covered with green and finally brown prickles; the husks split along two or four valves at maturity. Bright brown and shining, the nut is cylindrical, or flattened on the inner faces when there is more than one in a husk, and marked at base by a pale conspicuous scar. The shell is lined inside with hoary down, and the seed, thick and fleshy, has a sweet floury taste.

AMERICAN CHESTNUT

Castanea dentata (Marshall) Borkhausen

RANGE: Southern Maine and Massachusetts across southern and central New York to eastern Ohio, southeastern Michigan and southern Indiana and Illinois, south to Alabama and Mississippi.

All words about the American Chestnut are now but an elegy for it. This once mighty tree, one of the grandest features of our sylva, has gone down like a slaughtered army before a foreign fungus disease, the Chestnut blight. In the youth of a man not yet old, native Chestnut was still to be seen in glorious array, from the upper slopes of Mount Mitchell, the great forest below waving with creamy white Chestnut blossoms in the crowns of the ancient trees, so that it looked like a sea with white combers plowing across its surface. Gone forever is that day; gone is one of our most valuable timber trees, gone the beauty of its shade, the spectacle of its enormous trunks sometimes ten to twelve feet in diameter. And gone the harvest of the nuts, that stuffed our Thanksgiving turkey or warmed our hearts and fingers at the vendor's street corner. What chestnuts we still see come to us, for the most, from Italy.

It is believed that the blight came into this country on Chinese Chestnuts (*Castanea mollissima*), which despite a high percentage of infection show too a degree of resistance to it. No immunity existed in our American tree. From the time the blight was first detected, in 1904 in the New York Zoölogical Park, it spread with a sickening rapidity. Crossing New Jersey, it entered the great Chestnut stands of Pennsylvania; that state, thoroughly alarmed, appropriated a large sum for the control of the malady, in which the federal government joined. But all in vain. Destruction of infected trees proved ineffectual; new infections broke out at distant points.

For it was discovered that the spores are carried far by wind, and the disease was already scattered so far that quarantine lines were futile. The blight *(Endothia parasitica)* penetrates the bark at cracks in the crotches of limbs and where wood-boring beetles have made lesions; it then kills the entire cambium layer, and finally extrudes its fruiting bodies through the swollen and cracking bark, in a position to spread fresh infection on any passing breeze. At last the remotest stands of the tree, in southern Illinois, were reached. However, plantings in Wisconsin, Oregon, and California are said to be free of the disease.

It is often asked whether the little sprouts seen coming up from blight-killed trees will not perhaps show an acquired immunity. So far nothing so hopeful has been observed, and the spores of the disease are still lingering in the stumps themselves. Attempts are, however, being made, with some success, to create disease-resistant hybrids of the Chestnut and ours.

But never again will those proud forests rise. Quickening the decimation, lumbermen rushed in to salvage all the sound timber, whether from dead or living trees, doomed in any case. But if a king is wholly vanished from our scene, its absence is at least less depressing than were those years when its diseased hosts and gaunt, whitening skeletons saddened the forest prospect.

CHINQUAPIN

Castanea pumila (Linnæus) Miller

OTHER NAME: Chinkapin.

RANGE: From southern New Jersey to central and western Florida and west through the Gulf States to the valley of the Nueces River in Texas, ascending to 4500 in the southern Appalachians.

DESCRIPTION: *Bark* thick, light brown tinged with red, somewhat furrowed at the base of old stems. *Twigs* first bright red-brown, becoming olive-green by spring. *Leaves* 4 to 6 inches long, bright yellow-green. *Flowers* creamy white with a fishy odor. *Fruits* enclosed in spiny burs, the solitary nut thin-shelled, dark chestnut-brown, silvery downy. *Wood* hard, strong and medium-light, the heartwood dark brown, the sapwood scarcely distinguishable.

The first mention to be found of the Chinquapin is in Captain John Smith's account of Virginia. But the creatures of that wilderness

had known and appreciated it from time immemorial. Today it is chiefly as a wildlife crop that it can replace its vanished kinsman the Chestnut, though the sweet and abundant little nuts are sometimes to be seen in the markets of towns in our South. In that region it is useless as a timber tree, being indeed little more than a shrub, but west of the Mississippi it seems to be inspired by a new ambition and reaches heights up to 50 feet, with a diameter of two or three feet.

THE OAKS

(*Quercus*)

Oaks are usually ponderous and heavy-wooded trees, with scaly or furrowed bark, and more or less 5-angled twigs and, consequently, 5-ranked leaves, which in our area are deciduous, and marked by prominent branching veins which extend to or sometimes beyond the margin, or are united within the margin. The winter buds are clustered at the ends of the twigs, with numerous chestnut-brown scales which in falling mark the twig with ring-like scars.

The flowers of all our species bloom in midspring, with, or after, the appearance of the leaves. The male catkins are slim, stringy, drooping, and appear in clusters from buds in the axils of the leaves. Each floret consists in 2 to 6 stamens with yellow anthers, seated in a minute calyx which is usually 4- to 6-lobed nearly to the base. The female catkin is a solitary few-flowered spike appearing in the axils of the season. The tube of the minute, 6-lobed calyx is adherent to the ovary and more or less completely enclosed in a cup of overlapping scales which finally become the cup of the acorn. The nut is an acorn, marked at base by a large pale circular scar, with a thick shell.

The Oaks have extremely variable foliage, even on the same tree, where the leaves of a seedling or a sucker shoot may be quite different from those of the mature tree. There are also frequent wild hybrids between the species which produce leaves intermediate in form between the parents. So many of these hybrids have been described that they are now as numerous as the true species; to include them here would be beyond the bounds of the present work.

In identifying an Oak, an observer will first wish to decide which of the two great groups his specimen belongs to. For the genus *Quercus* is divided into the White Oak group (subgenus *Lepidobalanus*) and the Red Oak group (subgenus *Erythrobalanus*). The first 8 of the species in this book belong to the White Oak group and all the rest to the Red Oaks. The two groups may be distinguished as follows:

RED OAKS *(Erythrobalanus)*	WHITE OAKS *(Lepidobalanus)*
Leaves with the veins usually running out beyond the margin in the form of a bristle	Leaves never with the veins extending beyond the margins in the form of bristles.
Stamens 4 in each floret	Stamens 6 to 8
Cup scales rather thin	Cup scales more or less woody, and knobby at the base
Inner surface of the acorn shell lined with woolly hairs	Inner surface of the acorn shell smooth
Fruit in the first year minute ("baby acorns"), maturing the second year.	Fruit maturing the first year.

The characters for the two subgenera will not be repeated in the descriptions of the species that follow. The White Oaks are distributed all around the northern hemisphere, but the Red Oaks are found only in North America.

EASTERN WHITE OAK

Quercus alba Linnæus

RANGE: Southern Maine to the southern peninsula of Michigan, south-western Minnesota, eastern Iowa, and southeastern Nebraska, south to western Florida, through the Gulf states to the Brazos River of Texas and eastern Oklahoma and eastern Kansas. Rare on the southern coastal plains; ascending the southern Appalachians to 4500 feet, but becoming a bush at high altitudes.

DESCRIPTION: *Bark* light gray or nearly white, broken into numberless thin scales; on very old trunks becoming divided into flat, broad ridges. *Twigs* at first bright green tinged with red, during their first winter becoming red-brown, and ultimately gray. *Winter buds* broadly egg-shaped, small, obtuse, and red-brown. *Leaves*, 5 to 9 inches long, 2 to 4 inches wide, firm, on the upper surface shining and hairless, the lower surface with a whitish bloom. *Acorns* ¾ to 1⅛ inch long, shiny brown. *Wood* medium-heavy (48 pounds to the cubic foot, dry weight), very hard, very strong, durable in contact with the soil, light brown.

If Oak is the king of trees, as tradition has it, then the White Oak, throughout its range, is the king of kings. The Tuliptree can grow taller, and the Sycamore in the days of the virgin forest had gigantic boles, but no other tree in our sylva has so great a spread. The mighty branches, themselves often fifty feet long or more, leave the trunk nearly at right angles and extend their arms benignantly above the generations of men who pass beneath them. Indeed, the fortunate possessor of an old White Oak owns a sort of second home, an outdoor mansion of shade and greenery and leafy music. So deep is the tap-root of such a tree, so wide the thrust of the innumerable horizontal roots, that if one could see its whole underground system this would look like a reflection, somewhat foreshortened, of the giant above ground.

Like the detail of a cathedral, the White Oak's minor points are beauty too. When the leaves unfold they clothe the tree in a veil of vivid red gradually turning pink and then silvery white. In autumn this foliage is a rich winy color, and in its withered final state it tends to cling all winter. The acorns germinate soon after they fall, and before the cold weather their first little roots are in the ground — if they have not been harvested by squirrels or birds with which they are a favorite food. They were a staple of diet, too, with the Indians, for though a little bitter for eating out of hand, they sweeten after boiling.

When the first New England colonists saw White Oak on the shores of Massachusetts Bay, they recognized it gladly as a close relative of the English or Norman Oak (*Quercus robur*), which had for centuries built England's navy and merchant fleet and was a very synonym for staunchness. But that Oak which once covered most of England had been cut and cut; shortages were becoming evident in Queen Elizabeth's day, and increased with alarming rapidity. Cromwell, in sequestrating the Crown lands, and those of the Church and the nobles, saw a ready revenue in leveling the Oaks, and with them he built a great navy. But wooden ships decay faster than Oaks can grow; the proudest ships of the line had a life expectancy of but a few years. So the Cromwellian orgy of Oaken shipbuilding was followed by forest dearth.

This offered a great chance to the American colonies. Our White Oak, however, met with serious opposition from the British ship-builders and the inspection boards of the Royal Navy. Scornfully they maintained that it was weaker than their own as a structural timber, and that it was far more subject to decay. The truth of this lay simply in the haste of the cutting and carelessness of seasoning. No wood is so troublesome as Oak to season; it must be air-dried, over a long period, yet kept from exposure to sun and rain lest cracks and checks develop.

Indeed, the hastily rushed ships of English Oak were in as bad condition as those of our own Oak. Samuel Pepys describes his inspection of such a vessel in 1677 where he gathered from the boards "toadstools . . . as big as my fist." When Lord Sandwich inspected the ships at Chatham in 1771 it was necessary to shovel away the fungal filth before the timbers could be seen. Often the dry rot never appeared on the surface but, like termites, gnawed away the interior, especially in that most vulnerable place known to sailors as the futtocks or wales — just above the water line, where the heavy guns were carried. The famous disaster of the *Royal George* in 1782 was caused when the whole bottom of the ship dropped out from dry rot.

For all of this, the British loftily shook their heads at American White Oak as far inferior to their own. Well, if the mother country would not take our White Oak, we would build our own ships of it. The immortal frigate *Constitution* had a gun deck of solid White Oak of Massachusetts, her keel was the same wood from New Jersey, while knees of Maryland White Oak framed her keelsons. All-Oak ships became the pride of our shipbuilders; not good enough for the British Navy, they were just good enough to carry the New England sea captains around the world. Nor has White Oak entirely lost its place in the American Navy. The keels of our mine sweepers and patrol boats in World War II were still being laid in White Oak, and some of it came from Franklin D. Roosevelt's estate of "Hyde Park."

On land as on the sea, this great tree gave its strength to our people. Through two centuries the pioneers built their blockhouses of its stout timbers, their bridges, barns, and mills and log cabins. For this is the best all-around hardwood in America. True, White Pine warps and checks less, Hickory is more resilient, Ironwood is stronger, and Locust more durable; but White Oak would stand second to almost all these trees in each property in which they excel and, combining all these good qualities in a single species, it comes out in the end as the incomparable wood for nearly every purpose for which wood can be used. In a great table prepared by the Forest Service on the uses of woods, White Oak almost invariably occupies first, second, or third place under every item, except for wood pulp and plywood, tobacco

pipes, artificial limbs, and airplanes. Obviously it is too hard and too valuable for the first two, too heavy for the last two, and since it develops no burls is not made into pipes.

But "pipes," in quite another sense, were some of the first objects made out of White Oak by the colonists, for to them a pipe meant a cask for wine and other liquids. Today we speak of "tight cooperage," meaning barrels that will hold liquids, as contrasted with "slack cooperage" for barrels intended to hold solids. Oak of most sorts is ideal for tight cooperage. So the pioneer people rived their barrel staves out of White Oak by hand, and sent them abroad, especially to France for wine casks and to the West Indies for rum; even from the heart of the Middle West this oaken cargo went floating down the Mississippi to New Orleans for export. For generations, too, the early Americans employed great amounts of the bark in tanning. Unfortunately, the trees stripped for this purpose were taken in spring, the time of year yielding the highest tannin amounts but least favorable for logging operations, which are best performed in winter. So that the peeled logs were left exposed to decay and weathering which, in Oak, is the opposite of seasoning. Always, too, the White Oak has been a fireplace favorite, for as a fuel it is the best all-round wood we have, weight for weight. And it is the heaviest of all our Oaks, as well as marvelously durable in contact with the soil. Indeed, its durability is taken as a standard, other woods being measured in percentages of the durability of White Oak.

As material for furniture, Oak is thus more sturdy than it is graceful. In England it was the favorite during the centuries when solid wood was employed; up to and through the Jacobean period it was uncontested. Thereafter, Walnut and Mahogany came to dispute with it, and their introduction, as well as the use of veneers, gave the cabinetmaker scope for lovelier creations, and Oak began to yield its primacy. Yet it has often returned to favor; in America we still shudder reminiscently over "the golden Oak era." Golden Oak was the name for a high varnish, laid usually on quarter-sawed boards. A quarter-sawed plank of full breadth is one which has one edge at the center of the tree, the other under the bark, and its beauty in White Oak consists in the large size and silvery brilliance of its medullary rays which are properly seen only on this cut of the wood. When an entire room is paneled in quartered Oak, the effect is indeed striking, and it was a great favorite forty and fifty years ago in the houses of the newly rich.

The trouble with the "golden Oak era," however, was not with the noble wood, but in the ostentation of the costly display, the machine-made designs of the paneling, and that flashy varnish.

At present Oak as a furniture wood is chiefly used in office desks, though White Oak flooring remains unchallenged, and properly waxed Oak paneling will never cease to hold its high place. But quarter-sawed Oak is not satisfactorily cut from trees under 150 years old and, in general, dimension timbers must come from trees 100 to 300 years of age. So the supply of high-grade White Oak is running out, as the centenarian trees are cut or die.

Yet a hundred years is brief in the life of an old White Oak. There are members of this species still standing that were already tall when Columbus first raised his momentous landfall. In the Friends' Cemetery at Salem, New Jersey, there grows a White Oak that stood out as a landmark when the town was founded in 1675 and Quaker John Fenwick called the Indians together beneath its shade to make with them a treaty that, it is boasted, was never broken on either side. The whole region of the Jersey shore of the Delaware Bay is famous for its great White Oaks that line the streets of ancient towns like Salem, Mantua, Jefferson, and Mullica Hill, and shade the King's Highway which links them all to Philadelphia. The Tatum Oak at Mantua Grove was a giant said to have been 25½ feet in circumference at breast height, 87 feet tall, with a spread of branches 121 feet across. It is survived by its rival, the Hendrickson Oak of Mantua, which if not so large is not necessarily younger, for size in a tree depends in part upon the amount and closeness to the surface of the ground water. Its base spreads out in mighty buttresses that grip the earth. Half a dozen gigantic boughs sweep out and bend to the ground, with the weight of their years. Six generations of the same family have played here, where two thousand children could probably be gathered in this patriarch's shade. The supply of Indian arrowheads discovered in the soil in which it grows seem never quite exhausted. In the probable life span of this tree have been born, have mightily wrought, and died, William Penn and Benjamin Franklin, George Washington, Thomas Jefferson, Abraham Lincoln, and Woodrow Wilson, Peter the Great, Napoleon, and Beethoven. Thrones have crumbled and new empires arisen; great ideas have been born and great pictures painted, and the world revolutionized by science and invention; and still no man can say how many centuries this Oak will endure or what nations and creeds it may outlive.

Yet there are grander Oaks than this in our country. For reasons not clear, the largest and possibly the oldest are found on the Eastern Shore of Maryland. When, two hundred years and more gone by, the first colonists came to this region of long "necks" of land between the inlet bays and creeks, they built their manor houses in great White Oak forests. And though they long ago cleared, or cut for timber, the forest itself, they were an aristocratic people who appreciated the worth of the noblest old trees, and half a dozen standing today might lay claim to being the largest White Oak in the world.

Judgment on that would depend on one's standard. But the final honors generally go to two titans. The first is the largest of the seven Oaks in the churchyard of ivy-covered St. Paul's at Fairlee, built in 1713. Twenty-four and a half feet in girth, this tree is 118 feet tall and has a spread of 127 feet. Its rival, the great Oak at Wye Mills, is a monarch of superbly symmetrical beauty with a spread of 148 feet — a dimension unequaled by any other Oak in our sylva. The Wye Oak's appearance of utmost antiquity is enhanced by great "knees" three or four feet high that surround its base.

With trees such as these, it is no wonder that Maryland has adopted the White Oak as its state tree, or that it was to the Eastern Shore that naval architects turned, when the frigate *Constitution* was to be remodeled. There they would find White Oak timbers great enough to replace the original keelsons and futtocks and compass-timber that had been selected in the days of our forest abundance. Today the visitor who walks the deck of *Old Ironsides,* where she rests in honored peace in Boston Harbor, can feel an oaken-hearted strength, still sound, that is part of our American heritage.

POST OAK

Quercus stellata Wangenheim

OTHER NAMES: Iron, Box or Brash Oak.

RANGE: Cape Cod to Florida and west through southern Ohio, southern Indiana and central Illinois to southern Iowa, eastern Kansas and western Texas.

DESCRIPTION: *Bark* ruddy brown, divided by fissures into broad ridges. *Twigs* stout, at first orange to reddish brown, the next year brown to nearly black. *Leaves* 4 to 5 inches long, 3 to 4 inches broad, thick and firm, dark green above, with veins rather recurving and veinlets intricately meshed; lower surface finely downy. *Acorns* ⅜ to ¾ inch long, frequently striped longitudinally green and brown. *Wood* very heavy (52 pounds per cubic foot, dry weight), very hard, close-grained and durable, the heartwood light or dark brown, with thick paler sapwood.

You will know the Post Oak among its large tribe if you can see in the shape of its lobed leaves a sort of Maltese cross. When these leaves first appear in spring they are a deep and vital red; they mature to a dark green, thick and firm, and turn at last an uninteresting yellow or brown. Even then they will not give up their display, but often cling on, withered, until pushed off next spring by the new vivid growth.

Look for this Oak on poor or sandy upland soils, where it stands forth, bold but somewhat ungainly since it is a knotty tree whose dead limbs tend to adhere to the trunk. But its sturdiness commended it to the pioneers, who chose it for their fence posts and thus gave it a name. It might, however, as well be called Crosstie Oak, since some of the first rails in America were laid upon it, so that in its way it was a pioneer itself.

OVERCUP OAK

Quercus lyrata Walter

OTHER NAME: Swamp Post Oak.

RANGE: Southern Missouri and the Delaware peninsula, south to the valley of the Suwannee River in Florida and westward to eastern Texas and north in the Mississippi valley to southern Illinois and southwestern Indiana.

DESCRIPTION: *Bark* thin, brownish gray, with large, thick, irregular plates covered with thin scales, not, or scarcely, furrowed. *Twigs* green tinged with red, becoming orange or gray-brown the first winter and pale gray or light brown the next spring. *Leaves* 6 to 10 inches long, 1 to 4 inches wide, dark green and shining above, on the lower surface light green, coated thickly with silvery white hairs. *Acorns* light chestnut-brown, about 1 inch long. *Wood* very heavy (51 pounds per cubic foot, dry weight), tough, strong, very hard and durable, the heartwood rich dark brown, the sapwood paler.

If all the Oaks were as easy to identify as this one, they would not be the baffling lot that they are. The acorns are almost completely covered by the knobby cups, and the leaves are almost without rival, amongst the Oaks with lobed foliage, in being so long and so narrow, with such wide sinuses or bays between the lobes. These points distinguish it at once in the field.

The Overcup Oak is a lover of river swamps and low moist bottomlands; growing in the open, it is stockily short-trunked, with a great number of branches, forming a fine three-quarters sphere of a tree, handsome in full leafage and grateful, by its shade, on a hot summer day. In autumn the foliage blazes into yellow, orange, or scarlet, or all three colors on the same torchlike tree.

The wood is as strong as White Oak or stronger, and it is used for almost all the same purposes except as a beautiful cabinet wood. The growth is very slow, and a big tree usually represents the passage of four centuries; long ago the lumberman swept most such away, where they were not protected and beloved shade trees in farmyards and villages. Too often now the lumber that is being cut is short and knotty, but still its strength and endurance make the hardwood lumberman eye the 4,000,000,000 board feet which, it is estimated, represent the remaining stand, most of it in the South and west of the Mississippi.

SWAMP WHITE OAK

Quercus bicolor Willdenow

RANGE: New Hampshire westward through southern Ontario, and southern parts of Michigan and Wisconsin to southeastern Minnesota, and southeastern Nebraska, eastern Kansas, northeastern Oklahoma and northern Arkansas, south to Delaware, Maryland, northern and western Virginia, and northwestern Tennessee. Of rare and scattered occurrence in North Carolina and Maine, and absent from central and southeastern Kentucky and the northern Appalachians.

DESCRIPTION: *Bark* very thick, deeply and irregularly furrowed into broad, flat ridges covered with small gray-brown or red-tinged close scales, that on young stems and smaller branches turn back in papery, ragged scales to display the bright green inner bark. *Twigs* stout, shining, green, with pale lenticels, when they first appear, becoming light orange or reddish brown the first winter, then purplish brown overcast by a whitish bloom. *Leaves* 5 to 6 inches long, 2 to 4 inches wide, thick and firm, the upper surface dark green and shiny, the lower paler, often silvery white or tawny with slender yellow midrib. *Acorn* light chestnut-brown, ¾ to 1¼ inches long, ½ to ¾ inch thick. *Wood* medium-heavy (48 pounds per cubic foot, dry weight), medium-hard, medium-strong, tough, the heartwood light brown and the sapwood scarcely different.

As you tramp the woods with stick and dog, or even when you are rushing along, high over valleys and among mountain peaks, on the great Harrisburg-to-Pittsburgh turnpike, one Oak proclaims its unmistakable identity at a glance and at a distance. At least it does so if there is any free wind plowing through the summer foliage, for on the slightest provocation this beauty among the Oaks shows its white flounced petticoats — the silvery undersides of the blades which contrast so markedly with the upper surface. Hence the Latin specific name of *bicolor*.

This Oak can boast not only vivacious foliage (which in the autumn turns a dull brown or occasionally orange), but fine, fat acorns, usually occurring in pairs, some of the handsomest in all its tribe, and eagerly sought by squirrels all winter long. The years give it grandeur too; the lower branches are down-sweeping, the middle ones horizontal, the upper very numerous and bushily erect, making a broadly columnar outline, sturdily supported on the straight and massive trunk. So, living on for 300 and 400 years, a Swamp White Oak (which is not necessarily found in the swamp at all but merely in deep moist and fertile soil) becomes a beloved landmark wherever it is spared.

One of the most famous specimens of this tree is the Big Tree, towering 100 feet high with a circumference of 27 feet, which has for generations been the pride of the Wadsworth family and the village of Geneseo, in New York State. It was beneath this tree that Robert Morris, the early New York financier, who somehow found the money for Washington who somehow won the battles, purchased from the Senecas, by treaty in 1797, practically the whole of western New York State for the sum of $100,000. This, be it said to Morris's honor, was not turned over to them to turn over to the whiskey sellers, but was invested in United States Bank stock and held in trust by the President of the United States for the tribe.

The wood of Swamp White Oak is of the hardest and strongest, valued for tight cooperage, for mine timbers and crossties. But the tree does not occur in merchantable stands. The amount growing today is estimated to be no more than 1 per cent of the total of the lumber that the lumberman classifies together under the generic term of White Oak. And there can be few but wish that the sawmills may pass this lovely species by and leave it to the soil, the sunshine, and the wind.

CHESTNUT OAK

Quercus montana Willdenow

OTHER NAMES: Rock or Mountain Oak.

RANGE: From southern Maine to eastern Ohio and southern Indiana, and from the District of Columbia southward toward the Appalachians, following them, and on the high piedmont to Alabama and Georgia. Common as far west as central Tennessee, with a small outlying occurrence in southern Illinois.

DESCRIPTION: *Bark* a dark reddish brown becoming nearly black, nearly smooth on all but ancient trees when it becomes thick and rough. *Twigs* stout, at first purplish green, becoming in winter orange tinged with brown, and next year dark gray. *Leaves* 4 to 9 inches long and 1½ to 3 inches wide, firm and thick, rich yellow-green, paler beneath and finely downy. *Acorn* light brown and shiny, 1 to 1½ inches long, ⅝ to 1 inch thick. *Wood* medium-heavy (47 pounds per cubic foot, dry weight), close-grained, rather tough, medium-hard, medium-strong, the heartwood dark brown, the sapwood paler and thin.

This is a fine, soldierly sort of Oak, for the column of its trunk may rise 100 feet, and the long, unlobed leaves, softly shining, hang like green curtains from the spreading boughs, rather than in various planes like those of other Oaks. Even under forest conditions it is able to elbow out plenty of room for itself. And unlike most trees, it seems to grow more luxuriantly the taller it grows, at least on the rocky slopes it often chooses for its site.

So notable is it among its many relatives that it was one of the first Oaks reported to the Old World, by John Ray in his *Historia Plantarum* in 1688. Half a century later it was made much of by that *bon-vivant* and boaster, Colonel William Byrd of "Westover," who fathered a book to entice Germans and Swiss to settle on the lands in which he was so rich and yet so poor. The Chestnut Oak, he told his distant prospective tenants in his *Neugefundenes Eden,* is called so "because the acorns on it are as large and sweet as the best chestnuts." Only the squirrels, perhaps, would agree to this, and others would argue that the name derives from the resemblance of the leaves to those of the Chestnut tree.

"This tree is of terrific height," reported Byrd with relish, "since the trunk alone, to the branches, is fifty to sixty feet tall, and four to five feet thick on an average, so that one can make very beautiful boards or chests from them." But handsome as was the lumber to be sawed from the Chestnut Oak, its chief use, in the early days, was for tanning. Oak bark was deemed the best for preparing fine leather, and no other Oak of ours has so high a tannin content as this one. In our day, synthetic tannins are frequently used, and the process by which a hide becomes our shoe seems to us distant and savorless. In young America, however, the hide might have come from a beast you knew well, and the tannery that prepared it was, like the smithy, as natural and necessary a part of the community as the bakery is today. In his *Travels,* in 1802, François Michaux accurately describes this as he found it in North Carolina:

"The woods are in a great measure composed of different kinds of oaks . . . In all the towns that I have travelled through every tanner has his tan mill, which does not cost him above ten dollars to erect. The bark is put into a wooden arch, twelve or fourteen feet in diameter, the edges of which are about fifteen inches high, and it is crushed under the weight of a wheel, about one foot thick, which is turned by a horse, and fixed similar to a cyder-press. For this purpose they generally make use of an old mill-stone, or a wooden wheel, formed by several pieces joined together, and furnished in its circumference with three rows of teeth, also made of wood, about two inches long and twelve or fifteen wide."

To this primitive woodland tannery came great quantities of the bark of Chestnut Oak, which had been stripped from logs left then in the forest to rot, since the wood was not valued. Time has taught us better, for Chestnut Oak is tough, strong, heavy, close-grained, durable in contact with the soil though difficult to season. Indeed, when the first scarcity of White Oak began to show itself, it was the lumberman's second choice, sold under the other's name, but today it has a reputation in its own right.

BASKET OAK

Quercus Prinus Linnæus

OTHER NAMES: Cow, Swamp, Mountain, or Chestnut Oak.

RANGE: Southern New Jersey, southward to the coast and lower piedmont to central Florida, through the Gulf states to the valley of Trinity River, Texas, through Arkansas and southeastern Missouri, to central Kentucky and southern Indiana and Illinois.

DESCRIPTION: *Bark* silvery white or ashy gray, with thin, closely pressed scales. *Twigs* stout, at first dark green, becoming light orange-brown and finally ashy gray. *Leaves* 6 to 8 inches long, 3 to 5 inches wide, above dark green and shiny, the lower surface pale green or silvery white and more or less densely downy. *Acorns* 1 to 1½ inches long, ¾ to 1¼ inches thick, bright brown and rather shining. *Wood* very heavy (51 pounds per cubic foot, dry weight), tough, close-grained, very strong, very hard and durable, the heartwood light brown with thin, darker sapwood.

The Basket Oak is much more of a Southerner than a Yankee tree, and at its best it is a giant, towering up sometimes 100 feet with a trunk 3 to 7 feet in diameter. With its silvery bark, such a tree shines through the forest with a fatal charm for the lumber-camp foreman, who soon brings his black cohorts to send the monarch toppling, with a heart-rending crash that shakes the earth and shatters half a dozen lesser trees.

The Basket Oak's wood has the special property of splitting into fine yet tough ribbons of fiber. The splitting occurs along the spring wood, for the annual growth rings are broad, with the bands of spring wood and summer wood unusually distinct. Such a structure is ideal for the making of splints, and untold thousands of baskets were woven of this wood for toting cotton from the fields. That was in what Southerners like to call their Golden Age, and the wagons into which the cotton was dumped from the baskets were in those days also made of Basket Oak, for it stood up splendidly in every part — for axles, for felloes, hubs, hounds, tongues, spokes, bolsters, reaches, and bed-bottoms.

Tough, strong, durable, and hard, Basket Oak often takes the place of Hickory where great strain and violent shock must be endured, for it is a cheaper wood. So it is extensively used in the making of cant-hooks, those levers tipped with great iron hooks which lift whole trees in lumbering operations. It endures stoutly the heavy usage of cross-ties, for it holds spikes well, lasts long in contact with the soil, and stands up under the great loads that, freight or Pullman, go thundering and racking over it. The wood rives well, and so it is a favorite with the coopers for barrel staves. Braided, the splints make ideal cheap chair bottoms. Far from being an exquisite cabinet wood, like Walnut and Cherry Birch and Black Cherry, the Basket Oak may be; but none does more yeoman service.

The acorns are almost the only fruits amongst all the Oaks which are sweet enough to be eaten out of hand, without boiling to rid them of their tannic bitterness. Country children in the South know this well and so do the hogs, both of the domestic breeds and the razorback running wild. And though north of the Mason and Dixon line we are used to seeing cows that graze only on lush grass and clover, in the South the cattle are turned into the woods, where they get a large part of their browse from Oak leaves and, where this species grows, from its nuts. Hence the name of Cow Oak.

With all that is workaday, with all of its casting of its acorns before swine, Basket Oak is yet a beauty, its sturdiness somehow balanced by grace, its foliage almost like so much blossoming in early spring when, pink and silver, it first emerges, then dark and flashing during the long hot summer, and in late autumn a deep dark red that is like a cup of wine held against the light. Basket Oaks sometimes live to be 350 years old, having taken the first hundred years of their life to reach maturity, and, though the drain on this species for lumbering is great, its preferred habitat of swampy ground at least prevents it from being constantly cleared away, like the White Oak, to make more farmland.

CHINQUAPIN OAK

Quercus Muehlenbergii Engelmann

OTHER NAMES: Yellow, Rock, Chinkapin, or Chestnut Oak.

RANGE: Western Vermont to the neighborhood of New York City, thence southwestward through the District of Columbia to western Virginia and southward to western Florida, west through southern Ohio, southern Michigan, to southeastern parts of Minnesota and Nebraska, eastern Kansas, and eastern Oklahoma. Absent from the Delta country of Louisiana, from most of Wisconsin except the Mississippi valley and most of the southern Appalachians.

DESCRIPTION: *Bark* thin, on old trunks light gray and broken into thin, loose, silvery white flakes, but scarcely furrowed. *Twigs* slender, green, tinged with red, and velvety when they first appear, becoming reddish brown the first winter and finally brownish gray. *Leaves* 4 to 7 inches long, 1 to 4 inches wide, thick and firm, the upper surface yellowish green, the lower pale and downy. *Acorns* chestnut-brown, $\frac{1}{2}$ to nearly 1 inch long. *Wood* very heavy ($53\frac{1}{2}$ pounds per cubic foot, dry weight), very strong, very hard, close-grained and durable, the heartwood dark brown, the sapwood thin and paler.

Nobody will ever know how many million cords of Chinquapin Oak logs were split by the Homeric strength of our pioneering heroes into snake rail fences in the Ohio valley. Eleven feet long, mauled from the clearest, straightest timber that the aboriginal forest had to offer, these rails developed the muscle of a hardy breed of boys, and fenced in the early farms of Kentucky, Ohio, and Indiana. But the generations pass, farms are abandoned, and fences left to fall. And when, in the great days of Ohio river boating, steamships were first sent down from Pittsburgh to New Orleans, it was discovered that these old rails of Chinquapin Oak (along with many other Oak and Hickory fences, of course) made the best obtainable fuel for the devouring engines of the steamboats. So farmers came to heap them in great piles on the shore for sale to the engineers, and stops to take on these rails of seasoned,

completely combustible timber were as frequent and important as ever the stops at scheduled landings where goods and passengers waited. Liquid merchandise was commonly rolled onto the boat in barrels made of this same Oak, for though its pores look large, they are admirably plugged by nature and so proof against leakage. When the railways came chuffing to take away the business of the river boats, it was on ties of this strong, durable, shock-resistant wood that the first steel tracks were laid.

Unfortunately the Chinquapin Oak delights to grow on rich soil with a high water-table, so that it has been relentlessly pushed aside by the growth of Middle Western agriculture, and not so often now does one see a trunk 3 or 4 feet thick, and practically never trees that soar up 160 feet, as they did in the primeval forest. But still the traveler down the Ohio will admire the almost snow-white bark and, on a windy day, the fluttering of this Oak's lovely foliage, each crinkly blade handsome enough in itself, but superb in mass by the marked contrast of the dark and gleaming upper surface and the flashing white of the lower. Owing to the way the leaves hang upon the stalk, they are especially likely to flutter, almost as gaily as the Aspen's. When standing by itself the Chinquapin Oak often develops an immense number of shrubby forks after a height of about 20 feet, so that it has almost the vase-like shape of the White Elm — not so graceful, perhaps, but making of it a friendly tree in the pasture or the park.

BUR OAK

Quercus macrocarpa A. Michaux

OTHER NAME: Mossycup Oak.

RANGE: Manitoba and the Black Hills of South Dakota south to central Texas, east to southern Ohio, southwestern New Brunswick and southern Nova Scotia, and southward through New York State to Maryland, northern West Virginia, Kentucky, northwestern Tennessee, and Arkansas. Absent from southern Maine, New Hampshire, eastern Vermont, eastern Massachusetts, southern New England, Long Island, the lower Hudson valley, the Adirondacks, the mountains of West Virginia and Kentucky, and the north shore of Lake Superior.

DESCRIPTION: *Bark* of old trunks thick, grayish or reddish brown, flaky, deeply cut into wide fissures dividing broad straight ridges with more or less flat surfaces. *Twigs* greenish gray, turning light orange, and the following year dark brown with somewhat corky ridges. *Leaves* 6 to 12 inches long, 3 to 6 inches broad, thick, firm, the upper surface shiny dark green, the lower silvery green and downy. *Acorns* ¾ to 2 inches long, half buried in the strikingly fringed cup. *Wood* medium heavy (46 pounds to the cubic foot, dry weight), hard, tough, close-grained, with dark brown heartwood and thin paler sapwood.

When the pioneers of the Middle West had hacked their way through the forests of the Appalachians, they came, as they moved westward, to a new type of forest growth, something unknown in the aboriginal sylva of the Atlantic seaboard. This was the groves of wide-spaced trees, almost void of undergrowth, and carpeted with short, sweet grass. Between these trees, and under their great boughs, they drove their lumbering wagons easily; deer could be hunted through these groves on horseback; here the wind blew refreshingly free, driving away the plaguing horseflies and mosquitoes; here the ground was dry and the grass could not conceal snakes, nor were there ominous thickets to hide lurking savages. So our forefathers called these groves the Oak openings, and that is the title of one of James Fenimore Cooper's novels of primeval life in the old Northwest Territory, which now we call the Middle West.

The most characteristic tree which the settlers noted in the Oak openings was one which grows, indeed, to the eastward, but never comes there to its full grandeur or its characteristic park-like vistas. They knew it as the Bur Oak because the heavily fringed cups of the acorns look almost like the burs on a Chestnut, though the cups only half cover the nut. True that other Oaks are often found in the Oak openings, or prairie groves, of the Middle West, but ecologists consider them secondary successors; they have come in after the Bur Oak has conquered the prairie for them; and they in turn make way for a climax forest of Hickory, Walnut, Ash, and Linden.

But the Bur Oak seems, from all the geological and ecological evidence which can be collected, to be the pioneer in the advance of the forest upon the prairie. For the warfare of forest and prairie, of grass and wood, is an old one; probably it was going on, in the heart of North America, before ever the great glaciers came. Where those caps of ice rested, of course, they killed all life; when they retreated, as periodically they did, Oak and grass took up their ancient quarrel. As a Bur Oak may not reach productivity for fifty years, while the prairie grasses begin seeding themselves almost at once, it would seem that all the advantage must lie with the grass.

Yet that depends upon the climate of the inter-glacial periods (of which the present era is probably one), which have been alternately dry and moist. Whenever the climate tended to the dry side, the grasses advanced; in moister periods the forest advanced. Apparently a few thousand years before our time there was a dry period when prairies covered most of Illinois, but today "the prairie state," as it is called, has a forest climate. The result is that Bur Oaks have, where not actually kept back by destruction of one sort or another, advanced so rapidly, not only in Illinois, but in Wisconsin and Iowa, as to constitute a distinct agricultural problem in some localities.

Some ecologists believe that the only thing that prevented the Bur Oak from making forest states out of everything east of the Missouri was the constant firing of the region by the Indians in their hunting drives. For Bur Oak seedlings are more injured by fire than are grasses which come back readily. Though the coming of the white man put a stop to the firing, the introduction of cattle, which eagerly browse the leaves of Oak seedlings, and whose hooves pack down the soil so that the roots have most of their air supply cut off, has often held back the spread of the Bur Oaks.

Extensive studies have been made upon the root systems of the Bur

Oak, and they show that the taproot is comparatively short; like the trunk above ground, it soon gives rise to a large number of wide-spreading, horizontal primary branches, which in old systems are almost as thick as the great main lower boughs of the tree above. The primaries send off obliquely slanting secondaries in still greater numbers, and these give rise to tertiaries, which in turn send down numberless sinkers or slim roots that travel straight down. For all these thousands of sinkers there are tens of thousands of still finer rootlets called obliques, and on these are clustered the millions of fine capillary or thread-form rootlets. These capillaries may be very long, and in their search for water not only do they penetrate as widely as the widest spread of the great boughs above ground, and almost as deep as the tree is high, but others turn upwards and reach nearly to the surface of the soil in order to catch all the moisture that falls from light showers but never penetrates more than a few inches of the dust. So the underground system of the Bur Oak resembles a mirror image of the mighty structure above, and it is no wonder that a tree like this is able to go deep under the roots of the prairie grasses, extensive and tough though these are, and compete with them at their own level too.

But it follows that a tree with so mighty a root system has one serious competitor which can fight it with its own weapons — and that is another Bur Oak near by. So, perforce, Bur Oaks keep a respectful distance from each other; they hold each other off, not so much by their wide-spreading branches as by the fierce competition of their root systems. And that is the explanation of the Oak openings, the wide-spaced rooms where men drew their wagons to a stop with a slow, deep "Whoa!" and resolved: Here will I build me a house; here will my children grow up.

A grand old Bur Oak suggests a house in itself — for it is often broad rather than tall, and its mighty boughs, starting straight out from the trunk at right angles, extend horizontally 50, 60, 70 feet, bending with the weight of their own mass to the very ground, so that within their circle is a hollow room, its grassy floor littered with acorns, with the sloughed-off corky bark of the boughs, with a deep bed of leaves, and the birds' nests of many a summer, and the gold of many a flicker's wing.

No child who ever played beneath a Bur Oak will forget it, and if he was brought up by the right kind of parents, they showed him all its grand, elemental beauties, and perhaps found for him old portage trees of this species, bent down by the Indians a century and more ago, in their sapling stage, to mark the canoe carries from one of the slow, historic rivers or lakes to the next. For Bur Oaks live three centuries and four or more. At Sioux City, Iowa, still stands a mighty specimen of this race, the Council Oak, which, it is believed, was already 150 years old when Lewis and Clark saw it on their way up the Missouri and there held council with the Indians. At Exira, in northern Iowa, you can see the Plow Oak, where a plow that a homesteader leaned against the tree when he went off to the Civil War has been engulfed till only its handles wait for the hands that never returned to guide the share.

Most of us who have grown up among Bur Oaks will not leave among them even so much as a plow for the coming generations to remember us by, and when we are gone the rippling fox squirrels and the jeering crows will not remember us; the big dull yellow leaves of the Bur Oaks will cover the paths of our autumns. But these same trees will see our children and our children's children, and look to them the mansions that they are.

NORTHERN RED OAK

Quercus rubra Linnæus

OTHER NAME: Gray Oak.

RANGE: From Nova Scotia to Minnesota, eastern Kansas and northern Arkansas, south on the Appalachians to Georgia, also northern Alabama and central Mississippi. Absent from coastal plain and piedmont of the southern states, and from Kentucky and Tennessee except the mountainous parts.

DESCRIPTION: *Bark* dark brown, scaly. *Twigs* slender, light green and shining, becoming dark red changing to dark brown. *Leaves* 5 to 8 inches long and 4 to 5 broad, dark green above, pale below. *Acorns* 1 to 1½ inches long and ½ to ⅔ inch thick, pale brown and lustrous. *Wood* medium heavy (41½ pounds per cubic foot, dry weight), coarse-grained, medium-hard, medium-strong, the heartwood light brown or reddish brown with thin darker sapwood.

Lumbermen used to recognize only two sorts of Oak — "White" and "Red" — from the color of their respective woods. This classification coincides, in the species it includes, with the botanists' two subgenera listed under those names (for which see page 194). In the view of the veteran lumberman not only the color of their wood but their other properties divided all Oaks into these two general classes, with "White Oak" heavier, stronger, more durable and beautiful, and "Red Oak" weaker, coarser, and less resistant to decay. Gradually it became apparent at the mills that not all "White Oak" has the valuable properties of *the* White Oak (*Quercus alba*), and that much "Red Oak" is of high quality. One by one, the distinct botanical species have been receiving recognition by commerce, and while the statistics of the cut and sale of Oak lumber are still back in the primitive classification into two sorts, a good deal of nice sorting of Oak is now done in some hardwood lumber yards.

The present species is now generally accepted as *the* Red Oak. Not until White Oak was growing hard to come by was Red Oak heavily cut, since the wood is much lighter, even harder to season, and so porous that some claim smoke can be blown lengthwise through a piece 3 feet long! But when treated with preservatives it was early a favorite for crossties; nowadays it goes into rough lumber, clapboards, and slack cooperage. Fortunately the tree grows so rapidly that dimension timbers can be cut from the growth made during a man's lifetime — something that can be said of few Oaks of any value.

The leaves and acorn cups of Red Oak are so variable that it is hard to identify the tree, hard to describe it, and hard to illustrate it with certainty. But fairly distinctive is the large acorn with shallow cup enclosing only the base of the nut, and so is the smooth bark, which even in old age is never deeply furrowed. As for the leaves, they are pink when they first unfold, and in autumn they turn dull brown to bright orange. So that, with its frequent stature of 70 to 90 feet, and its broad, symmetrical crown, it is a handsome tree, recommended for planting in streets and parks. It is a favorite, too, in Europe, where it has been appreciated since the late seventeenth century, when the first Red Oaks were planted in Bishop Compton's garden, near Fulham.

SPANISH OAK

Quercus falcata A. Michaux

OTHER NAME: Southern Red Oak.

RANGE: From New Jersey to central Florida and eastern Texas and south-eastern Oklahoma; up the Mississippi valley to southern Illinois, Indiana and Ohio.

DESCRIPTION: *Bark* nearly black, divided by shallow fissures into broad ridges. *Twigs* stout, clothed at first in a thick rusty or orange-colored coat of clammy hairs, and dark red, becoming dark brown in winter and ashy gray the second year. *Leaves* 6 to 7 inches long and 4 to 5 broad, thin, firm, dark green and lustrous above but downy-coated below. *Acorn* orange-brown, about ½ inch long. *Wood* medium-hard, medium-strong, medium-heavy (41 pounds per cubic foot, dry weight), coarse-grained, not durable, with light red heartwood and thick paler sapwood. In the variety *pagodæfolia* the wood weighs 48 pounds per cubic foot, dry weight.

When, in the summer of August, 1683, William Penn squared his elbows to write a report on his new Commonwealth to The Free Society of Traders in London, he had already spent nearly a year in the province and could give a good account of its natural treasures. He lists them, fish, fowl, and beasts, flowers, crops, and trees, and among the latter he names Spanish Oak. So did the translator of the jocular William Byrd, half a century later, still speak of *Spannische Eiche,* in writing to persuade the Swiss whom Byrd wished as settlers on his acres.

But why Spanish? Was it in fancied resemblance to some Oak of Spain? Not only must Byrd and Penn have been unfamiliar with the sylva of that country, but indeed none of its Oaks much resemble this one. Some say this has its name because it turns the colors of the Spanish flag, but truth to tell in autumn it puts on not scarlet and gold but orange and brown. Others suggest that the form of the leaf looks like a Spanish dagger, which is more hopeful than helpful. But in the naming of plants fancy has a poet's license. "Spanish" Oak, for no good reason, it remains today, and it wears its title with a certain dash, due partly to the fine slashing curve of the leaf lobes, that seem drawn free-hand by the boldest of artists. On an autumn day, with the wind crying in its colored foliage, this is a handsome and gallant tree, not so knotty and sturdy as some of its kinsfolk, but straight-growing, in the field, and ambitious of height.

On the piedmont and coastal plain of Virginia, where every foot of ground, it sometimes seems, is steeped in memories of two wars and two great eras of peace, the Colonial and the Federal, the Spanish Oak is commonly the Chief Inhabitant and Oldest Settler. It is a poor country church indeed (in the land of our oldest and most beautiful country churches) that is not shaded by at least one great old Spanish

Oak. It is a rare Virginia courthouse (with attendant "lawyers' row" of little brick offices) whose mellowed walls and cupola are not dappled with the shadow and light from this tree's lively bicolored foliage — glossy green above, whitish or rusty-woolly beneath. On many a campus of Virginia's old colleges, the ancient boles of Spanish Oak are marbled with a growth of pale lichens till they look like columns. There are Spanish Oaks at "Mount Vernon," at "Stratford" the home of the Lees, in the historic streets of Williamsburg, at Yorktown, and at Appomattox, which, could they remember, might recall men with names to stir the heart, moving predestined by their greatness through decisive events. Yet historians have passed by this tree in their chronicles, and poets who chant of Weeping Willows and stately Elms, seem never to have observed our Spanish Oaks. But over and over, when a tree in Virginia draws the traveler to stop to admire it, it turns out to be a Spanish Oak. The grandest specimen so far reported is one at Sudley, Maryland, which measures 23 feet, 5 inches in girth, grows 105 feet tall, and shades a circle 129 feet across.

There is even a variety called Swamp Spanish Oak (variety *pagodæ-folia* Elliott) which has a scalier bark with a reddish tinge like a Cherry's, and grows in the same range but preferring to keep its feet wet. Its wood is a valuable timber, being harder, heavier, and stronger than the true species, which checks badly and is far from durable, though it too is used for telegraph-poles, crates, boxes, and Mission furniture.

SCARLET OAK

Quercus coccinea Muenchhausen

RANGE: Southern Maine westward through southern New York and southern Ontario to Indiana, southern Illinois and southeastern Missouri, southward to Georgia and Alabama. Rare on coastal plain, but ascending high in the Appalachians.

DESCRIPTION: *Bark* on young stems smooth and light brown, on old trunks darker and ruddier, shallowly fissured and irregularly ridged; inner bark bright red. *Twigs* slender, at first downy, becoming lustrous pale green, then in first winter light red or orange and next year light brown. *Leaves* 3 to 6 inches long, thin, firm, bright green and shining above with yellow midrib. *Acorn* ½ to 1 inch long and ⅓ to ⅔ inch thick, light reddish brown. *Wood* medium-heavy (42 pounds per cubic foot, dry weight), coarse-grained, strong and hard, with reddish brown or light brown heartwood and thick, darker sapwood.

The day when the storm-worn and weary *Mayflower* cast anchor in American waters was in bleak November, and only those trees which keep their foliage late had still some tattered banners to hang out in welcome. Of such is the Scarlet Oak, and since it grows abundantly on the shores of Massachusetts Bay, it must have been one of the first trees the Pilgrims saw. The scene to them was alien and disheartening, "for sumer being done, all things stand upon them with a weather-

beaten face; and ye whole countrie, full of woods and thickets, represented a wild and savage heiew." No "heiew" in the aboriginal forest
could have been more vivid, at that season, than the Scarlet Oak's,
since it retains its leaves until well into winter. When the big, slow
flakes of the first snowfall come driving through the still brilliant
foliage of the Scarlet Oak, there is no finer sight in all the range of
this tree. Winter — for the moment — seems a thing of vivid colors, of
glowing health.

Scarlet Oak is well named. In early spring the foliage is bright red,
just as in autumn it is the most burning note of red amongst all our
trees, rival to the orange of the Sugar Maple, the gold of Aspens. Even
in summer, when the leaves are glossy green, the red inner bark of the
Scarlet Oak sustains the reputation of its name, as you may see if you
will scratch with a penknife under the thin outer bark of a twig.

For an Oak the Scarlet is strikingly delicate in its fine twigs. The
crown is narrow; in forest-grown specimens it sometimes exceeds — or
it did in a more heroic sylvan age — 100 feet; the trunk may be four
feet in diameter. Though about as heavy as White Oak, the wood of
Scarlet Oak is considerably stiffer and stronger, and so has been in
demand for agricultural implements, boats, wagons, vehicles, slack
cooperage, and chair stock. Yet it is attractive enough in grain to have
seen use as an outside furniture material. Chair stock mills, which
clean up after a hardwood logger has taken out the big White Oaks,
seem glad to get all they can of the Scarlet Oak, a tree that has never
had its due, by name, from poet or business man.

SHUMARD OAK

Quercus Shumardii Buckley

OTHER NAME: Swamp Red Oak.

RANGE: Coast region of Texas from the Colorado River eastward along
the coastal plain to western and central Florida, north to southern
Maryland, northeastward through Arkansas and the Mississippi valley to
southeastern Kansas, Missouri, southern Iowa, southern parts of Illinois
and Indiana, and central Ohio.

DESCRIPTION: *Bark* thickish, ridged, broken into small scaly plates. *Twigs* gray or grayish brown. *Leaves* 6 to 8 inches long, 4 to 5 inches wide, the upper surfaces shiny and dark green, paler below, with large axillary tufts of hairs. *Acorns* ¾ to 1¾ inches long, ½ to 1 inch in diameter. *Wood* medium-hard, medium-heavy, coarse-grained, light reddish brown.

Shumard Oak is what can only be called a botanist's species, usually unrecognized by lumberman and layman, but an object of triumphant discovery to the botanical fraternity, wherever it is encountered on the borders of streams and swamps in moist rich soil. It seems closely related to the Red Oak except that the leaves are shining and not dull on the upper surface and 5- to 7-lobed, not 7- to 11-lobed. It also shows points of resemblance to the Pin Oak, but its acorns are more than ½ inch long, which is all that the Pin Oak can boast. Rising sometimes 120 feet high, with a long trunk clear of branches and sometimes as much as 5 feet in diameter, with muscular boughs spreading wide, this is a tree worthy of recognition by name.

BLACK OAK

Quercus velutina Lamarck

OTHER NAMES: Yellow, Dyer's, or Tanbark Oak.

RANGE: From southern Maine to southern Michigan, southern Wisconsin, southeastern Minnesota, southeastern Nebraska and eastern Kansas, and south to western Florida and the valley of the Brazos River in eastern Texas, ascending to 4000 feet in the southern Appalachians.

DESCRIPTION: *Bark* deeply furrowed and broadly ridged, the inner bark yellow or orange. *Twigs* at first woolly, by winter becoming smooth and reddish brown, darkening the next year. *Leaves* 5 to 6 inches long and 3 to 5 broad, thick and firm, dark green and shining above but yellowish or coppery beneath. *Acorn* light red-brown, frequently coated with soft rusty down, ½ to ¾ inch long. *Wood* medium-heavy (43 pounds per cubic foot, dry weight), hard, strong but not tough, coarse-grained, the heartwood light brown, with thin paler sapwood.

You may easily know this widely ranging and abundant Oak among
its kin, if you will scratch a twig with your thumbnail and see then
that the inner bark is yellow or orange. In the old days, before the
invention of aniline dyes, the intense yellow color this produced was
an important article of commerce, and native weavers may still use it
in the Appalachian coves. From the tanner's point of view this very
quality was a handicap, for the yellow had to be extracted before he
could use the bark, which is high in tannin content. The potter, it is
said, selected this tree in preference to others as fuel for his kiln.

The wood, used for flooring, boxcars, slack cooperage, and other
fundamental but prosaic purposes, probably passes as just "Red Oak"
when the lumbermen trouble to cut it. But too often the trunks are
short and crooked, knotty, cracked even in the living tree or, in trees
old enough to yield dimension timbers, inwardly decayed. And Black
Oak is too heavy in form, too narrow in the crown, too unkempt in its
winter outline, ever to be a favorite for planting. It has none of the
benignant grace that makes White Oak, Bur Oak, and Live Oak the
perfect dooryard trees, and it seems to have few civic or domestic associations. But as a forest tree, as part of the hard, untamed, original
sylva, it has a rough, unbending grandeur of its own, and in the
scraggly outline of its bare branches against the skyline of the moun-

tain ridge, in the war paint of its autumn foliage, in the color of its skin of inner bark, it seems an Indian among the Oaks.

PIN OAK

Quercus palustris Muenchhausen

RANGE: Western Massachusetts and the lower Hudson valley south to the piedmont of North Carolina and west generally to the Alleghenies, and from western Pennsylvania along both shores of Lake Erie to southern Michigan and southern Iowa, eastern Kansas, northeastern Oklahoma, northern Arkansas, and Tennessee. Absent from central and northern New York, from the western Alleghenies of Pennsylvania and the Virginias, and from the southern Appalachians.

DESCRIPTION: *Bark* hard and thin and so close as to appear tight, of light to dark grayish brown color, divided by shallow fissures into scaly, low, broad, ridges. *Twigs* slender, drooping, tough, dark red, and at first silvery downy, becoming smooth and green, and then shining dark red-brown or orange, and ultimately dark gray-brown. *Leaves* 4 to 6 inches long, 2 to 4 inches wide, thin and firm, the upper surface very shiny and dark green, the lower pale with big tufts of pale hairs in the axils of conspicuous veins and the stout midrib. *Acorns* light brown, commonly

striped, about ½ inch in diameter. *Wood* medium-heavy (43 pounds per cubic foot, dry weight), hard, strong, with light brown heartwood and thin darker sapwood.

The Pin Oak takes its name from the great number of pinlike or short spur-form branchlets on the main branches. This is an infallible distinguishing trait of the tree when one sees it close at hand. In outline, as it stands winter-naked, the Pin Oak is remarkable for having as a rule a single, mast-like shaft of a trunk going right up through the center of the tree. Unlike most Oaks, it does not give rise to heavy horizontal branches, but to a large number of much more slender ones that arch out gracefully and then, at least in the lower half of the tree, bend down, and branch out into unusually slim and un-Oak-like, almost whip-fine branchlets. As a result of all this branching, the wood of Pin Oak is unusually full of knots, and when the lumberman cuts it at all he marks it as an inferior grade of Red Oak.

But as a standing tree this one takes a high rank, not only for its gracious manner of growth, but for the glory that comes upon it when the world turns round to autumn. The light of Indian summer passing through its foliage then is like the shaft that gleams through a ruby or a garnet. This splendor is seen to perfect advantage amongst the Indiana dunes along the shore of Lake Michigan, and so gorgeous are the Pin Oak's colors that one is tempted to bear away a few of its boughs. But when they are brought into the house, one wonders what one saw in them, for their glory is departed. What one saw, of course, was the generous wealth of American sunlight, blue water between the white-gold of dune hills, and the purple spires of blazing-star in the little inter-dunal meadows; what one heard was the wind-torn scorn of the crows, the thunder of the surf, the hiss of the ever-lifting sand, the harsh lisp of the Pin Oak leaves themselves, as the still not unfriendly gale rattled their stiffened blades.

For an Oak, the Pin Oak is not too slow-growing; it is recommended by the experts as an admirable street tree throughout the eastern United States, since it is economical of room yet generous enough of shade, free of diseases, windfirm, tall-growing, gorgeous in autumn, and elegant in winter tracery.

NORTHERN JACK OAK

Quercus ellipsoidalis E. J. Hill

OTHER NAMES: Hill's, Black, or Yellow Oak.

RANGE: Southeastern Michigan, northern Indiana and Illinois to northern Missouri, northward to Lake Superior and northern Minnesota, westward through Iowa and Minnesota to the southeastern corner of North Dakota.

DESCRIPTION: *Bark* thin, smooth, divided by shallow connected fissures into thin plates, at the base of the tree dark brown, above dull gray-brown. *Twigs* at first bright reddish brown, becoming dark gray-brown. *Leaves* 3 to 5 inches long, 2½ to 4 inches wide, thin but firm, the upper surface shining and bright green, the lower paler. *Acorns* chestnut-brown, in a thin, light red-brown cup, ¾ to 1 inch long.

The Northern Jack Oak is but a stunted and scraggly tree found in the Middle West chiefly in the neighborhood of Lake Michigan, becoming abundant on the old sand ridges left by the lake when, in glacial times, it was larger than it is now, and piled up, with its waves and currents, beaches that it has since deserted. Commonly this Oak grows with the beautiful Pin Oak, but it has none of the same elegance, and in autumn the leaves turn only a dull gold or brown before they fall, leaving a tree peculiarly unkempt and formless in its winter nakedness. Perhaps the easiest way to identify it is to discover its yellow inner bark, a trait which it shares with few other Oaks.

But if you do not live in the region where it grows, it is a sure thing you will never see it in cultivation somewhere else, for it has no charms to recommend it, and it is no wonder that even after its native land had been settled and botanized for sixty years or more, no one got around to describing it for science, until E. J. Hill, that pioneer botanist of the Indiana dune country, perceived its distinguishing traits and gave the orphan species a name.

SHINGLE OAK

Quercus imbricaria A. Michaux

OTHER NAME: Northern Laurel Oak.

RANGE: Pennsylvania south on the upper piedmont to northeastern Alabama and west to the southern shores of Lake Erie, the southern parts of Michigan, southeastern Iowa, eastern Kansas, and western Arkansas. Absent from the Appalachian highlands and western Tennessee and eastern Arkansas.

DESCRIPTION: *Bark* on old trunks with broad ridges and shallow fissures, and covered by light brown, flattened scales. *Twigs* dark green, shiny, often at first tinged with red, soon becoming light reddish brown or light brown and in the second year dark brown. *Leaves* 4 to 6 inches long, ¾ to 2 inches wide, thin, dark green and very shiny above, pale or light brown and downy below. *Acorns* dark chestnut-brown, ½ to ⅔ inch long. *Wood* medium-heavy (47 pounds per cubic foot, dry weight), hard, the heartwood light brown tinged with red, the sapwood paler and thin.

The blades of this tree look more like those of a Laurel, but no Laurel bears acorns, and none as yet known sends up a fine, straight, ponderous shaft for 60 or 80 feet, spreading broad horizontal boughs. The Shingle Oak is so called (tradition has it) because when nearly two hundred years ago the first French colonists settled at Kaskaskia, Illinois, they discovered that the wood rives well. Any such wood —

one that can be split into comparatively thin sheets by the frow — is destined, if it has any power of resisting decay when exposed to sun and wind, to be used as shingles. And it seems that these Illinois Creoles covered their cabins with Oak shingles of this species. Such a sight greeted the eyes of the great French botanist and explorer André Michaux, when he came there in his "herborizing," to find to his disgust that the forty-five inhabitants had gone more native than the natives. He reports "the houses in ruins," so that one imagines the shingles missing in patches from the falling roofs. However that was, it was Michaux who translated the word shingle into Latin and gave us the name *Quercus imbricaria* for this tree. And in Tennessee they still rive shingles by hand from it.

WILLOW OAK

Quercus Phellos Linnæus

RANGE: Brazos County, Texas, north in the Mississippi valley to southwestern Illinois, east along the Gulf coast to western Florida, thence northward on the coastal plain and lower piedmont to Staten Island, New York.

DESCRIPTION: *Bark* thin, light red-brown, smooth or on old trees broken into shallow, narrow fissures with irregular scaly plates between them. *Twigs* reddish brown, roughened by dark lenticels, becoming in the second year dark brown tinged with red. *Leaves* 2½ to 5 inches long, ¼ to 1 inch wide, the upper surface light green and rather shiny, the lower dull and paler, conspicuously meshed with veinlets and marked by a slender yellow midrib. *Acorns* ½ inch in diameter, yellow-brown. *Wood* medium-heavy (46 pounds to the cubic foot, dry weight), coarse-grained, and strong but not hard, with red-tinged light-brown heartwood and a thin band of paler sapwood.

The visitor from the North who goes to Washington is struck — if he has an appreciative eye for the trees of the most beautifully planted of American cities — with an Oak which is likely to be new to him, the Willow Oak. For it is a tree of stately form, with foliage at once brilliant and delicate, in youth unusually well ordered for an Oak, in age remarkably symmetrical still, and if then it lacks the grandeur of Live Oaks and White Oaks, it is yet self-contained and noble in aspect. True to its name, the Willow Oak has remarkably willow-like foliage, but the veins run out beyond the margins of the leaves as fine bristles, like those of other Oaks in the Red Oak series; no Willow's leaves, of course, have such bristles. The slender, delicate, pendulous look of the foliage on young Willow Oaks is also like that of certain Willows — but where is the Willow that bears acorns? Those of this tree are eagerly eaten by jays and grackles and squirrels, yet at their ripest in late autumn, when the leaves turn a soft dull gold, are still bitter for the human palate.

Lumbermen almost never use the name of Willow Oak; they market the wood of this species as Red Oak, and it goes into almost as many uses as the versatile White Oak — for interior finish, newel posts, pulpits, church pews, bar tops, wagon axles, stairs, railings, balustrades, bedsteads, and flour barrels. The wood seasons very slowly, giving much trouble at the kilns and lumber yards, but once seasoned, it stays put and works easily.

In the South, where it is abundant, Willow Oak is almost everything you could ask a tree to be — a valuable timber crop, a rapidly growing ornamental, a dooryard and household friend. Its beauties in the old seaport cities of the South are most charmingly set forth when its late and lively foliage is contrasted with the rich dark green of the motionless and evergreen Magnolia.

BLACK JACK OAK

Quercus marilandica Muenchhausen

OTHER NAME: Scrub Oak.

RANGE: From Long Island westward to southern Indiana and Illinois, southern and eastern Iowa, southeastern Nebraska and eastern Kansas, south to Tampa Bay, Florida and west to western Texas.

DESCRIPTION: *Bark* of trunks thick, rough, deeply furrowed and nearly black. *Twigs* reddish brown when young, then ashy gray or brown. *Leaves* 6 to 7 inches long, dark green, leathery, lustrous above, but underneath hairy and yellowish. *Acorn* about ¾ inch long, light yellow-brown. *Wood* medium-heavy (46½ pounds to the cubic foot, dry weight), hard and strong, the heartwood dark, rich brown, the sapwood thick and lighter in color.

Not all of us can be handsome, or famous, or of distinguished lineage, and some trees too fill a humble station unadmired. One which is, in the words of Ancient Pistol, "base, common and popular" is the Black Jack Oak, which trudges along with Scrub Pine in places where otherwise you might have no trees at all. Its leathery leaves, though pinkish in spring, turn nothing but brown or dull yellow in the end; its trunk is short and apt to be crooked; so are the branches which form a compact crown or open irregular head. There is little timber to be got out of a tree which grows only 20 to 30 feet high (save in Texas, where most things come bigger, at least in the telling), and that is not much good save for fuel. But it is well that there are Oaks so poor they are worth little except to toss on the fire, since they save better trees from such a sacrifice.

For centuries Black Jack Oak has been correctly understood in the South as a sign of low-grade soil. A farmhouse among Black Jack Oaks is usually a poor one; the crops are stunted, the children ragged and pale. Far more valuable trees, which indicate good soils, have been hastily felled, or even burned down, to clear the land beneath them, while such a weed tree as Black Jack is left to flourish over hundreds of thousands of square miles. It comes up on abandoned fields, with Scrub Pine, and is a successor after fire, appearing too on erosion-ruined lands. So, as a pioneer in the tedious cycle of natural re-forestation (a little matter of two or three centuries) Black Jack Oak deserves some credit. There are even those of us who love it, for the lichens that gather quickly on its rough bark and mottle its dark surface with subtle tints and patterns, and for the queer, awkward-looking leaves that come to seem very friendly, to those who know them daily, as they glitter in the light.

The two illustrations show two markedly different leaf-forms of this variable species.

THE ELMS

(*Ulmus*)

Eʟᴍs have scaly and furrowed bark, and simple, alternate, stalked, deciduous leaves, which are usually unsymmetrical at the often very oblique base, with toothed margins and straight veins. From axillary buds near the base of the branch appear the small bisexual flowers on long, jointed stalks. The calyx, regular in form and 4- to 9-parted, encloses the 4 to 6 stamens; free from the calyx, the ovary is solitary and bears 2 styles. Fruiting takes the form of a samara — that is, a nutlet enclosed in a papery husk which is broadened into a sort of wing; the wings, light brown and more or less deeply notched at the apex, are veiny with meshed nerves.

WHITE ELM

Ulmus americana Linnæus

OTHER NAMES: American, River, Water, or Soft Elm.

RANGE: From southwestern Newfoundland to Manitoba, south to central Florida and central Texas, west to central Oklahoma and the extreme western parts of Nebraska and the Dakotas. Absent from mountain systems and high land, and in much of Oklahoma and Texas confined largely to riverbanks, extending on stream courses far out on the prairies.

DESCRIPTION: *Bark* ashy gray, deeply fissured and broadly ridged and covered with thin scales. *Twigs* slender. *Flowers* borne on long, slender, drooping twigs, in 3- or 4-flowered, short-stalked clusters. *Fruits* small, greenish and reddish, with little round wings. *Wood* medium-light (35 pounds to the cubic foot, dry weight), medium-soft, medium-weak as a beam, but very tough and difficult to split, and coarse-grained, the heartwood light brown, with thick lighter-colored sapwood.

"Why are there trees," asks Walt Whitman, "I never walk under but large and melodious thoughts descend upon me?" The answer, any New Englander would tell him, is that those trees must have been

White Elms. Wherever this tree grows, whether as a native or culti-vated beyond its aboriginal range, it is fairly sure to constitute itself Chief Inhabitant for miles around. It must have done so centuries before Thoreau climbed Poplar Hill in an autumn dusk to pick out unseen homes of his neighbors (whom he declares so much less estim-able than their trees) by the high domes of the "imbrowned" Elms, and the "hundred smokes" of the village chimneys twirling peacefully up through their noble crowns. For, long before the white men came, Elms were council trees for Indian tribes, later the meeting place for treaty-making between whites and reds, and then the favorite house site of the first settlers, who spared Elms when they razed all other trees.

So an Elm can scarcely grow to old age without collecting rich human associations around it. In this respect it has but two rivals in all the sylva of North America — the White Oak of the northern states and the Live Oak in the South. But a survey of all the historic trees of our country shows that among them Elms outnumber each of these Oaks nearly two to one. Summing up hundreds of accounts of such, one finds that in almost all cases it is the tree that makes some man or some event remembered. If you want to be recalled for something that you do, you will be well advised to do it under an Elm — a great Elm, for such a tree outlives the generations of men; the burning issues of today are the ashes of tomorrow, but a noble Elm is a verity that does not change with time. And though Elms too are mortal, great ones are remembered as long after they are gone as are great men. "On this spot stood once an Elm — " so begins many a marker, many a sentence in a book of local history, as one would say, "Here was born a man," "Here died a king."

This tree, so often a living monument, takes on several forms; there is what is called the Oak form, with heavy, more or less horizontal branches, and there is a "weeping" form and a "feathered" form; but typically the White Elm is vase-shaped. In this, the most beloved of all its outlines, the main trunk separates at fifteen to thirty feet above ground into several almost equal branches. At first these diverge slightly and gradually, but at a height of about fifty to seventy feet they begin to sweep boldly outward so that they form a great dome on the periphery of which the branches arch and the branchlets droop. Thus a great old Elm appears like a fountain of vegetation — the trunk as the primary jet gushing upward and forking as it rises, then the jets again forking, the forks spreading out and falling as if by gravity in a hundred branchlet streams that become a thousand streamlet twigs and a million drops of spattering foliage.

So, because of its fundamental architectural form, this is the ideal street tree, for its branches meet across the road in a vaulted arch that permits the passage of the highest vehicles. As a dooryard tree, it hangs above the roof like a blessing — clean of branches under the crown but shading the roof like a second air chamber above it. On a college campus a colonnade of Elms is a living stoa; the ancient Elms of Yale are sacrosanct in its deepest-rooted traditions, yet not more so than in colleges all across the country. The very way that the leaves hang accounts for the special quality of Elm shade. A big old specimen will have about a million leaves, or an acre of leaf surface, and will cast a pool of shadow one hundred feet in diameter. But, though umbraculate in shape, an Elm is fortunately not too perfect a parasol in function. The leaves hang more or less all in one plane on the bough, and they make a pattern roughly like a lattice. Hence the dappling of shadow and light that is full half the charm of many a fine old façade in Portsmouth and Portland, New Haven, Newburyport, and Salem, on Pleasant Street in Marblehead, on Brattle Street in Cambridge. Within an old room, the play of light and shade from elm leaves is like music without sound, a dance without dancers.

"What makes a first-class elm?" asked Holmes in *The Autocrat of the Breakfast Table*, and answered: "Why, size in the first place, chiefly. Anything over twenty feet of clear girth, five feet above the ground, and with a spread of branches a hundred feet across, may claim that title, according to my scale." Holmes mentions only six first-class New England Elms known to him, nor does he speak of the Elm of Cambridge Common under which, it is fondly told, George Washington took command of the Continental Army. This Elm, long a shattered wreck, died in the nineteen-twenties, and before the souvenir hunters had carried it quite away its rings were counted by an acknowledged expert. Alas for legend, it was found that this particular tree would have been little more than a sapling at the time of the siege of Boston. So, if Washington really stood under it, that third day of July, 1775, he must have picked it just because it was so small and young; he must have wished to give it a good start in life, to endow it with a legacy entailing his illustrious name. For Washington is perhaps the only man who ever added stature to an Elm.

Holmes makes no mention of Connecticut Elms, yet there are no New England villages so beautifully shaded by this species as Fairfield and Litchfield, Woodstock and Windsor, Woodbury and Wethersfield. The "Great Elm," at the last-named, is 102 feet high, with a spread of branches of about 150 feet, is 41 feet about at breast height (the correct place for measuring the girth of an Elm, by the way), and its age today should be 190 years. The Whipping Post Elm at Litchfield was used as a place of chastisement as late as 1815; today no culprit's arms could be tied around its doughty girth. When Sarah Saltonstall came from New London to be the bride of David Buck of Wethersfield, she intended to bring, after an old Connecticut custom, a bridal tree to plant, but ice on the river prevented the transportation of any gift except herself. Next spring she encountered an Indian bearing an Elm sapling in his hand, and after a pow-wow in sign language, secured it in exchange for a quart of rum. Perhaps more impressive than the fame and stature of Sarah's Elm is the mystery of how a church-going lady would have a quart of rum about her!

The Markham Elm at Avon, New York, is said to be almost 50 feet in girth and about 654 years old, which leaves the New England Elms rather in the shade! Nor are all the historic Elms found east of the Hudson; monarch among them was the Penn Treaty Elm that stood at Shackamaxon; here it was that William Penn made what was probably the only absolutely upright treaty ever offered the red man, certainly the only one scrupulously honored on both sides for as long as fifty years. This Elm blew down in a storm on March 3, 1810, but scions and grand-scions of this monument to integrity are scattered all over Penn's Woods.

George Washington's diary shows that he was constantly searching the bottom-lands along the Potomac for wild Elms to transplant to the grounds of "Mount Vernon." Today four of those set out by his hand still stand, the largest of them on the Bowling Green. But more venerable still is the Elm that young Mr. Washington, the surveyor, set out as the merest switch of a sapling at what is now Berkeley Springs, West Virginia, to mark the southern boundary of the land grant of Lord Fairfax. Elms and George Washington came naturally together throughout his life — at Valley Forge, at Brandywine, in the

churchyard at Alexandria where he worshiped, in the streets of Fredericksburg that he knew from boyhood.

There are so many Elms in Lincoln's life that it would be impossible to speak of them all even by name — the Elm above his mother's grave in Indiana, the Elms on the White House lawn, that must have known his sorrows, and best of all, perhaps, the Lincoln memorial tree at Atchison, Kansas, where the vast crowd that had gathered to hear him, and could not be accommodated inside the little church, sat under the shade while Lincoln spoke by the open window.

The great Elm of Boonesborough, in Kentucky, is gone now — indeed Boonesborough itself is nothing today but a cornfield, a patch of wood, and a lovely bit of stream. So wondrous was this tree they called it "the Divine Elm"; it stood at the heart of this ghostliest of ghost towns, with a turf of wild white clover making a carpet beneath it right to the mighty roots. On that sward gathered on May 23, 1775, the first legislature of Kentucky. See them there — Harrod of Harrodsburg, in his coonskin cap, cradling his long rifle, and Richard Henderson in his scarlet coat and powdered wig, Squire Boone and Daniel Boone and Calloway, the old fox — heroes of our Homeric days, who were founding a new state, in the American way. Transylvania they called it then — Kentucky, the Great Meadow, "beyond the woods."

In Missouri still stands the Justice Tree, an Elm where the aged Boone, as syndic of the Femme Osage district, dispensed the law to his consenting neighbors. At Le Claire, Iowa, the citizens still honor and protect The Green Tree, an Elm of enormous spread which was the "green hotel" of travelers and rivermen in the days of Mark Twain's boyhood. They say that Buffalo Bill played beneath this tree when he was a child. More importantly, The Green Tree is still the natural meeting place for all the folk of this old river town. When a railroad obtained a right-of-way through Le Claire, along the riverbank, its citizens stoutly refused to let it pass unless it routed its way around The Green Tree.

There are many Le Claires scattered over this country — little towns that worship big Elms, and all of them but prove the Elm does not belong to New England alone, not even to the national capital, although Washington is the most Elm-planted of all our cities.

The love of Elms goes naturally with the settling of a countryside, and belongs to the period that comes after the first fierce encounter of the pioneers with the wilderness. For the early settlers took, perforce, a utilitarian view of trees — they were a sign of good land or of bad, they filled a need or they were useless. Even today the pioneer psychology sometimes persists when the White Elm is mentioned. "They are the most useless piece of vegetation in our forests," one Iowan can still complain. "They cannot be used for firewood because they cannot be split. The wood cannot be burned because it is full of water. It cannot be used for posts because it rots in a short time. It can be sawed into lumber but it warps and twists into corkscrews and gives the building where it is used an unpleasant odor for years." [1]

But from simpler days to these of competitive lumbering, Elm has been of service. Country folk have long made ox whips by peeling the bark and braiding its long, supple, and stinging strength. The Indians fashioned canoes of the bark, and ropes. And the defects of White Elm are also its virtues. For it is at once a strong wood and supple. Technicians say that its modulous of rupture is 12,158 pounds per cubic inch, which, in simpler language, means that a weight of that amount will just suffice to break a White Elm stick $2\frac{5}{8}$ inches square resting on supports 1 foot apart. For these reasons Elm, from pioneer times, has been used for the hubs of heavy wagons where it resists all the pressure and friction that can be brought to bear on it. Large amounts are employed in agricultural implements and sporting goods, in shipbuilding and heavy-duty flooring, and wherever shock-resistance is essential. It is a leading wood for barrel staves and hoop poles. It holds screws better than almost any other wood, and so is valuable for boxes and crates. It makes ideal chopping bowls, and the more the housewife scours her woodenware of Elm, the whiter it shines. No wonder that the cut of White Elm in 1946 was some 200,000,000 board feet, most of it from Ohio and Wisconsin.

The lumberman's ideal of an Elm is somewhat different from the property owner's. The lumberman was delighted to find, in the Middle West of half a century and more gone by, a type of Elm growth that he prized for its straight, long, clean, columnar trunks, out of which boards could be sawed for fifty feet without encountering a branch. Such trees, of course, lack the fountain-like or vase-like form of the beloved street and dooryard tree. Yet they were forest kings. In the early days of lumbering in Michigan, the White Elms,

[1] C. A. Sheffield in *The Atlantic Monthly*, October, 1948.

according to the testimony of their chronicler Henry H. Gibson[1] were as lofty and straight and shapely as Tuliptrees. One splendid specimen, located near Jefferson, Pennsylvania, was 140 feet high, 5 feet in diameter at breast height, and had, though a forest-grown individual, a crown with a spread of 67 feet across. At the sawmill (for that, of course, is where this giant went as soon as it was discovered), it sawed out at 8820 board feet of lumber. There are no such timber Elms left, in Pennsylvania or anywhere else, nor will they grow again unless the American people vanish from the lands they have conquered, and the wilderness reclaims its own.

This is not to say that the Elm, in some of its forms, cannot reproduce itself abundantly. By taking refuge on the riverbanks and in the narrow bottom-lands of small streams where the farmer does not pass the plow, the Elm is secure along thousands of winding miles, in the company of Willow and Cottonwood and Sycamore. Its reproductive capacities are immense. Sometimes the little wafer-like fruits are almost ripe by the time the leaves begin to shoot, in early spring. Then every puff of wind carries them away on their glider-like wings by the thousands, and he who looks up may see the tiny air fleets flashing in the sunlight as they sail above the roof tops of the village. The seeds germinate readily, with a high percentage of viability, and the seedlings come up in shady sites and sunny, well able to compete with most sorts of natural vegetation.

By all these tokens, White Elm should be one of the most promising of trees for natural reforestation, able to hold its own even with man, since it can play skillfully upon his sentiments. But the Elm has long had serious pests and is prey, like human flesh, to many ills. The worst of them all is a new disease, or rather a combination, as we now know, of an insect pest which is also a carrier of a fungus disease. Their joint inroads are so swift and so full of menace for every White Elm in the country that, though this is not a book which makes any pretense at dealing with the pathology of trees, it is unavoidable to close these pages on the Elm without some account of the great tree's battle for its existence.

For the White Elm has proved shockingly susceptible to a fungus called *Graphium ulmi* that was first noticed some years ago in Europe

[1] *American Forest Trees.*

where it was ravaging the Elms which helped to hold the dykes of Holland and, no respecter even of majesty, had attacked the magnificent row of English Elms which line the long approach to Windsor Castle. Our quarantine authorities thought they had every avenue of entry blocked against the Dutch Elm disease. Yet it broke out in the heart of the country, in Ohio in 1930. Converging at once upon the local outbreak, sanitary forces exterminated it; but in 1933, 3800 diseased Elms were found in New Jersey and 23 in Connecticut, across the Hudson. Every year brought more alarming reports of spreading malady, and it was evident that, carefully though all living Elm stock was inspected at the ports of entry, *Graphium ulmi*, all unseen, was some way coming over here in lethal doses.

The locus of infection was found at last in logs of English Elm, which we imported wholesale for the manufacture of veneer. For some of the European Elms produce abnormal lumpy growths on the trunk, called burls, which when sliced by the veneer knives reveal fancy figures that unhappily pleased the public taste here. These logs were swarming with the Elm bark beetle (*Scolytus multistriatus*) who, disgustingly healthy himself, is the carrier of the disease. And since once it has gained entry within an Elm, nothing can be done save to fell and burn the tree, the war for the Elms has concentrated attack on the bark beetle.

If the beetle is present, you may find in the tree's crotches a lot of rust-colored frass, and also "shotgun holes" made where the larvae have emerged through the bark. Under the bark will be seen the characteristic "engraving" of centipede-like form — the broad galleries of the larvae. The presence of the fungus may be known by the shepherd's-crook curvature of the twigs, by the yellowing and falling of foliage even in spring and early summer, and in late summer and winter by the persistence of dead leaves at the tips of the branches. If you cut open the twig of an Elm diseased with this fungus, a cross-section will show brown streaks and discolored rings in the wood. Since all these symptoms are imitated by other maladies of the Elm, the layman should send doubtful specimens to his State Department of Agriculture for expert identification.

CORK ELM

Ulmus Thomasii Sargent

OTHER NAMES: Rock, Hickory, Corkbark, or Cliff Elm.

RANGE: Southwestern Quebec and southern Ontario, westward through Michigan and northern Wisconsin to the southern half of Minnesota, south to Vermont, western New York, northern New Jersey, Kentucky, Indiana, northern Illinois, Missouri, northeastern Kansas, Nebraska and Iowa.

DESCRIPTION: *Bark* gray tinged with red and deeply fissured with broad, flat, interbraiding ridges broken on the surface into irregular scales. *Twigs* at first light brown, becoming light reddish brown and shining in the first winter, and marked with scattered oblong lenticels and large hoof-shaped leaf scars, finally turning ashy gray and usually furnished with 3 or 4 irregular corky ridges or wings. *Winter buds* minute, with chestnut-brown scales which are hairy on the margin, the inner scales bright green below the middle, red-blotched in the center and with white papery tips. *Leaves* 2 to 2½ inches long, ¾ to 1 inch wide, firm and thick, dark green and shiny above, paler and softly downy below, especially on the stout midribs and numerous veins which run straight to the points of the teeth. *Flowers* on long, drooping, slender stalks in 2- to 4-flowered, elongated clusters, the calyx green and divided nearly to the middle into 7 or 8 rounded, dark red, papery lobes; anthers dark purple; ovary clothed in long pale hairs, with light green styles. *Fruit*....

½ inch long with a shallow, open notch at the tip, hairy on the margin of the broad wing. *Wood* medium-heavy (44 pounds to the cubic foot, dry weight), medium-hard, medium-strong, tough, close-grained, the heartwood clear light brown, often tinged with red, with thick paler sapwood.

Rocky slopes and the bluffs of rivers, dry gravelly uplands, and heavy clay soils are the habitat of this fine tree, which sometimes rises 80 or 100 feet tall, the trunk clear of branches in the forest for 60 feet, and attaining as much as 3 feet in diameter. If not so graceful as its close relative the White Elm, the Cork Elm is many-fold more valuable as a timber tree.

At an early date British contractors for the shipbuilding firms overseas began to appreciate this tree, which grows plentifully in southern Ontario and southern Michigan. The finest specimens and the largest stands occurred there, and large cuts were made at a time when no other Michigan hardwoods were equally appreciated, and exported through Canada to Britain. There the lumber was received with high acclaim, for even Hickory scarcely surpasses Cork Elm in toughness. With its interlaced fibers, it is almost impossible to split — and splitting was a serious consideration in the days of wooden battleships and sailing vessels. Under water it is particularly durable. Tradition states (but there are no definite figures to prove or disprove it) that the finest stands of Cork Elm were long ago cleared out of the country, and, as it is a slow-growing tree and the country that it chooses to occupy is forever being cleared of its forest, we have never seen a second growth of it comparable with the virgin stands.

Axemen of the old North Woods often preferred axe handles of Cork Elm to any other. In the early days of the automobile industry in Michigan, when much wood was going into car construction, large quantities of Cork Elm were used for hubs and spokes and in other places which had to take great strain. During the era when most kitchen furniture, including refrigerators, was wooden, this was a favorite, not only because it stood up under heavy usage, but because no matter how discolored the wood became, vigorous scrubbing with brush, soap, and water would always whiten it. Although Cork Elm is not usually listed as a furniture wood, great quantities have gone into furniture, as the hard core or stock on which more fragile and elegant woods are veneered. It is used in veneer form itself, not for the visible exterior, since it has no beauty of grain, but in the form of plywood — sheet after sheet glued together, to form boxes or the frames of trunks which are then covered by leather, cloth, or metal. Because of its stiffness, it has been used for a long time for flour barrels. To one rough usage, however, this stouthearted tree has never been put, surely. And that is a split rail fence; the steel edge of an axe would turn, the Ash handle break, before a sound log of Cork Elm would permit itself to be mauled.

WAHOO

Ulmus alata A. Michaux

OTHER NAMES: Winged, Mountain, Witch, Red, or Small-leaved Elm.

RANGE: Central Florida west to southern Texas, north on the coastal plain to southeastern Virginia, and in the Mississippi valley to central Missouri, southern Indiana and Kentucky.

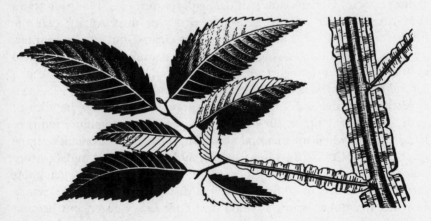

DESCRIPTION: *Bark* thin, light brown tinged with red, divided by irregular, shallow fissures into broad, flat, scaly ridges. *Twigs* slender, light green tinged with red at first, becoming light reddish brown or ashy gray, flecked with scattered orange lenticels and small, crescent-shaped leaf scars, usually furnished with two thin corky wings. *Winter buds* minute, dark chestnut-brown, slender, the inner scales tipped with a

minute point, thin, papery, light red above the middle. *Leaves* only
1½ to 3 inches long, dark green and smooth above, pale and softly
downy below, especially on the stout yellow midrib, thick, tough, and
almost leathery. *Flowers* on drooping stalks in few-flowered clusters,
calyx divided nearly to the middle into 5 lobes. *Fruit* ripening before
or at the time of the unfolding of the leaves, ⅓ inch long, tipped at
apex with slender, incurved bristles and covered with long white hairs,
especially on the thickened margin of the narrow wings. *Wood* hard,
heavy (47 pounds per cubic foot, dry weight), not strong, difficult to
split, the heartwood light brown, the sapwood thick and paler.

The curious name of Wahoo is said to come from the Creek Indian
language where the original word was *Uhawhu*. And what did it
mean? What else but this very tree, the Wahoo! Or so the dictionaries
tell us, though there have been those who trace this name to the
Yahoos in *Gulliver's Travels,* and others think it derives from the hoot
of an owl!

Next to its name, the most curious feature of this tree, of course,
is the corky wings which beset the twigs. The wings begin to form on
the twigs during the second year, and when the twigs are still small,
perhaps only a quarter of an inch thick, the wings have already
attained their breadth of half an inch on each side of the twig; however, as the twig enlarges the wings do not increase in proportion.
Usually the lowest branches, and those nearest the trunk, are most
heavily furnished with wings; sometimes no twigs on the tree display
this distinguishing mark. Since the Cork Elm also has winged twigs,
the difference between the two trees will be important for identification in the field. The wings of the present species are half an inch or
more broad, while the Cork Elm has generally narrower wings. In the
Wahoo the wings form two continuous lines opposite each other on
the twig, interrupted only at the nodes, where a leaf or secondary
twig emerges; in the Cork Elm there are usually three or four wings of
much less continuous occurrence.

On dry, gravelly upland or sandstone, the Wahoo is usually a short
and straggly tree, often an understory species as in the heavy timber of
the Great Smokies, but on the borders of swamps, on banks of streams,
and in bottom-lands occasionally inundated by rising rivers, it may
reach 80 or 100 feet with a trunk as much as 3 feet in diameter. Such
trees are usually found west of the Mississippi. In Texas, where the
heaviest cut is taken, the wood is used for table legs, tool handles, and

hubs of wheels; the inner bark has been made into rope for fastening the covers of cotton bales. In many a town in the lower Mississippi valley Wahoo makes a fine street tree, for under such conditions it develops the broad umbrella-like crown of the White Elm, with branches arching gracefully and meeting above the center of the street.

SLIPPERY ELM

Ulmus fulva A. Michaux

OTHER NAME: Red Elm.

RANGE: From southwestern Quebec to southern Ontario, northern Wisconsin, central Minnesota and southeastern South Dakota, south to northern and eastern Kansas and south-central Texas.

DESCRIPTION: *Bark* thick, divided by shallow fissures into braided ridges; inner bark notable for mucilaginous taste. *Twigs* stout, bright green, harsh to the touch, becoming light brown or orange and next year dark gray or brown; marked by large, elevated, semi-circular leaf scars. *Leaves* 5 to 7 inches long, 2 to 3 broad, dark green, and thick. *Flowers* with dark red anthers and reddish-purple stigmas. *Fruit* — nut surrounded by broad, thin, circular, veiny wings. *Wood* heavy (43 pounds per cubic foot, dry weight), hard, strong, close-grained, dark brown or red, with thin, lighter colored sapwood.

When that insatiably curious traveler, Prince Maximilian of Wied-Neuwied, arrived at New Harmony on the banks of the Wabash in 1832, he found plenty of oddities to engage him. For here on the frontier was not only an experiment in Utopian communism, but among these earnest social reformers in their pantaloon uniform were gathered also scientists renowned today as then. No wonder that the German prince lingered there two months, and among the observations he made at that time was a note on the use of a certain tree:

"A kind of bark, which is now used, is that of the Slippery Elm, (Ulmus rubra); if chewed or softened for a moment in water, it dissolves into a viscous slime, and is found very useful in dressing wounds,

as it is cooling, and allays the inflammation. It is said to have been applied with success in cholera, and is now sold, in powder, in all the apothecaries' shops. A teaspoonful of this bark, in boiling water, makes a very useful beverage, which is sweetened with sugar, and has the same effect as linseed."

The bark is peeled from the tree in long strips and the outer layers then shaved off; the mucilaginous inner bark, which is about ⅛ to ¼ inch thick, is then dried and put away for use, to be pounded to a pulp and moistened when needed as a poultice. Slippery Elm still figures in our pharmacopeia and is often prescribed by country physicians; undoubtedly it is a valuable demulcent now neglected in the days of synthetic medicines.

You will find that a nibble of the inner bark of twigs proves at once, by the mucilaginous taste, the Slippery Elm's identity. No other tree in the woods offers that gluey flavor except Sassafras, whose mitten-shaped leaves could never be confused with the Elm's foliage. Not often revered for beauty, like the White Elm, since it grows not more than 60 feet high, with a thick trunk and open broad crown, Slippery Elm is, as a commercial tree, still being exploited for even in this day of patent medicines there are still honest souls who prefer to trust their aches and pains to "slippery ellum."

THE HACKBERRIES

(*Celtis*)

THE HACKBERRIES are trees or shrubs with more or less warty bark and scaly buds, with alternate, deciduous, veiny leaves frequently obliquely unsymmetrical at base, and criss-crossed with veinlets. The flowers appear soon after the unfolding of the leaves on branches of the year, the male flowers in small dense clusters, the female solitary or in few-flowered clusters from the axils of upper leaves. The greenish yellow deciduous calyx is divided nearly to the base into 4 or 5 lobes; there are no petals. The 4 to 6 stamens are inserted on the margin of the disc at the center of the flower. The ovary of the female flower, green and shining, is topped by a short style divided into several lobes. Flowers of each sex contain the rudiments of the organs of the other sex, and usually some bisexual or perfect flowers are found. The fruit takes the form of a drupe, or stone fruit, with thick, firm skin, thin flesh, and a thick-walled, bony nutlet.

HACKBERRY

Celtis occidentalis Linnæus

OTHER NAMES: Sugarberry. Nettletree. Hoop Ash.

RANGE: From western New England (where rare) to Virginia and west to Iowa, southwestern Missouri, northwestern Kansas, and eastern North Dakota, the Black Hills of South Dakota and south to Texas. Absent from northern Michigan, northern Wisconsin, and northeastern Minnesota, the Hudson valley, the Louisiana Delta, and the coastal plain of the Carolinas and Virginias.

DESCRIPTION: *Bark* dark brown covered by warty excrescences or marked by long ridges. *Twigs* usually distinctly ridged, at first light brown, becoming darker next year; marked by pale oblong lenticels and oblong horizontal leaf scars. *Leaves* 2½ to 3½ inches long and 1½ to 2 broad, thin, and veiny. *Fruits* drooping upon short stalks, dark purple with tough thick skin and thin, sweet, orange-colored flesh, the thick-walled nutlet within containing a pale brown seed.

There is no disguise more baffling than the commonplace, no mystery greater than one in plain sight. So the "unknown bird," about which that most scientific of Presidents, Jefferson, wrote, turned out to be nothing more than the demure little chewink. And the "unknown tree" noted over and over in early descriptions of American

Nature, that tree that one knows so well yet does not know at all, usually proves to be the Hackberry.

The secret of this is quite open. The Hackberry simply does not look as though it belonged in its family; its berries do not suggest the fruit of an Elm, and its leaves, with three principal nerves from the base, are unlike most others in venation, and though they have a teasing resemblance to a Linden's, are perversely more like a nettle's than anything else. Even the Indians seem not to have bestowed on this species any good, ringing, colorful name, none, at least, that the colonists borrowed. Nor were the newcomers inspired to invent one. What it finally received was one of those nostalgic and inaccurate appellations which obscure so many identities. "Hackberry" is presumably a corruption of the Scottish "Hagberry," which, however, in Britain is given to the Bird Cherry (*Prunus avium*). Which completes the confusion in which the tree stands concealed.

Although in some places only a shrub, the Hackberry commonly becomes 50 to 60 feet high, the trunk usually not over two feet in diameter, the branches spreading and sometimes pendulous, forming a round-topped crown. The foliage in late autumn turns yellow. The seeds of the drooping dark fruits are distributed by birds, and no doubt by stream waters also, for this is a riverbank tree. So sturdy is its ability to withstand harsh conditions that it is highly recommended by the Forest Service for planting in the more southerly prairie states, where so many other kinds of trees fail to grow.

Though about 2,000,000 board feet are cut annually in the South, the greenish white wood of this tree is perhaps not appreciated. Its uses are chiefly for barrel hoops — since it is tough and flexible — and in cheap furniture, fence posts, kitchen cabinets, and the inevitable boxes and crates, but as it has a figure rather like that of Ash and takes a high polish, it might have its beauties if properly treated. Indeed, these are suggested in a pleasing recollection of pioneer life:

"The floors of the cabins were made of puncheons split as thin as desired from hunks of the hackberry tree, a very free-splitting wood of firm and beautiful grain, and white in color. The logs were cut in convenient lengths and split into pieces as wide as possible, which were straightened on the edges and hewed on the surface to be laid uppermost to a thickness that would make the floor when laid as even as possible; all of which being carefully and neatly done, made a floor nice enough to content any sensible housewife who could not afford carpets. It was satisfactory to my good mother for all the years of her early experience in our first home in the new country." [1]

Who would not tread more proudly a floor like this, well scrubbed, than any rug woven in Kirman or Tabriz?

Two varieties of the common Hackberry are widely recognized. Variety *canina* (Rafinesque) Sargent, differs in having long-pointed leaves, the blades 2½ to 6 inches long but only ¾ to 2½ inches wide. Growing to 80 or 100 feet, it is a much taller form than the true species, and inhabits bottom-lands and rich woody slopes and rocky ridges from Quebec to the coast of Massachusetts, south to northern Georgia and southwestern Missouri, west to eastern Nebraska and southwestern Oklahoma.

Variety *crassifolia* A. Gray, is taller still — 100 to 120 feet at maturity, with thicker leaf blades 3½ to 5 inches long, 2 to 2½ inches wide, long-pointed leaf tips, and the margins coarsely toothed, the upper surface rough, the lower downy on the heavy veins. This variety ranges from the southern Appalachians west to eastern Texas, and the panhandles of Texas and Oklahoma, and the Black Hills of South Dakota. This variety is notable for having the leaves distinctly roughened by small but numerous wart-like excrescences.

[1] Daniel Harmon Brush, *Growing Up With Southern Illinois.*

SUGARBERRY

Celtis lævigata Willdenow

OTHER NAMES: Mississippi or Sugar Hackberry.

RANGE: The lower Rio Grande valley and northeastern Mexico north to Oklahoma, southern Kansas, the neighborhood of Kansas City and St. Louis, Missouri, southern Illinois and Indiana, western Kentucky, southern North Carolina and Florida except the east coast.

DESCRIPTION: *Bark* gray-brown to silvery gray with corky ridges and warts, becoming scaly. *Twigs* zigzag, slender, at first greenish brown, becoming light reddish brown, and marked with many pale lenticels.

Buds only ¹⁄₁₆ to ⅛ inch long. *Leaves* 2½ to 5 inches long, 1 to 2½ inches broad, light green above, paler below. *Flowers* — the male in few-flowered clusters in the axils of the lower leaves, the female and bisexual flowers mostly solitary; calyx 4- or 5-lobed; stamens 4 to 6; ovary surmounted by a short style with two elongated, reflexed, hairy stigmas. *Fruit* an orange or yellowish spherical drupe ¼ inch long, with thick skin, thin flesh, and a wrinkled bony pit. *Wood* medium-light (36 pounds per cubic foot, dry weight), medium-hard, medium-strong as a beam, distinctly shock-resistant, the heartwood light clear yellow with thicker, paler sapwood.

This is predominantly a southern species, yet it attains its grandest dimensions in the Ohio valley, where it may grow 60 to 80 feet tall, with a short straight trunk as much as 3 feet thick, forming a broad open crown not without dignity as the spreading slender branches arch out, then droop with some grace at the tips.

The Louisiana French call this tree *bois inconnu* or unknown wood, just as the common Hackberry in the north is the "unknown tree" of English-speaking Americans. The fruits are doubtless water-borne, since they float readily, on the stream that is almost invariably curling, brown and lazy, past the feet of this tree. For in its distribution it follows the Mississippi and its infinite tributaries greater and lesser. Even when found well back from the river, it grows in low-lying sites, with other bottom-land trees, where sooner or later flood waters are sure to swirl. Birds too probably carry the seeds far and wide.

In autumn, in the South, the berries exude a sweet sticky substance which attracts millions of mealy-bugs. When overstuffed with it they secrete a honeydew of saccharine sweetness, known as ghost rain.

THE MULBERRIES

(*Morus*)

THESE TREES have scaly bark, and slender, roundish branchlets; the growth is by prolongation from one of the upper axillary buds. In falling, the inner scales of the winter buds mark the base of the twig with ring-like scars. The leaves, alternate and deciduous, are 3- to 5-nerved at base and may be unlobed or unequally 2-lobed (mitten-shaped) or 3-lobed at the apex. The flowers appear from the axils of deciduous bud scales of the lower leaves of the year; the female are densely clustered. The familiar Mulberry fruit consists in a mass of thin-skinned fruitlets with juicy, thick flesh surrounding the tiny nutlets.

RED MULBERRY

Morus rubra Linnæus

RANGE: From western Massachusetts to Miami and west to southern Michigan and southeastern Minnesota, eastern Iowa and up the Missouri valley to southeastern South Dakota, and southwest to Oklahoma and Valverde County, Texas.

DESCRIPTION: *Bark* irregularly divided into elongate plates separating into thick, close scales, dark brown tinged with red. *Twigs* zigzag and slender, dark green tinged with red at first and covered with straw-colored spots; by winter light red-brown, later darkening to orange, marked by pale lenticels and big, raised, roundish leaf scars. *Leaves* 3 to 5 inches long, 2½ to 4 broad, dark bluish green, paler below with short white hairs on the orange nerves. *Flowers* on stout stalks set in narrow spikes about 2½ inches long, with anthers and ovaries bright green. *Fruit* 1 to 1½ inches long, sweet and juicy and so dark a purple as to be nearly black. *Wood* medium-light (37 pounds to the cubic foot, dry weight), soft, weak, with light orange heartwood and thick nearly white sapwood.

The tree that from the recorded beginning of civilization has served to clothe the fortunate in silk is the White Mulberry, not native of our land. But this Red Mulberry of ours has its own wilderness romance. It is related of the Choctaws that:

"Many of the women wear cloaks of the bark of the mulberry tree, or of the feathers of swans, turkies, or India ducks. The bark they take from young mulberry shoots that rise from the roots of the trees that have been cut down; after it is dried in the sun, they beat it to make all the woody part fall off, and they give the threads that remain a second beating, after which they bleach them by exposing them to the dew. When they are well whitened, they spin them about the coarseness of packthread, and weave them in the following manner: they plant two stakes in the ground, about a yard and a half asunder, and having stretched a cord from one to the other, they fasten their threads of bark double to this cord, and then interweave them in a curious manner into a cloak of about a yard square, with a wrought border round the edges." [1]

Though often described in manuals as little more than a shrub, the Red Mulberry can grow in the southern Appalachians to 70 feet, with a trunk sometimes 4 feet in diameter, and it is then impressive, its stout, wide-spreading branches forming a thick and shapely crown. So it was easily noted, when in 1540 the *conquistadores* came plunging in their armor after DeSoto into the heart of the "Apalachen" country. Since in that savage day and place a man had to find in the forest the answer to his sometimes desperate needs, it was well for an explorer to have with him some keen botanical eye, and such there must have been among the Spanish gentlemen left leaderless when the great captain was buried in the night, in the middle of the Mississippi. They had to look about them, then, for means to save themselves, and their chronicler, "The Gentleman of Elvas," speaks of "Mulberry trees, apt to feed silk worms, to make silk; whereof there was such plenty in many places that though they found some hemp in the country, the Spaniards made ropes of the bark of them for their brigantines, when they were to set to sea for New Hispania." So, in boats built and rigged from the forest, they sailed out of the river by its dangerous mouth, coasted the Gulf, and reached Mexico.

In Jamestown the settlers not unnaturally had hopes that Red

[1] Le Page Du Pratz, *History of Louisiana*.

Mulberry would serve as had the White for so many centuries. In 1610 William Strachey reported that the colony was adorned with "some great mulberrye trees, and these in some parts of the country are found growing naturally in pretty groves; there was an assay made to make silke, and surely the worms prospered excellently well until the master workman fell sick, during which tyme they were eaten with ratts, and this wilbe a commoditie not meanely profitable."

But Red Mulberry leaves have never proved successful as food for the silkworm. As for the fruits, though not unpalatable, they are eaten chiefly by birds and squirrels. The wood, rather weak yet tough, coarse-grained but durable, finds a prosaic place in fencing and farm tools, boatbuilding and cooperage. The ways and the aims of men change, and it is a long time since the last Choctaw princess flaunted her Mulberry bark cloak.

THE TULIPTREES

(*Liriodendron*)

THESE ARE large, straight trees with tough outer bark and bitter inner bark. The twigs are marked by elevated leaf scars and narrow rings left by the stalks of the fallen leaves. The obtuse, compressed winter buds have papery, strap-shaped scales which are tardy about falling after the leaf expands. The leaves are 4-lobed or 6-lobed, the tip truncate or indented with a broad shallow sinus, the base heart-shaped or truncate. After the leaves, emerge the flowers; enclosed at first by a 2-valved, papery, deciduous scale, they appear when expanded as cup-shaped, showy, and erect blossoms, with 3 greenish white, re-curved sepals that soon fall, and 6 erect, thick, broad, blunt petals. The slender anthers are numerous and borne on short stalks; the over-lapping pistils are seated, closely crowded, on a spindle-shaped or conical receptacle. The fruit, narrow and cone-like, is formed by the overlapping of the ripened pistils; when mature in autumn these are deciduous from the axis of the fruit, which then remains on the branch all winter. The winged seeds are suspended on delicate threads.

TULIPTREE

Liriodendron Tulipifera Linnæus

OTHER NAMES: Tulip, Yellow, or White Poplar. Popple. Canoewood. Whitewood.

RANGE: From northern Florida to Rhode Island and central and western Massachusetts, and west through central and southern New York, the southern peninsula of Ontario, southern Michigan, to the Indiana dunes of Lake Michigan, southern Illinois, eastern Arkansas, and northern Louisiana. Ascends in the Appalachians to 5000 feet altitude.

DESCRIPTION: *Bark* when young thin, scaly, and grayish, becoming in age brown, thick, and deeply furrowed. *Twigs* erect, light yellow-green in first spring, turning reddish brown and lustrous in their first winter, and marked by pale lenticels. *Winter buds* ½ inch long, rich dark red with a bloom. *Leaves* 5 to 6 inches long and equally broad or broader, thick, rich green. *Flowers* borne at the tips of twigs, 1½ to 2 inches deep, with recurved, greenish sepals and rather thick and waxy erect petals; stamens pale yellow; pistil green and spindle-shaped. *Fruits* conspicuous, narrow, cone-like, dry, and light brown, borne erect on twigs, with winged seeds. *Wood* soft, very light (28 pounds per cubic foot, dry weight) with nearly white sapwood and pale yellow or brown heartwood.

This tree of stately beauty and immense practical use has a bewildering handful of folk names. The lumberman calls it Yellow Poplar or just plain Poplar, though of course it is no sort of a Poplar at all. However, to him Tulipwood means a tropical cabinet wood, so to do business with him one must use his terms. Country people call this wood Poplar too or, more easily, Popple, or Tulip Poplar, sometimes shortened to Tulip. Canoewood is heard in Tennessee. In pioneer days it was called Whitewood, and architects in New England sometimes specify it by this name for interior finish. The foresters prefer Tuliptree, and with reason, since this name brings to mind the glory of this species in spring, when its flowers, erect on every bough, hold the sunshine in their cups, setting the whole giant tree alight.

This is the king of the Magnolia family, the tallest hardwood tree in North America. In the southern Appalachians, where it is the most commercially valuable species, it attains its most superb dimensions, up to 200 feet tall, with a trunk 8 to 10 feet in diameter, clear of branches — in sound, old, forest-grown trees — for the first 80 or 100 feet. Its crown is then (as in its youth) narrowly pyramidal, giving a soldierly pride to the tree and an impression of swift upsurgence in growth. Under field conditions it takes a different form; the trees of the famous "Poplar walk" at "Nomini Hall" in Westmoreland County, Virginia, are known to be over 200 years old, and in these centuries their limbs have attained a magnificent weight and sweep, while their trunks measure as much as 20 feet in girth, at breast-height. The great mansion is gone; the sandy road which leads to this place is a remote by-path; the trees alone remain as monument to the Carter family. Beneath them passed the color and the vigor of a once baronial life, inimitably recorded by Philip Vickers Fithian in his journal. Frequently the young tutor speaks of strolling in the double avenue of these trees, which must have been noble even then and which today are giants of longevity, speaking, themselves, in many-leaved, elegiac voices, of how mayfly were the bright and vanished humans they knew.

But, despite the splendor of its dimensions, there is nothing overwhelming about the Tuliptree, but rather something joyous in its springing straightness, in the candle-like blaze of its sunlit flowers, in the fresh green of its leaves, which, being more or less pendulous on long slender stalks, are forever turning and rustling in the slightest breeze; this gives the tree an air of liveliness lightening its grandeur. So even a very ancient Tuliptree has no look of eld about it, for not only does it make a swift growth in youth, but in maturity it maintains itself marvelously free of decay.

This look of vitality comes partly from the vivid palette from which the Tuliptree is colored. The flowers which give it this name are yellow or orange at base, a light greenish shade above. Almost as brilliant are the leaves when they first appear, a glossy, sunshiny pale green; they deepen in tint in summer, and in autumn turn a rich, rejoicing gold. Even in winter the tree is still not unadorned, for the axis of the cone remains, candelabrum fashion, erect on the bare twig when all the seeds have fallen. No wonder that in the gardens of France and England this is one of the most popular of all American species.

The date at which it reached Europe is a very early one, at least 1687, when it was first described from a tree growing then in a Leyden garden. Certainly this is a species which the colonists would remark, and it must have been sent back to Europe many times in the early days. In America it was described enthusiastically by the rare cultivated traveler, and to the American himself proved picturesquely useful. As the eighteenth century opens, John Lawson, Surveyor-General of North Carolina, reports a Tuliptree "wherein a lusty Man had his Bed and Household Furniture, and lived in it till his labour got him a more fashionable Mansion." More commonly, the pioneer made a fine canoe of this straight-growing tree, hollowing out a single log to extreme thinness, for the wood is easy to work and one of the lightest in the forest. Such a canoe sixty feet long did Daniel Boone make, when his fortunes were low, and into it he piled his family and his gear and sailed away down the Ohio into Spanish territory, away from an ingrate Kentucky.

The pioneer sometimes built his house, too, of Tuliptree logs, and he lined his well with it, since it imparts no taste to water. That same quality makes it today an appreciated crate for perishable food stuffs. Light in color and weight, taking the shipper's stencil well, it is used in immense quantities for boxes, and even more goes into millwork. For though a hardwood, Poplar, as the lumberman calls it, is softer than any softwood in North America except Western White Pine and Alpine Fir. It is also one of the very lightest of our woods, hence easy to float in rafts on the river. Since so much of its bulk is in air, it is valuable as an insulating material, against sound as well as heat and cold. Though fairly flexible and tough, it is not strong as a beam or column, yet it takes paint excellently and holds up well as an outside finish.

Indeed, White Pine and so-called Poplar, regarded as standing timber, floating logs, boards at the mill, and lumber on the market destined to certain uses, are strikingly alike. Poplar has never engendered the wealth that Pine has, nor had so spectacular a history, but the drain upon it has been long and great. In the beginning of settlement it went down under the axe in sheer destruction, for it was taken as a sign of good soil, and simply felled to clear a field. So, like the Beech, it was widely dispossessed of its primeval holdings. Then, two decades after the Civil War, when railroads penetrated the southern Appalachians, and the great hardwood resources of these mountains were first tapped, Poplar was the prize of extensive selective logging. Only centenarian trees of great size were felled; those under 30 inches in diameter at the stump end would not have been cut, and only perfectly clear logs, containing upward of 400 board feet, were accepted at the mill in the eighteen-eighties. By 1905 the mills were beginning to be glad to get Poplar 14 inches at the stump end, which sawed out with 100 board feet clear. Today the portable sawmill is absorbing what is, for Poplar, almost sapling growth — logs 9 and 10 inches thick. Even the very young trees are now unfortunately cut, for pulp, since by the soda process Poplar can be made into high-grade book paper.

THE MAGNOLIAS

(*Magnolia*)

THE GROWTH of Magnolias is from large terminal silky buds of flower-bearing branchlets or by the upper axillary buds. The bark is aromatic and bitter; the commonly very large leaves (which in our species fall in winter) are alternate, the margins usually not toothed though often lobed at the base. The bisexual flowers are large, terminal, and solitary, and in the bud are enclosed in a deciduous, papery, big scale. The sepals and petals are inserted under the ovary; both stamens and pistils are numerous and of an indefinite number, in many rows; the stamens take their place below the pistils on the surface of a conical receptacle. This becomes a compound fruit, in appearance rather like a somewhat fleshy cone, actually composed of numerous 1-celled seed vessels which open to expose the large, usually scarlet seeds that hang suspended on threads before falling.

CUCUMBERTREE

Magnolia acuminata Linnæus

OTHER NAME: Indian-bitter.

RANGE: From western New York to upper Georgia and northern parts of Alabama and Mississippi, throughout Arkansas to eastern Oklahoma, extreme southern Missouri, southeastern Illinois, southern Indiana and southeastern Kentucky. Not found above 5000 feet in the southern Appalachians.

DESCRIPTION: *Bark* thin, furrowed, thinly scaly, and dark brown. *Twigs* at first coated with pale, soft, deciduous hairs, becoming bare, lustrous, and bright red-brown, marked with small pale lenticels, turning gray about the third year. *Terminal winter buds* small, slender, densely clothed in long lustrous hairs. *Leaves* 6 to 10 inches long and 4 to 6 broad, thin, yellow-green, paler beneath. *Flowers* erect, bell-shaped, greenish, odorless, with sepals shorter than the 6 petals, which are 1 to 1½ inches long, the outer broader than the inner. *Fruit* 2½ to 3 inches long, cucumber-like, greenish at first, ultimately covered with red seeds. *Wood* soft, not strong, very light (29 pounds per cubic foot, dry weight), durable and close-grained, the nearly white sapwood much thicker than the light yellow-brown heartwood.

In the rich mountain forests of the Carolinas and Tennessee, known as the cove hardwoods, flourishes this tree with the primitive flowers and the curious fruits that give it its name. Sixty to 90 feet tall, with a trunk 3 to 4 feet thick, this Magnolia makes a beautifully symmetrical, pyramidal tree, the middle and upper branches ascending sharply, the lower down-sweeping. Its greenish flowers are less lovely than others in its genus, but the "cucumbers" are notable, greenish at first, but as they ripen appearing dark red or scarlet. It is the seeds upon the fruit that take on this color, set as they are upon the surface like scanty grains of corn on a cob. They are not winged, neither are they palatable to any creatures of the forest, so that no means of dispersal seems provided to them. Furthermore, even when they are ripe the fruit seems reluctant to let them go, for instead of falling free they drop each on a small thread from one to three inches long and hang dangling there, as if uncertain of their fate.

Despite this awkward machinery of distribution, increased by the fact that half the flowers are apt to remain sterile, the Cucumbertree flourishes, not only in its mountain fastnesses but in parks and in city streets, for it has been popular in cultivation since the day of its discovery. This was in 1736, when John Clayton, Virginia's early botanist, found it; a few years later John Bartram sent the first plants to his patron Lord Petre, who grew them at his estate of "Thorndon Hall" in Essex, then considered the finest garden in England. In this era, toward the turn of the century, collectors in England and France became avid to obtain American Magnolias, a genus wholly new to Europe. Thus were these trees prominent among the treasures sought by François Michaux in our virgin wilderness, and he records the care he lavished on keeping their delicate seeds viable by putting them into fresh moss, constantly renewed throughout his travels. In July, 1802, on the banks of the Juniata River in Pennsylvania, he makes a dry observation on the Cucumbertree:

"The inhabitants of the remotest parts of Pennsylvania and Virginia and even the western countries, pick the cones when green, to infuse in whiskey, which gives it a pleasant bitter. This bitter is very much esteemed in this country as a preventative against intermittent fevers, but I have my doubts whether it would be so generally used if it had the same qualities when mixed with water."

It is said, too, that the pioneer people extracted the bitterness from the cucumber-like green cones and ate them, but the art, such as it was, seems to be quite lost. More enduring and profitable is the use of the wood, which in its properties so closely resembles that of its relative the Tuliptree that it is sold as "Poplar," though lumbermen know the difference and so do some of its buyers. Thus it is probably cut on a much greater scale than the scanty statistics under its own name would show, for it serves well for boxes, crates, slack cooperage, furniture cores, and interior finish of houses.

UMBRELLATREE

Magnolia tripetala Linnæus

OTHER NAME: Elkwood.

RANGE: Southeastern Pennsylvania to the coast of North Carolina and southward to southern Alabama and southwestward to southern Ohio, middle parts of Kentucky and Tennessee, and northeastern Mississippi. Also in central Arkansas and southeastern Oklahoma.

DESCRIPTION: *Bark* thin, light gray, smooth but marked with many small blister-like excrescences. *Twigs* stout, brittle, at first green, becoming bright reddish brown and very shiny and marked with large, oval, horizontal leaf scars, turning brown and finally gray. *Terminal winter buds* 1 inch long and purple covered with a bloom. *Leaves* 18 to 20 inches long, 8 to 10 inches wide, with thick midrib, the blades thin and stalks 1 to 1½ inches long. *Flowers* cup-shaped, creamy white, 2 to 2½ inches deep, with narrow, light green, reflexed sepals, and 6 or 9 thick concave petals 4 to 5 inches long and about 2 inches wide; stalks of the stamens bright purple. *Fruit* 2½ to 4 inches long, at maturity rose-colored. *Wood* very light (28 pounds to the cubic foot, dry weight), soft, weak, with brown heartwood and thick, white sapwood.

As you tramp or motor beside the roaring streams of Great Smoky Mountains National Park in May, the Umbrellatree, with its big, creamy-white flowers, repeats itself over and over, until the forest — made up of the most magnificent hardwoods of the North American continent — seems populated by a troop of wood nymphs.

Though so showy a tree in flower, the Umbrellatree is usually a straggling understory species, 30 to 40 feet high in the Great Smokies, where it attains its maximum, and often much less, with numerous shrubby stems from the base. The branches, commonly irregularly developed, are contorted or wide-spreading nearly at right angles with the stem. In autumn the foliage takes on no beautiful colors. It turns suddenly brown at the touch of frost and soon drops, but in summer the great, filmy, pale green leaves, clustered umbrella-fashion at the end of the stem, seem the very embodiment of the Appalachian forests' spirit, as they shine through the underwood, or stream on the fresh breeze that seems perpetually to sweep down the long valleys. Distance undoubtedly lends some enchantment to the flowers, for when one actually drinks of the odor in the deep chalice, it is strong and, to many persons, disagreeable.

But reproach this species as one will for its minor failings, it is still a beauty, and naturally it was introduced at an early date in the gardens of Europe, where the Magnolias of America created such a sensation in the eighteenth century. This species was first described by Mark Catesby in his *Natural History of Carolina,* published in 1743, but he must have seen it years earlier, when in 1712 this English naturalist first came to Virginia to visit his relatives and was so delighted that he remained for seven years.

Not the least of the charms of the Umbrellatree is its elusiveness, for it is by no means always present within the external boundaries of its range; in many areas it is lacking altogether, and over others it is distinctly a rare species. On the coastal plain it seeks the margins of the great swamps and the shade of lofty Swamp Chestnut Oak, Scarlet Maple, and Gum tree; in the mountains it loves the shady side of a deep gorge, and, with its roots buried in rich cool loam, it sends its stems to overtop banked masses of Rhododendron. Thus it has a habit of growing in memorable places and choosing beautiful associates, and is, each time one comes upon it, itself beauty-dispensing and unforgettable.

LARGE–LEAVED MAGNOLIA

Magnolia macrophylla A. Michaux

RANGE: Central and western Florida to western Louisiana and north to central North Carolina and the valley of the Green River, Kentucky.

DESCRIPTION: *Bark* very thin, smooth, light gray, and minutely scaly. *Twigs* stout, brittle, light yellow-green and conspicuously marked by large, irregular leaf scars, turning reddish brown the second year and gray the third. *Terminal winter buds* 1¾ to 2 inches long, covered with a thick coat of snowy, woolly hairs. *Leaves* 20 to 30 inches long, 9 to 10 inches wide, the upper surface bright green, the lower silvery and downy especially along the stout midrib and primary veins. *Flowers* cup-shaped, 10 to 12 inches across, with 6 concave, thick, creamy-white petals, each 6 to 7 inches long and 3 to 4 inches wide, or those of the inner row somewhat narrower. *Fruit* 2½ to 3 inches long, bright rose-color when ripe, and downy. *Wood* medium-heavy (33 pounds to the cubic foot, dry weight), medium-hard but not strong, the heartwood light brown, with thick, light yellow sapwood.

The wide range of this species gives little conception of its scarceness. It occurs only at scattered stations through the southern states, and only enters the circumscription of this book in the southern Appalachians and in Kentucky. Even in the few localities where it is known to occur, it is generally represented by but few individuals and these seem to hide away (as well as such a showy tree can) in deep swamp woods, or in valleys sheltered from the wind, the roots thrust deep in rich soil and the straight spindling trunk rising to scarcely more than understory height, 30 to 40 feet.

But the trained eye of the great French naturalist and explorer André Michaux could not miss a tree, rare though it might be, which had the largest leaves in the entire sylva of temperate North America, as well as superb white and intensely sweet flowers, the petals curving back at the middle and revealing at the base of each a rich rose-colored blotch. For it was in full flower in the month of June when first Michaux encountered it near Charlotte, North Carolina. Having once discovered so notable an addition to this continent's famous list of native Magnolias, Michaux was forever watching for it. And thus he found again this queenliest of all the deciduous Magnolias while he was passing through "the wilderness" of the Cumberland Mountains, through which Daniel Boone, only nineteen years before, had cut the Wilderness Trail. Those were the days when one was still wise to wait, as Michaux did, until a party of armed travelers became sufficiently numerous to give one another protection, before attempting the lonely forest-ringed road.

On June 4, 1795, Michaux started from Knoxville with a company of travelers, and four days later, "alternately ascending and descending the mountains," he spied in the bottom-lands this rare and exquisite tree. On the 15th he came to the house of a "Mr. Jackson" — none other than the immortal Old Hickory, then an obscure lawyer and planter. A year later, Michaux found himself near Jackson's birthplace, south of Charlotte, where, he says, he remained all day to "pull shoots of a new Magnolia with very large leaves, auriculate, oblong, glaucous, silky, especially the young leaves; the buds very silky; Flowers white, Petals with a base of a purple color. Stamens yellow, etc." It grew, this tree, along a creek, Michaux noted, with Mountain Laurel, Yellow Violet, Slippery Elm, Silverbell-tree, and Mountain Camellia — a company of princesses for this queenly tree.

Magnolia macrophylla is probably rarer today than even in

Michaux's time, and the lucky amateur of trees who can boast that he has ever seen it in its native setting is himself a rare specimen. When encountered, it symbolizes, more perhaps than any other tree, that lost and pre-Columbian America, that lush, sweet, upland sylva of the South, that was seen in its days of innocent perfection by those lucky first explorers Bartram, Fraser, and Michaux.

MOUNTAIN MAGNOLIA

Magnolia Fraseri Walter

OTHER NAMES: Fraser Magnolia. Ear-leaved Cucumbertree.

RANGE: From southwestern Virginia to the high country of Georgia, and from northeastern Kentucky to Alabama. Ascends to 4000 feet altitude.

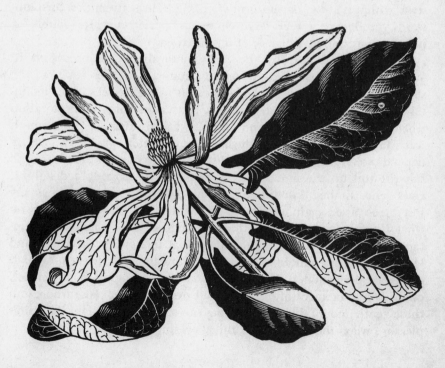

DESCRIPTION: *Bark* very thin, dark brown, and smooth in youth except for minute, warty excrescences, but in age covered with little scales. *Twigs* lustrous, brittle, and stout, soon turning bright red-brown and marked by numerous minute pale lenticels; in the first winter ringed by crowded leaf scars, in the second turning grayish. *Terminal winter buds* 1½ to 2 inches long, dark purple. *Leaves* 10 to 12 inches long, 6 to 7 wide, or larger, bright green. *Flowers* 8 to 10 inches across, pale yellow, fragrant. *Fruit* cone-shaped, bright rose-red, 4 to 5 inches long, 1½ to 2 thick. *Wood* medium-light (31 pounds per cubic foot, dry weight), soft, weak, close-grained, nearly all a thick, creamy-white sapwood.

In the coves of the southern Appalachians, cooled by the breezes set astir by ever-falling water and fresh with fern and saxifrage, this lovely tree is most at home, its flowers shining forth serenely as water-lilies floating in the forest green. Its leaves are borne all at the ends of the branches, which gives the Mountain Magnolia a wilder and more careless look than the cultivated species familiar in the garden. Indeed, it has proved too tender for gardens as far north as Massachusetts, and is happiest in the rich, humid soils to which it is native. There it rises some 18 to 30 feet in height, in many stems from one source, its "crooked wreathing branches arising and subdividing from the main stem without order or uniformity, until their extremities turn upwards, producing a very large rosaceous, perfectly white double or polypetalous flower, which is of a most fragrant scent."

So it was described by the lucky naturalist who discovered it, William Bartram, the first American botanist who ever explored the southern Appalachians. On the headwaters of the Keowee in the mountains of South Carolina he found it, in that morning of exploration when this land was young and half its wealth unnamed. The month was May, the year that in which a young nation was to declare independence, but the happy naturalist was far from any human struggle but the toil up the mountains. When he had crossed "a delightful river" and climbed "swelling turfy ridges, varied with groves of stately forest trees, then again more steep grassy hill sides," he rested at last on what he conceived to be the highest ridge of the "Cherokee mountains," which he named Mount Magnolia, in honor of the new and lovely species he had found here so abundant and in such "a high degree of perfection." There is but one first recognition, in science, one Adamite moment of discovery, but over and over those who climb those gentle mountains in the spring can share old William Bartram's pleasure when they come upon this flowering tree.

Its history, indeed, may be said to antedate by eons a May day in Revolutionary times. For Mountain Magnolia is a descendant of one of the oldest (excepting the Conifers) of all trees; systematists used to believe it was certainly the most primitive of them all, and many are coming back to that view. Its antiquity is visible in its flower structure, which is primitive, and so is that of the fruit and of the wood. And Magnolia fossils are found, to a total of perhaps 23 species, in the lower Cretaceous rocks, which would place them as far back as any trees we have save the Conifers. At that time the genus was represented from western Greenland to Texas and Nebraska. In the middle Cretaceous there are fossil Magnolias from Vancouver, Portugal, and Moravia, and in the Late Cretaceous from Tennessee and Wyoming.

From the Eocene come 12 known species of Magnolia, from Spitzbergen to Alaska, Tennessee, and Louisiana, and all over the Rocky Mountain and Pacific coast states, as well as central Europe. The Oligocene has yielded only 8 species, mostly from Italy, the Miocene 16 from Europe and North America, while the Pliocene, which is almost never represented by American fossils of any sort, showed 11 species in Europe and Pacific Asia. The Pleistocene glaciation wiped Magnolia out of Europe and our western states, leaving eastern Asia and eastern North America in possession of the surviving species. Like similar locations in far China and Japan, the wild sweet glens of the Appalachians keep for us a flora of strangely ancient lineage, and Mountain Magnolia is one of the loveliest plants in it that have come down to us, by the winding ways of evolution, from an unimaginable antiquity.

THE PAWPAWS
(*Asimina*)

MEMBERS of this group have slender twigs marked by conspicuous leaf scars and minute buds covered with ashy-downy deciduous scales. The alternate, deciduous leaves are feather-veined, with meshed veinlets, and when crushed emit a bad odor. Solitary and nodding on short stalks, the flowers are bisexual with rather fleshy and mesh-veined petals, the 3 outer alternate with the 3 green and recurving sepals, the inner shorter, erect, and opposite the sepals. The stamens appear densely packed on the receptacle; 3 to 15 pistils project from the globular mass of the stamens. The thick-skinned, heavy, custardy fruit is pear-shaped, with the compressed seeds in one or two ranks, the seed coat shining, smooth, and brown.

PAWPAW

Asimina triloba (Linnæus) Dunal

OTHER NAMES: Wild Banana. Custard Apple. Fetidshrub.

RANGE: From northern Florida to western New York State, the northern shores of Lake Ontario, southern Michigan and southwestern Iowa, and west to southeastern Nebraska, eastern parts of Kansas and Oklahoma and eastern Texas.

DESCRIPTION: *Bark* thin, dark brown, marked by large ash-colored blotches, covered by small, wart-like excrescences, and divided by long, shallow depressions. *Twigs* light brown tinged with red marked by narrow, shallow grooves. *Winter buds* ⅛ inch long, clothed with rusty brown hairs. *Leaves* 10 to 12 inches long and 4 to 6 broad, light green, paler below. *Flowers* nearly 2 inches across, pale green becoming brown, then maroon or purple. *Fruit* 3 to 5 inches long, becoming dark and wrinkled when ripe, with custardy flesh. *Wood* very light (25 pounds to the cubic foot, dry weight), soft, weak, spongy, and coarse-grained, with light greenish yellow heartwood and darker sapwood.

The first reference to this curious species of an otherwise notably tropical family occurs in the chronicles of DeSoto's expedition in the Mississippi valley in 1541, for naturally an edible fruit of such size was important to a host of *conquistadores* always near starvation. But, after that, for two centuries the Pawpaw flourished unknown save by wild animals and red men, until Mark Catesby delineated it in his *Natural History of Carolina*, that master work whose plates are fresh with wilderness still.

Once abundant in the Mississippi valley, where it formed dense thickets of wide extent, the Pawpaw is today in the northeastern states only a scattered understory tree, though to the south it may become 30 to 40 feet tall, with a straight trunk more than a foot in diameter. Everything about it is odd and unforgettable. The leaves are among the largest in our sylva, and in autumn, when they turn a butter yellow, they are the mellowest of the season's tones. The flowers, with their exotic look borrowed from tropical relatives, hardly seem to belong to the cool vernal world on which they open. At first green, the petals soon turn brown, and then they become a dark winy color, with an odor to match, a remembrance of fermenting purple grapes. As to the fruit, the better it grows, the uglier, for it is only when it is thoroughly mature, in late fall, that it is edible. At first the skin is greenish yellow; gradually it darkens, and when it is nearly black, wrinkled, and looks unappetizing — in October or November — at last the yellow or orange flesh is soft, custardy, and palatable.

Pawpaws have had their enthusiasts from the days of the Creeks, Cheraws, and Catawbas, who often planted them, to the present. Such wood-wise people know that there are good and bad trees, as to flavor, and have long insisted that selection would soon result in marked improvement of the fruit; in general, the orange-fleshed variety is considered much more tasty. Pawpaws were made into a jelly by the early settlers, and still in southern towns sometimes appear in the markets. The seeds contain a powerful alkaloid which, it has been noted, has a stupefying effect on the brains of animals, yet opossums are great Pawpaw eaters, and raccoons and gray squirrels also appreciate the fruit.

For the wood there are no uses, but the inner bark was woven into fiber cloth by the Louisiana Indians, and the pioneers employed it for stringing fish. In its range a characteristic part of American country life, the Pawpaw, for all its exotic kinship, seems an intensely native tree, above all in the frosty autumn, when the leaves droop withering on the stem and the great plashy fruits hang preposterously heavy on the twigs.

THE SASSAFRASSES

(*Sassafras*)

THESE aromatic trees which arise from creeping, spongy, thick roots have whip-like twigs which are marked by half-circular elevated leaf scars, and contain mucilaginous pith. The flowering buds are terminal, with 9 or 10 scales loosely overlapping, the innermost the largest and bright yellow-green, turning dull red before falling. They open more precociously than the buds of the alternate, deciduous, mucilaginous leaves. A single tree usually displays only male or female flowers, hence male trees never bear the bead-like little stone fruits (drupes) on the thick elongated stalks. The flowers are found in long drooping spikes, with the little calyx pale green-gold and divided to the middle into 6 convex lobes; the stamens in our species number 9, inserted on the edge of the calyx tube; in the female flower the stamens are reduced to dark orange stalks without anthers and pollen. The ovary is light green and narrowed to a long style.

SASSAFRAS

Sassafras albidum (Nuttall) Nees

OTHER NAMES: Saxifraxtree. Sassafac. Aguetree.

RANGE: From southern Maine through southern Vermont and southern Ontario, central Michigan, northern Indiana, northern Illinois, and southeastern Iowa to eastern Kansas and Oklahoma, southward to central Florida and the valley of the Brazos River in Texas; ascending in the southern Appalachians to 4000 feet altitude.

DESCRIPTION: *Bark* when young thin, reddish brown, divided by shallow fissures, when old covered by thick scales and broad ridges separated by shallow furrows. *Twigs* slender, brittle, rough or warty, vivid light green gradually turning reddish brown with the years. *Leaves* 4 to 6 inches long, 2 to 4 broad, yellow-green, shining above, with a bloom below, mucilaginous. *Flowers* inconspicuous, clustered on stalks about 2 inches long. *Fruits* ⅓ inch long, blue, on long stalks. *Wood* soft, weak, medium-light (32 pounds to the cubic foot, dry weight), with light sapwood and dull orange-brown heartwood.

Against the Indian summer sky, a tree lifts up its hands and testifies to glory, the glory of a blue October day. Yellow or orange, or blood-orange, or sometimes softest salmon pink, or blotched with bright vermilion, the leaves of the Sassafras prove that not all autumnal

splendor is confined to the northern forests. Deep into the South, along the snake-rail fences, beside the soft wood roads, in old fields where the rusty brook sedge is giving way to the return of forest, the Sassafras carries its splendid banners to vie with the scarlet Black Gum and the yellow Sweet Gum and other trees of which the New Englander may hardly have heard. The deep blue fruits on thick bright red stalks complete a color effect in fall which few trees anywhere surpass.

In spring the leafing-out is late — later at least than the inconspicuous pale gold flowers that bloom on the naked wood. But once they burst their buds, the heavy glossy leaves form swiftly. On old boughs they are simple in outline — boat-shaped and rather small; but on young trees and vigorous new growth they grow large and take on their characteristic mitten shape — with one "thumb" lobe and a larger terminal lobe. Or they may have three terminal lobes, the middle one a little longer, a strong vein running through each lobe. Such a blade is almost unique in our flora, and could be mistaken for nothing else save perhaps the leaf of our wild Mulberry. But the Mulberry's mitten-shaped leaves are thin, dull, dark green, harsh above, and many-toothed. The Sassafras blade is thick, waxy-glossy and yellow-green above while chalky white below, and it has no teeth on the margin. More, the Sassafras leaves, when chewed, at once set up a mucilaginous slime in the mouth, like that of Slippery Elm twigs, which country children love to taste; the hot and thirsty botanist, as well, has been known to resort to chewing Sassafras to promote salivation, when no water was to be found on his dusty tramps.

In the North, Sassafras is usually a small tree. Yet in the South it may reach 80 feet, with a trunk 6 feet thick, and stout branches leaving the trunk at right angles to form a strong rather than a graceful out-line. On the Lake Michigan dunes of Indiana, Sassafras growing out of pure shifting sand may be a mere shrub, its stems only limber green canes. In northern Illinois the Sassafras seems to be gaining ground, much as is the Red Cedar, and is present now in places from which it was unreported by the first botanical explorers. Because its bright blue fruits are eagerly eaten by birds and the seeds carried and then voided, and because the Sassafras does best not in forest country but in lands opened up by agriculture, it seems destined to continue to increase its range, while so many other trees are losing ground.

Its rôle in American folklore and early exploration is unique.

About it have clung fantastic hopes and promises of gain, and superstitions that have not yet wholly departed. The wood, which has less shrinkage in drying than any other hardwood (10 per cent), is not only durable, so that it appealed to the pioneer for fences, and is still esteemed for small boats, but its odor was reputed to drive away bedbugs; hence many bedsteads were made of it, in a more innocent age and the more innocent states of Arkansas and Mississippi. Negro cabin floors in Louisiana were often laid in Sassafras for the same reason. In Kentucky, where soap is still sometimes a home product, it is often supposed that the kettle must be stirred with a Sassafras stick to make a good quality of soap. In West Virginia it is believed that Sassafras hen-roosts keep out chicken lice.

But it has been the bark on the roots of the tree, yielding an oil once prized beyond all reason, that gave the Sassafras its fame. As a demulcent and emollient, oil of Sassafras has never completely ceased to be of some importance in the manufacture of soaps and perfumes; it disguises the bad taste of some medicines and may perhaps still be employed in the flavoring of candy. At one time, however, especially in Virginia, roots were grubbed out by the ton for the production of this essence, thereby clearing cut-over land for the farmer and at the same time yielding a paying harvest. But the old belief in Sassafras as a tonic that would prolong life has yielded place to acceptance of radio advertisers' claims for vitamins to do the same, and it is probable that Sassafras at the moment is at an all-time low in its chequered career.

Yet no other American tree was ever exalted by such imaginary virtues, in expectation, as Sassafras, or has fallen so far in esteem. Its reputation was launched upon the world in 1574 by Nicholas Monardes, "physician of Seville," in his work on the resources of the West Indies (translated into the English by Frampton), with the delightful title *Joyfull Newes Out of the Newe Founde Worlde*. And these are some of his glad tidings:

"From the Florida, which is the firme Lande of our Occidentall Indias, liying in xxv degrees, thei bryng a woodd and roote of a tree that groweth in those partes, of greate vertues, and great excellencies, that thei heale there with greevous and variable deseases.

"It may be three yeres paste, that I had knowledge of this Tree, and a French manne whiche had been in those partes, shewed me a peece of it, and told me merveiles of his vertues. . . .

"After that the French menne were destroied,[1] our Spaniards did beginne to waxe sicke, as the Frenche menne had dooen, and some whiche did remaine of them, did shew it to our Spaniardes, and how theei had cured them selves with the water of this merveilous Tree, and the manner which thei had in the usyng of it, shewed to them by the Indians, who used to cur theim selves therewith, when thei were sicke of any grief . . . and it did in theim greate effectes, that it is almoste incredible. . . .

"The name of this Tree, as the Indians dooeth name it, is called *Pauame,* and the Frenche menn doeth call it Sassafras."

Monardes goes on to say that Sassafras is a sovereign remedy for "Quotidian Agewes [malaria], large importunate fevers . . . it comforteth the liver and the Stomacke . . . it dooeth make fatte . . . doth cause lust to meate." It is also good for "Tertian Agewes, griefes of the breast caused of cold humours, griefes of the head," for "them that bee lame and creepelles and them that are not able to goe."

Such a panacea as this was certain to raise high hopes in the Europe of that day, when almost no disease was correctly understood in either its origin or its treatment, so that credulity might mount untrammeled. It was the easier to believe in a cure-all that came from the New World and had never failed — because it had never been tried except by the Indians. Indeed, the early Spanish, French, Portuguese, Dutch, and English were as gullible about "Indian medicine" as the Americans of a later date. The great value of Sassafras to the red men (aside from the undoubtedly soothing effect that the mucilaginous properties of its sap would have on raw mucous membranes) was doubtless in its aromatic nature. A plant with a strong pleasant smell was supposed to ward off evil, and evil, rather than bacteria, is believed still, among the Chinese, Indians, and certain American sects, to be the real cause of sickness.

This conception of the curative, since evil-dispelling, nature of an odor is very ancient; it goes back to Egyptian and druidical ceremonies, and was strongly believed in by Europeans during the bubonic plague, when doctors wore great nose-beaks filled with spices; indeed, it survived to our own times in the only recently abandoned theory of fumi-

[1] Reference is had to the attack by the Spanish of St. Augustine, Florida, upon the French Huguenot colony at Port Royal, South Carolina, when the French, after surrendering, were coldly butchered by the Spanish.

gation. The American Indians believed, above all, in the efficacy of tobacco smoke, and it was as a curative that tobacco was first introduced into Europe; Catherine de' Medici took tobacco for a cold in the head! Such then is the background, the psychological preparation, which greeted the first arrivals of Sassafras in Europe. It rated with the spices of Ormuz and Araby as a precious substance.

Impatient to secure adequate supplies of it, the English charged their early explorers to search for it. Thus when Philip Amadas and Arthur Barlowe dropped anchor in Pimlico Sound, North Carolina, in 1584, they immediately began the search for Sassafras. In 1602 Bartholomew Gosnold was sent out to explore what is now the coast of New England for the marvelous tree, for the price of Sassafras in England had risen to £336 sterling the ton. Then in 1603 the merchants of Bristol, urged thereto by Richard Hakluyt, the celebrated historian and anthologist of early exploration, formed a company to send to Virginia for the sole purpose of gathering Sassafras. They sailed in two vessels "plentifully victualled for eight monethes, and furnished with slight Merchandizes thought fit to trade with the people of the Countrey, as Hats of divers colours, greene, blue and yellow, apparell of coarse Kersie and Canvasse readie made, Stockings and Shooes, Axes, Hatchets, Hookes, Knives, Sizzers, Hammers, Nailes, Chissels, Fishhookes, Bels, Beades, Bugles, Looking-glasses, Thimbles, Pinnes, Needles, Threed and such like."

After a long voyage they reached land, probably in the neighborhood of what is now Old Orchard, Maine. Meeting with no Sassafras there, they continued southward, always hunting for it, and first encountered it on the Connecticut shore of Long Island Sound. Here they spent a month filling the hold of the bark with Sassafras and then sent her home to England " to give some contentment to the Adventurers," that is, satisfy the stockholders. The remaining company continued to cut Sassafras and load it into the larger ship, but either this aroused the jealousy of the Indians or the redskins decided the foreigners had stayed long enough. Several surprise attacks were made, ambushes were laid, and treachery attempted, but the stout banging of a brass "Peece" (cannon) and the fear inspired in the natives by two mastiffs belonging to the Bristol men drove off the Indians, and a fair wind brought the Sassafras cutters away at last in safety to Bristol and, we hope, returned great profit to the gentlemen "Adventurers."

Sassafras was one of the first exports sent by Captain John Smith from the Jamestown colony, and as late as 1610 it was still demanded from Virginia, like tribute, as a condition of the charter of the colony. But soon it began to share the fate of other panaceas. It wasn't curing all the ailments it was claimed to cure. A disillusioned public lost its faith in Sassafras — but not in panaceas! So, through the years, Sassafras as a medicament sank to the position of a tonic to "purify the blood" — a continuation, of course, of the notion that our ailments originate in some inner evil. Thus for generations it was administered, in connection with black cherry and various other unpleasant ingredients, to pioneer children as the dreaded "spring tonic." Older people left out the unpleasant ingredients and simply sipped Sassafras tea.

Even that placid custom is becoming a part of the past — that long American past in which the Sassafras tree shone boldly forth, just as today when it is only a bright reminder of the time when everything here was wonderful and new.

THE WITCH HAZELS
(*Hamamelis*)

THESE little trees have naked buds, zigzag twigs, scaly bark, and alternate, deciduous leaves with more or less unsymmetrical bases, straight primary veins, and rounded teeth on the margins. The flowers occur in 3-flowered terminal clusters from buds appearing in the summer, on the curved, short stalks from the axils of the leaves of the year. Each flower appears surrounded by 2 or 3 scales, the outer slightly united at the base to make a 3-lobed cup. Four-parted, and yellow or red, the little calyx is persistent on the base of the ovary, with reflexed lobes. The bright yellow petals, inserted at the edge of the cup-shaped receptacle, are strap-shaped, and 4 in number. There are 8 stamens inserted in 2 rows on the edge of the receptacle, those opposite the petals smaller and reduced to strap-shaped scales. The female organ consists in 2 carpels inserted at the bottom of the receptacle, only partly adhering to the calyx, and tipped by spreading styles. The fruit is a capsule (seed pod) which is 2-beaked at the tip and bears at the base the remnant of the calyx and the cup of floral scales; the woody, thick, outer layer splits from above before the opening of the bony, thin inner layer. The shining, chestnut-brown, bony seeds are forcibly discharged when ripe by contractions of the valves of the outer walls of the seed pod.

WITCH HAZEL

Hamamelis virginiana Linnæus

OTHER NAMES: Winter, or Snapping Hazel. Winterbloom.

RANGE: From the Maritime Provinces of Canada south to northern Florida, and west to southeastern Minnesota, eastern Iowa, eastern Texas, northern Louisiana, and central Mississippi; ascending to 4000 feet in the Appalachians.

DESCRIPTION: *Bark* thin, light brown, often scaling off to show reddish-purple inner bark. *Twigs* slender, flexible, at first coated with rusty hairs, becoming smooth, light orange-brown marked by white flecks, turning dark brown the second year. *Winter buds* acute, narrow, slightly curved. *Leaves* 4 to 6 inches long and 2 to 2½ broad, dull dark green above, paler and lustrous below. *Flowers* opening in late fall, petals yellow, ½ to ⅓ inch long. *Fruit* ½ inch long, hairy, dull orange-brown. *Wood* medium-heavy (44 pounds to the cubic foot, dry weight), with thick white sapwood and light reddish brown heartwood.

An understory tree is the Witch Hazel, whose faintly fragrant flowers venture forth only when its dull yellow leaves have dropped and the late autumn airs are beginning to grow chill. They have twisted, crinkled petals of pale greenish gold, and the fruits are stranger still, for those of last year are just ripening at the time that this year's flowers appear. More, they eject their shiny, hard, black seeds with violence; the tree, which seldom grows more than 20 feet high, can send its seeds much farther. Reliable observers, who have kept the pods in the house and could measure the distance of the ejection precisely, report 25 and 30 feet. The viability of these little missiles is high, and thus the wintry-blooming Witch Hazel, of ancient geologic lineage, is still today well able to maintain itself.

Though the wood is hard and close-grained, very much like Sweet Gum wood, it never grows to saw-timber size and so has no commercial possibilities. There is, however, a business in the extraction of the essence, which began with the Indians, who probably had the same mystical faith in it, as an aromatic plant, that they put in Sassafras. High hopes were once entertained of Witch Hazel extract as a curative for all sorts of diseases. It was still being advertised as an antiseptic and gargle a few years ago. But modern chemistry has found that Witch Hazel is quite inert, and any value the extract may have as an astringent and antiseptic may well reside in the alcohol in which the aromatic essence is embodied. Nevertheless it has never ceased to be in some demand as an after-shave lotion and toilet water, on account of its cleanly aroma. The southern Appalachians are the chief source of the dried leaves which supply the material for the extract; in New England, however, the bark, twigs, and sometimes the entire plant are often used.

Naturally an aromatic tree from the New World was certain to attract the interest of the early botanists. Witch Hazel was first noticed by John Banister, the English missionary to Virginia (where he died about 1692). Then, in 1695, Plukenet published in his *Almegastum Botanicum* the first printed notice of this strange plant. Peter Collinson, the Quaker plantsman and linen draper, grew Witch Hazel in 1736 at his garden near Mill Hill, where so many American plants were raised for the first time. Our *Hamamelis* continues still to be one of the curiosities of European botanical gardens, for its November flowers and exploding fruits.

Witch Hazel is usually said to have its name from a confusion in the minds of the early settlers between this plant and the true Hazel, and there is some resemblance between the leaves and the appearance of the young fruits in the two species. The Hazel of Europe was famous for its magical properties; some legends say that one can find witches by means of it, and others that with its help witches can find water, or gold, or other desirable subterranean things. Philologists like to dispute this source of the name, saying that it comes from the word *wych* which has nothing to do with witches but is related, according to various and sundry authorities, to Anglo-Saxon *wicken,* meaning to bend, or Old English *wick,* meaning quick or living, or possibly even to the modern word, switch.

However all that may be, it is certain that, in early days in America, Witch Hazel was used in local witchery, to find water or even mineral deposits. You took a forked branch, one whose points grew north and south so that they had felt the influence of the sun at its rising and setting, and you carried it with a point in each hand, the stem pointing forward. Any downward tug of the stem was caused by the flow of hidden water or the gleam of buried gold. And if there are people still who believe in water-witching, theirs is one of the most harmless and pleasing of fallacies.

THE SWEET GUMS
(*Liquidambar*)

THE TREES of this group possess balsamic juices and scaly bark, and the twigs are often winged. The alternate, deciduous leaves form a characteristic star-like outline, being deeply lobed as well as finely toothed. The buds are scaly, not naked. Usually unisexual, flowers of the two sexes appear, however, on the same tree, in spherical heads, those of the male flowers grouped in long spikes while those of the female are generally solitary in the axils of upper leaves. Male flowers show no calyx or corolla; stamens of an indefinite but large number are interspersed with little scales. The female flowers possess each a minute calyx, 4 aborted or non-functional stamens, and a pistil of 2 united carpels terminating in long, recurved, persistent, and numerous styles; the ovary is partly adherent to the calyx. Fruits take the form of capsules or seed pods united in a dense spherical head. They are made prickly by the elongated, incurved, hardened styles. The seed has a bony coat which is winged at the apex.

SWEET GUM

Liquidambar Styraciflua Linnæus

OTHER NAMES: Red or Star-leaved Gum. Gumtree. Liquidamber. Alligatorwood.

RANGE: From western Connecticut and Long Island to the southern parts of Ohio, Indiana, Illinois, and southeastern Missouri, and south to central Florida, eastern Texas and southeastern Oklahoma. Ascends to 4000 feet in the Appalachians. Occurs in Mexico, in the mountains of Veracruz, Puebla, Hidalgo, Oaxaca and Chiapas, and in Guatemala.

DESCRIPTION: *Bark* furrowed into narrow sometimes flaky ridges. *Twigs* slender, pithy, many-angled, light orange at first, becoming reddish brown and marked by large leaf scars and occasional minute dark lenticels, with corky ridges appearing the second year. *Leaves* 6 to 7 inches broad, lustrous light yellow-green, emitting pungency when crushed. *Flowers* clustered on stalks 2 to 3 inches long. *Fruit* 1 to 1½ inches in diameter. *Wood* medium-heavy, (37 pounds to the cubic foot, dry weight), straight, hard, close-grained, with thick white sapwood and pink or ruddy heartwood.

Out of a bizarre and dramatic moment of history comes, like a puff of pungent smoke, the first reference to this American tree. It is written by a witness of the ceremonies between Cortez and Montezuma, and he says, of the Emperor: "After he had dined, they presented to him three little canes highly ornamented, containing liquidamber, mixed with an herb they call tobacco, and when he had sufficiently viewed and heard the singers, dancers, and buffoons, he took a little of the smoke of one of these canes."

This remarkable author and soldier, Don Bernal Díaz del Castillo, who accompanied Cortez in 1519 on the conquest of Mexico and became its most celebrated historian, published his account (here translated by Keating) in 1632. He must have recognized the burning liquid-amber (in spite of its being called by the Aztecs *xochiocotzoquahuitl!*) by its odor, since, though no *Liquidambar* is native to Europe, the gum of an Asiatic species was well known in the pharmacopeias of western civilization, and was prized as an incense in Christian churches and Indian temples. The plant which produced it, however, was for a long time quite unknown to science, and the gum arrived mysteriously in the markets of Constantinople either as a resin floating in water and sewed up in goatskin bags, or as a bark in camel's-hair bags. Retailed over Europe at advanced prices, it was valued both in perfumery and incense, and in the treatment of diphtheria and gonorrhea. Ultimately Europe learned that the gum was derived from *Liquidambar orientalis,* which grows in the mountains of southern Anatolia, Turkey, and was gathered by wandering bands of Turcomans.

The American species which produces a like resin was described to Europe by Francisco Hernandez, the first great herbalist of Mexico, who dwelt in that country from 1571 to 1575. He speaks of it aptly as having leaves "almost like those of a maple," and a resin of which the "nature is hot in the third order, and dry, and added to tobacco, it strengthens the head, belly, and heart, induces sleep, and alleviates pains in the head that are caused by colds. Alone, it dissipates humors, relieves pains, and cures eruptions of the skin. . . . It relieves wind in the stomach and dissipates tumors beyond belief." [1]

This account of the learned, if credulous, Hernandez did not see print until about 1651. Yet over twenty years earlier the Sweet Gum tree, as most Americans call it, had been recognized — for the first time on the soil of the present United States — by Alvar Núñez Cabeza de Vaca. This bold, Christian, and observant adventurer was a member of one of the most desperate of the Spanish expeditions into the

[1] Translated in Paul Standley's *Trees and Shrubs of Mexico.*

New World, and so it was he found himself in 1528 near the present Appalachicola, Florida. "The country," says he, "where we came on shore to this town and region of Apalachen is for the most part level, the ground of sandy and stiff earth. Throughout are immense trees and open woods, in which are walnut,[1] laurel [2] and another tree called liquid-amber, cedars,[3] savins,[4] evergreen oaks, pines, red oaks and palmitos [5] like those of Spain." Now this account was apparently published for the first time in 1542, long after Cabeza de Vaca had returned home after shipwreck, Indian captivity, near-starvation in the wilderness, and further incredible hardships. A man must have a keen eye and mind to recollect so clearly a tree he had seen in a distant place long ago, and still more astonishing is it that he knew it when he saw it, for he could only have recognized it by its gummy exudation.

Yet this Sweet Gum is a noble tree, that might well impress anyone new to the sight of it. And the sight is a common one, for it grows along any fence row, in piedmont Virginia, beside any country road of the Carolinas, in any field abandoned by agriculture and growing up to Scrub Pine and Dogwood. It comes up in company, in these upland sites, with Sassafras and Red Cedar, and may be known by its beautiful star-shaped leaves. Their upper surface has a star-like glister, but unlike most shining leaves, those of the Sweet Gum are not dark at maturity but a light, gay yellow-green. Crushed in the fingers, they give out a cleanly fragrance; on the tongue they have a tart taste. Foliage so odd and yet so attractive would make any tree conspicuous.

But even when the leaves have turned a deep winy crimson and fallen, Sweet Gum is striking by reason of the broad corky wings on the twig. True, one might confuse them with those of some of the Elms, but the fruiting heads of woody spiny balls, hanging all winter on the slim stalks after the winged seeds have escaped, are unique among all American trees. In the eastern states and on uplands, the Sweet Gum is often a small tree, sturdy rather than graceful, 20 to 40 feet tall. In the deep gumbo soils of the Mississippi Valley, in the swamps of Missouri's Tiwappatty Bottom, Sweet Gum becomes a giant, up to 140 feet high, with a trunk 5 feet thick.

There is something about Sweet Gum that looks like a living fossil, like a member of some family more abundant in another and far dif-

[1] Probably White Hickory. [2] Probably Magnolia. [3] Probably Bald Cypress.
[4] Red Cedar. [5] Scrub Palmetto.

ferent sylva than ours, and that is exactly the case. Today there are three extant species of *Liquidambar* — one in Formosa and one in Turkey, beside our own. Such a disparate distribution bespeaks a long story of spread over the planet, then a history of tragic extinctions. Twenty extinct species are known, the oldest found in the Upper Eocene rocks of Greenland, in an age when that continent had a sub-tropical climate, some 55,000,000 years ago. Later fossils turned up in Italy, Siberia, Colorado, and in great numbers in the Miocene lake beds of Switzerland. From the Pleistocene or Glacial Period, we distinguish Sweet Gum leaves in much the same regions the living species are found in today — as in Formosa and North Carolina.

To the lumberman the heartwood of this tree is Red Gum, and the sapwood, which is marketed separately as if it were a different wood, he calls Sap Gum. Country folk refer to it simply as Gum tree, and to furniture salesmen the wood is plain Gum, or Gum wood, which is confusingly ambiguous, since many trees are called so. In the pharmaceutical trade the name for the exudate of this tree is liquid-amber, or copalm balm, or, incorrectly, storax. The gum, which is considered identical in its properties with the oriental gum, flows from the tree in the form of bitter-tasting but sweet-smelling balsamic liquid. It is then semitransparent and yellowish brown, but on exposure to the air it hardens into a rosin-like and darker solid. From pioneer times it was used in the South for the treatment of sores and skin troubles, for a chewing gum, for catarrh, and in the treatment of dysentery was much favored by doctors in the Confederate armies.

However, in the years that followed the Civil War, American copalm sank into insignificance, for Oriental storax could easily undersell it. During the First World War, interest in the native gum revived, only to languish again. In the Second World War, with Formosa (whence it had been coming chiefly) completely cut off, it became definitely important as a needed base of salves, adhesives, perfuming powders, soaps, and tobacco flavoring, just as in the days of Montezuma. Clarke County, Alabama, which had retained from the first World War a memory of the technique of tapping the trees, became the center of the industry.

The operation is reported by a local agent to yield one-half to one pound of the resin from a tree each year, with the amount greatest from trees with the most green leaf surface. When the leaves are fully spread in the orchards in spring, the trees are expertly peeled, and the gum slowly gathers as an exudation, to be scraped off after some days. Then it is heated — carefully, since it is highly inflammable — strained and canned. A tree will produce like this for three to five years, and the young and healthy ones then grow new bark and can later be cut for lumber.

Not strong enough for a structural timber, the wood of Sweet Gum has only recently come into the place its beauty deserves. For though the very thick white sapwood is rather featureless, the pink or ruddy heartwood, which develops in trees over 60 or 70 years old, may sometimes show handsome figures on the quarter-sawed cut. All the wood is capable of taking a high polish, and can be stained to look like even nobler woods. Thus it happens that the lumber often leaves this country as Red Gum, is received in England as "Satin-Walnut" (forsooth!) and after various transmogrifying rites have been performed upon it, it may return to America as a Mahogany, Rosewood, or Circassian Walnut antique. The bands of distinctly darker wood in natural figured quarter-sawed Gum especially lend themselves to substitution as Circassian Walnut.

Obviously, everything about Red Gum points to its use as a cabinet wood. But only in the last half-century has it risen from the most despised position in the list of hardwoods to second place amongst them, inferior only to Oak in the amount cut in this country, far outstripping Birch and Maple. With an annual cut of something like 690,000,000 board feet a year, Red and Sap Gum (which are only one species) show a higher cut than any other species of deciduous hardwood. The cut is wholly in the southern states, with Louisiana and Mississippi far out in the lead.

One reason for this new popularity is the conquest, by technological processes, of some of the difficulties inherent in the wood of Sweet Gum when seasoning. The sapwood dries easily enough, but the heartwood warps badly, and has a tendency to stain. Through the use of modern scientific drying methods, Sweet Gum's seasoning difficulties have been largely overcome, so, although at first considered fit only for crates and boxes, the wood of Sweet Gum now shows its best face in the veneer of furniture, and promises a fine commercial future.

THE SYCAMORES
(*Platanus*)

Sʏᴄᴀᴍᴏʀᴇs have thin, scaly bark, on the branches and young trunk,
which constantly drops, in large thin plates, exhibiting the inner bark
of contrasting colors; the pithy twigs, which grow by prolongation
from an upper axillary bud, are zigzag. The smooth and shining
winter buds, axillary in position, appear nearly surrounded at base by
the narrow leaf scars and are covered by 3 deciduous, strap-shaped
scales, which, falling at maturity, mark the base of the branchlets
with narrow, ring-like scars; the outer scale splits longitudinally as the
buds expand, the second scale, light green, exudes a fragrant gummy
secretion and encloses a bud in its axil, while the third remains coated
with long rusty hairs.

Alternate and deciduous, the leaves display 5 principal nerves, all
arising from the point of attachment to the stalk and running out to
the tips of the broad shallow lobe; a few large low teeth with shallow
sinuses between them mark the margin between the points of the
lobes. The veinlets branch and arch, becoming united near the
margin, and are connected by still finer veinlets which are intricately
meshed. When young, the leaf blades are clothed like the twigs, in
branching, star-shaped, gray or rusty or silvery hairs. In winter the
leaves turn dull yellow or merely brown before falling.

Appearing at the time of the unfolding of the leaves, the minute
flowers are clustered into dense, unisexual, stalked spherical heads, the

male and female heads usually on separate stalks. The male flowers have each a minute calyx divided into 3 to 6 scale-like sepals and 3 to 6 papery petals, the stamens as numerous as the petals and alternate with them. The female flower heads, on long terminal stalks, have each a calyx divided into usually 4 sepals, and show the same number of petals; the ovaries are as many as the divisions of the calyx and are gradually narrowed upward into bright red styles and surrounded at base by a tuft of hairs. In fruit the head of female flowers becomes a "button ball," each nutlet deeply buried among woolly hairs; at the time of the breaking up of the fruiting head at maturity, the nutlets, surrounded by the down, disperse upon the wind.

SYCAMORE

Platanus occidentalis Linnæus

OTHER NAMES: Buttonwood. Buttonball-tree. Plane. Planetree. White-wood. Water Beech. Virginia Maple.

RANGE: Rare and local, but apparently indigenous, in Maine; thence westward at low altitudes across southern New Hampshire and Vermont, New York, southern Ontario, Michigan, in Wisconsin northward to the lower Wisconsin River, southern Iowa, eastern Nebraska and Kansas, south to central parts of Texas, Mississippi, and Alabama and to the Gulf states, but absent from the Appalachians above 2500 feet.

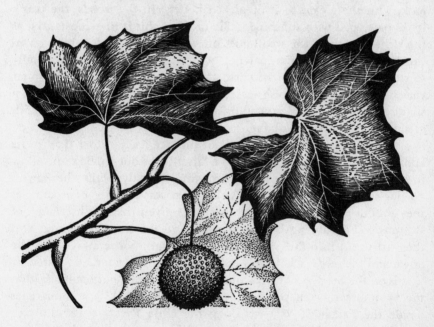

DESCRIPTION: *Bark* flaking off in large, irregular patches, on old trunks deeply furrowed and warty, usually clay-yellow. *Twigs* dark green, thickly downy at first, becoming smooth with small oblong lenticels, turning in first winter lustrous and dark orange-brown and by second summer smoke-gray. *Winter buds* small, nearly surrounded at base by narrow leaf scars. *Leaves* usually 4 to 7 inches long and as broad, sometimes twice as large, thin, firm, and plane, bright green above, paler and woolly beneath. *Flowers* — male flowers borne in leaf axils, dark red; female on long terminal stalks, greenish. *Fruits* "buttonballs" about 1 inch thick on slender, drooping stalks 3 to 6 inches long, with nutlets clothed in downy hairs. *Wood* medium light (35 pounds to the cubic foot, dry weight), hard, tough, difficult to split, fuzzy in texture, with light brown heartwood and thick, pale tan sapwood.

By the beautiful bright smooth bark, the Sycamore is known as far off as the color can be descried; it shines through the tops of the forest even in the depth of summer when the leafy crowns are heaviest. In winter against a stormy sky it looks wonderfully living, amidst all the appearances of lifelessness in other deciduous trees. Yet seen as a snag in the Mississippi, with the bleaching timbers of some wreck piled on it, the white bark looks deader than any other dead tree can look, with the gleam to it of picked bones. In the woods, the trunk looks patterned with sunshine. The cause of this is that constantly, as the swift growth of the wood goes on, the bark keeps sloughing off in thin plates and irregular patches. On close inspection, one usually sees three different colors of bark; the outer light gray and the inner variously pale tan, greenish, or chalky white, but the impression at a slight distance is that of an exquisitely mottled tree, as if dappled with green shade and pale sunlight.

Thus the beauty lies in the body of the tree itself, rather than in its adornments of flowers or foliage; the latter turns but a pale dull yellow in autumn, becoming brown or browning directly, while the flowers do not catch the eye of any but the observant admirer of trees. Yet they produce the curious fruits that have given the tree the name of Buttonwood — hanging balls that persist on the tree over winter and then break up into fluff, when the fruitlets are borne away upon the down and the seeds thus widely distributed both by wind and water.

It is on the borders of rivers and lakes, and in rich bottom-lands, that the Sycamore takes happy root. With the Black Willow it marches beside the Father of Waters; along the Ohio River it was the outstanding riverbank tree of the primeval forest, unsurpassed in picturesque grandeur and in the cooling depth and mighty spread of its shade. Wide groves of it covered the rich bottom-lands, as far as the eye could see up and down the stream, while upon some bend or

promontory of the river, or on some island in its flood, stood forth here and there a Sycamore so gigantic in its girth that the marveling traveler wrote of it half doubting he would be believed. For the Sycamore is, in girth of trunk, the largest deciduous hardwood of North America, and in those early days there were indeed giants in the earth.

To the pioneer the sight of it was welcome, since in general its presence and enormous growth were correctly taken to denote rich soil. However, from its predilection for low grounds, where malaria also was harbored, it often worried the early prospector for lands; well might it be a warning, he felt, of ague, chills and fever. He dreaded, too, its proximity because of the down that grows on the underside of the leaves; to his mind it was this, producing a constant though imperceptible irritation of the lungs, that brought consumption to any rash enough to live beneath it. Though we smile at this, we may find some reason in this distrust of the abundant deciduous hairs upon the leaves, for being at once very light and sharp, they float long in the air and undoubtedly some people are allergic to them.

But in a sturdier day hay fever was the least of a man's problems, and the Sycamore answered many practical ones. Though not strong in the position of a beam or column, and with little resistance to decay, its wood is hard, fairly tough, and almost impossible to split. So the pioneer cut trunks of great dimension into cross-sections which he then bored through the center, to make primitive solid wheels for his ox cart. If the trunk were hollow, as it often was, he sawed it in lengths of three to four feet, nailed a bottom in it, and so had a stout hogshead for grain. As time went on, and American civilization evolved into the sophistication of barber poles and wooden washing machines and lard pails, Sycamore was a favorite for such things. The very broad panels that could be sawed out of Sycamore recommended it for use in Pullman cars — in the days of wooden Pullmans. Stereoscopes used to use immense amounts of Sycamore wood in the days when Americans used immense amounts of stereoscopes! Slats of the ubiquitous Saratoga trunks were commonly of Sycamore, and formerly piano and organ cases and phonograph boxes employed this light-hued wood. Today, though it is used for crates and boxes and in some furniture manufacture, the place you are most likely to see it is at the butcher's, since it can be endlessly hacked without splitting.

So on the block ends a noble once undisputed in the virgin Ohio valley forests! It had great fame, and it had great friends. André Michaux wrote of a Sycamore growing on a little island in the Ohio "the circumference of which, five feet from the surface of the earth . . . was forty feet four inches, which makes about thirteen feet in diameter. . . . Twenty years prior to my travels, George Washington had measured this same tree, and had found it nearly of the same dimensions." And Michaux's own son, François, coming after him in 1802, found an Ohio Sycamore which beat his father's record, "the trunk of which was swelled to an amazing size; we measured it four feet beyond the surface of the soil, and found it forty-seven feet in circumference. By its external appearance no one could tell that the tree was hollow; however, I assured myself it was by striking it in several places with a billet." Most Sycamores over one hundred years old are hollow at the heart, which of course does not prevent the tree from continuing to expand through the years. So it was that pioneers often stabled a horse, cow, or pig in a hollow Sycamore, and sometimes a whole family took shelter in such an hospitable giant, until the log cabin could be raised.

Long before there were any chimneys to send up a twirl of smoke in lonely clearings, these hollow Sycamores were home to the chimney swift — "swallow," as the pioneers often called it. On an evening of July, not far from Louisville, Kentucky, there came to such a tree John James Audubon. "The sun was going down behind the Silver Hills," he remembers, "the evening was beautiful; thousands of Swallows were flying closely above me, and three or four at a time were pitching into the hole, like bees hurrying into their hive. I remained, my head leaning on the tree, listening to the roaring noise made within by the birds as they settled and arranged themselves, until it was quite dark, when I left . . . .

"Next morning I rose early enough to reach the place long before the least appearance of daylight, and placed my head against the tree. All was silent within. I remained in that posture probably twenty minutes, when suddenly I thought the great tree was giving way, and coming down upon me. Instinctively I sprang from it, but when I looked up to it again, what was my astonishment to see it standing as firm as ever. The Swallows were now pouring out in a black continued stream. I ran back to my post, and I listened in amazement to the noise within, which I could compare to nothing else than the sound of a large wheel revolving under a powerful stream. It was yet dusky, so that I could hardly see the hour on my watch, but I estimated the time which they took in getting out at more than thirty minutes. After their departure, no noise was heard within, and they dispersed in every direction with the quickness of thought. . . . "

Not only swallows (swifts, more exactly) loved the Sycamore, but a now-vanished bird of the primeval woods. The men of Long's great expedition to the Rockies noted, as they passed through, that "the fruit of the sycamore is the favorite food of the paroquet, and large flocks of these gaily-plumaged birds constantly enliven the gloomy forests of Ohio." The Carolina paroquet, only member of the parrot family native in the United States, is extinct now, and so are the gigantic Sycamores of the virgin forest. Long ago the great trees were cut down recklessly, to clear the land, to feed the sawmill; the merest shadows of their great dimensions are all that we see today. But nothing of our past is wholly lost that still is treasured in the American saga.

THE APPLES
(*Malus*)

THESE TREES have scaly bark and branches marked with conspicuous ring-like scars of the overlapping bud scales and by the leafstalk scars, which are narrow and horizontal. Alternate and deciduous, the leaves have toothed margins; on flowering shoots the blades are un-lobed, but are more or less lobed or deeply double-toothed on vigorous sucker shoots. The flowers and fruit are borne on much shortened lateral spur-like branches which are sometimes terminated by a short spine. The tube of the calyx is inversely conical, its lobes reflexed in flower but erect on the fruit. The 5 petals are contracted at base into a claw. The stamens are numerous in several rows and inserted on the edge of a conspicuous disk that lines the bottom of the calyx tube. Inferior in position to the calyx, the pistil consists of 5 carpels united at base to form a 5-celled ovary. In the drooping fruit the carpels become the apple core; they are tough, parchment-like, or papery, not bony or nut-like, and contain the acute seeds with their shining brown coats.

WILD SWEET CRAB

Malus coronaria (Linnæus) Miller

OTHER NAMES: Sweet-scented, American, or Fragrant Crab. American Crab Apple. Garlandtree.

RANGE: Western New York through southern Ontario to Missouri, south through Pennsylvania to northern Delaware and along the Appalachians to North Carolina, where it ascends to altitudes of 3300 feet.

DESCRIPTION: *Bark* thin, fissured, with red-brown scales. *Twigs* bright red-brown and flecked with a few small pale lenticels the first winter, becoming stout, spur-like, and often spine-bearing. *Winter buds* with bright-red papery scales and dark hairy margins. *Leaves* 2 to 3 inches long, about 1½ inch wide, yellow-green above, paler below, with prominent midrib, those at the ends of shoots often larger, lobed, and veiny. *Flowers* in few-flowered clusters on long stalks, the blossoms about 1½ inches across; calyx tubes downy, with long slender lobes. *Fruit* yellow-green, about 1 inch long, a little broader. *Wood* medium heavy (44 pounds to the cubic foot, dry weight), not hard or strong, heartwood brown to light red, sapwood thick and yellow.

Long after the orchard Apple trees have come into bloom, the Wild Sweet Crab still stands in its dense thickets on the edges of abandoned fields, along fence rows, behind the moving dunes of the Great Lakes, naked, leafless, dark, secretive, and spiny, as if it intended never to awake to the seduction of spring. Then, when the petals of the culti-vated Apple are falling, this Crab at last puts forth its little new leaves, tinged red and very downy when they unfold from the bud, and at the same time the flowers open swiftly. So swiftly, indeed, that suddenly the dead-seeming thicket seems to burst into bloom upon the naked wood. And what bloom! — petals at first daintily flushed with shell pink, becoming at last pure white, and breathing a fragrance that the wind may carry far. It is an odor like that of Apple blossoms but more tart and wild and more penetrating. Those who have known it in childhood never forget it. It steals out to us from our earliest memories of things that we were wise enough then to consider precious — the bluebird's throaty whistle, the soaring trill of treetoads calling up a spring thunderstorm, the finding of a golden woodpecker's feather and the first wood turtle of the season.

Later in the season every youngster who knows where there are wild crab apples sets his teeth in them, and not even the intense acidity seems to discourage him from trying again and again. For the little pomes are so tempting, the apple odor of their waxy coating so delicious, that he is sure that he must eventually encounter one that is truly ripe. But ripeness in Nature's view of things does not neces-sarily measure up to civilized requirements, and the crab apple is never truly mellow until, at the end of winter, it is pretty well rotted and would be palatable to animals only. Grosbeaks and deer, among others, devour the fruits.

Yet in pioneer times it was common practice to press the crabs for cider, and the early settlers had a high opinion of this drink, though François Michaux, a native of northern France, confided to his diary that he pities the Americans for never having tasted fine Normandy cider. Sometimes still the country farm wife makes jelly of the wild crab, and it is one of the tangiest that ever finds its way to the table.

The Wild Sweet Crab grows from 15 to 30 feet in height, and old trees may have a trunk a foot in diameter. In general the trunk forks at about a foot above the ground in a shrub-like way and, repeatedly forking thereafter, this understory tree makes an intricate, hedge-like, impenetrable growth, a favorite nesting site for song-birds, who appre-ciate the density of the shelter and armament of thorns.

As a cultivated tree this Crab is well named the Garlandtree; the ravishing blossoms are fit, indeed, for the head of a May queen. The early colonists in America planted it by their dooryards just for the sake of its enchanting, innocent odor. When you come upon the tree in the wild, you see it, usually, from afar, shining through the woods like a lovely nymph.

Several varieties and numerous closely related species have been described. Some have the leaf blades much narrower (*Malus lancifolia* Rehder) or with truncate (*Malus glaucescens* Rehder) or heart-shaped (*Malus glabrata* Rehder) bases, and some have fruits markedly flat on the sides, or nearly spherical or distinctly broader than high (*Malus platycarpa* Rehder). All of these are grouped here together as one variable species, since by insensible gradations the most extreme forms merge into each other.

IOWA CRAB

Malus ioensis (Wood) Britton

OTHER NAME: Bechtel Crab

RANGE: Indiana to eastern Nebraska, Missouri, and southeastern Minnesota, and southwestward to Arkansas, eastern Oklahoma, the Edwards plateau of Texas, and south to Louisiana.

DESCRIPTION: *Bark* thin with red-brown scales. *Twigs* somewhat spiny, bright red-brown and marked with a few small pale lenticels. *Leaves* 2½ to 4 inches long, 1 to 1½ inches wide, with slender midrib, thick and firm, the upper surface dark green and shining, the lower pale green and usually downy. *Flowers* in 3- to 6-flowered clusters, 1½ to 2 inches across, on slender downy stalks, the calyx covered with hoary down, with long narrow lobes, the petals white or rose-colored, about ½ inch wide. *Fruit* on stout, downy stalks, greenish yellow when ripe, about 1 inch long and slightly broader.

   This little tree, never more than 30 feet tall, is perhaps the loveliest
of the native American Crab Apples — in flower the fairest and the
most sweetly scented, in fruit, if not the largest, at least the most
fragrant and handsome in color and tempting to the eye. Tingling
though its intense acidity is to the palate, the sharp sweet odor, like
that of apple skins but far more intense, is a bouquet so delicious that
the proper way to eat an Iowa Crab is to carry it about as you tramp
through the autumnal groves of Oak and Hawthorn and Wild Plum,
fingering its waxen smoothness, appreciating its strange greeny-golden
color, and passing it back and forth under your nose, only taking an
occasional cautious nibble — just as one drinks a fine old cognac by
smelling a great deal and sipping just enough to let it volatilize upon
the tongue.
   The Iowa Crab blooms at the same time as the cultivated Apple tree,
but no Apple that grows has such beautiful blossoms, the warmest
pink in the bud, nearly white in full maturity, and a blood-pink as
they fade. The odor alone would justify the frequent cultivation of
this lovely wildling, under the name of Bechtel Crab as the nursery
men like to call a particularly deep-colored variety. Indescribable, the
odor is yet incomparable — not a drugging odor or a honeyed, but
innocent and pervading, flung on the spring air in invisible swirling
ribbons of scent that draw you upwind to the odor, as the bees are
drawn, to find the shining source of this mysterious fragrance. Perhaps
it will never be captured in alcohol and corked up in a bottle — one
hopes, indeed, that it will not — but if it were, the perfume would
probably disappoint us, for like most things in Nature it is bound up

with its setting and association. With the cool, sequestered sound of mourning doves, with the finding of white violets by the slough, with the aching blue of the sky bent in a faultless arc, and the bubbling cricket-like din of spring peepers in the pond.

SOUTHERN CRAB

Malus angustifolia (Aiton) A. Michaux

OTHER NAME: Narrow-leaved Crab.

RANGE: From southeastern Virginia near the coast to western Florida and western Louisiana, inland to the Appalachian foothills.

DESCRIPTION: *Bark* dark reddish brown, furrowed by deep fissures into narrow, scaly ridges. *Twigs* at first palely downy, becoming smooth and by the first winter brown tinged with red, the second year light brown flecked with orange-colored lenticels. *Winter buds* minute, chestnut-brown. *Leaves* 1 to 2 inches long, ½ to ¾ inch broad, dull green, paler beneath. *Flowers* in 2- to 5-flowered clusters, the petals deep pink in bud, becoming white blushed with pink. *Fruits* ¾ to 1 inch in diameter, broader than long, pale yellow-green, with tartly fragrant skin. *Wood* hard, close-grained, and medium-heavy (42 pounds to the cubic foot, dry weight), with heartwood light brown tinged with red and thick yellow sapwood.

These are the little Crab trees that George Washington planted in the shrubberies of "Mount Vernon," and in his diary he speaks with pleasure of their fragrance. It is a tart perfume that, in April when the deep pink buds open into paler bloom, may often be perceived from farther than the tree itself can be seen, shining with feminine grace through the woods. The fruits, too, carry a like tang in their waxy skins. Though so sour and hard on the tree, in the old days they were made into cider or preserved, with plenty of sugar.

Pioneer orchardists often dug up small Crabs in the wild and planted them on the home lands, then grafted on them their Apples. In time, the Apple would cover the entire Crab stock with its own bark, leaving the roots and hidden stock to impart their hardiness to the more tender exotic Apple. This may have been a practice of very early origin, for in 1610 William Strachey, author of *Historie of Travaile into Virginia Britannia*, found this species growing near the Jamestown colony and regarding it suggested: "Crabb trees there be, but the fruict small and bitter, howbeit, being graffed upon, some we might have of our owne apples of any kind, peares, and what ells."

Even left flowering free and unserviceable, as an understory tree of our southern forests, this Crab seems to lend a wild and hardy sweetness to the prosaic modern road that passes by.

THE ROWANTREES
(*Sorbus*)

T REES of this group have smooth bark, the twigs marked by conspicuous ring-like scars of the big bud scales. The alternate leaves are
compound, with an odd number of leaflets which are seated in opposite
pairs directly on the central axis, except for the long-stalked odd one
at the tip of the frond. The flowers are numerous in terminal, broad
flat, leafy clusters, each flower with 20 stamens in 3 rows and usually
3 carpels with 3 styles making up the compound pistil. The small
nearly round pomes are borne erect in broad flat-topped clusters, while
the seeds are enclosed in a core of rather tough carpels and have
shining chestnut-brown coats.

AMERICAN ROWANTREE

Sorbus americana Marshall

OTHER NAMES: Rowantree. Mountain Ash. Mountain Sumac. Winetree.

RANGE: Newfoundland and Quebec, southward to northern Massachusetts, Connecticut, New York, Pennsylvania and Maryland, and on the mountains to North Carolina and Tennessee, westward through Michigan, Wisconsin, Minnesota and Manitoba, rare in northern Illinois and northeastern Iowa.

DESCRIPTION: *Bark* thin, light gray, smooth or slightly scaly. *Twigs* round and stout, red-brown, becoming dark brown and marked by large leaf scars and oblong lenticels. *Winter buds* terminal, dark red with gummy exudations. *Leaves* 6 to 8 inches long in over-all dimensions, with 13 to 17 leaflets, these 2 to 4½ inches long and ¼ to 1 inch wide, thin, dark yellow-green above, paler and sometimes with a bloom beneath. *Flowers* creamy-white, very numerous in flat-topped clusters that are 3 to 4 inches across. *Fruits* ¼ inch in diameter, bright orange-red with thin flesh and pale chestnut-colored seeds. *Wood* medium-light (34 pounds to the cubic foot, dry weight), soft and weak, the heartwood pale brown, the sapwood pale yellowish brown.

The Rowantree in full flower in early summer looks something like an overgrown Elder and lights up with unwonted delicacy the somber aisles of the North Woods. But it is in autumn that this tree comes into its glory, when the big yellow fronds of its foliage are turning a pale clear gold and falling, and the hundreds of shiny red berries — or really little pomes, miniature apples — gleam in the tingling air of a northern Indian summer. Then the little tree — it is seldom more than 25 feet high, with slim trunks and narrow straggling head, a mere understory species — shows itself in true loveliness. Its fruits are the holly of the North Woods, for if the birds do not get them they last all winter. They form, however, an important article in the diet of the sharp-tailed grouse, the blue grouse, and the ptarmigan. Nobody, certainly, but a bird would care to try their intense astringency. But the fragrant inner bark is a staple in the diet of the moose. Your North Woods guides may, indeed, call this tree Missey-moosey, or Moose-miss, or even Indian Mozemize.

In Tennessee the name of Peruve is, or used to be, heard for the Rowantree, and probably this odd word is a reference by analogy to Peruvian bark, that is, the bark of the quinine tree. For any bitter and aromatic bark used to be considered antimalarial, and many were the substitutes — imaginary or real — for quinine, sought and employed by our pioneer ancestors. Probably some of the first of them retained memories of the supernatural associations of the closely related European Rowantree. It was believed to be powerful in exorcising witches and was known as Witchwood. But the witches who crossed the ocean with the first colonists, by stowing away in the heads of certain people, were soon exorcised by the very air and the sky of the New World.

The homeopathic uses that country doctors once had for the astringent inner bark are doubtless forgotten. This lovely little tree, which reaches its greatest perfection north of Lakes Huron and Superior, serves no purpose now but to cheer the unbroken wastes of the forests. Yet one who has seen it there will never forget it; he will remember how, when it flowered, the hermit thrush, the most magical singer of the North Woods, perhaps of the world, was twirling his slow notes in the high clerestory of forest, like some angel in a celestial choir. And how in autumn the berries shone through the changing wood, while the voice of the whitethroat whistled his autumn song — that last farewell to the departing traveler.

THE SHADBLOWS

(*Amelanchier*)

These trees have scaly bark and slender twigs with acute buds, the inner scales bright colored as they enlarge. The leaves, alternate and deciduous, are simple and never lobed or at most only a little doubly toothed. From the axils of slender scales the long flower stalks develop, forming the nodding terminal spike. The calyx tube, cup-shaped, adheres to the ovary, with the lobes reflexed in flower; the petals are 5, long and slender, not clawed at base. There are 20 stamens in 3 rows; the 5-celled ovary bears 2 to 5 styles that are united below. The fruits, little pomes, contain a core of rather soft or papery carpels, and the 5 or 10 seeds bear dark chestnut-brown, leathery, mucilaginous coats.

SHADBLOW

Amelanchier arborea (F. Michaux) Fernald

OTHER NAMES: Shadbush. Serviceberry. Juneberry.

RANGE: Rare in eastern New England, becoming common from the valley of the Connecticut River, westward through New York and southern Ontario to southeastern Minnesota, the eastern parts of Nebraska, Kansas, and Oklahoma, south to tidewater Virginia, thence on the piedmont to northwestern Florida and southwestern Mississippi.

DESCRIPTION: *Bark* shallowly fissured on old trunks, with broad ridges covered with fine scales. *Twigs* at first covered by a dense mat of white hairs, becoming smooth and the first winter bright red-brown, then darker in the second year and flecked with many pale lenticels. *Winter buds* large, green tinged with brown. *Leaves* 1½ to 3 inches long. *Flowers* with long white petals, in conspicuous masses. *Fruit* about ¼ inch thick, maroon-purple, often persisting on the tree through the winter.

In early spring, "when the shad run," according to tradition, Shadblow bursts into flower upon the naked wood, before the leaves appear or when the foliage is still just budding out and covered with silvery down. The contrast, then, of the long, delicate white petals with the bright red of the scales that hang from the flower stalks is vivid, and no daintier flowers than these, in their season, star the forest aisles.

In the South the Shadblow may be little more than a shrub, but in western New York and southern Michigan it may grow to 60 or even 70 feet, the short branches forming a narrow, round-topped head. So pleasing a tree was early noted by the botanically curious in America, among whom one of the chief was that assiduous John Clayton who added to his duties as clerk of the court of Gloucester County those of correspondence with and collection for the great Linnæus, and was the author, too, of the *Flora Virginica* published in 1736. Perhaps owing to his notice of the Shadblow, it was first grown by Archibald Campbell, third Duke of Argyll, at his villa near Hounslow. Horace Walpole called him "the tree mongerer," and the Duke's famous collection of exotic plants was ultimately removed to become the nucleus of Kew Gardens.

To those so minded, such associations come to adorn a tree of our native forests like the delicate and modest plants that grow about its roots.

SARVISSTREE

Amelanchier laevis Wiegand

OTHER NAMES: Sarvissberry. Servicetree. Serviceberry. Shadbush. June-berry.

RANGE: Newfoundland, southern Quebec and Ontario to northern Wisconsin and eastern Minnesota, south to central Iowa, northern Illinois, southern Indiana, Ohio, Pennsylvania and Maryland, thence south on the Appalachians from Virginia to Georgia, ascending to 5550 feet.

DESCRIPTION: *Bark* dark reddish brown and fairly thick, shallowly fissured, broadly ridged, and scaly. *Twigs* reddish brown darkening the first winter and becoming dull gray the second season, flecked with dark lenticels. *Winter buds* as much as 1 inch long, outwardly green tinged with red, the inner scales bright red above the middle. *Leaves* 2 to 2½ inches long and 1 to 1½ inch broad. *Flowers* with long white petals. *Fruit* about ½ inch thick, dark purple or blackish. *Wood* strong, close-grained, very heavy (52 pounds to the cubic foot, dry weight), the heart-wood dark brown tinged with red, the sapwood thick and lighter brown.

While the fruits of the preceding species are inedible, to all bipeds but birds, those of this slender little tree are pleasant enough to find favor sometimes with ever-hungry country youngsters. François Michaux says that in his day the berries appeared in the markets of Philadelphia, but adds that they were bought only by children. It is from the fruits that the Sarvissberry takes its name, for the word is a transformation of the *sorbus* given by the Romans to a related kind of fruit. Sarviss is a good Shakespearean English form of the most classic Latin, whereas Serviceberry is meaningless as a name, or is at least a genteel corruption of an older and more scholarly form.

The wood of the Sarvissberry tree, though it reaches but 20 to 30 feet in height and may indeed be only a shrub, ranks with that of the Persimmon as the heaviest in our northern sylva, or indeed in the United States outside the tropics. It is the fifth hardest of all our woods and it takes a beautiful polish, so that it would be a more valuable cabinet wood than White Oak if only the trees grew large enough for lumbering. But that is like wishing a nymph of the forest might do duty as a sturdy farmwife!

THE HAWTHORNS
(*Cratægus*)

THESE TREES or shrubs have dark scaly bark, and tough, zigzag, slender twigs, marked by pale oblong lenticels and small leaf scars. Thorns are frequent and often long and slender; they are borne below or opposite the leaf, especially on sterile shoots. The winter buds have shining, light brown outer scales and enlarging green or rosy inner scales. The alternate deciduous foliage is simple or on sterile shoots sometimes distinctly lobed. The usually fetid white flowers occur in simple or branched round-topped clusters, the lowest stalks commonly arising from the axils of the uppermost leaves. Inversely conic, the calyx has lobes reflexed in flower. The petals are not clawed at the base; there are 5 to 25 stamens, and the pistil may have 1 to 5 carpels and adheres at base to the calyx tube. The fruit, a pome, contains a nest of as many nutlets as there are styles. Usually the nutlets appear flattened on the two inner faces and are rounded and ridged on the back.

RED HAW

Cratægus mollis (Torrey and Gray) Scheele

OTHER NAMES: Downy Hawthorn. Thorn Apple.

RANGE: Northern Ohio and southwestern Ontario to northern Missouri, eastern South Dakota, eastern parts of Nebraska and Kansas, and south to central Tennessee.

DESCRIPTION: *Bark* light gray, in long close strips. *Twigs* thick, gray, becoming olive and shiny at the tip, with straight, dark chestnut-brown and somewhat shining or dull gray thorns 2 to 3 inches long, or few or none. *Leaves* dull grass-green above, the lower surface with downy wool in the axils of the veins, but otherwise hairless, thickish and firm in texture, 3 to 4 inches long and about as broad, or those on vigorous sucker shoots 5 or 6 inches long and broad, on stalks 2 inches long and often downy and crimson, as is the midrib on the lower surface. *Flowers* in downy, many-flowered, branched clusters, the calyx lobes glandular-toothed; stamens 20 with white anthers fading brownish-pink; styles 4 or 5. *Fruit* in drooping clusters on stout stalks, ¾ to 1 inch in diameter, scarlet, at first downy, becoming finally smooth and sometimes shiny, tipped with the persistent remains of the calyx; flesh yellowish, usually sweet but acidulous and more or less juicy, enclosing the 4 or 5 thin, light-brown, rounded, and obscurely ridged nutlets. *Wood* very heavy (50 pounds to the cubic foot, dry weight), hard and close-grained, but not especially strong, the heartwood light reddish brown, with thin, paler sapwood.

Almost everyone who ever had a midwestern childhood knows about Red Haws. Their tiny apples may be eaten without stint by experimental small boys, from the moment they ripen in early September until the last of them has fallen in late October, and little girls may string them into necklaces, a jewelry better than rubies, since it can be devoured at any time. The Red Haw — Thorn Apple is usually the farmer's name for the tree itself — which has its seeds distributed by all fruit-eating birds and every little wild rodent, comes springing up joyfully along the fence rows and especially in the Oak openings between the tolerant Bur Oaks. Like them it spreads relentlessly out from the woodland upon the prairies, being another forerunner of the encroaching forest itself, forever at war with the great grass lands. When fully grown, a Red Haw may be 40 feet high and 60 feet broad, and its wide-spreading limbs may reach out so far that they rest their tips upon the ground, making a great ball-shaped mass inside of which the farm child finds a roomy house, where she can play at her woman duties.

The leaves burst their buds in midspring, and two weeks later flowering begins when the leaves are half grown, continuing in fine style for a fortnight more. Toward the end of summer the fruit is just beginning to turn a dull crimson with a purplish bloom, and at that time the Hawthorn thickets take on their colorful appearance, which reaches a height in the first and second weeks of autumn, when these trees may be loaded from top to bottom with clusters of bright red fruits. These then begin to fall swiftly; there are none left by the end of the month. During the dropping of the fruit, the leaves have begun to turn color, generally yellow or orange or a coppery hue, rarely dark red or purplish. Leaf fall is apt to be swift, and soon the trees stand quite naked, the bright harvest of pomes scattered in a circle beneath the boughs.

Here they generally lie all winter, for apparently animals prefer them after they have been softened, though children like to eat them from the tree. With respect to their edible quality, they are variable just as apples are. Some are rather dry and tasteless, and others hard and sour. But no apples could be finer than the best specimens of this species, which lack only in size. So Hawthorn fruits are often preserved by farm wives.

A curious circumstance in the germination of this species, and perhaps other kinds of *Cratægus*, is the phenomenon known as after-ripening. It appears that the seeds are not capable of germinating till a high degree of acidity has developed in the embryo. This increase in acidity seems to be aided by low temperatures, so that it is likely that the ripening of the seed goes on upon or in the ground during the winter. The same effect can be produced by removing the seed coat and immersing the kernel in a weak acid solution. Gardeners report that seeds of native species of Hawthorn commonly do not germinate for two or three years; but whether this is true of the same plants under wild conditions is not certain. Apple seeds, too, exhibit after-ripening; it may be said of their seeds that they are "green" or immature when they fall from the tree in the fruit. Apples are more successfully reproduced from the seed by planting outdoors in the winter than by trying to sprout them in the greenhouse with high temperatures. It is the same with this Hawthorn, and it would seem that it simply cannot sprout without a cold winter.

The Red Haw is host to a large number of little creatures. The song sparrow, mourning dove, indigo bunting, yellow warbler, and goldfinch nest, feed, and sing in the Hawthorn groves all summer long. Cattle browse the foliage eagerly, as high as they can reach, and often trim back the young trees severely into a sort of uncouth rustic topiary. The haws are a favorite food of squirrels, and field mice devour and store the seeds. The seeds themselves are digested by the field mice, not voided, but probably many a cache is forgotten or never reclaimed by its little miser, and eventually some seeds in it sprout. Sometimes a tree is completely stripped of its fruits by animals before they are even wholly ripe, causing chagrin to the botanist who may have marked that very tree and collected its flowers and waited patiently for months to collect it in fruit.

It is under the Hawthorn that the pine mouse often passes his obscure life in tunnels around the roots, on the bark of which he nibbles all winter under ground. The round-headed apple borer is a longhorn beetle whose larvae work in the base of the trunk in large groups, pushing their telltale sawdust piles out of their burrows. The larvae of the Tineid moth (*Ornix cratægifolia*) misspend their youth in rolling up the edges of the leaves; leaf-miners, burrowing in the tissues, write little cabalistic letters there, and gallflies make cockscomb galls on the leaves and globular galls on the midribs.

Under the dense shade cast by these old Red Haws grow happily some of the sweetest and most familiar wildflowers of the Middle West

— the tall bluebell, the white snakeroot, touch-me-not, sweet cicely, and the nodding waterleaf. So each Red Haw tree and each grove of Thorn Apples is a little world in itself, and in all the world there is nothing precisely like it — quaint, yet subtle and self-contained.

PILGRIMS' WHITETHORN

Cratægus submollis Sargent

RANGE: Quebec (city) and Montreal to the valley of the Penobscot river and Gerrish Island, Maine, to the eastern coast of Massachusetts, and west through northern New York to southern Ontario.

DESCRIPTION: *Bark* light gray-brown and scaly. *Twigs* smooth, shining, and red-brown, becoming dull ashy, slender, zigzag, with orange lenticels, and slender, bright chestnut-brown, shining spines 2½ to 3 inches long. *Leaves* 3 to 3½ inches long and 2 to 2½ inches wide, thin, dark yellow-green, rough above, pale below and minutely downy, with thick yellow midribs. *Flowers* 1 inch across, in broad, many-flowered, many-branched clusters, the calyx tube white-hairy, and the lobes with stalked red glands; stamens 10, with small, light yellow anthers. *Fruit* in many-fruited clusters, drooping on long, thin, hairy stalks, pear-shaped, ¾ inch long, with bright orange-red lustrous skin marked by pale scattered dots, thin, mealy, dry or rather acid flesh, and 5 nutlets that are rounded or slightly ridged on the back and ⅓ inch long.

This was the first American Hawthorn known to the early colonists, for it grows around Plymouth, Massachusetts. The Pilgrims called it Whitethorn, which is another name for *Cratægus Oxyacantha,* the "May" of old England, or Mayflower, for which their famous ship was named. The Pilgrims' Whitethorn forms a tree up to 25 feet tall, with a trunk sometimes 1 foot thick. With its ascending branches it makes a handsome broad head. The flowers appear in early summer when the leaves are half formed. The fruits are inedible — dry and small.

A closely related Hawthorn is *Cratægus anomala* Sargent, which differs in having rose-colored anthers, the leaves smooth above and the fruit crimson. It forms a bushy tree up to 20 feet in height, and grows on limestone ridges of Quebec, western Vermont, and northern New York State.

SCARLET HAWTHORN

Cratægus pedicellata Sargent

RANGE: Quebec, Ontario, Vermont, and Massachusetts, south to Tennessee and west to Michigan and Illinois.

DESCRIPTION: *Bark* scaly and ruddy brown. *Twigs* slender, at first dark chestnut-brown, thorns about 2 inches long. *Leaves* 3 to 4 inches long, 2 to 3 inches broad, thin, dark green and rough above, paler below, the stalks with minute glands. *Flowers* in lax, drooping, many-flowered clusters, the blossom ½ inch across, with coarsely glandular-toothed calyx lobes, 5 to 10 stamens bearing pink or rose anthers, and 5 styles. *Fruit* drooping on long, bright red stalks, shiny and bright scarlet, flecked with many dark dots, ½ inch thick or a little more, the calyx persistent on the fruit, much enlarged; flesh dry and mealy, thin and nearly white, containing 5 sharp, grooved nutlets.

Linnaeus, father of botany, would be astounded to know that a thousand species of *Cratægus* have been described from North America, where he knew of only three. This Hawthorn was one of the three of which he received specimens, in far-off Upsala, the university where

he taught in Sweden. Loving brevity, he described this species in just as few words as he could, to distinguish it from the other two American Hawthorns which he knew, and referred, in publication, to a picture in an older author's book. This should make everything perfectly clear, one would think, yet the description is *so* brief it might fit fifty species as we know them now, and it does not tally with the heterogeneous specimens in his herbarium, nor does either agree with the picture! So the old Linnaean species, which he named *Cratægus coccinea,* meaning Scarlet Hawthorn, had to be dropped as a hopeless confusion, and a new name, the earliest of the many synonyms, was adopted.

By whatever name you call it, Scarlet Hawthorn is an attractive little tree, reaching about 25 feet in height, with a trunk as much as 1 foot thick, forming a symmetrically rounded crown. The flowers bloom in midspring when the leaves are about one third grown. The fruits ripen early in autumn.

Cratægus Pringlei Sargent, is a related species, with the dull red fruit on stout stalks, and oval leaves drooping on the stem and conspicuously concave. It is found from New Hampshire and western Massachusetts to Connecticut, southern Ontario, Michigan, and northern Illinois.

Cratægus Holmesiana Ashe, differs from *Cratægus pedicellata* in having 5 to 7 stamens with dark reddish-purple anthers and crimson fruit. It ranges from Quebec to Pennsylvania, Ontario, northern Illinois and Wisconsin.

EGGERT HAWTHORN

Cratægus coccinoides Ashe

OTHER NAME: Eggert's Thorn.

RANGE: From southern Illinois and St. Louis, Missouri, to eastern Kansas, and south to Washington County, Arkansas.

DESCRIPTION: *Bark* scaly, dark brown. *Twigs* stout, nearly straight, bright chestnut-brown and very shiny, armed with thick, dark-reddish-purple, shining spines 1½ to 2 inches long. *Leaves* 2½ to 3 inches long and 2 to 2½ inches wide, thin, firm, and stiff, dull dark green above, lower surface paler, with thin pale midrib. *Flowers* large, in dense 5- to 7-flowered clusters; stamens 20 with large, deep rose-colored anthers and 5 styles. *Fruits* in few-fruited, compact, erect clusters on stout stalks, dark crimson, very shiny and marked with large pale dots, ¾ inch long and ⅞ of an inch in diameter, with the calyx much enlarged, erect, and spreading on the tip of the fruit; the flesh thick, acidulous, firm, and reddish; nutlets 5, about ⅓ inch long.

This is an exceptionally beautiful species. True, it only grows about 20 feet high at the most, but the flowers are perhaps the largest in the entire genus, and the big, bright, shiny pomes load the tree in

October with glory. They persist for a month or six weeks, falling gradually, and as they go, the foliage takes on the most brilliant tones of scarlet and orange.

A closely related species is the New London Hawthorn (*Cratægus dilatata* Sargent) which differs in having smaller flowers in loosely 6- to 12-flowered clusters and drooping bright scarlet fruit flecked with numerous small dark dots. The New London Thorn is native from eastern Massachusetts and the coast of Rhode Island to Albany, New York, to Montreal, and western Vermont. It is especially abundant in Connecticut.

VARIABLE HAWTHORN

Cratægus macrosperma Ashe

RANGE: Nova Scotia and Quebec to Minnesota and Illinois, and south in the Appalachians to Georgia and Alabama.

DESCRIPTION: *Bark* dark gray, scaly, separating into plates, sometimes exposing the yellow inner bark. *Twigs* stout, flexible, armed with numerous curved, blackish brown or grayish spines 1 to 3 inches long. *Leaves* 1 to 3 inches long, and almost as broad, dark yellow-green above, and hairless, the teeth tipped with black glands, the leafstalks very slender. *Flowers* in 5- to 10-flowered clusters, the blossoms about ½ inch across, with 5 to 20 stamens bearing pink or purplish anthers, and 3 or 4 styles. *Fruit* drooping, scarlet, sometimes with a bloom, about ½ inch thick, the flesh soft, containing 3 or 4 nutlets having a sharp keel on the inner face.

There is nothing about this little tree to tell the layman why botanists should have lost their heads with species-making, wherever they encountered it over its wide range. But, as you nibble at its edible little apples, you may find food for thought too in the knowledge that Messrs. Sargent, Ashe, and Beadle were able to make about 70 species grow where none at all had grown before. The purpose of all this? The layman would be inclined to hazard that it was to give Messrs. Eggleston, Britton, and Palmer the pleasure of reducing all

those species back to one! That, at any rate, is what has fortunately happened, but the name that botanists were bound — by the rules of the game of nomenclature — to accept was not particularly appropriate but merely the first given. Admittedly this is a variable species, with a number of valid varieties, but it is no more variable than the common Apple. Think how many new species there would be if we gave Latin names to the Baldwins, Jonathans, Grimes Goldens, Winesaps, and all the others!

Cratægus basilica Beadle, the Alder Hawthorn, differs from the above in having drooping fruit and hairless flower stalks. It ranges from Vermont and New York to the mountains of South Carolina.

GROVE HAWTHORN

Cratægus lucorum Sargent

RANGE: Northern Illinois and southern Wisconsin, also Vermont and New York State.

DESCRIPTION: *Bark* reddish brown and close. *Twigs* at first dark green, then dull brown, finally dark gray-brown, armed with shiny red-brown spines 1 to 1½ inches long. *Leaves* about 2 inches long, 1¼ inches wide, thin, smooth, dark dull green on the upper surface, pale yellow-green below with thin yellow midrib, the teeth tipped with bright red glands, the leafstalks slender, glandular. *Flowers* in compact, narrow, small downy clusters, the blossoms ¾ inch across, the calyx lobes coarsely glandular-toothed, the stamens 20 with small dark purple anthers, the styles 4 or 5. *Fruit* borne erect on short stout stalks, shiny, crimson, about ½ inch long with thick, dry, yellow flesh and 4 or 5 thin, rounded nutlets.

As you travel from Chicago toward Madison, Wisconsin, through fertile, pleasant country half prairie and half woodland, Hawthorns of bewilderingly many species are the smallest but sometimes the commonest trees that you will see. If you stop and enter the odd little Thorn forests that encircle the tall groves of Oak and Hickory and invade the prairie, you will find that one of the commonest of them, the Grove Hawthorn, makes a fine tree 20 to 25 feet tall, with a straight trunk and slender, ascending branches that form a narrow head. You can distinguish it from almost any other Hawthorn you will see there by the fact that the fruits are borne erect, not drooping.

Formerly Grove Thorn was thought to be a purely local species; it was described in the great rush of species-making in this genus that came about 20 and 30 years ago. But careful studies since that time have shown that a number of eastern species are later synonyms of this one. As a result, we now know that the Grove Hawthorn is common in parts of central New York State and occurs also in Vermont. Tree students of southern Ontario, of Ohio, and of Michigan should watch for it, for in all likelihood it will be found there too.

FROSTED HAWTHORN

Cratægus pruinosa (Wendland) K. Koch

OTHER NAME: Waxy-fruited Thorn.

RANGE: Southwestern Vermont to Ontario and northern Illinois, south through eastern Pennsylvania to Delaware.

DESCRIPTION: *Twigs* slender, at first bright chestnut, then dark reddish brown, furnished with light chestnut-brown thorns 1 to 1½ inches long. *Leaves* 1½ to 3 inches long, 2 to 2½ inches broad, rather thick, with glandular teeth, dark blue-green, and often with a bloom on the upper surface. *Flowers* in few-flowered clusters on long, slender stalks, the blossom 1 inch across, with calyx lobes finely glandular-toothed below the middle; stamens 20 with big rose-colored anthers; styles 5. *Fruit* drooping on long, thin, bright red stalks, in few-fruited clusters, at first green and appearing heavily waxy or frosted, at length bright shining red, with thick, light-yellow flesh and 5 deeply grooved nutlets acute at tip, rounded at base.

One of the many Hawthorns that love the limestone soil, the Frosted Hawthorn, forming a compact bushy tree 15 to 20 feet tall, is fond of associating with its own kind in little dense thickets where the flowers in midspring, appearing when the leaves are half developed, quite cover the boughs with generous bloom. Not until late October are the fruits ripe, but by then the frosted appearance which gives this plant its name has disappeared, for it is a characteristic only of the "green" fruit.

Very similar is a related species, *Cratægus rugosa* Ashe, which differs in its broader leaves and somewhat larger flowers and fruit. It is found in thickets, pastures, and borders of woods, usually in well-drained soil, from New York to Iowa, southward to North Carolina and Missouri.

Cratægus filipes Ashe, is a related species of the Connecticut Valley and New York State, having 7 to 10 anthers and erect fruits.

GREENTHORN

Cratægus viridis Linnæus

OTHER NAME: Tree Haw.

RANGE: Eastern Texas to Florida, north on the coastal plain to Virginia, and in the Mississippi valley to Missouri and Illinois.

DESCRIPTION: *Bark* very thin and scaly, with large plates which peel off to reveal the cinnamon-colored inner bark. *Twigs* ashy gray to light red-brown, unarmed or with only a few short, slender, sharp, pale spines. *Leaves* 1 to 2 inches long and half as wide, dark green and shining above, paler below with tufts of hair in the axils and thin midrib. *Flowers* in many-flowered clusters, the corolla ¾ inch across, the stamens 20 with pale yellow anthers, the styles 2 to 5. *Fruit* small, ⅛ to ¼ inch thick, drooping, on long slender stalks in many-fruited clusters, bright scarlet or orange, with 5 minute nutlets.

In the broad river-bottoms of western Louisiana the Greenthorn forms thickets of vast extent, rising 25 and even 35 feet in height — higher, perhaps, than any other Hawthorn — and early in March the trees fume with blossoms, as fair as ever wild Plum, wild Cherry, or Crab Apple. Flowering does not take place in Missouri until May. But lovely as the flowers are, more gorgeous still is the brilliant scarlet of late autumnal foliage. Sargent in his *Silva of North America* asserts that it is the finest on the continent, and, as we have the most splendid of all autumns, that should make Greenthorn's foliage the most brilliant in the world. The bright scarlet fruits, though little, make a brave show, too, and persist on the naked tree all winter.

In view of the fact that the Greenthorn is a tree of the interior of our continent, it is remarkable that it is one of the three North American Hawthorns known to Linnaeus when he published his great *Species Plantarum* in 1753. This is explained by the fact that John Clayton, clerk of the court of the quaint old town of Gloucester in Virginia, found Greenthorn growing somewhere in the tidewater country near Norfolk (which is its northeasternmost extension) and sent it to the great Swedish botanist for identification.

SHINING HAWTHORN

Cratægus nitida (Engelmann) Sargent

RANGE: Western Illinois, eastern Missouri, and Arkansas.

DESCRIPTION: *Bark* of close plate-like dark brown scales. *Twigs* slender, at first shiny orange-brown, becoming pale reddish brown, then gray, unarmed or furnished with a few short, thin, shiny chestnut-brown spines. *Leaves* 2 to 3 inches long, half as broad, thick and leathery, the upper surface dark green and shining, the lower pale and dull with a prominent red midrib. *Flowers* in mid-spring, opening when the leaves are almost grown, in many-flowered, broad, compound clusters, the blossom ¾ inch across, with 15 to 20 stamens having pale yellow anthers, and 2 to 5 styles. *Fruit* drooping on long slim stalks in many-fruited clusters, about ½ inch long and ⅓ inch thick, covered with a heavy frosted bloom and containing 2 to 5 light-colored nutlets that are rounded or ridged on the back.

Every ardent student of trees, when he knows he is going to new country, makes a study of the species that he expects to find there. He reads all about them and tries from descriptions and pictures to fix them in mind, so that he will recognize them when he sees them. The Shining Hawthorn, confined to the middle reaches of the Mississippi valley, growing to a height of 30 feet in rich bottom-land, with a straight tall trunk a foot and a half thick, is a tree worth watching for, since it is a rare beauty — rarely beautiful and rare in the experience of most people. Its northernmost outpost appears to be the little town of Hannibal, Missouri, famous as the birthplace of Samuel Clemens and the home town of his immortal Tom Sawyer and Huckleberry Finn. But it grows too in the old French settlements like Ste. Genevieve and Cape Girardeau. Or you can see it on the Mississippi bottom-lands near St. Louis.

The best time of year to visit that region, on all counts, is Indian summer, which comes in late October. Then the Shining Hawthorn, a tree of comely shape, is seen in all the splendor of its red and orange and bronze foliage. The fruit is not really brilliant, a dull brick-red overcast with a soft bluish-white bloom — but it loads the tree with its wild harvest. Because of its striking loveliness, Shining Hawthorn is becoming a favorite in cultivation, with those who appreciate our native plant material, and has proved perfectly hardy at the Arnold Arboretum in eastern Massachusetts.

MARGARET HAWTHORN

Cratægus Margaretta Ashe

RANGE: Western Pennsylvania and Ontario to Michigan and Iowa, south to Missouri and Tennessee.

DESCRIPTION: *Bark* dark gray-brown and thin. *Twigs* slender, orange-green, becoming shiny chestnut-brown and at length gray, almost unarmed or again furnished with bright chestnut-brown thorns about 1½ inch long. *Leaves* about 1¼ inch long and almost as broad, rather leathery, dark green and shining above, pale below with yellow midrib, the leafstalks slender and beset with dark red glands. *Flowers* in 3- to 12-flowered clusters, the blossom ¾ inch across, the calyx lobes finely gland-toothed, the stamens 20 with small bright yellow anthers, the styles 2 or 3. *Fruit* in few-fruited, drooping clusters, ½ inch long and dark red or rusty orange-red; with thin, dry, mealy, yellow flesh enclosing 2 or 3 nutlets that are acute at one end, broad at the other, and prominently ridged and grooved on the back.

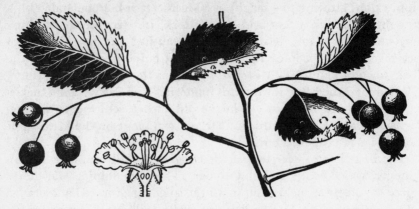

Sometimes 25 feet high, this tree grows on rocky slopes, sandy or gravelly moraines, pastures and thickets, and borders of woods. It was named by its discoverer Mr. William Ashe, of Forest Service, for Mrs. Margaret Wilcox of North Carolina, who later became Mrs. Ashe and had more species of trees named for her, by this prolific species maker, than any other woman in history. In fact, Mr. Ashe described so many species of trees that other botanists were incredulous. Some of them are undoubtedly valid, yet when his private collection, which was usually inaccessible in Mr. Ashe's lifetime, was at last examined, it did not contain type specimens for all his many published species, so that many of them must remain enigmatic.

ROUNDLEAF HAWTHORN

Cratægus chrysocarpa Ashe

RANGE: Newfoundland and Nova Scotia and southern Quebec to Saskatchewan, south to Colorado in the Rockies, to Nebraska, central Minnesota, northern Illinois, northern Indiana, eastern Pennsylvania, and south in the mountains to North Carolina and Tennessee.

DESCRIPTION: *Bark* scaly, dark reddish brown. *Twigs* slender, at first light green, then red-brown and shiny, finally ashy gray, beset with numerous stout, shiny chestnut-brown thorns 1 to 1½ inches long. *Leaves* 1½ to 2 inches long, 1 to 1½ inches wide, thick, dark green and shiny above, paler below with thin midrib and 4 or 5 pairs of veins running almost straight to the points of the lobes, the teeth tipped with minute dark glands. *Flowers* ¾ inch across, in many-flowered, broad, branched clusters, the calyx lobes coarsely gland-toothed, the stamens 10 with small pale yellow anthers, the styles 3 or 4. *Fruit* ½ inch thick, drooping on short, strong stalks, dark crimson flecked with pale dots, and tipped with the enlarged bright red calyx lobes; flesh yellow and sweet, but thin and not juicy; nutlets 3 or 4, rounded at the ends.

There has never been a satisfactory definition of a tree which will distinguish it clearly from a shrub. If we insist that a tree is a woody growth which has a single trunk, not forking from the very base, then Willows a hundred feet high would sometimes be shrubs! If we require that a tree be over a certain height — say, 20 feet — then we must declare that a plant of woody growth 19½ feet high is a shrub, while if it grew 6 inches taller it would be a tree. Fortunately most trees are trees, and no doubt about it, but amongst the Hawthorns there is doubt in fully half the cases, and this is one of them. But we can say, at least, that Roundleaf Hawthorn very commonly forms a handsome round-topped bushy tree up to 25 feet tall. The leaves are about half formed before the flowers open in late spring; the fruit is ripe by August in the north, and by October farther south.

Cratægus Jonesæ Sargent, is common along the rocky shores of sounds and bays on the coast of Maine, New Brunswick, and parts of Quebec. It differs from the above in rose-colored anthers and carmine-red fruit.

BOYNTON HAWTHORN

Cratægus Boyntonii Beadle

RANGE: Nothern Georgia and Alabama to Kentucky, New York, and Vermont; ascends in the southern Appalachians to 3000 feet.

DESCRIPTION: *Twigs* green at first, then light orange-brown and smooth and shiny, finally grayish, armed with numerous brown thorns 1½ to 2 inches long. *Leaves* 1 to 2½ inches long, thick, smooth, the upper

surface yellow-green, the lower pale, the stalks beset with light red glands. *Flowers* in midspring when the leaves are almost half grown, in compact, 4- to 10-flowered clusters, ¾ inch across. *Fruit* dark-dotted, in erect, few-fruited clusters, ½ inch thick, with 3 to 5 nutlets embedded in the unpalatable flesh.

Most of our Hawthorns prefer the great limestone areas of the Middle West, but the Boynton Hawthorn accepts the sterile granite of the Blue Ridge and the mountains of western New England. It grows in open woods and borders of fields, and because of its comely shape it is tolerated around the farm dooryard. Boynton Hawthorn blooms in midspring when the leaves are half grown. In autumn the foliage turns yellow or brown.

WASHINGTON THORN

Cratægus Phænopyrum (Linnæus the Younger) Medicus

OTHER NAMES: Virginia or Maple-leaved Hawthorn.

RANGE: Mountain valleys from the upper Potomac to Georgia and Alabama, Missouri and Arkansas, and southeastern Illinois along the Wabash. Widely naturalized as an escape from cultivation.

DESCRIPTION: *Bark* light brown, thin, smooth or finally scaly. *Twigs* zig-zag, shiny, smooth, and light brown, armed with sharp, spreading spines 1½ to 2 inches long. *Leaves* about 2 inches long and almost as broad, thin, firm, the upper surface dark green and shiny, the lower pale, with orange veins, the teeth gland-tipped. *Flowers* on slender branching stalks in many-flowered hairless clusters, the stamens 20, with rose anthers, the styles 2 to 5. *Fruit* small (1/4 inch thick), scarlet and shining, with 3 to 5 narrow, sharp, minute nutlets. *Wood* red-brown with thick paler sap-wood, hard, close-grained, very heavy (45 1/2 pounds per cubic foot, dry weight).

Of all the Hawthorns of America, and there are hundreds of them, this is by all means the daintiest, with its brilliant little fruits drooping and bobbing on the stalks, and the finely cut-leaved, three-lobed foliage. Its slender, upright branches form an elegant small tree, the head narrow or sometimes rounded. Clipped into hedges, it is responsive to topiary effects, and even the spines, drawn out to needle-fine points and cruelly pungent, add to its exclusiveness.

Washington Thorn must have been remarked for its charms at a very early date, for it was first described to science in 1691, from garden specimens which had been growing in England we know not how long. Thus some unknown or forgotten botanical explorer must have brought this tree out of the Appalachian wilderness and cherished it on the long voyage home. At a later date it became popular in cultivation around Washington, D.C., and thence it was brought, under the name of Washington Thorn, to historic Chester County in Pennsylvania, where it was more cultivated for hedges than any other plant. Today it is almost forgotten in American gardens, but in foreign countries it is not without honor, being highly appreciated by horticulturists in Germany, France, and England.

The flowers, in the northern states, open in the last days of May after the leaves are fully grown. Very late in the autumn, after most trees have dropped their leaves, the Washington Thorns at length turn bright scarlet and orange; when they fall, they reveal the tree laden with its dainty freight of fruits. Until the snow flies, these retain their color; then, dun and sodden, they cling on until the spring.

FLAT–TOPPED HAWTHORN

Cratægus punctata Jacquin

OTHER NAME: Dotted Haw.

RANGE: Montreal and westward through Ontario and southern Michigan to southern Wisconsin, southeastern Minnesota, central Iowa, northern Illinois, northern and eastern Indiana, and southward through western New England and New York to Delaware, and along the Appalachians to northern Georgia at high altitudes.

DESCRIPTION: *Bark* gray, closely flaky, the inner bark yellowish, showing through the cracks of the outer bark. *Twigs* slender, dull olive-green, mostly erect or ascending on the horizontal branches, with very slender gray spines 1½ to 2½ inches long. *Leaves* 2 to 3 inches long and ¾ to

1½ inches wide with broad and prominent midnerve, the upper surface grass-green, slightly shiny, with impressed nerves, paler and veiny beneath, with short, broadly winged stalks, those on sucker shoots much larger and lobed. *Winter buds* with long, conspicuous red scales. *Flowers* in 5- to 20-flowered broad, branched clusters, the blossoms ½ to ¾ inch across, small, with long, slender calyx lobes which are green and not toothed nor glandular; stamens 20, with rose-colored or pale yellow anthers; styles 3 or 4. *Fruit* drooping on long stalks, large (1 inch long), the skin dull brick-red to deep garnet-red or dull yellow, flecked with small dots, the flesh green, hard, and acid until ripe; nutlets 3 or 4, about ¼ inch long. *Wood* hard, very heavy (48 pounds to the cubic foot, dry weight), the heartwood bright red-brown, the sapwood thick and pale.

From Montreal almost throughout the Great Lakes basin and the upper Mississippi valley, the North American continent is covered by a vast geological stratum known as the Niagara limestone, giving rise above it to particularly fertile, deep, dark soils. So this was a region which, when it was not already prairie, was soon stripped of its primeval forests to make way for a rich agriculture, as well as the great industrial population naturally centered along the Great Lakes. As the overshadowing virgin woods were cut down, there emerged from them a little understory tree which may not have been especially important before the coming of the white man. But today the Flat-topped Hawthorn, over all this area, is frequently the commonest species of its genus, and not seldom is this the dominant tree. It is certainly so in many sections around Niagara Falls, southern Ontario, northern Illinois, and southern Wisconsin.

Flat-topped Hawthorn may grow 20 or 30 feet high, with a trunk as much as a foot in diameter, but under field conditions is usually 18 to 20 feet tall, and its long, almost horizontally spreading or gradually ascending branches give it a broadly flat-topped appearance which is unmistakable in the landscape, resembling little else in our sylva and reminding one, rather, of those Thorn trees (Acacias) which one sees in pictures of the savannas of central Africa, usually with a herd of giraffes browsing among them.

But central North America, too, has its thorn forest, though even ecological botanists often neglect to point it out. For around all the great Oak and Hickory groves of the Chicago area, for instance, there is always a ring of thorny trees of smaller stature than the members of the true groves. This thorn forest consists in Crab Apple, wild Plums,

cultivated Pears and Apples which have gone back to the wild and developed thorniness, in thorny English Buckthorn which has become naturalized, brambles and, predominantly, the many kinds of Hawthorn. The two leading Hawthorns there are the dome-shaped Red Haw (*Cratægus mollis*) and the present species.

No tree is more active than this in invading the prairie. Its pioneers may be seen far out ahead of the groves of other trees, those nearest the groves grown full size, and so on, in descending steps, until on the farthest periphery of the encroaching woodland there are hundreds of little seedlings only a few inches high. And if no stately giraffes are seen browsing upon them, dairy cows do so abundantly, despite the armory of thorns.

The flowers are very late in blooming — not till well into June in the latitude of Chicago — and the fruits do not ripen until late October, and even then are not edible. They are sour, hard, and gummy to the palate, up to the moment when they suddenly become dry, soft, mealy, and tasteless. But animals are less demanding than we, and the birds and rodents devour the fruits abundantly in the spring, after the little pomes have been frost-bitten and rain-soaked. This seems to be Nature's form of cookery, bringing the fruits to the taste of animal epicures all in good time. It is likely that a process of after-ripening goes on with the seeds of this species, just as described for the Red Haw.

The same birds love to nest among the Flat-topped Hawthorns as those mentioned for the Red Haw, and the same fox squirrels hop among the boughs, and pine mice burrow about the roots, devouring the bark. The stems of this species are apparently the favorite for the apple borer, a beetle whose larva gives great trouble to orchardists. It makes gall-like swellings in the stems of this tree and these thus become a permanent locus of infection for Apples. In fact, the apple grower has a long list of just grievances against this Hawthorn, so long and grave that the lover of our native trees prefers to forget it, and to remember, rather, that this little tree is one of the most picturesque in all our sylva, striking at all times of the year but especially so in autumn when the heavy crops of fruit are on the tree and the leaves are turning bronze, gradually becoming clear gold, or sometimes deep claret red.

A closely related species, the Sandhill or Foothill Thorn (*Cratægus collina* Chapman), is distinguished by the fact that its fruit is spherical or nearly so instead of being short-oblong, and that the stalks of the fruit and flower clusters are densely woolly. It ranges through the southern Appalachians from Virginia to Georgia and central Alabama above 2500 feet.

COCKSPUR THORN

Cratægus Crus-galli Linnæus

OTHER NAMES: Newcastle or Pine Thorn. Thorn Plum.

RANGE: Montreal south to Delaware, along the Appalachian foothills to Asheville, west to Minnesota and Arkansas.

DESCRIPTION: *Bark* dark brown and scaly. *Twigs* light brown or gray and armed with stray chestnut-brown or gray spines 3 to 4 inches long. *Leaves* 1 to 4 inches long, ¼ to 1 inch wide, on short stalks, toothed only above the middle, thick leathery, dark green and shining above, pale below, with prominent meshed veinlets, the midrib and principal nerves concealed within the tissue of the leaf. *Flowers* numerous, in much-branched clusters ⅔ inch across, stamens 10, with rose or pale creamy white anthers; styles 2. *Fruit* drooping, ½ inch long, dull red often covered with a bloom; nutlets 2 or rarely 1, plump, blunt, prominently ridged in the back.

All the year round Cockspur Thorn makes a fine display. In spring the young leaves wear a vivid blush, and by May a wealth of flowers covers this little tree on every bough, rivaling the English May itself. After they have faded, the leathery glittering leaves impart, all summer, an appearance of garden-like formality; in autumn they turn bright orange or deep garnet-red, and when they fall each twig is laden with the pomes that gleam through the snow itself (for birds do not seem to eat the fruit in winter) until spring comes again.

Sometimes 25 feet tall, in the rich soil of wooded hillsides where it delights to grow, the Cockspur Thorn in gardens is trimmed into the form of a hedge, and was so used even in colonial times. With its fierce thorns and intricate twigs, it is impenetrable and has found more favor as a garden subject than any other American Hawthorn.

Engelmann's Hawthorn (*Cratægus Engelmannii* Sargent) is a related species, differing in having the leaves, twigs, and flower stalks distinctly downy, the leaf blades only 1 to 1½ inches long, and the fruit bright orange-red. It is found on dry limestone ridges from the neighborhood of St. Louis, Missouri, south to Kentucky and Arkansas.

Cratægus algens Beadle, is closely related to Cockspur Thorn, but has yellow anthers, veiny leaves with blades only somewhat leathery and only 1½ to 2 inches long, and very small fruits dull red, or green flushed with red. It is found in fields and borders of woods around Asheville, North Carolina, and thence to northern Georgia, central Alabama, and eastern Tennessee.

PEAR HAWTHORN

Cratægus Calpodendron (Ehrhart) Medicus

OTHER NAME: Sugar Haw.

RANGE: New York State and Ontario to Minnesota and Arkansas, and south to the mountains of Georgia.

DESCRIPTION: *Bark* smooth and pale gray, or dark brown, flaky and
furrowed, the trunk often armed with triple spines. *Twigs* slender, at
first hoary, then dark orange, finally ashy gray, mostly without spines, or
with occasional spines 1 to 1½ inches long, straight, dull gray-black and
slender. *Leaves* thin, dark dull green above, downy below, at least on
the nerves, with wavy margins, on long wavy-margined stalks. *Flowers*
in 16- to 60-flowered, many-branched, downy clusters, very small, the
calyx lobes toothed and downy, not glandular; stamens 20, the anthers
white or rose; styles 2 or 3. *Fruits* erect, small, dull, light red with the
calyx lobes spreading and persistent, the flesh thin, dry, and mealy, enclosing two nutlets each with deep cavities on their inner faces.

The Pear Hawthorn is a tree about 20 feet tall, with a trunk about
½ foot thick, at the most, its slender spreading or nearly horizontal
branches forming a wide, rather flat crown. The flowers bloom in
early summer when the leaves are practically full grown. The little
fruits, too small for eating, are early deciduous from the tree, or
gobbled by birds, well before the leaves turn brilliant orange or
scarlet. Pear Hawthorn grows by the banks of streams, in prairie
groves and open forests.

Chapman's Hawthorn, *Cratægus Chapmanii* (Beadle) Ashe, differs
in having 5 to 10 stamens, and fruits bright orange-red in drooping
clusters. It is found in the Appalachians from Virginia to Georgia and
in southeastern Missouri.

Cratægus succulenta Schrader, is a relative of the Pear Thorn, having leathery leaves, 10 to 20 stamens with rose-colored anthers, and succulent fruit. It grows from Massachusetts to southern Ontario and northern Illinois and Pennsylvania. It has very thorny twigs and a bushy habit of growth.

BRAINERD HAWTHORN

Cratægus Brainerdi Sargent

RANGE: Quebec and New Hampshire to Pennsylvania, Wisconsin, and Iowa.

DESCRIPTION: *Twigs* dark chestnut-brown becoming ashy gray, flecked with long pale lenticels and armed with slender spines 1 to 2½ inches long. *Leaves* 1½ to 3½ inches long, ¾ to 2½ inches broad, bright green above, downy on the veins beneath. *Flowers* ¾ inch across, in hairless clusters, the stamens 5 to 20, with pink anthers, the styles 2 to 4. *Fruit* drooping, scarlet or cherry red, ½ inch thick; nutlets 2 to 4, with shallow pits on their inner faces.

One of the things that has caused the greatest perplexity to everyone who has ever tried to identify a Hawthorn is the way in which the various species hybridize. The progeny of these hybrids then hybridize again, and so on through untold generations, creating the most bewildering mixtures of traits. Before this was realized, eager botanists had described innumerable species based on what seemed like new forms, sometimes in their zeal for accuracy describing a single tree so minutely that the description actually fits no other in the world! When the realization that a vast number of specimens of Hawthorn are really hybrids began to circulate in the scientific fraternity, almost all species were thrown into doubt, for who could pronounce offhand which was a true or pure species, and which a hybrid? Worse, many of the hybrids proved a very temporary lot, not reproducing themselves in the least. Yet there are certain species of Hawthorn which, though they look like hybrids, exactly combining the features of two other well-known subgenera, nevertheless faithfully reproduce themselves in large numbers over a great range. So, having all the fixity of good species, they may be credited as such.

Such a one is the Brainerd Hawthorn. It has the thin, deeply cut leaves of the *macrosperma* group, and the pits on the inner faces of the nutlets of the Pearthorn group. It is found in light woods, on steep rocky banks and open groves, and forms a tree or very tall intricate shrub up to 20 feet high. The flowers bloom in midspring, and the fruit ripens and falls promptly in September. In taste it is mealy or succulent, but very acid.

THE PLUMS AND CHERRIES

(*Prunus*)

The members of this group have astringent bark and simple alternate leaves, which in our species are deciduous. The flowers occur in spikes or branched and round-topped clusters, from buds borne separately from those of the leaf. The petals are usually clawed, and the stamens number 15 to 30, in 2 or 3 rows. There is a single ovary which is free from and superior in position to the calyx, and a single style. The fruit is a 1-seeded drupe, that is, a bony stone or nut filled with the seed, and enclosed in flesh and an outer skin.

CANADA PLUM

Prunus nigra Aiton

OTHER NAME: Horse Plum.

RANGE: Western New Brunswick to the southern shore of Georgian Bay, the northern shore of Lake Superior, west to the valley of the Winnipeg in Manitoba, southward to northern New England, western and central New York, southern Michigan, central Indiana, northeastern Illinois, southern and western Wisconsin.

DESCRIPTION: *Bark* very thin, light gray-brown, very smooth, the outer layers peeling away in papery plates and falling to display the darker inner bark. *Twigs* stout, bright green, at first marked by numerous pale warts, becoming dark brown tinged with red, spur-like and often tipped with a stout spine. *Winter buds* chestnut-brown. *Leaves* 3 to 5 inches long, 1½ inches wide, firm and thick, the upper surface dull dark green, the lower paler with pale conspicuous midrib, the leafstalk with 2 large dark glands near the apex. *Flowers* appearing in the early spring before

the leaves, large (1½ inches across), in 3- or 4-flowered clusters on slender dark red stalks; calyx lobes reflexed after the flowers open, petals white, fading to pink, narrowed at base to a short claw. *Fruit* 1 to 1¼ inches long, with thick, tough, orange-red skin and yellow flesh; stone 1 inch long, compressed, thick-walled and acutely ridged on one surface, slightly grooved on the other. *Wood* hard, medium-heavy (43 pounds to the cubic foot, dry weight), with a rich ruddy heartwood and thin pale sapwood.

When Jacques Cartier sailed into Chaleur Bay (where, five centuries before, the Norsemen had spent their first winter in America), the Indians coming out to meet him in their canoes brought him red plums, the Canada Plum. On his second voyage he landed, in September, 1535, on the island of Orleans (in the St. Lawrence) which he named Isle de Bacchus, because of the wild grapes he found growing in the woods, and here he first encountered this Plum tree laden with its handsome fruits.

Still today the Canada Plum is commonly cultivated in the gardens of French Canada, both for the delicious plums themselves and for the beauty of the flowers, the largest of the genus amidst all our native species. They are slightly fragrant, and in all respects this fine cleanly tree, which grows 20 to 30 feet high, the trunk commonly forking about 6 feet from the ground into a number of stout upright branches, has everything to recommend it and nothing against it except its comparative scarcity. It is rare in many a region within the external periphery of its boundaries, and quite absent from the sterile sandy soil of the Lake Michigan region, from the burned-over and cut-over second growth of northern Wisconsin and the northern peninsula of Michigan.

The strength of the wood enables the tree to hold up under heavy snows and severe ice storms, with much less injury from breaking than most trees, and on all counts the Canada Plum deserves more cultivation than has ever been given it. The fruits are still commonly sold in the markets of Canadian cities, but horticulturists have given this Plum little attention and as yet few named varieties have been bred from it.

WILD RED PLUM

Prunus americana Marshall

RANGE: From central Massachusetts and central Vermont west through central New York to southern Michigan and northwestward across central Wisconsin to Minnesota and southern Manitoba; west to eastern Montana and through Wyoming, except in the mountains, to Logan, Utah. In Colorado and New Mexico confined to intermediate altitudes on the Front Range of the Rockies and the Sangre de Cristo Mountains; not found on the high plains of Colorado and Kansas, but appearing in central Kansas and northwestern Arkansas. Ranges south to the Gulf coast of Mississippi and Alabama but absent from the coastal plain of the Carolinas. Known near Savannah but not in Florida except the extreme northwest part. Absent from the high Appalachians.

DESCRIPTION: *Bark* dark brown, thick and rugged, exfoliating in little plate-like scales. *Twigs* chestnut-brown at first, turning gray, knotty or zigzag. *Leaves* 3 to 4 inches long, thick, firm, rather wrinkled, dark dull green above and pale beneath. *Flowers* white, in few-flowered, open clusters, the blossoms 1 inch across. *Fruits* less than 1 inch thick, green at first, then orange with a red cheek, finally bright red, with thick, tough bitter skin having numerous pale dots, the flesh yellowish, acid, and juicy. *Wood* hard, strong, medium-heavy (47 pounds to the cubic foot, dry weight), with deep rich red-brown heartwood and paler sapwood.

Where, throughout its large but irregular range, the Wild Red Plum grows profusely, spring has a special loveliness. For the Plum thickets, early in the year, foam with white blossoms piling like snow upon the naked wood. And in such places — in clearings, on the edge of woods, on warm hillsides or on bottom-lands — the first frail wild-flowers of spring draw close to the slim Plum boles, in a carpet where spring-beauties may make the warp, and the weft be adder's-tongue and yellow violet, hepatica and even Dutchman's-breeches. Alone, or as an understory tree beneath hardwoods, this Plum is a lacy note in the forest pattern. Though it grows usually little higher than 12 to 15 feet, and is commonly a mere shrub 6 to 12 feet tall, its branches are comparatively wide-spreading, and even somewhat drooping, forming a broad-topped head. Since it sends up many sprout stems, it spreads wherever it finds the opportunity, and there the odor of the blossoms freights the spring sunshine — an odor faintly fetid yet not wholly un-pleasing to any who played as children in those flowering and but sparsely thorny thickets.

Such fortunates will remember how in summer the fruits lay scat-tered in bright largesse under the trees, and how acid was a bite into the tiny red cheek of one. For in the East the fruit does not become sweet, though when preserved with cane sugar it makes one of the most tangy and fragrant of all preserves. But it is said that in the western part of its range the fruit is excellent for eating out of hand, and used to provide a precious crop to the Indians, pioneers, and wild animals. How much the red man prized this forest harvest is suggested by the DeSoto narrative of May 30, 1539, in which mention is made of a plum that, from the locality given, and the time of year, seems to be this species as discovered near the present site of Tallahassee: "There were other towns, where was a great store of maiz, pompions, french beanes, and plummes of the countrie which are better than those of Spaine and they grow in the fields without planting."

The Wild Red Plum is not only abundant in a wide range, but it has given rise to more pomological varieties than any other native species. The horticulturists distinguish some three hundred culti-vated varieties derived from this species. Botanists are accused of being hair-splitting theorists, but they point to the present instance to illustrate how the horticulturists, who pride themselves on being such practical people, have broken all records for making endless names based on fine pomological distinctions.

The Woolly-leaf Plum, *Prunus americana* variety *lanata* Sudworth, ranges from southern and western Indiana, southern and western Wisconsin, and southern Iowa southward to Texas and Alabama. It differs in having the undersides of the leaves completely covered with a whitish wool, the leafstalks woolly all the way around and bearing one or two glands, the calyx lobes woolly, and the fruit reddish with a distinctly bluish bloom. It intergrades with the true species to such an extent that it is not tenable as a species distinct from the Red Plum.

PURPLE SLOE

Prunus alleghaniensis Porter

OTHER NAMES: Allegheny Sloe. Porter's Plum.

RANGE: Southern Connecticut and central Pennsylvania on limestone bluffs of the Little Juniata in Huntingdon County, northward through the barrens and westward over the Alleghenies to Bear Mountain, Elk County.

DESCRIPTION: *Bark* dark brown, the fissured surface broken into thin scales. *Twigs* at first dark red and shining, later becoming nearly black, flecked with pale lenticels, occasionally armed with stout spur-like spines. *Winter buds* bright red, minute. *Leaves* 2 to 3½ inches long, ⅔ to 1¼ inches broad, rather thick and firm, dark green above, paler below.

Flowers appearing with the unfolding leaves, ½ inch across, petals pure white, contracted at base into short claws, fading pink. *Fruit* borne on stout downy stalks ⅓ to ⅔ inch in diameter with thick, tough, dark reddish purple skin covered with a bloom; flesh yellow, clinging to the turgid stone which is ¼ to ½ inch long, pointed at both ends. *Wood* hard, medium-heavy (44 pounds to the cubic foot, dry weight), the heartwood brown tinged with red, the sapwood thin and pale.

The most famous of this little tree's few known stations is in Huntingdon County, Pennsylvania, on the dry plateau, 10 or 12 miles broad, between the Little Juniata River and Tussey's Mountain on the east, and Bald Eagle Mountain on the west. Forming dense shrubby thickets, the Purple Sloe rises sometimes to tree size — some 20 feet in height — producing an enchanting profusion of flowers in May and, in mid-August, great quantities of fruit which load down the branches. The flesh is juicy but puckery. As yet almost no selective work has been done with this promising plum, yet there is every reason to suppose that, like so many other species of *Prunus* in America, it is just as capable of being brought to perfection as any of the cultivated plums and cherries of the Old World.

GARDEN WILD PLUM

Prunus hortulana Bailey

OTHER NAME: Hortulan Plum.

RANGE: From southeastern Iowa across the southern two thirds of Illinois to the southwestern half of Indiana and western Kentucky, south to northern Tennessee, northern Arkansas, northeastern Oklahoma, and southeastern Kansas.

DESCRIPTION: *Bark* thin, dark brown, separating into papery plates which display the light brown inner layers. *Twigs* rigid, stout, marked with small pale lenticels, at first dark red-brown, armed on vigorous sucker shoots with stout chestnut-colored lateral spines. *Winter buds* with chestnut-brown scales, the inner ones enlarging and becoming glandular too. *Leaves* 4 to 6 inches long and 1 to 1½ inches wide, thin but firm, the upper surface dark and shining, the lower with a broad orange-colored midrib and tawny hairs in the axils of the primary veins; leaf-stalks orange and beset with numerous scattered dark glands above the middle. *Flowers* ⅔ to 1 inch in diameter, in 2- to 4-flowered clusters, appearing when leaves are ⅓ grown in midspring, the calyx lobes reflexed when the flowers are fully opened, the petals contracted below into a long narrow claw, white sometimes marked with orange close to the base, often ragged or fringed around the margins. *Fruit* ¾ to 1 inch in diameter, the skin thick and dark red or sometimes yellow and shining, the flesh thin, the stone turgid, ⅔ to ¾ inch long, markedly ridged on the one suture and deeply grooved on the other, thick-walled, conspicuously pitted and rough, compressed at the end.

The banks of streams and rivers and the low-lying alluvial flood plains, where in the spring floodwater regularly inundates the terrain, are the favorite habitat of this fine little tree, which is sometimes only a shrub with many upright stems forming thicket-like clumps, but again, in the richest of soil, may be a tree 20 to 30 feet high with a slender, usually leaning trunk ½ or 1 foot thick; commonly there are several forks from near the ground which spread out into stout branches. In such situations the Garden Wild Plum delights to grow with the typical trees of the Mississippi River banks, Swamp White Oak, Green Ash, Box Elder, Red Birch, Pawpaw, Sweet Locust, Sycamore, Hackberry, and the stately Kingnut. The flowers, in the neighborhood of St. Louis, where this tree is particularly abundant, appear by the end of April or early May and the fruits ripen in September and October. In the typical tree the flesh is thin, austere and hard. This is, of course, the case with most wild fruits, but few of our native plums have given rise to such valuable garden forms as has this one, and these were only selected and propagated because individual trees were discovered which had large fruits and fine flavors. According to tradition, the "Miner" variety was discovered by

Captain William Dodd at the Horseshoe Bend of the Talapoosa River in Alabama in 1813, at a time when that part of the state was well within "Injun country." Indeed, since that region is far outside the natural range of the species, it is assumed that this, like so many of our native plums, was cultivated there by the Indians. One year later, Captain Dodd returned, in the army of General Andrew Jackson, and on this same spot Jackson's Tennessee militia and his Chickasaw and Cherokee allies disastrously defeated the Creeks in what has been called the greatest Indian fight in history, in point of numbers engaged on both sides. Yet even while campaigning, Dodd found time to hunt again for his delicious plum, and with the aid of a friendly Chickasaw chief he secured a lot of seed and bore it back to Knox County, Tennessee. There he planted it and raised the first tree.

He called this variety sometimes "Old Hickory" and sometimes "General Jackson." About 1823 Dodd removed to Springfield, Illinois, and brought with him sprouts which he planted in newly broken prairie sod; his plants did so poorly there at first that he wrote his brother in Tennessee to come to Illinois the next spring and bring with him more sprouts of "Old Hickory." This brother started out with the plums, but instead of going to Sangamon County, he did not stop until he reached Galena, where fertile land was going cheap. Here he planted his little trees. In the meantime William Dodd's trees had revived from the root and, their fruits becoming famous among his neighbors, they were distributed from farmer to farmer under the name of "William Dodd" and "Chickasaw Chief." In Galena the plums were also given away to (among others) a Major Hinckley, so that this plum also became known as the "Hinckley" and, variously, the "Townsend" and "Isbell." Further to confuse the tangle, the plum came into the hands of an enthusiastic horticulturist who firmly named it the "Miner," in honor of his father-in-law, a Mr. Miner of Lancaster, Wisconsin. Perversely enough, it is by this name that the heroic William Dodd's plum is chiefly known!

The "Miner," which thus entered into American horticulture by popular acclaim and hand-to-hand dissemination for 50 years before it was taken up by professional nurserymen, is an especially large plum, in shape roundish, with rather thick dull red skin, the stone short and broad, smooth or nearly so and very short-pointed, the front edge rather sharp, the stone clinging to the flesh. The large leaves are heavy, inclined to be broadest above the middle, and rather long-pointed. It is one of the latest ripening of all the plums in its class.

A famous yellow-skinned variety of the Garden Wild Plum is the "Golden Beauty," first introduced in 1874 by Gilbert Onderdonk of Nursery, Texas. This nurseryman relates that a German of Gonzales County, Texas, whose name is now lost to history, fled during the War of Secession from conscription by the Confederate Army. Most of the German immigrants of central Texas were anti-slavery, though as passionately pro-Texas as any others. When a body of Germans from Fredericksburg tried to leave the country for Mexico, they were set upon by secessionist Texans and killed. Warned, perhaps, by this, the German of Gonzales County slipped away by himself to Fort Belknap on the Indian frontier. Here he found this plum in cultivation among the Indians and on his return he brought it with him and called it the "Late Yellow Chickasaw." It was not a Chickasaw Plum at all, in the modern restriction of that term to a species which does not reach the circumscription of this book in the form of a native tree, but belongs as we now know to the present species.

By such odd and fortuitous ways have come to us one after another of the named varieties of this horticulturally promising species. Nor is there any reason to think that the story is over. New and better varieties yet unknown will in the future be discovered, though perhaps none of them under circumstances so romantic as the desperate fighting at the Horseshoe Bend or the flight of the liberty-loving German from the armies of slavery and secession.

WILD GOOSE PLUM

Prunus Munsoniana Wight and Hedrick

OTHER NAME: Munson Plum.

RANGE: Northeastern Tennessee to central Missouri, westward to southeastern Kansas and central Oklahoma, and south to northern Mississippi and northeastern Texas.

DESCRIPTION: *Bark* thin, gray or grayish-brown, separating into thin, plate-like scales on older trunks. *Twigs* slender, smooth, shining and red-brown, flecked with many pale lenticels, rarely spine-bearing. *Winter buds* chestnut-brown, minute. *Leaves* 2½ to 4 inches long, ¾ to 1¼ inches wide, thin, pale green and shining above, paler on the lower surface, the leafstalk slender, bright red, usually bearing 2 glands near the apex, the groove on the upper side white-downy. *Flowers* appearing after the leaves, in 2- to 4-flowered, branched clusters, the petals white, ¼ inch long, abruptly contracted to a short claw. *Fruit* ripening in July and August, ¾ inch long, bright red with a slight bloom and flecked with pale dots, the skins thin, the flesh yellow, juicy, fragrant; stone about ½ inch long, compressed, pointed at the tip, irregularly roughened and grooved on the sutures.

The botanical species, *Prunus Munsoniana*, was first described in 1911 in that classic book of American orchardists, *Plums of New York,* by Hedrick. But the true first discovery of this little tree, which sometimes rises 20 feet high with a stem half a foot thick, was made probably in the eighteen-thirties by a Captain Means of Nashville, Tennessee, who, having shot a wild goose, discovered in its craw a plum seed. Out of curiosity he planted it. It grew rapidly and fruited the third year, and, being convinced of its superior qualities, Means turned it over to various nurserymen for propagation. In this way the "Wild Goose" has been widely disseminated, with marked success in the latitude of Maryland, Kentucky, and Kansas. Many other varieties have been developed from the Wild Goose, including the "Goose Egg," "King of Plums," the "Tennessee," and the "Nolan." The Wild Goose is particularly to be recommended for size, quality, firmness, high productivity, early bearing, rapid growth and long duration, and adaptability to shipping long distances.

In native form this little species is usually found on rich soil, stream banks, and the alluvial flood plains of the rivers of the Mississippi valley. Commonly it forms dense thickets of which only the central stems actually reach tree size. By gradual diminution the thicket at its periphery may be only knee-high, so that the whole of the little grove forms a dome-shaped mass that is very lovely in spring when it is covered with flowers, and full of promise for the amateur horticulturist when the boughs are weighted with fruit in summer.

FIRE CHERRY

Prunus pensylvanica Linnæus the Younger

OTHER NAMES: Bird, Pin, Pigeon, Red or Wild Red Cherry.

RANGE: Newfoundland and New England, south to Pennsylvania and thence on the high Appalachians to North Carolina and Tennessee, west through the St. Lawrence basin to northern parts of Ohio and Indiana, to the Black Hills, the eastern slopes of the Rockies (south to Colorado) and the eastern slopes of the Coast Range in British Columbia and the valley of the Fraser River.

DESCRIPTION: *Bark* on trunks ½ inch thick, separating by horizontal strips into papery mahogany-colored plates flecked with irregular bands of orange lenticels and covered with small scales. *Twigs* at first bright red and shining, with pale raised lenticels, becoming the second year thick, short, spur-like and dark red with light orange lenticels, the outer bark peeling easily to show the brilliant green inner bark. *Winter buds* bright red-brown. *Leaves* 3 to 4½ inches long, ¾ to 1¼ inches wide, shining above, paler below, the leafstalks often glandular above the middle. *Flowers* appearing in midspring when the leaves are half grown (or late June at high altitudes), the calyx lobes red at tip and reflexed after the flowers open, petals creamy white, contracted into a short claw, about ¼ inch long. *Fruit* ripening in summer, ¼ inch thick, with thick light red skin and sour thin flesh, the stone thin-walled, only ³⁄₁₆ inch long, ridged on the upper suture and pointed at the apex. *Wood* soft, close-grained, medium-light (31 pounds to the cubic foot, dry weight), the heartwood light brown, sapwood thin and yellow.

When fire or lumbering has swept away the aromatic groves of Red Spruce and Southern Balsam which crown the highest peaks of the southern Appalachians, the growth that springs up in their place is not, at first, their own seedlings but this tree, the Fire Cherry. It grows 30 or 40 feet high on the Great Smokies, with a trunk sometimes 20 inches thick, and produces a mass of long, slender, nearly horizontal branches that elbow out a great deal of room for this swift-growing invader species.

Not without charm when in full flower, the little white blossoms foaming all over the naked wood, and superb in autumn, with fiery red, Fire Cherry is, however, nothing but a woody weed to the lumberman, for there is no practical use, except for the making of jelly from the acid, tangy little cherries, to which this little tree can be put. And when one thinks of the cool and noble groves of conifers it succeeds, and their lovely associates the elvish-seeming lichens, the delicate and gleaming mosses, the fair-faced mountain oxalis, Fire Cherry cuts a sorry figure indeed. Its associates are chiefly fireweed and brambles, and other sorts of trees that, like itself, are swift-springing, soft, and weak.

It is at least a virtue in Fire Cherry that it is short-lived. In time it gives way to Canoe and Yellow Birch and other hardwoods. Often, in the Canadian North Woods, Spruce and Balsam may finally return, but within the confines of the United States this is seldom the case, for these conifers are remnants of a colder age, and have only lingered on as an over-mature stage in ecological succession. The modern geologic age is one of hardwoods, and when once the çonifers are forcibly displaced, the ground they held is often taken over permanently by the hardwood trees. To say that this is uniformly good or bad would be to pass judgment in a purely human way. The fact remains that the increasing spread of Fire Cherry in so many parts of the country is the first act in a profound and often irreversible change.

CHOKE CHERRY

Prunus virginiana Linnæus

RANGE: Newfoundland south to the valley of the Potomac River and northern Kentucky, thence southward on lower slopes of the Appalachians to North Carolina and Alabama, westward through Labrador to the shores of Hudson Bay, Saskatchewan, and eastern parts of the Dakotas and Nebraska, northern Missouri, and Kansas. Also in the Black Hills.

DESCRIPTION: *Bark* very thin, slightly if at all fissured, marked with irregular pale warts and dark brown persistent red scales. *Twigs* slender, smooth, red-brown or orange-brown and shiny, flecked with pale lenticels, becoming in the second year dark red-brown. *Winter buds* with pale chestnut-brown scales with papery margins, the inner ones strap-shaped and glandular-toothed and about 1 inch long. *Leaves* dark green and shining on the upper surface, pale green below, 2 to 4 inches long, 1 to 2 inches wide. *Flowers* in erect or nodding spikes 3 to 6 inches long, white, the petals rounded, contracted to a short claw. *Fruit* ¼ to ⅓ inch thick, shining, bright red at first, becoming at maturity scarlet and finally dark winy red or nearly black and crowned with the persistent remnants of the calyx; flesh dark, juicy; stone broadly ridged on one suture and acute on the other. *Wood* heavy, hard, close-grained, rather weak, the heartwood light brown and the thick sapwood paler.

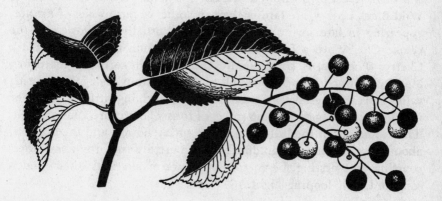

Most boys with a country or suburban childhood have probably tried the Choke Cherry — and concluded that it is well named. As a rule the flesh is astringent and acid, yet many writers have testified to their own experience that individual trees may bear fairly palatable fruit, the chief fault of which lies in the thinness of the flesh and the large size of the pits. These are defects which have been corrcted, in a limited way, by propagation of the most promising strains. Some such strains may produce fruits as much as an inch in diameter. Cooking removes the astringency. In Quebec the *habitants* have long cultivated the Choke Cherry and have selected strains that may be eaten out of hand, like the best orchard cherries, or as preserves or jelly.

Choke Cherry holds its ripe fruit on the tree better than the cultivated Cherries of European origin, and ripens in late July or August, long after other cherries are gone from the market. The fruit is borne densely and compactly, is hence easy to pick, and holds up well in shipping. As a stock, this tree is far hardier, north, than the Old-World Cherry.

In the field, Choke Cherry is apt to be mistaken for Wild Black Cherry, yet this little tree may readily be distinguished from that lofty one by the disagreeable odor of the inner bark of the twigs, by the fact that the petals are roundish rather than broader above the middle, and that the leaves are short-pointed or nearly obtuse instead of long-pointed, while the fruit of the Black Cherry, unlike this one, is crowned with the persistent remains of the calyx.

Sometimes only a shrub 2 or 3 feet tall, the Choke Cherry, in rich deep soil — especially in the southern Appalachians — may grow to be a tree 20 to 30 feet high with a straight trunk 6 to 8 inches in diameter, and small, erect or horizontal branches. The flowers, like those of the Wild Black Cherry, are tardier than any other of our species of *Prunus*, appearing in late spring or early summer; usually the flowers of the Choke Cherry are a full two weeks earlier than those of the Black Cherry. The fruit is, correspondingly, a fortnight earlier in maturing. Margins of woods, fence rows and roadsides, sunny clearings and rich valley soils are the favorite habitat of this charming little species. For in full flower the gay nodding spikes of foamy flowers are a lovely sight. They come out in the lull between the spring flowers and the summer, about the time that the goldfinches, who are always tardy about their courting and nesting, begin to fill the warm airs with their golden song and their looping flight.

Variety *demissa* (Nuttall) Torrey, differs in having the lower surface of the leaves, the twigs, and the flower stalks distinctly downy. It is a western variety ranging from California and British Columbia east to Texas and Indiana, becoming quite frequent on the Indiana sand dunes. Commonly only a shrub, it is, like the true species, sometimes of tree size. Especially in the West this variety is apt to have larger and less bitter fruit, and was often gathered and eaten by the Plains Indians.

WILD BLACK CHERRY

Prunus serotina Ehrhart

OTHER NAMES: Rum, or Whiskey Cherry.

RANGE: From Nova Scotia to the north shore of Lake Superior and the eastern parts of the Dakotas, Kansas, Nebraska, and Oklahoma, and into central Texas; south to central Florida, but absent from the highest Appalachians and from the Louisiana Delta and the Texas Gulf coast.

DESCRIPTION: *Bark* aromatic, dark red-brown on old trees, becoming broken into irregular scaly plates divided by braided fissures. *Twigs* slender, stiff, and smooth, at first pale green or bronze becoming bright red or dark brown with a red tinge, or gray-brown, flecked with many minute pale lenticels during the first winter; next year bright red.

Winter buds bright chestnut-brown. *Leaves* 2 to 6 inches long, dark green and lustrous above, paler below, firm, thick and smooth. *Flowers* ½ inch in diameter, white. Fruit ⅓ to ½ inch thick, dark red becoming almost black when ripe, with thin skin and juicy, dark purple flesh usually with a bitter winy taste. *Wood* weak, medium-hard, medium-light (35 pounds to the cubic foot, dry weight), with pink or light brown heartwood and thin yellow sapwood.

In the forest this, the tallest of all Cherries and the most precious cabinet wood in the rose family, may rise to a noble 100 feet in height, with a trunk clear of branches for 30 feet and attaining 4 or 5 feet in diameter, the small horizontal branches forming a narrow oblong head. In the days when our woods were rich with such fine old Cherry trees, the Appalachian pioneers invented a drink called cherry bounce; juice pressed from the fruits was infused in brandy or rum to make a cordial which, though bitter, was in high favor among the old-time mountaineers. Bears were plentiful then in the Appalachians, and the ripening of the cherry crop was a signal for an ursine congregation. The cubs of the year learned to climb trees by following their mothers up them, to reap the wild cherry harvest. "Cherry bears" were considered especially mettlesome and best left strictly alone.

Still today it is claimed that even the cultivated cherry does not have more juice than this one, and the ripe fruit is sometimes employed as a flavoring for alcoholic liqueurs. The bitter aromatic bark has a distinct odor of bitter almond or hydrocyanic (prussic) acid, which is also found in the leaves. As an astringent, the medicinal properties of the bark are even today in use for cough medicines, expectorants, and the treatment of sore throat.

But it is for its beautiful smooth-grained wood that this Cherry has found highest favor. As long ago as 1820, a traveler on the Ohio writes, "When we reached Brown's Island, five miles from the Wabash, and four from Shawneetown, the wind obliged us to anchor on the left side, close to three large flat boats, loaded with flour, bacon, whiskey, tobacco, horses, and pine and cherry planks, for the Orleans market." [1] It thus appears that sawn Cherry was transported from Henderson, Kentucky, all the way to New Orleans, and the presumption is that the price was even then fairly high, and esteem for the wood great, to justify such a long haul.

[1] John Woods, *English Prairie in the Illinois Country.*

So from pioneer times, Cherry has grown steadily rarer. The assault upon it was twofold, just as in the case of Beech, Tuliptree, and Sycamore, in that the land on which Wild Black Cherry grew being counted the best agricultural soil, the trees were disposed of as fast as possible, even to the extent of girdling magnificent virgin growth, or burning it down, while at the same time there was a constant culling-out of all the finest specimens for the sawmills. In the days of wooden Pullmans, wooden streetcars, and fine carriage-making, Cherry was of the utmost importance. It is astonishing to remember that only fifty years ago a city could order a whole fleet of streetcars paneled in superb Cherry, when today boards of such dimensions might not be obtainable at the price of Rosewood or Ebony.

Indeed, by the close of the last century, hardwood buyers were cruising the country in a tree-to-tree search for Cherry of fine dimensions. They were so successful that dimension timber is now harder than ever to find. True, the tree is prolific, and birds devour the fruits and so scatter the seeds over the countryside, with the result that large numbers are coming up along the roadsides where the seeds are voided by the birds perching on the telephone wires and fences. But these field-grown specimens are limby, knotty, and short-trunked. Only under forest conditions are wild Black Cherries forced by competition into splendidly tall, straight growth producing saw timber. For this reason alone has Cherry sunk to twenty-eighth place among native trees, in the amount cut, and ranks at the bottom of the native cabinet woods.

Yet its virtues as such are many. Though it is weak — weaker than Black Willow — when used as a beam, it is fairly hard, and furthermore it is very smooth-grained, takes a handsome finish, shrinks but little in seasoning and warps not at all after it is seasoned, no matter what the temperature and moisture changes in the air. True that it rarely develops a fancy figure, but compensating for that is the splendid way the tree grows under forest conditions, producing wonderfully knot-free, clean, broad planks. Thus it is that Cherry came to rank second in cost only to Black Walnut, as the finest cabinet wood of temperate North America.

Cherry wood, fresh cut, is not at all cherry-colored. While its pinkish tone will darken somewhat with age, stains and varnishes are commonly used to give it a "Mahogany red," which is itself, of course, not the natural hue of fresh Mahogany wood. Indeed, Mahogany and

Cherry in their natural state are much alike in tone, and when both are finished off with a deep stain they are difficult to tell apart. The readiest distinguishing mark is that a smoothly cut end surface of Mahogany shows pores visible without a magnifying glass; in Cherry the pores are not visible without a magnifying glass. However, where only a veneer of these woods is used on a core of a less noble cabinet wood, these points of difference are not available. Hence, in the days when Cherry was cheaper, it used to be possible to substitute Cherry for Mahogany in a way to baffle experts. But Cherry has been so severely overcut that it is sometimes almost as expensive as Mahogany, and in its turn Cherry is imitated by skillful staining of Black Birch!

As it would no longer pay anyone to imitate Mahogany with Cherry, it will not lead us into temptation to describe the method by which it was done: "A well-known and perfect method of making cherry look like mahogany is to have the wood rubbed with diluted nitric acid, which prepares it for the materials subsequently to be applied; afterwards, to a filtered mixture of an ounce and a half of dragon's-blood dissolved in a pint of spirit of wine, is added one-third that quantity of carbonate of soda, the whole constituting a very thin liquid which is applied to the wood with a soft brush. This process is repeated at short intervals until the wood assumes the external appearance of mahogany." [1]

The greatest use of Cherry at the present time is for showcases, counters, and bars, closely followed by weighing apparatus, on account of its ability to "stay put" under all conditions, never throwing the metal fittings out of alignment; for the same reason it is almost always the wood used for spirit levels, and is exclusively sought for the backs of electrotypes in the printing arts. Fourth most important use of cherry is planing-mill work such as paneling and interior finish. After that there is a sharp drop to much lower figures, in board feet, to furniture which comes in fifth place; next, scientific and other precision instruments; then handles; then backs of hairbrushes; then musical instruments (actions for organs) and the list virtually ends with caskets. If many woods outrank Cherry for this last purpose, in number of board feet cut, this does not mean that most of them are better but rather that the cost of Cherry is now so high. The perfect

1 Gibson and Maxwell, *American Forest Trees.*

joinery possible with such a stable wood, and the satiny smoothness with which the lid of a Cherry casket can be made to glide in the groove of the box, all recommend it highly. It is related that the immortal Daniel Boone made himself several Cherry caskets, and used occasionally to sleep in them, in his old age, but gave up all but his last to needy corpses.

THE REDBUDS

(*Cercis*)

THESE ARE small, scaly-barked trees, without thorns; growth is by prolongation from an axillary bud. Marked by numerous pale lenticels, the twigs show elevated horizontal leaf scars. Small and axillary, the winter buds have chestnut-brown scales. The long-stalked, deciduous, simple and heart-shaped leaves show margins without teeth, and 5 to 7 prominent principal nerves arising together from the base. Borne in simple or branched clusters on thin, jointed stalks from branches of the previous year, or on the trunk itself, the bisexual flowers appear in early spring, before the leaves. The calyx is small and bell-shaped. The petals form a flower somewhat like a sweet pea; at base they are clawed and slightly lobed on one side. The 10 free stamens are grouped in 2 rows, while the short-stalked pistil inserted at the bottom of the calyx tube terminates in a fleshy, incurved style with obtuse stigma. The fruit takes the form of a tough papery, stalked pod of which the lower edge is curved and the upper straight, the tip showing the thickened remainer of the style. It opens tardily by the back suture, to reveal the compressed, bright reddish-brown seeds suspended on slender stalks.

REDBUD

Cercis canadensis Linnæus

OTHER NAME: Judastree.

RANGE: Southern Connecticut and New York westward through extreme southern Ontario and southern Michigan, northern Illinois to southern Iowa and eastern Nebraska, southward to the Gulf of Mexico and northeastern Mexico.

DESCRIPTION: *Bark* bright red-brown and scaly, becoming deeply fissured in old age. *Twigs* somewhat angled and slender, in their first season shiny brown, becoming eventually dull dark grayish brown. *Leaves* 2 to 6 inches long, and as broad as or broader than long. *Flowers* appearing before the leaves, rose-purple or magenta-colored, ⅓ to 1 inch long in short clusters. *Fruits* 2 to 3 inches long, ½ inch wide, dark red-purple, shining, several seeded. *Wood* hard, close-grained, medium-light (39 pounds to the cubic foot, dry weight), the heartwood dark rich brown tinged with red, the sapwood paler.

Tree-planting Mr. George Washington of "Mount Vernon" confided many times to his diary that he had transplanted Redbuds from the woods to his garden, and when they filled the land with their flowering, he liked to tell us, in his unsentimental way, of the lovely sight. For

Redbud blooms in the first fine weather — in February in the far South, in May at its farthest north, generally about the same time as the Peach trees and when the Wild Plums are clothing themselves in shining white. But Redbud flowers, which bloom on the naked twig, are neither Peach pink nor Plum white, nor red like the clay soils of the piedmont country that they love; they are a striking purplish pink or magenta. And though this is not a color which blends well with most gardens, it is one of which Nature seems to be particularly fond in the flora of eastern North America. When the Redbud flowers, the still leafless deciduous woods display its charms down every vista; it shines in the somber little groves of Scrub Pine; it troops up the foothills of the Appalachians; it steps delicately down towards swampy ground in the coastal plain, flaunts its charms beside the red clay wood roads and along the old rail fences of the piedmont. Inconspicuous in summer and winter, Redbud shows us in spring how common it is. It is notable that wherever Redbud, Dogwood, and Mountain Laurel grow, the local population believes that it has the finest display of these trees in the world. The people of eastern Texas will sincerely urge Virginians to come to the Lone Star State if they really want to see Redbud!

Once the Redbud has put out its leaves, and the flowers have faded, and all the woods are leafing out, Redbud is forgotten till in autumn the foliage turns a clear bright yellow. When the tree stands winter-naked, the pods persist on the boughs almost till spring. Yet even in summer the Redbud is a gracious little thing, with its heart-shaped, softly shining foliage. In general this is but an understory tree, never over 40 feet tall, and elbowing out little room for itself. For these reasons, and for the precocity of its blooms, Redbud is a favorite garden tree for the small property.

A passage in John Lawson's *History of North Carolina,* published in 1708, speaks of salads made of the blossoms, and in Mexico the flowers are still fried and eaten as a great delicacy. As a result of its presence in Mexico, the Redbud was first distinguished and described by Francisco Hernandez, author of the *Historia de las Plantas de Nueva España* (1571–75). Who sent the first specimens from America we do not know, but it was described in 1696 by the herbalist Leonard Plukenet, so that it is likely that his correspondent, John Banister the Virginia missionary, was the first to send Redbud to England.

Judastree is the older but more foreign name for this tree. It is sometimes transferred to our American species from the related plant of the Mediterranean zone (*Cercis Siliquastrum*) which was called Judastree in accordance with an old belief that it was the wood on which Judas Iscariot hanged himself. Wherefore its flowers, stated in the myth to have been formerly white, turned red either with shame or blood. But the name Redbud was already in use in North Carolina by 1700, for it is thus that John Lawson spoke of it. George Washington and Thomas Jefferson called it Redbud too, and that should be good enough for any American.

THE COFFEETREES

(*Gymnocladus*)

S TOUT thornless blunt twigs and thick pith, deeply fissured, rough bark, and fleshy thick roots characterize the Coffeetrees. The minute buds are found sunk in hairy cavities in the bark, 2 of them in the axil of each leaf, the lower nearly surrounded by the enlarged base of the leafstalk, each with two scales coated with thick, dark-brown wool. The alternate deciduous leaves are twice-compound, the primary, opposite divisions of the compound leaf bearing many small, thin, deciduous leaflets having untoothed margins. The regular flowers have a narrow, tubular 5-lobed calyx, the lobes erect, nearly equal, and alternate with the petals which are inserted on the margin of the disk and spreading or reflexed. Inserted with them are the 10 stamens. In the female flower the ovary is stalked, and terminates in a short erect style with 2 broad, oblique stigmas. The several-seeded, 2-valved pod has thin but tough and woody sides thickened on the margin into narrow wings. Pulpy within, the pods enclose the thick, bony, brown seeds suspended by slender threads.

KENTUCKY COFFEETREE

Gymnocladus dioica (Linnæus) K. Koch

OTHER NAMES: Coffeenut. Coffeebean. Nickertree. Stumptree.

RANGE: Scattered in central New York, eastern Pennsylvania and Maryland, Ohio, southern tip of Ontario, southern Michigan and Wisconsin, southeastern Minnesota and eastern South Dakota, south to Alabama, Arkansas and Oklahoma.

DESCRIPTION: *Bark* dark gray tinged with red, deeply fissured and roughened by small scales. *Twigs* at first very blunt, dark brown and marked with orange-colored lenticels and large, broadly heart-shaped, pale leaf scars. *Leaves* 1 to 3 feet long in over-all dimension, with 5 to 9 principal divisions and 6 to 14 leaflets, each about 2 to 2½ inches long and 1 inch wide, dark green above, pale yellow-green below. *Flowers* small, greenish purple, unisexual, the male in short clusters, the female in elongated spikes, the petals 4 or 5, the stamens 10, of two alternating lengths, with bright orange-colored anthers. *Fruit* a pod 6 to 10 inches long, 1½ to 2 inches wide, on stout stalks 1 to 2 inches long; seeds ¾ inch long, and imbedded in a sweet dark-colored pulp. *Wood* medium-heavy (41 pounds to the cubic foot, dry weight), medium-soft, strong, the heartwood rich light brown tinged with red, the sapwood thin and paler.

When the first settlers and explorers crossed the Alleghenies, chiefly between 1775 and 1825, into what was then the wilderness of the

Middle West and Middle South, the simplest intelligences as well as
the best-trained noted that a new sylva had been encountered. The
trees they found on the limestones and deep soils of their new homes
included Sycamores, Black Locust, Sweet Locust, Buckeye, Catalpa,
Kingnut, and the present species, the striking Kentucky Coffeetree —
all rare or new in their experience. Eagerly the botanical explorers
collected seeds or slips for trial, while the pioneers, with axe and saw
and knife, tested the qualities of the new timbers to make themselves
cabins, fences, furniture, tools, and every object in their markedly
wooden culture, from cradle to coffin.

It is not known now who first sufficiently appreciated the Kentucky
Coffeetree to send back specimens to Europe, but at an early date it
was known there as a botanical curiosity from America. The pioneers
left us but scant account of any use they made of the handsome
cabinet wood produced by the Coffeetree, and today it does not appear
in lumbermen's statistics at all. Perhaps this is because, though it
grows to be a fine tree 75 to 100 feet in height, in the rich bottom-land
of the Ohio, it forks close to the ground, so that thick trunks are
seldom found to tempt the sawmill foreman. But because the wood is
so durable in contact with the soil it has from the first been used for
fence posts wherever it was common enough for the farmer to obtain
it.

The appearance of the beans or seeds, rather than the taste, must
have induced the pioneers to roast and brew them to make what can
only by imagination and forbearance be called coffee. As soon as the
first settlers were able to obtain real coffee they troubled this curious
tree for its beans no longer. Yet the Coffeetree is cultivated far beyond
its natural range. Perhaps, indeed, the Indians, who valued the pods
as a crop, had already done much to spread it before the palefaces
came.

On the lawn the forking habit of the trunk, to which the lumberman objects, only adds to the grace of the specimen. But it is late in
leafing out in spring. The flowers are not unattractive, but two years
out of three they scarcely show at all. Lovely though the broad fronds
of its foliage are in summer, they turn yellow at the first touch of
autumn and promptly drop. After the leaflets are gone, the naked axis
of the branches of the compound leaf drops too, so that the tree seems
to be shedding its very twigs. Only the great pods cling on, like open
purses, their contents scattered in a spendthrift's gesture.

THE SWEET LOCUSTS

(*Gleditsia*)

CHARACTERIZED BY thick, fibrous roots and furrowed bark, the Sweet Locusts are usually armed both on the trunk and branches with stout, often branched spines developed from buds imbedded in the bark. The minute winter buds, 3 or 4 together, are almost surrounded by the base of the leafstalk, the upper and largest covered by small scurfy scales. Deciduous and long-stalked, alternate or often clustered in the earlier axils, the leaves are once-compound or twice-compound, with leaflets of an even number (no terminal leaflet). The thin, numerous, small leaflets have irregularly and minutely scalloped margins. The minute green or white flowers are regular, not pea-like, in simple or clustered spikes. The bell-shaped calyx is 3- to 5-parted with nearly equal narrow lobes. With the 3 to 5 petals are inserted on the margin of the disk the 6 to 10 stamens, their stalks free from each other. The ovary terminates in short styles with dilated stigmas. Flowers may be wholly male, wholly female, in any given spike, or the two sexes mixed in the same spike, but seldom bisexual. The compressed pod contains 1 or many thin-coated, flattened seeds on long slender threads.

SWEET LOCUST

Gleditsia triacanthos Linnæus

OTHER NAMES: Thorny, Honey, or Black Locust. Thorny, or Three-thorned Acacia. Honeyshucks.

RANGE: Central New York and eastern Pennsylvania to northern Florida, west through southern Ontario, Michigan and Wisconsin to southeastern Minnesota and eastern South Dakota, and along the Gulf of Mexico to eastern Texas, with its western limits in Nebraska and Oklahoma. Extensively planted, and the exact limits of its natural range difficult to determine.

DESCRIPTION: *Bark* iron gray, thick, and divided by deep fissures into long narrow longitudinal ridges roughened with small tough scales; sometimes very thorny. *Twigs* marked with minute lenticels, at first light reddish brown, becoming a shiny red with a green tinge, and by the second year greenish brown; thornless or beset by simple or branched thorns. *Leaves* in over-all dimensions 7 to 8 inches long, dark shiny green above, dull yellow-green below. *Flowers* inconspicuous, odorless, and greenish. *Fruits* flat rich brown pods 12 to 15 inches long, hanging in clusters, with seeds hard, shiny brown, and flattish, about the size of navy beans. *Wood* very durable, very hard, medium-heavy (44 pounds to the cubic foot, dry weight), with red or bright red-brown heartwood having a thick bright yellow ring of sapwood around it.

Down in Florida this tree is still sometimes called by the obsolete name of Confederate Pintree, because its formidable spines were used to pin together the tattered uniforms of the southern hosts in the war of the Blue and the Gray. Honeyshucks is the name used in some parts of Virginia, and very appropriate it is on account of the sweet pods eagerly eaten by cattle and sometimes by nibbling country boys. True that Honey Locust is the name given it almost throughout our horticultural, botanical, and forestry literature, but as country people usually apply Honey Locust to *Robinia Pseudo-Acacia* (*q.v.*) because of its showy as well as fragrant flowers, both trees lay nearly equal claim to this as a name. Thus the best thing to do, in the interests of clarity, is to apply it to neither, since both have other, and usually different, titles. The word Locust, of course, is a transposition to a New World tree of an Old World name. When Saint John went into the wilderness he lived on "honey and locusts," says the Bible, and by a later transposition the name of the noisy insect became attached to the rattling, edible pods of Carob (*Ceratonia Siliqua*), often called St. John's-bread.

Not unnaturally a sweet-tasting pod on an American tree received the name of Locust. The pods are eagerly eaten by cattle when they can find them on the ground, though it is not easy for the animals to browse them from the thorny branches, and thus the tree is spreading far in its range, as the voided seeds are distributed by the cattle from pasture to pasture. In such open places, the ponderous trunk of this tree soon forks with many erect secondary trunks. The gradually spreading limbs and branchlets tend to droop at the tips, while the crown is generally open and rather flat-topped — a habit rare in a lofty tree. And Sweet Locust, on the rich bottom-lands of southern Illinois, is said to grow 140 feet high, or it did, at least, in the days of forest virginity. A tree in Dayton, Ohio, has a spread of more than 100 feet in diameter, with a girth of nearly 15 feet.

Although sometimes the stout trunk of the Sweet Locust is devoid of thorns, other specimens are beset by a horrendous armory of long, triple-branched thorns that may be a foot long, and are sharp as bayonets. Not even when closely pressed by dogs, it is said, will a squirrel attempt to climb such a tree. While the thorns of the Black Locust are superficial and easily picked off, those of the Sweet Locust arise from the wood and cannot by any means be pulled out. At first they are bright green, then bright red, and when mature a rich chest-nut-brown that shines as if it had been polished. In the days when the southern mountain folk had to use the natural resources at hand, they employed these thorns in carding wool, and for pinning up the mouths of wool sacks.

Even the twigs may bear thorns, especially the lower ones and those on little trees, though some trees are prickly to the very top. Some-times the thorns bear leaves, proving that they are modified branches. This is a slow tree to leaf; long after other citizens of the forest are clothed in foliage, the fiercely thorny, dark-barked Honeyshucks stands naked and secretive, as if refusing to yield to the persuasions of spring. At last the tender, airy, feathery foliage begins to appear, which early in autumn turns clear yellow, then falls, leaving the tree bare for an-other six months.

Bare save for the strange fruit. In late summer one begins to notice the clusters of hanging flat pods, a foot or more long. Gradually twisting and contorting (for some time without opening), they remain on the tree most of the winter, where one can hear them rattle dismally in the wind. At last they fall, before spring.

The wood can boast a remarkable durability — 80 to 100 per cent of that of White Oak. A knot-free or thorn-free board, where one can be found, ranks second in strength under pressure as a beam only to Black Locust, among all our trees. Far less than Black Locust is this tree attacked by borers; in fact, it seems entirely repellent to them. Yet with all these stalwart qualities, which should place it with Hickory, Ash, White Oak, and Black Locust as a heavy-duty lumber, Sweet Locust is rarely cut, and has even been sent to market as Sycamore! Some say that it is weakened by the trunk thorns, others report that it is considered too coarse for any but the roughest uses. True that it makes excellent railway ties and fence posts, on account of its durability, but many a wood can now be creosoted and preserved against decay, which makes this virtue less precious. A kind of antique honor remains to the wood of Sweet Locust, from the fact that, before they adopted firearms, the proud and intelligent Cherokees of Tennes-see chose to make their bows of it.

WATER LOCUST

Gleditsia aquatica Marshall

RANGE: From south-central Florida to the coastal plain of South Carolina along the Gulf coast to the Brazos River, Texas. Northward in the Mississippi basin to central parts of Kentucky and Tennessee, and southern and west-central Illinois and extreme southern Indiana.

DESCRIPTION: *Bark* thin, smooth, reddish-brown or dull gray, shallowly fissured and covered with small scales. *Twigs* orange-brown, in the second year armed with flattened, branched or simple and dark red-brown and shining spines 3 to 5 inches long, the bark of the twigs then becoming reddish-brown or gray and marked by a few large, pale lenticels. *Leaves* in over-all dimensions 5 to 8 inches long, once-compound or twice-compound (if the latter, then with 3 or 4 pairs of branches), the leaflets numbering 12 to 20, remotely or slightly scalloped on the margin or quite entire, the upper surface shining yellow-green, the lower dark green, each leaflet about 1 inch long and ⅓ to ½ inch wide. *Flowers* appearing after the leaves are fully grown, on stout purple stalks, in slender spikes 3 or 4 inches long, the calyx tubes covered with orange-brown down, the petals green and erect, the anthers large and green. *Fruit* pendant in graceful clusters, thin and flat, 1 to 2 inches long, 1 inch broad, the walls bright chestnut-brown and shining, tough and papery with thickened margins, the interior without pulp and containing usually only a single roundish orange-brown seed. *Wood* medium-heavy (45 pounds to the cubic foot, dry weight), very hard, very strong, the heartwood bright brown tinged with red, the sapwood very thick and clear yellow.

One of the features of the North American sylva which most profoundly impressed foreign travelers, like Prince Maximilian of Wied, Nuttall, the two Michaux, and even the earliest *conquistadores* like DeSoto and Cabeza de Vaca, was the solemn grandeur of the forests which inhabited the land regularly inundated by the annual floodwaters of the Mississippi and its great tributaries. On such low-lying land where the spring floods stood long in numberless sloughs and bayous and ox-bow lakes, grew the Cypress, the cane, the Sycamore, Bottom Hickory, Sweet Gum, Black Gum, Swamp Cottonwood, and the present species, the Water Locust. It formed an understory tree beneath the towering Cypresses, and yet was 50 or 60 feet high, and sometimes made up densely thorny groves. The short trunk usually divides a few feet from the ground into stout, spreading and contorted branches to form a wide, irregular flat-topped head, something like the Mesquite of Texas. The spines can be formidable indeed — simple or triple-branched and half an inch thick at base, clothing sometimes the entire tree. Such was not a vegetable with which the pioneers cared to try force, as they threaded their way through the ancient timber of the primeval bottoms.

The flowers do not appear until the leaves have completely grown, in May or June; the fruit is fully ripe in August. At almost all times during the summer one may see a handsome glossy red growth of new foliage putting out. The Water Locust would not be a bad-looking tree in cultivation, but its demand for a high water-table will probably confine it forever to the kingdom of the water moccasin and the no less deadly malarial mosquito.

A fine polish is taken by the wood of Water Locust, and it should make an excellent cabinet wood, but when lumbermen cut it at all they never seem to send it to market under its own specific name, so that it is impossible to say how much of it is ever used. Farmers in the region where it grows have, because Water Locust is so durable in contact with soil, made fence posts of it for more than a century.

THE YELLOWWOODS

(*Cladrastis*)

MEMBERS of this genus have smooth bark, slender, roundish twigs without a terminal bud, and compound deciduous leaves of an uneven number of a few large leaflets, the margins not toothed. The axillary buds are naked of covering and, overlapping and flattened by mutual pressure into a pointed cone-like mass, they are inclosed collectively in the hollow base of the leafstalk. The sweet-pea-like flowers are bisexual, and droop in graceful elongated clusters; the cylindric-bell-shaped calyx, enlarged on the upper side and obliquely top-shaped at base, has 5 nearly equal teeth, the upper 2 slightly united; the white petals have a pale yellow blotch at the base of the lateral pair; the 10 stamens are free from each other, not connected by their stalks; the bright red ovary terminates in a long, slender, incurved style. The fruit takes the form of a much flattened pod which finally opens by its sutures, to expose the 4 to 6 seeds on their slender stalks. The seed coat, thin and papery, is dark brown.

YELLOWWOOD

Cladrastis lutea (F. Michaux) K. Koch

OTHER NAMES: Virgilia. Yellow Locust. Yellow Ash. Gopherwood.

RANGE: Rare and local in extreme southwestern North Carolina and eastern and central Tennessee, northeastern Georgia, western Alabama, Kentucky, and very rarely in central Indiana. Reported from Missouri, Arkansas and Oklahoma, but not certainly as a native.

DESCRIPTION: *Bark* thin, silvery gray. *Twigs* brittle, zigzag, at first very smooth, pale and shining and marked by many dark lenticels, becoming red-brown the first winter and warty with large, elevated leaf scars surrounding the buds; finally dull, dark brown. *Leaves* 8 to 12 inches long in over-all dimensions, the leaflets 3 to 4 inches long, 1½ to 2 inches wide. *Flowers* with clawed petals, the uppermost nearly circular, reflexed above the middle, scarcely longer than the oblong, straight wing petals; keel petals free from each other, oblong, nearly straight. *Fruit* hairless, short-stalked, the upper margin slightly thickened, tipped with the remnants of the style, the walls of the pods thin and papery. *Wood* bright clear yellow, changing on exposure to light brown, with thin, nearly white sapwood; very hard, very strong, close-grained, with smooth satiny surface, medium-light (39 pounds to the cubic foot, dry weight).

An icy rain was falling — a rain that presently turned to blinding snow — and the roaring creeks of Tennessee were rising fast, on the last day of February, 1796, when André Michaux stopped his horse, somewhere in the lonely woods twelve miles from Fort Blount, to examine a curious tree. True, the leaves must have been off it then; it stood winter-naked, but with its smooth silvery gray bark shining like some wood nymph through the drear forest. With his experienced plantsman's eye, this wandering Frenchman, whose romantic life included adventures in Persia, Mesopotamia, and the Trans-Caspian regions and had even embraced curing the daughter of the Shah of a mysterious malady, now added to his long list of first discoveries of American tree species what is one of the rarest trees of eastern North America. For the Yellowwood has a most restricted range, and even within the described limits of that range it is often a distinctly rare tree. But André Michaux, that cold and nasty day in 1796, was recognizing by his native flair something neither he nor many other white men had ever seen — the only American species of this strange genus which is best represented in the mountains of China and Japan.

The plantsman remained over at Fort Blount seeking an opportunity to pull young shoots of his new tree, but the ground was so covered with snow that he was unable to get any. A young officer stationed at the fort obligingly cut down some trees for him, and from them Michaux was able to gather seeds. He also cut off some of the roots of the felled trees to replant in his acclimation garden near Charleston, South Carolina. Thence he would one day send them, with his Magnolias and Rhododendrons and so many other of his American discoveries, to France. But no happy fate awaited them there; it is said that Queen Marie Antoinette dispatched a large part of Michaux's collection, which was sent to Versailles (since he was a royal botanist), to her father, the Emperor of Austria, after which all trace of them is lost. Others were banished to Marly, that simple little country place which the kings of France had established to get away from the fatigues, splendors, and lack of privacy at Versailles (which had also started out as a simple country place). But Marly soon came to rival Versailles in cost and splendor, though it was never popular, and there Michaux's collection of living trees from America probably shared the fate of the whole of Marly's ostentatious, overreaching scheme, since almost from the first Marly was neglected, especially the planting. Later, François Michaux, the son, when he was in Nashville, gathered seeds of Yellowwood and it is told that their descendants grow still in the Tuileries gardens in Paris.

The elder Michaux's own life was to be thrown away, when he left America, on the far-off island of Madagascar, but of his fate and that of his trees he could know nothing now, as he sat down to write to Territorial Governor Blount an account of his discovery, with the information that the inner bark of the roots yielded a dye which he thought must be valuable.

And so the pioneer Tennesseeans came to learn. They reduced the roots to chips with the axe; the women then boiled the chips, and the yellow coloring matter was thus extracted. Many a yellow stripe in a piece of old-time homespun must have been dyed by this lovely tree, before synthetic dyes became cheap at the stores.

Yellowwood soon attracted the attention of the menfolk as well. Its lightness, combined with unusual strength, and the beautiful pale wood which takes so high a polish, made a unique gunstock, for in those days mountaineers were accustomed to buy the metal fittings and barrels from the gunsmith and blacksmith, but it was each man's pride to whittle out his own stock. If only Yellowwood did not habitually fork from near the base into several thin stems, no one of which would repay the cost of felling it, in terms of board feet, this would be a superb cabinet wood. But then, if Yellowwood were a merchantable tree it would long ago have grown rarer than it is.

Fortunately its lovely appearance, with that mottled bark, the graceful fronds of foliage, the milk-white spikes of drooping flowers like wistaria, and the clear sunset gold of the leaves in fall, have all combined to make this tree a favorite in cultivation. Not, to be sure, as the hardy Black Locust is popular — with the millions — but amongst the knowing who choose trees for their refinement and rarity.

THE LOCUSTS

(*Robinia*)

THE MEMBERS of this genus have zigzag twigs without a terminal bud, and small clusters of buds below the leafstalks which are protected by a scale-covering that embraces all the buds in clusters. The once-compound, alternate leaves have an odd number of medium-sized opposite leaflets (and one terminal one) which show untoothed margins and meshed veinlets. The drooping spikes of flowers are borne on long stalks from the leaf axils. The bell-shaped calyx tube is topped by unequal lobes; the wistaria-like corolla has the upper petal enclosing (not enclosed by) the lateral ones, in bud; the petals are short-clawed at base, the uppermost erect and reflexed at tip and, though large, barely longer than the other petals — the oblong-curved wing petals and the incurved obtuse keel petals. Of the 10 stamens, 9 are united by their stalks into a tube surrounding the styles, the tenth one free. The slender style is inflexed and bearded along the inner side near the tip. The drooping pods are thin and papery, nearly stalkless, long and narrow and compressed. The hard-coated seeds are oblique and attached by a stout persistent stalk.

BLACK LOCUST

Robinia Pseudo-Acacia Linnæus

OTHER NAMES: Yellow, White, Red, Green, Post, or Honey Locust. False, or Bastard Acacia.

RANGE: Originally, perhaps, only in the southern Appalachians, Virginia, the lower Ohio valley, and the Ozarks, at present naturalized as an escape from cultivation over most of the eastern United States, sometimes in the western states and Europe.

DESCRIPTION: *Bark* very thick and dark-brown or tinged with red, furrowed and sometimes cross-checked. *Twigs* at first coated in silvery woolly hairs which, dropping off, leave the twigs pale green, becoming by autumn reddish brown and flecked with small, scattered pale lenticels; thorns usually found at the base of the leafstalks and deciduous with them. *Leaves* compound, in over-all dimensions 8 to 14 inches long, with 7 to 19 leaflets, these dull, dark green. *Flowers* in midspring drooping on slender stalks in loose spikes 4 or 5 inches long, with milk-white petals, the uppermost having a large yellow blotch. *Fruit* a flat pod 3 to 4 inches long, ½ inch broad, with bright red-brown sides opening at the end of winter to release the dark orange-brown, spotted seeds. *Wood* medium-heavy (49 pounds to the cubic foot, dry weight), very hard, very strong and stiff, the heartwood brown, the sapwood paler and very thin.

When in 1607 the first Englishmen to make a permanent settlement in the future United States of America landed upon a little island in the James River, Virginia, moored their ships to some great trees leaning over the bank, and faced the forest wilderness of the New World, there wasn't an axeman or carpenter in this well-dressed shipload of fortune hunters, younger sons of prominent families, and ne'er-do-wells. Yet there have been illustrators and historians who represent them as building log cabins (no mean feat!) for their first habitations. Here, however, is the testimony, as to the first homes of these Virginians, by Mark Catesby, the British naturalist who visited Virginia only a century after the founding of Jamestown:

"Being obliged to run up with all the expedition possible such little houses as might serve them to dwell in, till they could find leisure to build larger and more convenient ones, they erected each of their little hovels on four only of these trees (the Locust-tree of Virginia), pitched into the ground to support the four corners; many of these posts are yet standing, and not only the parts underground, but likewise those above, still perfectly sound."

These words attest to two significant points — the great durability of Locust wood in contact with the soil, and the lack of any notion of log cabins. That form of domestic architecture did not exist in Britain, and these colonists had presumably not only never seen a log cabin but never even heard of one. For the log cabin was brought to us by the early Swedish colonists of Delaware, many decades later, and formed no part of the architecture of Jamestown, Plymouth, or most of the earliest European settlements on the Atlantic coast. Those early colonists first lived, as Mark Catesby says, in "hovels," and when they had time to make themselves houses they laboriously hewed out and tongued and tenoned the structural beams and covered them with clapboards.

Apparently the name of Locust for this species was given it first in Jamestown, for we have the evidence of William Strachey in his *Historie of Travaile into Virginia Britannia* (1610) which tells us of "a kynd of low tree, which beares a cod like to the peas, but nothing so big; we take yt to be locust." By this he meant that the James-towners supposed it to be the Old-World Locust tree (*Ceratonia Siliqua*) of the Mediterranean zone, the Carob, or St. John's-bread. Obviously Strachey and the others had never seen St. John's-bread, but the name of Locust has stuck to our tree. There is no substitute for it except by calling on another analogy, as the English do, and titling it False Acacia. But country people today, almost everywhere in the northern states, call this tree Honey Locust because of the sweet breath of the blossoms. Yet the botanical and horticultural works all try to confine the name Honey Locust to the Sweet Locust *Gleditsia tricanthos*. This confusion, which has persisted a century or so and promises to continue, is best circumvented here by designating our tree as the Black Locust, a name in good standing with the foresters.

Under any name, this tree is impressive, when it grows to a soldierly 80 feet, the trunk 3 or 4 feet thick and the topmost branches often spreading the ferny foliage high above the surrounding trees. When the Locust flowers, in late spring, its pendant spikes of honey-sweet blossoms look as though some white wistaria had climbed in the stalwart tree and let down fragrant tassels of bloom.

Among the Locust's numerous familiar charms, most famous is the so-called sleep of the leaves. At nightfall the leaflets droop on their stalklets, so that the whole leaf seems to be folding up for the night. Physiologists assure us that the mechanism of this "sleep" is the loss of cell turgidity or sap pressure in the little secondary stalks that bear each leaflet. Because some minds require that all things in Nature shall serve some useful purpose, as from a human point of view we understand usefulness, it has been asserted that the sleep of the Black Locust's leaves is a habit that has been acquired as a means of avoiding too great loss of moisture. But this can scarcely be so, since the leaves fold at night when the moisture content of the air normally rises and its warmth diminishes. In the heat of the day, when the leaves should be in the greatest danger of withering, they are fully expanded. So the "sleep" has not yet been explained in purposive terms.

It is not certain when Black Locust was first introduced into Europe. Either Jean Robin, herbalist to Henry IV of France, or his son Vespasien, grew seeds of this tree and sent them between 1601 and 1636, presumably from Louisiana. At any rate, the generic name *Robinia* does honor to these Robins. Toward the end of the eighteenth century in Europe the growing of Black Locust became a rage. No other American tree has so extensive a foreign literature. Senator de Neufchâteau, in 1803, published a 315-page book extolling its virtues and explaining its cultivation to the French. William Cobbett, famous English publicist, anti-Jacobin, politician, rural economist, having fled to America, took to growing Black Locust, between 1817 and 1819, on his farm on Long Island where there was then a vogue for the culture of this tree, the hope being to supply the British Navy with treenails. For the Locust nails of many an old-time vessel were stronger than the strongest hulls, and far longer-lived; the British gave as one excuse for their defeat on Lake Champlain, in the War of 1812, the superiority of Locust in our hastily built fleet.

But Cobbett made America too hot to hold him, by libeling the famous Dr. Rush for having allegedly killed George Washington by malpractice, so he returned to England with a quantity of Black Locust seed — and the corpse of Thomas Paine. This he had dug up from its neglected grave in New Rochelle, intending to inter it in a splendid monument, to atone for his former attacks on the author of *The Rights of Man*. The monument was never erected; on Cobbett's death, the coffin was auctioned off to a furniture dealer, and the renowned corpse inside was lost to history!

But Cobbett, if he failed to inter Paine nobly, did wonders keeping alive the popularity of Black Locust. His panegyric on this tree in his widely read *Woodlands* (1825) aroused sanguine hopes. To satisfy the demand he himself had created, Cobbett imported immense quantities of seeds from America and sold over a million plants. Even this did not suffice, and he exhausted the London nurseries to satisfy the clamor of his customers.

"The evidence of Cobbett's activity is very marked in the gardens around London and all other cities and towns throughout Great Britain . . . British-grown Acacia has been used occasionally in old furniture, and will compare favorably with satinwood for such work. Exposure to light and air improves the colour, and it is often mistaken for the latter wood. The burrs [burls], cut into veneer, although lighter in colour, compare favorably with Amboyna. On more than one estate the owners have planted Acacia trees for more than three generations for estate work, and have always refused to sell any as they have recognized the value of the timber for estate purposes." [1]

Long before Cobbett's day our pioneer ancestors learned that no other wood in America has more high qualities than the Locust's. In the first place almost the entire woody cylinder of the trunk is heartwood, always the strongest part of a tree. It is the seventh hardest in all our sylva and, as to strength in the position of a beam, Locust is the strongest in North America outside the tropics. It is the stiffest of all our woods, exceeding Hickory by 40 per cent. Of all important hardwoods, Black Locust shrinks least in drying, losing only 10 per cent in volume though 20 per cent in weight. It is the most durable of all our hardwoods; taking White Oak as the standard of 100 per cent, Black Locust has a durability of 250 per cent. The wood takes such a high polish as to appear varnished. The fuel value of Black Locust is higher than that of any other American tree, exceeding even Hickory and Oak, being almost the equal, per cord at 20 per cent moisture content, of a ton of anthracite coal.

Yet with all these splendid qualities Black Locust is not even

[1] A. L. Howard (1946), *Trees in Britain*.

mentioned in the usual lumbering statistics. The chief reason is that the Locust borer beetle (*Cyllene robiniæ*) is so ruinous in many regions that Black Locust is too seldom found in sound condition. In North America, but not in Europe, the infection is all but universal and no measures of control have had any effect. Locust boards are therefore almost unknown, and the only common use has been for fence posts, railway ties, and small articles such as rake teeth, tool handles, ladder rungs, and (in the days when such things were in common use) buggy hubs and policemen's clubs.

Not until 1936 did botanists get around to describing, as a distinct variety (variety *rectissima* Raber), a form of the Black Locust known as Shipmast Locust which farmers of New York State and New Jersey and estate owners of Long Island had, for a hundred years or more, recognized by its distinguishing points and superior qualities. The Shipmast Locust takes its name from the fact that the main stem grows straight up through the branches, without forking till near the top, like the mast of a ship, or like the stem of a Spruce. The lateral branches are few in number, and after leaving the main stem they rise upward at a sharp angle of 60 degrees to 90 degrees with the main axis. Commonly the lateral branches do not taper out to the end in the gradual and uniform manner of most trees, but instead they narrow down abruptly, somewhat in the manner of Japanese dwarf trees. Especially in winter is the Japanese look of the trees apparent. The shipmast habit and the short branches are found not only in close groves of these trees but even where the Shipmast Locust is growing alone on a lawn with all the space it needs to develop.

In the common Black Locust the bark, though deeply furrowed, has the horizontal lines of the furrows broken by many "cross checks," but on the Shipmast Locust there are none such and the massively heavy bark is very deeply furrowed, the ridges straight or somewhat twisted and standing out like the muscles of a Titan's leg, reminding one in its grain of the bark of the California Redwood save for the gray color. Flowering in the Shipmast Locust is comparatively sparse, and the calyx is usually green or yellowish green, not reddish or reddish brown as in the common Locust. Futhermore, the pistils seem too commonly infertile so that seed is scarce. Although there is no difference in the microscopic structure of the wood, the Shipmast produces a yellowish, not a reddish-brown heartwood. But most important of all, the wood of Shipmast Locust, in the neighborhood of New York, endures much longer in contact with the soil than that of the common sort, which ordinarily lasts fifteen years, while a surveyors' stake of Shipmast Locust, dated 1881 and dug up in 1942, was found to be in perfect condition.

Apparently Shipmast Locust is never found apart from cultivation; with its almost total lack of seeds, this could hardly be otherwise, and it appears that for generations a small but knowing group in the Hudson valley and on Long Island have been propagating this valuable tree.

Those who know it well call it sometimes the "Old-fashioned" and sometimes Yellow Locust. Where this variety originated and when is not known but it is most abundant in the oldest-settled parts of Long Island. To take a single example, the great Shipmast Locusts still standing at Roslyn, on the grounds of "Washington Tavern," the former residence of the old Dutch family of the Bogarts, are mentioned in an article in *The Long Island Farmer* for March 6, 1879, and stated then to have been planted about 1700 and probably introduced by Captain John Sands of Sands' Point. They were enormous and ancient trees in 1791, according to the memoirs of a member of the family.

The Shipmast Locust may not be as beautiful as a lawn specimen, but as a timber tree it is distinctly more valuable and less subject to borers than the typical Black Locust. If ever we come to our senses and start planting and growing our valuable hardwoods instead of cutting them down faster than they can be replaced, Shipmast Locust might well be one of the first varieties on which to concentrate.

The discovery of a possible ancestral form of the mysterious Shipmast Locust was announced in 1948 by the federal Department of Agriculture, as a result of a prolonged investigation by Dr. Henry H. Hopp of the Bureau of Plant Research in the quest of a beetle-free strain of Locust having the qualities of fine saw timber. In Randolph County, West Virginia, Dr. Hopp discovered scattered stands of tall, straight Black Locust, the finest quality in the country, producing trunks of arrowy straightness, free of branches for fifty feet or more. These trees are highly resistant to the attacks of borers and yet, unlike the Shipmast Locust, they seed heavily under forest conditions. Seeds are now being propagated by the Conservation Commission of West

Virginia and will be distributed for afforestation purposes. This strain is said to possess properties that make it particularly advantageous for mine props, millions of which are used in the state's great coal mining industry.

ROSE–FLOWERING LOCUST

Robinia viscosa Ventenat

OTHER NAME: Clammy Locust.

RANGE: Mountains of Pennsylvania south on the Appalachians to Alabama.

DESCRIPTION: *Bark* smooth, very thin and dark reddish brown on the trunk and on the slender, wide-spreading branches. *Twigs* bright red-brown, at first clammy and sticky, covered with small black lenticels, becoming by the second year dry and light brown. *Leaves* 7 to 12 inches long in over-all dimensions, consisting in 13 to 31 leaflets each 1½ to 2 inches long, ⅔ inch wide, with yellow midrib beneath. *Flowers* in thick, heavy, drooping spikes, the corolla ¾ inch long, pale or deep pink. *Fruit* a narrow winged pod about 2½ inches long with very small, dark reddish-brown and mottled seeds. *Wood* hard, close-grained, very heavy (50 pounds to the cubic foot, dry weight), the heartwood dark brown, the sapwood pale and thin.

The discoverer of this little tree (which is sometimes 20 feet high) was the first great American nature writer, William Bartram, whose classic *Travels,* first published in Philadelphia in 1791, was a favorite of Wordsworth and Coleridge, profoundly influencing them with its description of pure wilderness, so that the Lake Poets dreamed at one time of removing in a body to found a Poets' Perfect State on the banks of the Susquehana (chosen for its poetic name). Of Bartram's book, Carlyle wrote to Emerson that "all American libraries ought to provide themselves with that kind of books and keep them as a future *biblical* article."

William Bartram, himself the son of a famous botanist, old John Bartram of Philadelphia, was the first plantsman who ever collected in the southern Appalachians, and many were the trees which he, first of all white men, beheld. Often without guides, quite at ease even in the midst of the hostile Cherokees in the summer of 1776, William Bartram gives us this picture of Blue Ridge scenery on the day when he first collected the Rose-Flowering Locust:

"My next flight was up a very high peak, to the top of the Occonne Mountain, where I rested; and turning about found that I was now in a very elevated situation, from whence I enjoyed a view inexpressibly magnificent and comprehensive. The mountainous wilderness which I had lately traversed, down to the region of Augusta, appearing regularly undulated as the great ocean after a tempest; the undulations gradually depressing, yet perfectly regular, as the squama of fish, or imbrications of tile on a roof; the nearest ground to me of a perfect full green; next more glaucous; and lastly almost blue as the ether with which the most distant curve of the mountains seemed to be blended."

Of the little tree itself he says: "This beautiful flowering tree rose twenty to thirty feet high, with a crooked leaning trunk; the branches spread greatly, and wreathing about, some almost touching the ground; however there appears a singular pleasing wildness and freedom in its manner of growth; the slender subdivisions of the branches terminate with heavy compound panicles of rose or pink coloured flowers, and amidst a wreath of beautiful pinnated leaves."

In 1790 André Michaux collected the Rose-flowering Locust in the same region (the mountains of South Carolina) and introduced it into his acclimation garden at Ten Mile Station near Charleston. Thence the plants were sent to Michaux's son François in Paris, and the first plantation of which we know in Europe was made from descendants of these plants by Louis Guillaume Lemonnier in his garden near Montreuil. Then, from the time of the elder Michaux for nearly a century, Rose-flowering Locust disappeared from scientific ken. It became a lost tree even as was John Bartram's famed Franklinia, and Michaux's own little flower, Shortia. Not until 1882, or 97 years after it was first found, was the Rose-flowering Locust rediscovered, on Buzzard's Ridge near Highlands, North Carolina, by the distinguished Baltimore collector, bibliophile, and philanthropist John Donnell Smith.

Presumably the wood of this tree would be valuable if ever the trunks grew large enough, in view of its strength and hardness, but a species so outstandingly pretty in flower need neither toil nor spin. It does, however, have high value because of its extensive creeping roots and the many sucker shoots it sends out; these make an excellent binder of soil on railroad and highway embankments and road cuts. At the same time, it beautifies the raw spots it thus covers, so that this plant has come into great vogue all over the country. It is now escaped from cultivation northward to Nova Scotia and Wisconsin and extensively on the piedmont of Carolina.

In midspring the flowers appear, and though the blossoms have no odor, they make up for this in size and in grace of form and above all in color; the flesh-tinted strains are not so pleasing to some eyes, but the rich rose-hued are unsurpassed in depth and warmth. So brilliant and large are they that they quite transform the roadsides where they are planted, and when encountered in their native wilds they look like garden flowers bred by the most premeditated art; it seems at first hard to believe that they had already attained to such positively showy perfection when first discovered so long ago by Bartram.

THE PRICKLY ASHES

(*Zanthoxylum*)

The Prickly Ashes are trees or shrubs with commonly prickly twigs and leafstalks, and alternate compound leaves that are translucently dotted, the mostly unisexual flowers small and greenish, in axillary or terminal branched clusters. The petals number 3 to 5, the male flowers with 3 to 5 stamens and the female with 1 to 5 distinct pistils and rarely some stamens. The fruit is a fleshly, 2-valved, 1- to 2-seeded pod with oblong, black and shining seeds.

TOOTHACHE–TREE

Zanthoxylum americanum Miller

OTHER NAMES: Prickly Ash. Wait-a-bit. Sting-tongue. Angelica-tree. Suterberry. Hercules'-club. Spitberry.

RANGE: Southern Quebec and extreme southern Ontario to Virginia, westward through the Lower Peninsula of Michigan, Wisconsin, central Minnesota to the central Dakotas, south to Georgia, Missouri and eastern Kansas.

DESCRIPTION: *Bark* thin, smooth, gray or brownish. *Twigs* usually armed with a pair of spines beneath each leafstalk, bearing reddish flower buds. *Leaves* 2 to 9 inches long in over-all dimensions, with 3 to 11 leaflets (always with an odd number), each 1 to 3 inches long, dark green above, paler beneath. *Flowers* with the sexes usually in separate trees, a few bisexual, in axillary branched clusters borne on the wood of the previous season, appearing before the leaves; calyx none; petals 4 or 5; pistils 2 to 5. *Fruit* a berry-like pod about ½ inch long, on short stalks, 1- to 2-seeded. *Wood* very soft, medium-light (35 pounds to the cubic foot), pale brown.

One does not expect to find a member of the Citrus family in our northern sylva, and a first glance at this odd little tree or tall shrub (it sometimes reaches a maximum of 20 feet in height) suggests an

Orange or a Lemon tree. With leaves like an Ash's (though of course this is no true Ash), with inconspicuous flowers and a cluster of the oddest little hard, red fruits clinging close to the bare wood, it is not much like any other tree in one's experience. Yet one of the earmarks of the Citrus family is its aromatic and bitter properties, as in the rind of the lemon or orange. And one whiff of the lemony odor of the fruits of the Toothache-tree, or one nibble on their skin — which first completely benumbs the palate and then fiercely bites it — will inform your senses that you are making the acquaintance of something with an exotic flavor. Perhaps the odor should be described as partly lemony but also with some of the heavy odor (which is disagreeable on second thought) of rue.

The bark too is aromatic, and everything about the little tree naturally suggests that it must contain medicinal properties. Indeed the alkaloid called xanthoxylin pervades many parts of the tree and has been used as a stimulant and diaphoretic and in the cure of flatulence and diarrhea. The bark and the berries, especially the latter, are the parts sought by commercial collectors. Your druggist may still carry Prickly Ash berries, for they appear in the *U.S. Pharmacopoeia*, ninth edition, and in the fifth edition of the *National Formulary*.

The name Toothache-tree derives from the use of the berries and bark in the home treatment of toothache, and there is certainly a sort of anesthetic effect upon the nerves when the fruits are taken into the mouth. But, if swallowed, they are said to produce a burning sensation in the stomach.

Toothache-tree forms a much-branched, sprawling, and rather broad-headed growth, and is found in dense thorny thickets, around old Tamarack bogs and in low wet woods or occasionally on rocky wooded slopes. It also grows in little isolated groves as an invader of the prairie. The flowers attract no attention when they appear in April or May, and the leaves, which follow them, little enough. It is not until the fruits begin to load down the branches, and the leaves turn early a soft dull yellow, that one realizes how curious a plant in our midst is this one. The fruits, about the size of very small peas, are at first bright red; as they dry they turn brown, then burst, and each one forcibly discharges a black, shining seed.

Lepidopterists search every twig of Prickly Ash for a caterpillar known down south as the orange dog. Somewhat injurious to young Citrus trees, it has been spreading north and west, in recent times, in the Prickly Ash and Hoptree. It is sought for the beauty of its imago, or adult form; the larva, however, looks like nothing so much as a bird dropping, and if you molest it, it throws back its head and extrudes a pair of "horns" (red glands) which exude an odor unpleasant as the rotting rinds of orange or lemon. But collectors prefer to raise their own butterflies from the larval stage, since that is the best way to obtain undamaged specimens. From the ugly orange dog emerges in due time the giant swallowtail, one of the most curious and magnificent species of *Papilio*. Brown above, but bright yellow below, the wings of this butterfly make a brilliant contrast, as it floats along with strong, leisurely flight.

Not the least of the strange things about this butterfly is that when its wings are placed in contact with a photographic plate in complete darkness, a perfect image of the wings is imprinted there when the plate is developed. The nature of this secret emanation is unknown; but, according to Austin H. Clark,[1] a specimen of a giant swallowtail which had been dead for forty years gave, after thirty days of exposure to the photographic plate, a ghostly but recognizable image.

1 *The Butterflies of the District of Columbia and Vicinity.*

THE HOPTREES

(*Ptelea*)

THESE LITTLE TREES or shrubs grow by axillary buds. The twigs appear marked by the inversely heart-shaped narrow leaf scars; the long-stalked leaves are compound with 3 to 5 leaflets. The flowers appear in terminal branched clusters, some unisexual and others bisexual, the stamens in the female flowers aborted, while in the male flowers the pistil is small and not stalked. The male flowers possess 3 to 4 stamens as long as the 4 to 5 petals, while in the female flowers the ovary is stalked, flattened, and solitary with a short style and a 2- to 3-lobed stigma. The fruit takes the form of a broad-winged, papery-inflated, hop-like veiny sack around the seed.

HOPTREE

Ptelea trifoliata Linnæus

OTHER NAMES: Wafer Ash. Aguebark. Quininetree. Swamp Dogwood. Pickaway Anise. Shrubby Trefoil. Wingseed.

RANGE: Southern New York, westward through the southern tip of Ontario, southern Michigan, to the southeastern corner of Wisconsin, eastern and southern Iowa and eastern Kansas, Utah and California, south to Florida, the Gulf Coast, Texas, New Mexico and Arizona, and Mexico.

DESCRIPTION: *Bark* smooth, with a fetid odor. *Twigs* slender, dark brown, shining, marked with watery excrescences. *Leaves* compound, with leaflets 4 to 6 inches long and 2½ to 3 inches broad, the middle or terminal usually larger than the lateral, thick, dark green and lustrous above, paler below. *Flowers* small, greenish, ill-smelling, appearing usually before the leaves, on slender stalks. *Fruit* 1 inch across, thin-winged, borne on stalks, with little dark red-brown seeds. *Wood* hard, close-grained, and very heavy (51 pounds to the cubic foot, dry weight), with yellowish brown heartwood and thin sapwood.

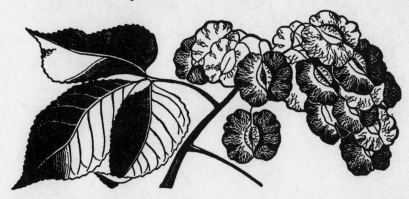

This curious little tree with a wide but eccentric range rarely achieves more than 20 feet in height, though the trunk grows straight and slender, and for the most it is no more than a shrub. Its branches are short; its leaves remind one of poison ivy in their arrangement;

its bark has a decidedly unpleasant odor, and so have its flowers, which are sought out by the carrionflies and pollinated by them. The fruits, which droop all winter on the tree and finally break off to sail by their wings on the wind, were once in high repute as a substitute for hops. As to the wood, the little tree's growth is too insignificant to make it of value.

In its roots lie the qualities that have given it whatever importance it may ever have had, aside from its use as an ornamental — in which it finds more popularity in England than at home. The root is aromatic and to the taste bitter and pungent; it contains the alkaloid berberine. Our ancestors imagined that anything sufficiently bitter might be a substitute for quinine; Hoptree root has also been used as a remedy for dyspepsia and as a mild tonic promoting the appetite. That handy compendium of folk-lore *materia medica, The Herbalist*,[1] observes that "The bark of the root of Hoptree is officinal, and yields its virtues to boiling water." But it might be well to add that there is a difference between "officinal," meaning on the market as a "remedy," and "official," meaning recognized by medical authority.

[1] By Joseph E. Meyers, Hammond, Indiana (1934).

THE SUMACS

(*Rhus*)

Thick, pithy twigs, and fleshy roots and, in our species, compound leaves characterize the members of this group. The sexes are usually separated, not only in different flowers, but frequently a given tree bears only male or only female flowers; sometimes both are found on the same plant, and bisexual flowers occur occasionally with the unisexual. The calyx coheres with a conspicuous disk at the bottom of the flower, but the ovary is free from both and has 3 styles rising from its center. In the male flower the 5 stamens are inserted on the margin of the disk and alternate with the 5 petals. The sometimes velvety-hairy, sometimes smooth and more or less resinous skin of the fruit (a little drupe) contains a bony stone embedded in pulp.

STAGHORN SUMAC

Rhus typhina Linnæus

OTHER NAMES: Velvet, Virginia, or American Sumac. Vinegar-tree.

RANGE: From the Maritime Provinces and Quebec to Minnesota, south to Maryland, Virginia, West Virginia, northern Kentucky, northern Indiana and Illinois to northeastern Iowa, and in the mountains to North Carolina.

DESCRIPTION: *Bark* thin, smooth, and dark brown on the trunk. *Twigs* containing milky juice, downy in first year with deep velvety brown hairs, marked in second season by large leaf scars and orange lenticels persisting into the third and fourth years, when the twigs, now thick and lumpy, become smooth. *Leaves* compound, measuring 1¼ to 2 feet long, with a long, stout, red, downy stalk enclosing at its enlarged base the axillary bud; leaflets 11 to 31, in opposite stalkless pairs except the short-stalked terminal one, the middle leaflet usually the longest (about 5 inches), exuding milky juice when broken. *Flowers* in very large, densely flowered, compound, erect clusters, opening one after another; clusters of male flowers 1 foot long, 5 to 6 inches through, with wide-spreading

branches, the petals greenish red, thin, strap-shaped; anthers bright orange. Female flowers in smaller, denser, less branched clusters, the petals green, thick, short, hooded, the disk bright red. *Fruit* red-purple or maroon, covered with dense velvety coating of acrid crimson hairs, with a hard, pale brown stone. *Wood* very light (27 pounds to the cubic foot, dry weight), very soft, brittle, and coarse-grained, with thin orange heartwood streaked with green, and thick white sapwood.

The richly velvety, thick, branching twigs, so like the antlers of a stag when they are "in the velvet," have given this handsome little tree the first part of its popular name. The second half, which is spelled, according to your taste, Sumach, Summaque, Shumac, Shumack, and probably with even more variation, is said to derive from the Arabic title for another species (*Rhus coriaria*) of the Mediterranean zone, which is *simmâk* according to some, and *summaq* if you follow Webster. Still others there are who insist that the word is simply a corruption of "shoe-make," in reference to the tree's properties useful in tanning fine leather. The name *typhina* is an allusion to the supposed medical virtues of the plant, applied in the past by country folk in the treatment of typhoid fever. As for the name *Rhus,* you may — if you are one of the happy quibblers who enjoy such innocent detection — trace it all the way back to ancient Greece, where the great botanist Diocorides had a word for it.

There is a Danish proverb that says "a dear child has many names," and certainly the varied titles of this tree and its relatives show the interest in which they have been held through the ages. Yet there is nothing in Europe to compare with the American Sumac, and of all the Sumacs of the New World the Staghorn is the most striking. In autumn gorgeous, often mottled shades of orange, crimson, or purple may be seen on the same tree, and with them other leaves which have not yet turned, but keep a deep green on the upper surface and a silvery underside. No wonder this tree caught the eye of some of our very first colonists, who must have sent it back to Europe in the sixteenth century; at least, it was described by Caspar Bauhin, the celebrated physician and botanist of Basle, Switzerland, in 1596, in a work whose modest little title was *Pinax Theatri Botanicorum seu Index in Theophrasti, Diocoridis, Plinii, et botanicorum qui a sicula scripserunt opera.*

Sumac is one of the chief plants to give to our Indian summer scene a sort of mellow savagery, a colorful wilderness character like that of a "good Injun" in a childhood storybook. It was, indeed, a part of the redskin's peace pipe. For the leaf of the tobacco plant was seldom smoked by him unadulterated; to him a "smoke" was understood to be a blend of cured leaves among which Sumac was a most important ingredient. For our own folk, in the days when our land was young, the plant had a friendly place in daily life. A cooling drink like lemonade was made out of the fruits, whose acidulous hairs contribute a pleasant sour taste. The country people of the Appalachians, especially in Maryland and the Virginias, used to bring Sumac to the tanneries, for its leaves and twigs are rich in tannin; the finest grades of leather, at one time, were cured with Sumac.

With synthetics and progress those simple uses are over. But still in summer, unchanged, the Staghorn Sumac lifts its immense panicles of vivid flowers among the great frond-like pinnate leaves, and still in autumn the brilliant fruits, the most variously brilliant foliage, shout out their color to the dying year. Flaunting orange, war-paint vermilion, buttery yellow, or sometimes angry purple may be seen all together on a single tree. More, it commonly happens that half of a compound leaf, or even half of a leaflet may retain its rich, deep, shining green, in calm contrast to the flaming autumnal hues. And at all times the lower surface of the foliage keeps its pallid, glaucous cast that, when early frost has brushed it, turns silver. Probably no tree in the country, perhaps in the world, may exhibit so many and such contrasting shades and tints, such frosty coolness with its fire.

POISON SUMAC

Rhus Vernix Linnæus

OTHER NAMES: Poison Dogwood. Poison Elder. Poison Ash. Poisontree. Poisonwood. Thunderwood.

RANGE: Florida to central Maine, southern Vermont, rarely in southern Quebec, the southern tip of Ontario, throughout Ohio and Indiana, southern Michigan, northern Illinois, to Wisconsin and Minnesota, and in the South westward through Mississippi and Louisiana to eastern Texas; largely absent from the Mississippi basin except as listed above.

DESCRIPTION: *Bark* thin, smooth, light gray. *Twigs* covered with many raised lenticels, flexible, smooth, stout and gray. *Leaves* compound, 7 to 14 inches long in over-all dimension, alternate, deciduous, the leaflets 7 to 13 in number, 1½ to 5 inches long, opposite, dark green and shining above, pale below. *Flowers* with the sexes usually on different trees, very small, yellowish, in open slender clusters near the ends of branches in the axils of leaves. *Fruits* yellowish or ivory white, nearly spherical, less than ½ inch thick, in drooping, slender clusters, with solitary ribbed stones and thin flesh. *Wood* very light (27 pounds to the cubic foot, dry weight), soft, the heartwood light yellow streaked with brown, the sapwood paler.

Every American child, unless he has been confined exclusively to city life, has been taught to recognize poison ivy by means of the old ditty: *Leaflets three, quickly flee.* He knows that poison ivy is either a climbing vine or a sprawling shrub, found in fence rows, woods, and thickets. And once he has learned to recognize the plant and has had, perhaps, some painful experience with touching it, he is on the watch for it. But the ditty does not describe Poison Sumac, tree-sized relative of poison ivy, as witness this testimony of a well-known tree student:

"I had been botanizing in some bottom lands of Mad River on an October afternoon and had been successful in finding several rarities; as I turned to leave the swampy ground, I noticed a tall shrub with most exquisitely colored leaves; I worked my way carefully over the soft muck and, on reaching the bush, found that it was new to me. I cut off several shoots, some with their clusters of beautiful red-purple leaves and others with a few whitish berries, intending to look up the little tree in my books when I reached home. I put the branches with

my other specimens into a long box, tied it securely and hastened . . .
home. . . . I eagerly took up the unknown specimen and again admired
the lovely, glossy red and purple leaves with their brilliant crimson
stalks set on a twig of soft, creamy gray — an unusually charming
complex of colors. Having no flowers to help me identify this lovely
thing, I began to trace it down in the leaf-key of Sargent's *Trees of
North America*; I had almost reached the end of this long analytical
key when my eye fell upon the line leading to the genus *Rhus* and
then came the shocking realization that I had been playing with fire —
my beautiful little tree was the Poison Sumach!" [1]

Poison Sumac resembles poison ivy distinctly in flower and in fruit,
but fruit and flower are both small and have each their passing season.
Much of the time Poison Sumac would only remind one, by its
foliage, of the common and harmless sorts of Sumac. But no innocent
Sumac grows in swamps, like the poison kind. The harmless species
have erect, dense, and many-branched clusters of fruits covered with
greenish or reddish or rusty, velvety hairs. The fruit of the poisonous
species is of a dead, unhealthy-looking, waxen whiteness, or yellow like
old ivory. Unfortunately there is just enough resemblance to the
berries of mistletoe to deceive some persons, and it is well to remember
that true mistletoe is a little shrub with greenish twigs which grows
perched upon the branches of high trees. The gorgeous coloration of
the autumnal leaves of Poison Sumac, too, tempts the fingers. It is
best to recall that the "good" Sumacs have, most of them, finely
toothed leaves while the "bad" kind show only a few low scallops on
the margins.

There is general agreement that the sap of this species is the most
intense and virulent of all contact poisons in the American sylva, save
only the tropical Poisontree of Florida. The poisonous principle in
the sap is an amber-red, clear, sticky resin; it floats in water and is not
a volatile substance; hence its particles cannot float on the air and give
susceptible persons dermatitis without contact, as is often supposed.
The pollen, for instance, may be rubbed on the skin, or swallowed,
with no injurious effect and even the bark, plant hairs, and surface of
uninjured leaves, though intensely poisonous, may be rubbed on the
skins of susceptible persons, providing that the tissue is not broken.

[1] William B. Werthner, *Some American Trees.*

For it is only the sap that is poisonous and it is secreted by special poison canals which are found in the bast of the stem, in the veins of the leaves, and around the seed in the fruit. A new set of canals forms with each spring and autumn growth of the wood, each separate canal being surrounded by secretory cells which pour their poison into the canals; even the flowers have them, and the slightest injury to the plant sends the sap pouring out.

Iron chloride salts in a solution of alcohol is the easiest remedy to apply, once poisoning has set in. This is essentially the formula of the common "D.D.D." of the drugstores. Calamine lotion is also good. Where the case is serious and widespread, physicians often bandage the lesions with sugar of lead. The Public Health Service has recently announced a vanishing-cream preventive, which can be rubbed invisibly on the hands and face and is supposed to impart immunity to persons going into the woods. Many country folk have long believed that the best treatment is to swallow some of the leaves. This sounds dangerous indeed, and perhaps no physician would recommend it; yet on the principle of "a hair of the dog that bit you," modern medicine has also tried the "shock treatment": the poisonous oleoresin is given in gelatine capsules which are swallowed, and the skin thereafter is said to be desensitized to the poisoning, just as in the case of the treatment of many other allergies.

When the poisonous sap flows from an injured part of the plant, it soon hardens on exposure to the atmosphere into a sort of black varnish and has indeed been used in the preparation of a durable and shiny varnish similar to that obtained from the Lacquertree (*Rhus vernicifera*). Japanese lacquer workers, it has been reported, are often the victims of constant poisoning, though tradition has it that immunity is acquired — after the first seven years! All over the main island of Japan and in some districts of Kiushu and Shikoku the Lacquertree is cultivated, and in the valley of Tadami-gawa whole villages of lacquer workers are embowered in groves of this beautiful venomous tree. Why there has never arisen a lacquer industry based upon our probably equally valuable Poison Sumac, no American needs to be told.

But many will ask, perhaps, if the world would not be a better place without so toxic a tree in it. Undoubtedly this were so, if the ideal were a world in which all of Nature should be sweet and refined,

harmless and useful, park-like and tame. But Nature is not thus —
certainly not American Nature, certainly not the aboriginal wilderness.
And it is in the bogs and swamps, so hostile to human encroachment,
that wilderness still lingers close to the city, the village, and the farmhouse. If one longs for the Nature of strange and far-off places, where
curious vegetation waves its fronds, if one would like to see the
"deadly Upas Tree" of travelers' tales — one does not have to cross the
sea. As strange, as poisonous, as beautiful a tree as anything the
tropics have to show grows down there in the old swamp, with the
chain fern, the sphagnum moss, and the Black Gum.

THE HOLLIES

(*Ilex*)

THESE TREES and shrubs have scaly buds and simple leaves. The flowers are small, greenish white, inconspicuous, and unisexual, with the sexes on separate trees; the calyx is 4- to 6-lobed, and the 4 to 6 petals are free or united at base into a corolla. The stamens are as many as the petals, and the pistil is compound with a 4- to 8-celled ovary, a short style or none, and as many stigmas as there are cells of the ovary. The fruit is a drupe containing as many bony nutlets as there are carpels, imbedded in thin flesh.

CHRISTMAS HOLLY

Ilex opaca Aiton

OTHER NAMES: American, Prickly, or Evergreen Holly.

RANGE: St. Augustine and Charlotte Harbor, Florida, north near the coast to Quincy, Massachusetts, and up the Mississippi valley to southeastern Missouri, and to the lower slopes of the southern Appalachians, west to Arkansas and southeastern Texas; in Kentucky only in the mountains, but common in Tennessee up to 3000 feet altitude.

DESCRIPTION: *Bark* roughened by little warts, greenish or grayish but not furrowed or scaly. *Twigs* at first rusty-downy but soon hairless and pale brown. *Leaves* 2 to 4 inches long, usually prickly-margined, dull yellowish-green above and paler green beneath, remaining on the twigs 3 years. *Flowers* in short clusters from the axils of young leaves, on slender stalks, the male clusters 3- to 9-flowered, but the female only 1- or rarely 2-flowered, blooming in midspring, small and greenish. *Fruit* a shiny red berry. *Wood* nearly white, very hard, strong, tough, fine-textured, medium heavy (40 pounds to the cubic foot, dry weight).

No one needs a description of the appearance of the Christmas Holly's leaves and berries. But so relentless has been the attack upon the female trees in fruit that only far from cities is the Holly a common tree. Low altitudes are its favorite habitat, yet it does not grow on wet ground. Sometimes it is scattered in with Pines, Magnolias, Hickory, Sweet Gum, and Sassafras; again, the traveler in the South may find himself in a beautiful little forest of pure Holly. With its inescapable associations of the great festival, such a grove seems all dressed up for Christmas — at any time of year! Down south the Holly sometimes grows 100 feet tall with a trunk 4 feet thick, but in the circumscription of this book it is a little tree, densely pyramidal in shape, with a short trunk about 2 feet in diameter at best, and only 20 to 40 feet high. Though sometimes the prickles are lacking on the margins of the leaves, Holly is still the only tree within the area embraced by this book, except in the southern Appalachians, which is at once broad-leaved and evergreen. All our other evergreens, of course, are needle-leaved. The broad-leaved evergreen habit is characteristic of tropical trees, yet we associate Holly in our minds with cold and snow.

The problem of conservation of the Christmas Holly from destruction will never be settled until the public stops buying more than it needs, and the law begins to police the market. For the real problem is that too much of the Holly on the market is simply stripped from the trees by professional pickers who violate the property rights of the owners of the woods. True that the owner has a legal right to sell all the Holly he wants, but in many cases the owner is never consulted by the vandals who relieve him of his property. If boughs of Holly are to be removed, they should be sawed, but ordinarily they are torn off, thus opening the way to disease and death. The Wild Flower Preservation Society recommends that Christmas Holly, when purchased, be shellacked. This will preserve it from decay, and in that way the same Holly can be used year after year, just like Christmas-tree ornaments, lights, and other fittings, thus aiding in conservation.

A study of all the colonial gardens of Virginia shows that Holly was a favorite in most of them, for, slow though its growth, Holly deserves a place of the first honor wherever the climate permits. The number of entries in George Washington's diary concerning the Christmas Holly is surprisingly large. It seems that the master of "Mount Vernon" was devoted to this tree. For Holly has exactly that formal elegance which we should expect to please the taste of George Washington. In one year he tells of transplanting many little Hollies from the woods. In another he confesses to his diary (what so many gardeners are unwilling to confess even to themselves) that his experiment was a complete failure; all the Hollies had died. On a March day Washington notes "received a Swan, 4 wild Geese, and 2 Barrels of Holly Berries (in Sand) from my brother John." These he sowed on the seventh of April, in the South Semicircle in the rear of the mansion; but he was still delighted, on March 28, 1786, to receive from Colonel "Lighthorse Harry" Lee of "Stratford" (father of Robert E. Lee) a number of small Holly trees boxed with earth, and these he set out with his great Holly planting in the South Semicircle. Today thirteen of the Hollies which Washington planted still stand.

As a valuable cabinet wood, Christmas Holly has never been appreciated by the buying public, although the wood technicians and some lumbermen understand its value. Harder even than Black Locust, almost as hard as Dogwood, Holly is yet only in the medium-heavy class. Its texture is so uniform throughout the woody cylinder that its growth lines are practically indistinguishable in the greenish-white wood; this is due perhaps to the fact that Holly is primarily a sapwood tree. Such a hard, pale, even-grained wood is ideal for taking dyes. Practically all the white and black inlaid lines in musical instruments and furniture and much of the colored wood in marquetry are Holly. Modern styles in elaborate furniture sometimes call for the use of bizarre shades impossible to find in natural wood; Holly fills in these lacks by obligingly taking any sort of stain or dye. It is unexcelled for taking enamel finishes. Sliced $\frac{1}{60}$ to $\frac{1}{16}$ inch thick, it makes an ideal veneer. Because it is so hard, it can be used for all sorts of turnery, knife handles, and, dyed black, for black piano keys. Engravers, because of its whiteness and even texture, demand it in art work; more nearly than any other American wood, it approaches ivory in color. It is fortunate that it yields so little lumber that it is not heavily cut, since the depredations of the Christmas-green pickers take toll enough.

MOUNTAIN HOLLY

Ilex montana Torrey and Gray

RANGE: Western Massachusetts and the uplands of New York State, southward in the Appalachians to eastern Tennessee and central Georgia, rare near Charleston, South Carolina, in western Florida, northeastern Mississippi, and West Feliciana Parish, Louisiana.

DESCRIPTION: *Bark* very thin, light brown, roughened by many lenticels. *Twigs* zigzag, pale reddish brown becoming dark gray. *Leaves* deciduous, thin, 2 to 5 inches long, 1½ to 2½ inches wide, light green above and pale below. *Flowers* in small clusters crowded at the ends of spur-like side twigs of the previous year, or solitary on branchlets of the year. *Fruit* bright scarlet, ½ inch thick. *Wood* hard, medium-heavy (40 pounds to the cubic foot, dry weight), creamy white.

We always think of Holly — any Holly — as being an evergreen, but this one, like most of our northern hardwoods, is deciduous. Often only a shrub, at most a tree 30 to 40 feet high with a short trunk and slender branches forming a narrow pyramidal head, the Mountain Holly blends into the mass of Appalachian forest greenery as thoroughly as a plain-clothes detective is supposed to merge himself anonymously in a crowd. So successful was Mountain Holly at this concealment in plain sight that botanists had been combing the eastern seaboard for a hundred years or more before, in 1840, this modest tree was first distinguished, in the Catskill Mountains, and made known to science. The flowers appear in June when the leaves are more than half grown, and the pretty berries shine out for a while when the leaves are yellowing and dropping in the early fall; then the tree becomes winter-naked and even more completely blended in with all the trunks and stems of our deciduous and hardwood forests.

THE MAPLES
(*Acer*)

MAPLE LEAVES are opposite on the twig and simple and deeply
lobed, or pinnately compound in the case of one species, the Box
Elder, with 3 to 7 principal nerves arising from the base. In falling,
the leafstalks leave small U-shaped scars on the roundish twig. The
buds are scaly, the inner scales marking the base of the twig with
ring-like scars. The flowers are regular and usually have the sexes in
separate flowers or on separate trees, or frequently some perfect or
bisexual flowers are found amongst the unisexual. The calyx, which
is generally colored, has 5 separate or united sepals. The petals are
lacking, or, if present, are 5 in number and distinct from each other.
In the center of the flower is a ring-like fleshy disk. The stamens
number 4 to 10. The ovary is 2-lobed, with 2 styles between the lobes,
which are coherent below but divergent above into 2 stigmatic
branches. The fruit is composed of 2 separable samaras (the familiar
"keys" of Maples) which consist in nut-like, laterally flattened carpels
furnished with a long, papery, veiny wing which is broader near the
outer end.

SUGAR MAPLE

Acer Saccharum Marshall

OTHER NAMES: Hard or Rock Maple. Sugartree.

RANGE: Maritime Provinces and eastern Quebec westward north of the Great Lakes to Minnesota, and southward to New Jersey and Pennsylvania and along the mountains to Georgia, westward through Tennessee, Kentucky, Illinois and northern Missouri to central Iowa and Minnesota.

DESCRIPTION: *Bark* of old trunks brownish or grayish and finely scaly, becoming deeply furrowed. *Twigs* at first smooth and green, soon becoming brown or orange-brown and marked with the V-shaped leaf scars. *Leaves* thin, dark green above, paler green or whitened beneath, 3-lobed or 5-lobed with a main nerve running to the tip of each lobe, 3 to 6 inches long and broad. *Flowers* appearing with the leaves in clusters at or near the ends of the twigs of the preceding season, drooping, the male and female in separate clusters or sometimes on separate trees, or, again, with some bisexual flowers amongst the unisexual; calyx 5-lobed; petals none; stamens about 7. *Fruits* 1 to 1½ inches long, the wings markedly veiny and parallel or slightly divergent. *Wood* very tough, strong, medium-hard, medium-heavy (44 pounds to the cubic foot, dry weight), the heartwood light brown tinged with red, the sapwood thin and paler.

The most magnificent display of color in all the kingdom of plants is the autumnal foliage of the trees of North America. Over them all, over the clear light of the Aspens and Mountain Ash, over the leaping flames of Sumac and the hell-fire flickerings of poison ivy, over the war-paint of the many Oaks, rise the colors of one tree — the Sugar Maple — in the shout of a great army. Clearest yellow, richest crimson, tumultuous scarlet, or brilliant orange — the yellow pigments shining through the over-painting of the red — the foliage of Sugar Maple at once outdoes and unifies the rest. It is like the mighty, marching melody that rides upon the crest of some symphonic weltering sea and, with its crying song, gives meaning to all the calculated dissonance of the orchestra.

There is no properly planted New England village without its Sugar Maples. They march up the hill to the old white meetinghouse and down from the high school, where the youngsters troop home laughing in the golden dusk. The falling glory lights upon the shoulders of the postman, swirls after the children on roller skates, drifts through the windows of a passing bus to drop like largesse in the laps of the passengers. On a street where great Maples arch, letting down their shining benediction, people seem to walk as if they had already gone to glory.

Outside the town, where the cold pure ponds gaze skyward and the white crooked brooks run whispering their sesquipedalian Indian names, the Maple leaves slant drifting down to the water; there they will sink like galleons with painted sails, or spin away and away on voyages of chance that end on some little reef of feldspar and hornblende and winking mica schist. Up in the hills the hunter and his russet setter stride unharmed through these falling tongues of Maple fire, that flicker in the tingling air and leap against the elemental blue of the sky where the wind is tearing crow calls to tatters.

As a street tree, Sugar Maple is surpassed in form adapted to traffic only by the White Elm; and it is far less demanding of water, less injured by disturbance to its roots when pipes and drains are laid. But it suffers from city smoke and industrial gases; that is what keeps it a village tree, a tree of old colonial towns. On the lawn it develops, from its egg shape in youth, a benignant length of the lower limbs which is ideal for the play of children. The fine tracery of the tree in winter stands revealed in all its mingled strength and elegance. In spring the greenish-yellow flowers appear at the same time that the leaves

begin to open like a baby's hand. The full spread of its foliage in summer gives what is perhaps the deepest, coolest shade granted by any of our northern trees. Not until fall do the "keys," the winged fruits, mature. When they drop at last, they go spinning away, joined like Siamese twins, on their veiny, insect-like wings, with a gyroscope's motion.

Under forest conditions, Sugar Maple may grow to 120 feet, with a 3- or 4-foot trunk clear of branches half the way — a cylinder of nearly knot-free wood almost unrivaled among our hardwoods. It is immensely strong and durable, especially the whitish sapwood called by the lumberman Hard Maple; a marble floor in a Philadelphia store wore out before a Hard Maple flooring laid there at the same time. Few are the standard commercial uses for lumber where Hard Maple does not figure, either at the top of the list or high on it. Tough and resistant to shock, it becomes smoother, not rougher, with much usage — as you will notice if you look at an old-fashioned rolling pin.

And Sugar Maple can produce some notable fancy grains. There was a day that might be called the Bird's-eye Maple Era. Some of us were young then, and may have believed it when we were told that the figure in the best bedroom set was made by woodpeckers. But woodpeckers work over a trunk in a straight line, and that is not how bird's-eye is found in Maple. It is due, say some botanists, to the presence of hundreds of bark-bound buds; others believe the effect is produced by fungal growths; in either case, when the saw passes through these, on a tangential plane, the dainty effect is seen on the cut surface. Familiar to all is the figure displayed by curly Maple, for it is the wood used for the backs of fine fiddles. Produced by dips in the fibers, it gives a striped effect that the violin makers insist upon procuring, rare though the figure is. In the age when an American made his own gunstocks, curly Maple was his favorite.

But even the featureless, straight-grain wood has been in demand for furniture since the earliest cabinetmakers of New England plied their tools. Today it is more popular than ever, in designs good, bad, or indifferent. The cut of Sugar Maple is probably in the neighborhood of 480,000,000 board feet a year. In Vermont, where the New England hurricane of 1939 downed an estimated million Maples, only the increasing farm abandonment keeps the young sugar bush growth ahead of the saw, in the state that is, above all others, famous for its maple sugar production. For the pressure for Maple logs at the sawmills has forced the price up, of recent years, as high as thirty dollars a thousand feet. When that happens, even Vermont farmers stare hard at their grand old Sugartrees, and begin to do a little figuring in their hard heads. Maple sugar extraction costs have been steadily rising. Why not sell the trees for their stumpage value — five or six dollars when the market is high? The lumber companies will even come in and cut the trees for you, and hand you cash. So the last sweet sap oozes from the bleeding stump when spring comes vainly back.

Plant physiologists tell us that the very glory of the Maple's autumnal leaves is due in part to the sweetness of this sap, no less than to the acidity of New England soils, the dryness and sharpness of her swift autumns. That sweetness amounts in the Sugar Maple to 2 per cent or even 6 per cent of the sap. But of course the yield of sap varies much with the method of tapping, the size of the tree, and the given season. Yet from 5 to 40 gallons of sap may be drawn yearly from each tree. As it takes about 32 gallons of sap to yield one gallon of syrup or 4¼ pounds of sugar, the yield of a tree in a season (9 to 57 days at the end of winter) will be 1 to 7 pounds per tree; the average would be 3 pounds.[1]

As early as 1663, the great English chemist, Robert Boyle, told the learned world of Europe that "There is in some parts of New England a kind of tree . . . whose juice that weeps out of its incisions, if it be permitted slowly to exhale away the superfluous moisture, doth congeal into a sweet and saccharin substance, and the like was confirmed to me by the agent of the great and populous colony of Massachusetts."

The early colonists, both English and French, learned the art of sugaring, of course, from the red man for whom maple sugar was the only sweet. The Indians had their sugar camps, just as the white man, though it was usually, no doubt, the women who did the work. Their method was to slash a gash in the tree, when the sap was rising, and insert a hollow reed stem or a spile of hollow Sumac twig or a funnel of bark. The sap was then allowed to pour from the spile into a bark bowl or bucket or a gourd shell, and this in turn was emptied into a large vessel of Elm bark or a tree trunk hollowed out to form a trough. Having no metal vessels to endure direct contact with the fire, the

[1] Figures from *Sugar and Sugar-making* by James B. McNair, Field Museum of Natural History. Chicago, 1927.

Indians let the sap freeze and took off the ice from time to time (thus, in effect, concentrating the syrup), or they boiled it by dropping hot stones in the sap troughs. Some of the hot syrup might then be poured out on the snow for the children, who ate it as a sort of candy. But for future use the sugar was stored in bark boxes. Often on the frontier "barks of sugar" were bartered from the Indians by the pioneers. Maple sugar formed a sauce for much Indian cookery, especially (however odd it seems to us) with meats.

Captain John Smith is merely the first of a host of explorers who mention sugar making by the Indians. In no time at all the colonists had adopted maple sugar enthusiastically into their diet. It was the opinion of the famous Congregationalist, the Reverend Samuel Hopkins of Waterbury, that of all sugars that from the Maple was the most wholesome. And modern medical opinion is inclined to bear him out. For maple sugar is the only sweet except honey which contains the bone-building phosphates that cause calcium retention. It has therefore been used in the dietetic treatment of rachitic and tubercular children. It has even been asserted by doctors that certain New England farmers and their families could do twice or three times the work performed by others because of maple sugar in their diet.

The wise in these matters say that certain Maples yield more and better sugar, precisely as Apple trees give each their own special apples. The age of the trees, the particular season, the nature of the soil, the general climatic conditions play their part. That grove is best, some say, which stands on a slope with a south exposure, in sandy soil; heavy soils and north exposures make a cloudier syrup with a coarser flavor. Yet one might add that sugar is best which is most quickly reduced from sap to syrup, and with the cleanest equipment.

The Vermont farmer of today may make his own maple sugar into cakes and sell it on the roadside or by mail order direct to the customer. Or he may dispose of it to producers of maple syrup, maple cream, maple flavoring, and confections. The destiny of some maple sugar is to be blended with corn syrup or even (*horribile dictu*) molasses. Sizable amounts of maple sugar have been absorbed by the tobacco business, for flavoring the Virginian weed. The wholesale dealers scatter barrels in January at the country stores of Vermont; the farmer picks them up, fills them, is paid (none too well, he says), in cash at the store, and the filled drums are then retrieved by the wholesalers. On most farms today tractors have replaced the picturesque oxen or horse teams pulling the filled drums over the snow on sledges, and on some farms mechanical efficiency in the sugar bushes has banished hand-emptied buckets by introducing aluminum-painted lead pipes that run from the tree downhill to the evaporator!

The flavor of sugar making as an old-time Vermonter knows it is given in the following passage contributed by Thomas Ripley, lumberman, Yale man (class of 1888), and author of the delectable volume *A Vermont Boyhood:*

"The spring snows begin to melt, leaving soft, wonderful-smelling bare patches about the Maple trunks in the sugar bush. The Vermont farmer cocks his eye at the sun in its northwest passage, feels something stirring in his insides and turns his thought to the sugar shanty and the sap buckets. A nippy frost at night freezes little blobs of ice at the ends of the Maple twigs. A prodigal sun melts them and warms the bare patches. 'Sap's runnin'!' The mysterious signal is sounded and the annual miracle is on. Every boy and girl in the village knows that sap's runnin'. Teacher knows it, too. For in the kinship with the Maples, human sap as well as vegetable is rising.

"A wonderful transformation takes place in the sugar bush; with a stroke of heaven's wand, the winter-bound grove becomes a fairyland of blue and gold, picked out with red and green sap buckets like Christmas tree ornaments. It was good to see and hear the drip of the sap. It seems to me that I can remember particular days when the sap ran in a trickling stream, so bounteous was the store.

"With the advent of our pioneer ancestors, the American passion for efficiency set in and the new-comers proceeded to show those redskins a thing or two. It seems there were various ways of 'boiling down,' each succeeding way an improvement on the old. In my boyhood, I read of the 'good old times' when two long logs were laid parallel to each other ('side by each,' as undoubtedly it was described), between which the fire was lighted. And over the fire a row of kettles, a big one at the end, to receive the sap, a smaller one next and then a still smaller one down to the littlest of all. Dipping from kettle to kettle, the finished syrup was dipped from the little kettle.

"The long fire and the row of kettles had given way to the march of improvement before ever I came on the scene. I seem to remember a big flat receptacle over a fire, an evaporator, I think it was called, into which the sap was poured. It bubbled and threw off the most delightful smells while the fire was stoked underneath with the dry 'dead and down' wood that the bush yielded. Though it was watched and skimmed from time to time, a lot of smoke and cinders floated into the boiling, and the finished product emerged a bit gritty, coarse in texture when compared with the modern stuff, but with the tang of woodsmoke in it.

"As the boiling down proceeded, the boys and girls crowded in for 'sugaring off' parties. Big dishpans and eathenware bowls were packed hard with snow on which the hot syrup, fresh from the boiling, was spooned. It coagulated into the most heavenly chew. Patterns were made, preferably hearts and arrows with initials of boy swain or girl flutterer.

"New methods inevitably have been adopted in the making and marketing of Vermont maple sugar. As bit and brace took the place of the barbarous old ax-slash, metal spouts replaced those made by hand from the sumac, and then the old wooden buckets gave way to galvanized pails. I don't suppose a boiling kettle could be found today from Swanton to Brattleboro. The sugar shanty of yesterday has been transformed into a scientifically managed sugar factory with instruments, the very names of which would have caused head-shakings in the bush of a generation ago. Thermometers! Hydrometers! Color standards! And I hear rumblings which presage even more dreadful things. The spirit of Henry Ford has invaded the bush with something which suggests the assembly line to supplant even the lidded galvanized iron pails. 'Sap's runnin' — right from the tree to the sugar factory. Such is the penalty and the burden of Vermont's leadership!" [1]

[1] *The Atlantic Monthly*, March 1949.

BLACK MAPLE

Acer nigrum F. Michaux

RANGE: New England and Montreal across southern Ontario, southern Michigan, southern Wisconsin and Minnesota to the northeastern corner of South Dakota, south through Pennsylvania to West Virginia, Kentucky, and southern Illinois to western Missouri; usually occurring with the Sugar Maple and with intermediates, mostly very rare eastward but increasingly common westward and nearly replacing the Sugar Maple in Iowa.

DESCRIPTION: *Bark* on old trunks deeply furrowed, thick, sometimes nearly black. *Twigs* stout, flecked with oblong pale lenticels, orange-green when they first appear, but becoming shining and orange-brown the first winter and the following season dull pale gray-brown. *Winter buds* small, with dark red-brown scales, the inner becoming when they open bright yellow and 1 inch long. *Leaves* 5 to 6 inches long and wide, with drooping sides, dull green on the upper surface, yellow-green and softly downy, especially on the yellow veins below. *Flowers* yellow, the male and female in the same cluster or in separate clusters, or on different trees, with broadly bell-shaped, 5-lobed, partly united calyx; petals none; stamens 7 or 8, twice as long as the calyx or in the female flower much shorter and aborted; ovary pale green. *Fruit* with wide-spreading wings ½ to 1 inch long. *Wood* like that of the Sugar Maple.

This is a rare tree in the eastern states, but west of the Alleghenies it grows more frequent, and beyond the Mississippi it is the commonest of the Sugar Maple group, sometimes reaching a height of 80 feet with a trunk nearly 3 feet thick. Middle Western farmers often maintain that it yields more and better sugar than the true Sugar Maple. Some botanists believe that it is identical with the Sugar Maple, but other and very close students of trees point out the following differences between the Black Maple and Sugar Maple. The leaves of the present species are usually 3- lobed, not 5- lobed, and with drooping sides, and the under surface of the blades is definitely velvety.

Lumbermen make no distinction between the two trees, and from the point of view of street planting the Black Maple boasts all the fine qualities of the Sugar Maple — it is long-lived, stately, gorgeous in its autumnal coloration and fairly free of disease.

SILVER MAPLE

Acer saccharinum Linnæus

OTHER NAMES: Soft, White, River, Water, Creek, or Swamp Maple.

RANGE: Western New Brunswick and southern Quebec to northwestern Florida, westward through southern Ontario, Michigan, northern Wisconsin and Minnesota to southeastern South Dakota, and in the south to Louisiana (where rare), eastern Oklahoma, Kansas and Nebraska.

DESCRIPTION: Bark of young trees smooth and gray, becoming on old trunks thickish, reddish brown, furrowed, and thinly scaly. *Twigs* brittle, drooping, pale green and flecked with lenticels at first, becoming bright chestnut-brown, smooth and shining, and in the second year gray tinged with red or pale rose. *Winter buds* with thick bright-red outer scales, the inner becoming yellow or pale green and about 1 inch long at the time of opening. *Leaves* 6 to 7 inches long and nearly as broad, thin, bright pale green above, silvery white below, with 5 prominent nerves. *Flowers* greenish yellow, opening before the leaves in the short axillary ciusters or on spur-like shoots of the previous year, the male and female in separate clusters on the same or on different trees, the corolla lacking, calyx slightly 5-lobed, greenish yellow, the stamens 3 to 7, much longer than the calyx, the ovary thickly downy, with styles united only at base and long stigma lobes. *Fruit* 1½ to 3 inches long, the thin wings sometimes ¾ inch broad and meshed-veiny and pale brown. *Wood* medium-light (33 pounds to the cubic foot, dry weight), hard and strong but rather brittle, the heartwood pale brown, with very thick sapwood.

When the traveler first looks out of his train window in the Ohio valley he will, if he has any eye for trees, see a magnificent Maple with short columnar trunk and long branches which, at least in the lower half of the tree, sweep grandly down toward the ground, then lift again near the tip in a gesture of airy grace. In the upper half of the tree the branches are apt to be ascending, so that the outline, especially in winter, is somewhat pagoda-like. Fine old specimens — and the Ohio valley is the place to see them — impart to every stream and bank where they grow, to every big red Hooiser barn and little white farmhouse, to all the village streets and the long straight roads where they have been planted, an air at once of dignity and lively grace, a combination rare in a tree as in a human.

All our best and most beloved species in the northern sylva present a drama throughout the year, and the Silver Maple has a leading rôle in every act. In winter the fine, flaky, gray bark of the trunks shines almost silvery; the elegant down-sweeping of the boughs, the graceful upturning of the twigs seem etched by the strokes of the finest engraving tool, and as one tramps the woods of the Middle West, perhaps through some chill morning mist, the Silver Maples take solid shape more slowly than the more ponderous trees; there is always something wraith-like about them at such a time.

The snow has usually not departed when the first twigs high over head begin to brighten, and the shy apetalous flowers, too high above one's eyes to see clearly at all, bloom in an upper atmosphere, chill and beeless, so that one wonders how they are ever going to set fruit. Yet the fruits, daintly meshed as dragonflies' wings, are already twirling from the twigs when the leaves, themselves distinctly precocious, put forth from the buds, so silvery white at first that they are often mistaken for flowers. As the leaves uncrumple from the constrictions of the bud, the fruits go spinning away on those odd wings in the last fury of some spring gust.

In summer the full beauty of the Silver Maple's leaf expands; very deeply lobed, each pointed lobe again deeply jagged with coarse teeth and these again finely fringed with smaller ones, the Silver Maple's blade is what nurserymen call a cut-leaved type; in other species, as in European White Birch and even English Elm, cut-leaved strains are usually sports or freaks for which there is a demand among the sort of tree planters for whom Nature is seldom good enough but must be prettified. But the Silver Maple comes by such charms naturally. The mighty tree has the strength to wear them without being made effeminate.

Like some of the Poplars, the Silver Maple suspends its leaves on very long, somewhat flattened stalks, so that every breath of wind is sure to set the foliage to spinning, or fling it over. Then the contrast in the hues of the two surfaces is seen to greatest advantage; when composed, the tree seems clothed in dark green foliage (which, however, is filmy and delicately poised, never heavy). In the next moment the whole of one bough, or one half-side of the whole tree, will suddenly turn silver, as the blades are reversed, and show their under sides. Then, the summer breeze having sighed away, the tree regains its green composure, and again one hears that rolling, fluting whistle from the bluejays in the orchard, carrying piracy to the blue summer airs. But when begin those day-long gales that are destined to blow summer quite away, the Silver Maples along every stream are whipped into continuous whitecaps, threshing and seething and flashing their silver in more torment than delight.

The Silver Maple lacks the autumnal splendors of the Red and Black and Sugar and Mountain Maples, for the orange and scarlet tints are quite absent. It turns only a pale clear yellow. But the blades are likely to retain their silver under-surface even then. So that the greenback leaf of yesterday becomes a bank note — redeemable only on such banks as the Muskingum, the Thornapple, the Sangamon, the Scioto and Miami, the Rock and the Fox and the Kentucky, in the silver of hoarfrost and the gold of Indian-summer noons.

A tree with so many charms has naturally been planted far beyond its natural range, and everywhere within it. In the South, where it is rare as a native tree, it is common as a street tree. In the West, even in southern California where deciduous trees usually find little favor, it is a favorite, for it cannot grow without lending grace to any spot; it makes a railroad station look like a home, and adds a century to the appearance of a village street. It is the fastest growing of all our

Maples, one of the fastest amongst all trees suitable to our climate, be they native or exotic. It is as charming in its childhood as in age, and in its youth goes through no awkward stage.

Yet landscape architects have little good to say of it. They complain of the insect pests that attack it, and of its comparatively short life, as well as the breakage of its brittle and too-long boughs under wind and ice damage. They urge that it be planted, if at all, in the full knowledge that its quickly achieved effects will not last long, and that more permanent if slower plantings be started at the same time. It may be that we should always listen to cautious and sensible people, and not allow ourselves to think too highly of a tree that will perhaps only live three times as long as we do.

François Michaux found that, in his day, the Middle Western farmers tapped the Silver Maple for its sugar and got a much finer grade than is yielded by the Sugar Maple. Unfortunately the amount of flow is too small to compete commercially with that of the more abundantly yielding species.

Lumbermen have so far cut comparatively little Silver Maple; they say that a small proportion of the wood that goes to market simply as "Maple" is cut from this tree, especially in the South, but it has little reputation of its own and goes for the most plebeian of uses. It is, however, a wood with many fine qualities, except for its tendency to split, and should the supply of Sugar Maple become much more sharply curtailed, perhaps the industry will begin to stare at this tree with speculative gaze.

RED MAPLE

Acer rubrum Linnæus

OTHER NAMES: Swamp, or Scarlet Maple.

RANGE: Maritime Provinces and eastern Quebec, westward through the Upper Great Lakes region to southern Manitoba and Minnesota, south to Florida and westward to central Texas, central Oklahoma, central and southern Missouri, and Illinois.

DESCRIPTION: *Bark* on old trunks thin, dark gray, with scaly ridges, and shallowly furrowed. *Twigs* slender, dark red or green at first, becoming dark or bright red and shiny by the end of the summer, and flecked with numerous white longitudinal lenticels. *Winter buds* small, blunt, with dark red and thick outer scales rounded on the back and fringed with hairs, the inner scales bright scarlet at the apex, becoming showy in spring. *Leaves* 3 to 6 inches long and practically as broad, light green above, paler below, with 3 to 5 lobes, on long slender red stalks. *Flowers* in early spring, scarlet or yellow, appearing before the leaves, in pairs of opposite clusters, each on a long slender stalk, the male and female in separate clusters or on separate trees. Stamens 5 to 8, very long and scarlet or yellow; in the female flower the stamens aborted or very short; both sepals and petals present. *Fruit* on drooping stems 3 to 4 inches long, yellow, brown, dark red or scarlet, with thin wings ½ to 1 inch long, ¼ to ½ inch wide. *Wood* medium-soft, medium-light (38 pounds to the cubic foot, dry weight), rather weak, very porous, close-grained, the heartwood light brown tinged with red, the sapwood paler and thick.

At all seasons of year the Red Maple has something red about it. In winter the buds are red, growing a brilliant scarlet as winter ends, the snow begins to creep away, and the ponds to brim with chill water and trilling frog music. So bright, in fact, that if one takes an airplane flight anywhere across the immense natural range of this tree (the most widespread of all our Maples), one can pick out — as far below as the color can be detected — the Red Maples, by the promise of spring in their tops, for no other tree quite equals them at this season in quality or intensity of color. The flowers too are generally red, sometimes yellow, and, minute though they are, they stand out brilliantly because they bloom upon the naked wood before ever the leaves appear. This may be as late as May; around Washington, D.C., February brings the Red Maple to bloom; down on the Gulf coast, January or even December may call the flowers forth. The most conspicuous feature of the showier male flowers is the long scarlet stamens; the petals and sepals scarcely count at all. Unlike the Sugar Maple, which does not bear its fruit until August, the Red Maple's "keys," twirl on their slim stalks a month after flowering and while the leaves are still very small. These early leaves have a positively autumnal brilliance — scarlet or crimson — as they unfold from their fanwise crumpling in the bud. Even in summer the leafstalks are very red. And in autumn the foliage turns crimson or winy red, and is second in splendor only to the Sugar Maple.

The Red Maple loves swamps and river flood plains and low woods where spring pools form from the melting snow or the overflowing streams. When Red Maple grows up into the hills and even ascends the Appalachians, it likes deep ravines, the shady side of cliffs and high mountain coves. With its cool, deep, yet not oppressive umbrage, and its elegant leaves, it ranks wherever it is found with the first choice of our finest shade trees.

In height, it may attain 100 or even 120 feet, especially in swampy situations, with a trunk 3 or 4 feet thick. The branches tend to be upright, so they form a narrow head, those near the halfway mark of the tree being generally the longest; thus the outline is rather diamond-shaped when the tree is growing in the open, with a short trunk. Though slower growing than the Silver Maple, and more demanding of water than the Sugar Maple, this species is yet a fine street and lawn tree, with columnar trunks of a beautiful, almost Beech-like bark, and a generous pool of filmy shade.

If Red Maple were as valuable a timber tree as Hard Maple, it would, with its immense range and abundance, be a national resource of the first class, but the wood is only three fourths as strong and yet weighs almost as much. It is said that Red Maple is sometimes sold as Hard Maple, sometimes as Soft Maple, but never goes to market under its own name. It is made into box veneer, interior finish, flooring, kitchenware, clothes hangers, and clothes pins. Curly and wavy grains occasionally occur and some bird's-eye grain is also found. Sugar may be drawn from Red Maple, though in smaller quantities than from Sugar Maple. Our pioneer ancestors made ink by adding sulphate of iron (copperas) to the tannin extracted from Red Maple bark. If, instead, alum was added, a cinnamon-colored dye was produced; the use of both alum and sulphate of iron with the bark extract produced a black dye. The Indians seem to have had still other uses for this tree. John Josselyn in *New-Englands Rarities Discovered* (1672) wrote:

"The Natives draw an Oyl, taking the rottenest Maple Wood, which being burnt to ashes, they make a Lye therewith, wherein they boyl their white Oak-Acorns until the Oyl swim on the top in great quantities."

Peter Kalm, Linnaeus' greatest student, who visited America in 1750, especially in the old Swedish settlements in Delaware and Pennsylvania, records of this tree and of his countrymen, that "out of its wood they make plates, spinning wheels, spools, feet for chairs and beds, and many other kinds of turnery. With the bark they dye both worsted and linen, giving it a dark blue color. For this purpose it is first boiled in water, and some copperas, such as the hat makers and the shoemakers commonly use, is added before the stuff (which is to be dyed) is put into the boiler."

The Carolina Maple (variety *tridens* Wood) is strikingly different from the true Red Maple in foliage, but not in flowers or fruit. The bark is remarkably smooth even on old trunks, reminding one of Beech boles. The leaves are thicker, almost leathery, a darker green and shining above, and coated below with a heavy bloom and with persistent cottony tufts in the axils of the main nerves which are very prominent beneath. In autumn the foliage commonly turns yellow, not crimson.

The lobes of the leaves are usually three, rarely five, and rather broad, the two lateral ones somewhat divergent, with wide-angled sinuses between them. The teeth are not nearly so close or numerous as in the true Red Maple, except near the base, and are not especially sharp or fine. The Carolina Maple, confined to a somewhat more southerly range, is still included, in its distribution, within the wide range of the true Red Maple and cannot be considered a separate species but only a variety of it.

STRIPED MAPLE

Acer pensylvanicum Linnæus

OTHER NAMES: Whistlewood. Moosewood. Striped Dogwood. Goosefoot, or Northern Maple.

RANGE: Maritime Provinces and southern Quebec westward to the Upper Peninsula of Michigan, south to northern New Jersey, western New York, rarely in northern Ohio, and the northern part of the lower peninsula of Michigan, and south on the mountains to northern Georgia.

DESCRIPTION: *Bark* thinnish, reddish brown, marked longitudinally by pale broad stripes, and roughened by many warty points. *Twigs* at first pale greenish yellow, bright reddish brown the first winter, after 3 years becoming longitudinally striped, like the trunk, with broad pale lines. *Winter buds* with the terminal one much longer (½ inch) than the axillary, and conspicuously stalked, covered by 2 thick, bright-red, boat-shaped, keeled outer scales, the inner green and leafy, becoming 2 inches long and bright rose or yellow at the time of opening. *Leaves* with 3 prominent nerves from the base, thin, pale green above, paler below, 5 to 6 inches long, 4 to 5 inches wide. *Flowers* opening when the leaves are nearly grown, brilliant yellow, in long-stemmed spikes 4 to 6 inches long, the male and female usually in different spikes on the same plant; sepals ¼ inch long, petals a little longer; stamens 7 or 8; ovary purplish brown, the styles united almost to the top and branching into the curved stigmas. *Fruit* in graceful drooping spikes, with thin wings ¾ inch long. *Wood* light brown, with a thick layer of paler sapwood, soft and medium-light (33 pounds to the cubic foot, dry weight).

In the deep cool woods of northern New England, under Sugar Maples, Beeches, Canoe and Yellow Birches, and Hemlock, the Striped Maple sometimes forms full half the undergrowth, and anything daintier than the bright, white-and-green-striped twigs, the fresh-looking foliage, and the brilliant canary yellow of the flowers, one cannot find. It is, however, only on the Great Smokies of Tennessee and North Carolina that the Striped Maple attains its full stature of 30 or 40 feet, with a trunk sometimes 10 inches thick. The flowers generally open toward the end of May or early June and the fruit matures in summer. In autumn the leaves do not take on the gorgeous tint of the Mountain Maple but turn an almost ethereal clear gold, very lovely after a night of autumn rain, when the soft sunlight passes through them.

Cottontail, deer, moose, and beaver all live upon the bark, especially in winter.

MOUNTAIN MAPLE

Acer spicatum Lamarck

OTHER NAMES: Moose, Low, or Water Maple.

RANGE: Newfoundland and Labrador to Hudson Bay, Manitoba and Saskatchewan, southward to Minnesota, northern Iowa, locally in southern Wisconsin, northern part of the lower peninsula of Michigan, and Ohio, and along the Appalachians to North Carolina and Tennessee at high altitudes.

DESCRIPTION: *Bark* very thin, smooth, reddish brown. *Twigs* slender, light gray at first, becoming bright red the first winter and pale brown or gray the following season. *Winter buds* with bright red outer scales

more or less coated with hoary hairs, the inner scales at maturity growing long, pale and papery. *Leaves* with 3 principal nerves, thin, 4 to 5
inches long and broad. *Flowers* opening after the leaves are fully grown,
¼ inch long, the male at the top and the female toward the base of the
many-flowered, long-stemmed upright spikes; calyx lobes yellow, much
shorter than the yellow petals; stamens 7 or 8; ovary hoary, its columnar
style almost as long as the petals. *Fruit* bright red or yellow when ripe.
Wood light brown tinged with red, with thick paler sapwood, soft,
medium-light (33 pounds to the cubic foot, dry weight).

Only on the Great Smokies of Tennessee and North Carolina does
the Mountain Maple become a bushy tree sometimes as much as 30
feet tall with a trunk 8 inches in diameter. Elsewhere Mountain
Maple is only a shrub but a beautiful one, the leaves wondrously
fresh-looking and large in proportion to the bush, and the graceful
spike of flowers large in proportion to the leaves. Rocky woods, cool
ravines, high coves in the mountains and the neighborhood of white
and singing water — these are the chosen habitats of the Mountain
Maple. There are no commercial uses for the wood of so small a tree,
but deer and moose browse the bark, and beaver too, when Aspen
fails, while the buds are eaten by ruffed grouse. The flowers open in
June and the fruit ripens in July and is already turning brown by the
time that the autumnal leaves take on their gorgeous shades of orange
and scarlet.

BOX ELDER

Acer Negundo Linnæus

OTHER NAMES: Ash-leaved or Manitoba Maple. Sugar Ash.

RANGE: Southwestern New England, westward through central and western New York, Ohio, Michigan, northern Wisconsin, Minnesota, southern Manitoba, south to Florida and central Texas; also in Colorado Springs, Colorado, the Black Hills of South Dakota, and Nez Percé County, Idaho. Replaced elsewhere in the West by varieties.

DESCRIPTION: *Bark* thin, light brown or pale gray, soon scaly and furrowed. *Twigs* slender, limber, and pale green or bluish gray or violet, with scars left by winter buds encircling the twig. *Leaves* compound, with 3 to 11 leaflets, the terminal often very deeply 3-lobed; the leaflets 2½ to 4 inches long and 1½ to 2½ broad, light green above, paler and sometimes hairy on the veins of the lower surface. *Flowers* expanding just before or with the leaves, male and female always on separate trees, the female in drooping spikes, with the style separating from the base into 2 long stigmatic lobes, the male in close clusters each with 4 to 6 stamens; calyx greenish and 5-lobed. *Fruit* ("keys") drooping in long spikes, the nutlets narrow, the wings broad, veiny, and rather convergent.

Wood soft, close-grained, weak, brittle, and very light (27 pounds to cubic foot, dry weight), with sapwood and heartwood nearly white and scarcely distinguishable.

The Box Elder probably takes its name from its elder-like leaves and its wood like that of the Box tree. The foliage would make one think of some sort of cut-leaf Ash tree. Yet its nearest relatives are undoubtedly the Maples, as is shown by its flowers, pendant on long stalks in early spring, and its autumnal crop of fruits, the typical double samara of the Maples.

But Box Elders are the Maple's poor relations. They have little of the strength and grace, little of the autumn splendor and beautifully figured wood of their noble kin. Somewhat sprawling in growth, short-lived (the top of the tree often begins to die just when full and promising stature is obtained), Box Elders inhabit chiefly the banks of the slow, coffee-colored streams of the Middle West and the Great Plains; they are not neighbors to clean and singing waters; their associates are the common Cottonwood, Willow, Hackberry, and Red Birch. No one could call them aristocratic trees.

Yet Box Elder, which is a small and insignificant tree east of the Mississippi, begins to look good, the farther one goes up the Missouri and its vast system of tributaries. Perhaps any shade would do so, but the form of the Box Elder in the Great Plains states is actually finer; it develops into a broadly rounded or dome-shaped head, with short trunk and wide-spreading branches. Sometimes 70 feet tall with a trunk 4 feet thick and a crown often broader than tall, this species, despised in lands with richer sylvas, is a true friend of man and beast in the West. Able to endure extremes of climate, drought, wind, dust, abuse of all sorts, it germinates with great freedom, and grows so swiftly that in a few years it is shading a doorway or some drinking trough for the cattle or a roadside which before was sunbitten and wind-parched. It is, after all, not such a reproach to a tree that it is short-lived, especially when, like this one, it can so readily be replaced by planting new generations every decade or so. True that the foliage turns only sear in fall; in summer it is genuinely lovely and in spring precocious. Even in winter the tree is handsome by reason of its twigs — sometimes a bright green, again violet or glaucous, and its seeds are a favorite food of those winter visitants, the evening grosbeaks. We need not ask a tree, even one dependent chiefly on its ornamental charms, to be what it is not, or to compare it with more noble species which, however, could not endure the harsh conditions supported by this one.

Odd as it sounds to easterners, the Box Elder yields a sugar, not despised even today by Middle Western farmers, and welcome, surely, on the Great Plains, where no Sugar Maple could endure. Elliot Coues, the distinguished naturalist, mentions this in his *New Light on the Early History of the Great Northwest*: "This small bastard maple (box-elder or ash-leaved maple, Negundo aceroides) begins to run. . . . The sap yields a fine white sugar, but it is not so sweet as that of the real maple, and more is required to make the same quantity of sugar."

THE HORSE CHESTNUTS
(*Æsculus*)

THE MEMBERS of this group have ill-smelling inner bark and opposite, palmately compound and deciduous leaves which in falling mark the stout twigs with big triangular leaf scars. The flowers are unisexual, the male and female found on the same tree but in separate flower clusters, though sometimes perfect or bisexual flowers are found near the base of the cluster. Usually the calyx is 5-lobed, the lobes often unequal, oblique, and inflated on the back. There are 4 or 5 petals, narrowed at base to a claw, and usually 6 to 8 stamens of unequal length but all free from each other and inserted on the disk. The ovary is 3-celled with a long, slender, curved style. Fruit takes the form of a roughened, leathery, thick-walled capsule, opening by 3 valves to allow the fall of the big chestnut-brown, dark, smooth, and shining seeds.

OHIO BUCKEYE

Æsculus glabra Willdenow

OTHER NAMES: Fetid or Stinking Buckeye.

RANGE: Western Pennsylvania on the west slopes of the Alleghenies to northern Alabama, and westward to northeastern Kansas, southeastern Nebraska, and central and southern Iowa.

DESCRIPTION: *Bark* on old trees thick, ashy gray, broken into thick scaly plates and densely furrowed. *Twigs* orange-brown, becoming reddish brown and flecked with scattered orange lenticals. *Winter buds* with triangular pale brown scales, the inner surface of the outer scales bright red toward the base, the inner pair prominently keeled on the back and at maturity 2 inches long and bright yellow. *Leaves* with 5 to 7 leaflets, 4 to 6 inches long and 1½ to 2 inches wide, yellow-green above and paler on the lower surface, with conspicuous yellow midribs, the leafstalks 4 to 6 inches long. *Flowers* ½ to 1½ inches long, appearing after the leaves, pale yellow-green, the calyx bell-shaped, petals nearly equal in size, the superior pair sometimes marked with red stripes; stamens 7 on long curved stalks, with orange anthers; ovary covered with slender prickles. *Fruit* 1 to 2 inches long, the husk bluntly prickled; seeds 1 to 1½ inches thick. *Wood* very light (28 pounds to the cubic foot, dry weight), weak, soft, the heartwood nearly white, the sapwood dark and thin.

Ohio, the Buckeye State by its own account, has adopted this sprawling shrub or small tree which rarely reaches as much as 70 feet in height with a trunk 2 feet in diameter, for its floral emblem. But Americans seldom take their emblems seriously, and there is a bit of crude pioneer humor in the choice of the Stinking Buckeye, as it is called on account of the nauseating odor of the bruised bark. Probably much capital has been made of this by Ohio's neighbors, but the retort might be made that the wolverine is a thoroughly disgusting animal, and the sucker an ugly and not too tasty fish, and so the score be paid off with Michigan and Illinois respectively.

But the Buckeye has its hour. As soon as the first warmth comes stealing up from the south, its great buds begin to swell, the inner scales thrusting aside the outer brownish ones and showing a lovely greenish tint with an inner surface of deep rose. Then, like the petals of some large flower, the scales fold back and the first frail young leaves and the flower buds themselves push outward. At first each leaflet is folded, fanwise; looking almost like green grapes, the crowded clusters of flower buds emerge from among the five-fingered little leaves. If the good weather keeps up, the leaves fairly rush into full foliage while, all about, the Hickories and Oaks, the Locusts and Ashes remain closed in winter's steely secrecy. Soon the flowers, borne stiffly in open clusters at the ends of the upturned clumsy twigs, make their appearance, the color of pale spring sunshine. In early summer the prickly pods split into 3 valves, and from them drop the big seeds, shining and dark brown, rather like the gleaming coat of a fine horse, and beautified by that large pale scar that is seen on each one.

Many an Ohioan in the old days probably carried a Buckeye in his pocket to ward off rheumatism, and at one time, at least, an extract of the bark was used as a stimulant of the cerebro-spinal system. Bark and fruits are both poisonous, though it is probable that, as in the other species of this genus, the poison is driven off the seeds by boiling, when the starchy meat would become edible. The seeds, which look too large, surely, for any but the clumsiest method of distribution, are so light that doubtless spring floods carry them along, leaving them on many a Middle Western stream bank when the water subsides. Squirrels are not known to eat them, and it is doubtful if any bird tackles this bitter fruit. The poisonous qualities of the fruit are counted by some farmers as a distinct menace to their cattle, and in certain localities an unremitting warfare is waged against this strange tree.

Because the wood is so light it has been much used for artificial limbs, the more especially as it does not readily split. Buckeye logs in short sections used to be hollowed out and cut into troughs, especially for catching maple sap. Pioneer babies of the Middle West were rocked in cradles hollowed out of a thick Buckeye log, and it is related that the first settlers used to make summer hats from Buckeye shavings.

"The farmers would take a straight Buckeye limb 4 to 6 inches in diameter, 15 to 18 inches long and plane off fine shavings. They would then drive 5 or 6 pins through a board about 1/8 of an inch apart, the points coming about a quarter of an inch above the surface of the board, and the shavings, while being drawn over the pins, would be divided into proper width for plaiting. A hat made in this way would wear for a long time." [1]

[1] John F. Edgar, *Pioneer Life in Dayton.*

SWEET BUCKEYE

Æsculus octandra Marshall

OTHER NAME: Big Buckeye.

RANGE: From the mountains of southwestern Pennsylvania south along the Blue Ridge to extreme northern parts of Georgia and Alabama, thence west to northern Mississippi, northwestern Louisiana, northeastern Texas, and eastern Oklahoma, and north to extreme southern Illinois, Indiana, and Ohio.

DESCRIPTION: *Bark* dark brown and scaly rather than furrowed, the outer scales often glaucous, the inner bright yellow or scarlet. *Twigs* at first orange-brown and without hairs, becoming next year pale brown and flecked irregularly with many lenticels. *Leaves* compound, the leaflets on stalks 4 to 6 inches long, the terminal leaflet largest (4 to 6 inches long), the lateral pair smaller, the basal pair smallest, dark yellow-green and semi-shiny above, duller below. *Flowers* in big, branched, loosely flowered clusters; petals yellow, sometimes red, pink, or cream-colored;

calyx bell-shaped, the 4 petals converging but very unequal, the upper
pair rather erect, the lateral pair with large blades and shorter claws;
stamens usually 7, shorter than the petals. *Fruits* 2 to 3 inches long with
thin, pitted husks, generally 2-seeded, the seeds large and shiny brown
with big pale scar. *Wood* very soft, weak, yet difficult to split, very light
(25 pounds to the cubic foot, dry weight), the heartwood creamy white
and hardly distinguishable from the very thick sapwood.

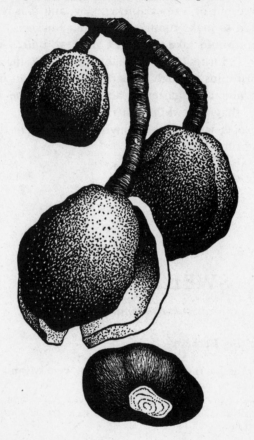

Country folk have named this tree for its big shiny brown seed
which, with the large pale scar upon it, has looked to them like the
eye of a deer. They are seeds pleasing to look at and satisfying to hold,
but there is poison in them, as there is in the young shoot leaves. Pigs,
horses, and cattle — even children who were tempted by the seeds —
have been repeatedly reported as poisoned by them, with symptoms of
inflammation of the mucous membranes, vomiting, stupor, twitching,

and paralysis. The glucoside aesculin is one, at least, of the poisonous elements involved.

Yet with this bitter principle removed, the very starchy seeds are both edible and nourishing. "The Indians roasted the nuts among hot stones, thus loosening the shells, peeled and mashed them, and then leached the meal with water for several days." [1] Thus there was left to them a highly nutritious meal. The very presence of the poison, however, serves to make the seed useful in another way; bookbinders prefer above others a paste made of its starch since it is not eaten by the insect enemies of books.

The tree that bears this tempting and dangerous seed is a beautiful thing in the forest, growing sometimes 90 feet high, with a trunk up to 3 feet thick. The big, branched clusters of bloom which appear in late spring, when the leaves are half grown, light up the whole tree with their yellow petals; in autumn too the tree glows again, when the foliage turns clear yellow.

But in the lumberyard Buckeye is rated so low it scarcely dares to pass under its own name. Softest of all the woods in our sylva, including even the so-called "softwoods," it is also the weakest of them, nor does it resist decay. It has an ill odor when green, shrinks more than any other wood (50 per cent of weight in drying), and though it does not warp excessively, holds nails well, and works easily, it is surprising that it is even at the bottom of the list of the 35 leading timbers of the United States. Most of it goes, naturally enough, for crates and boxes, since its lightness lessens the cost of shipping merchandise in it. Commonly Buckeye is graded and sold in the lumber yard as sapwood of Tulip Poplar — not with intent to defraud but because most lumbermen see no difference.

A superb variety of this tree with rose-red or purple flowers was first discovered, near the mouth of the Cheat River in what is now West Virginia, by none other than George Washington. It was on the occasion of his visit in 1784 to Colonel Morgan Morgan of Morgantown (where now the University of West Virginia is located) to confer with him on the possibilities of an inland waterway or land route to the Ohio (for Washington, founder of the Union, was ever fearful that

[1] Fernald and Kinsey, *Edible Wild Plants of Eastern North America.*

the lands beyond the Alleghenies might lose touch with the country and break off from it unless communications were improved). Probbly these trees were noted by the tree-loving general on some of his own lands; his holdings in the Ohio basin were great. At any rate, he collected seeds and planted them the following year at "Mount Vernon" where four of them may still be seen in the Serpentine. For many years they were thought to be the only known examples of this splendid flowering tree, but careful search has now shown that wild specimens still occur in Ohio, Tennessee, West Virginia, and presumably, eastern Kentucky and southwestern Virginia.

THE LINDENS
(*Tilia*)

THESE TREES have rather stout twigs, without terminal buds, and rather large, flattened, pointed and axillary buds with many scales. The juices are somewhat mucilaginous; the inner bark is tough and fibrous. The leaves, alternate and deciduous, are heart-shaped at base or truncate, and frequently oblique and unsymmetrical. In general their veins are branched only on the side toward the base of the blade.

The long leafstalks, in falling, leave big, elevated, horizontal scars. The fragrant flowers, small but numerous, occur on slender stalks in branched clusters. The stalk is always adherent for part of its length to the leaf-like, veiny, strap-shaped bract which accompanies both flowers and fruits, even when the fruits finally fall, bearing them away on it as on a wing. The petals, white or yellow or creamy, usually have a nectar-bearing gland at the base of the petal. The sepals, of the same number (5) as the petals, are hairy, and like the petals distinct from each other. The stamens, inserted on the receptacle, unite at base with each other into 5 clusters, each at base cohering, in the American species, with a spatulate, petal-like scale, the staminodium. The fruit, rather woody and nut-like, takes the form of a capsule enclosing 1 or 2 light reddish-brown seeds.

AMERICAN LINDEN

Tilia americana Linnæus

OTHER NAMES: Common Basswood. Bass. Lin. Lime. Limetree. White-wood.

RANGE: New Brunswick and southern Quebec to the eastern shore of Lake Superior and west to the Assiniboine River of Manitoba and the central parts of the Dakotas and Nebraska, south to northern Missouri, central Illinois, Indiana, eastern Kentucky, West Virginia, the District of Columbia, and Delaware.

DESCRIPTION: *Bark* thick, deeply furrowed, light brown. *Twigs* slender, light brown or light gray, and marked with many dark lenticels in the first year, becoming in the second dark brown or dark gray, and by the third heavily marked by the elevated leaf scars and with wrinkled bark. *Leaves* 5 to 6 inches long, 3 to 4 inches broad, firm, thick, the upper surface dull dark green, the lower paler and shining, with tufts of rusty brown hairs in the axils of the principal nerves; leafstalks 1½ to 2 inches long. *Flowers* ½ inch long, on slender, smooth gray stalks which are free from the bract for 3 or 4 inches, the bract itself 4 or 5 inches long, 1 to 1½ inch wide, the sepals densely hairy on the inner surface and as long as the scales (staminodia) and ⅓ as long as the creamy white petals. *Fruit* covered with a rusty down, ⅓ to ½ inch long. *Wood*

very soft, very light (26 pounds to the cubic foot, dry weight), weak, brittle, readily decaying, the heartwood light brown to almost pure white, the sapwood very thick and hardly distinguishable from the heartwood.

When the shade begins to be heavy and the midges fill the woods, and when the western sky is a curtain of black nimbus slashed by the jagged scimitar of lightning, when the wood thrush seldom sings except after rain and instead the rain crow, our American cuckoo, stutters his weary, descending song — an odor steals upon the moist and heavy air, unbelievably sweet and penetrating.

It is an odor that comes from no bed of stocks, no honeysuckle. More piercing, yet less drugging, than orange blossoms, it is wafted, sometimes as much as a mile, from the flowers of the Linden. All odors have evocative associations to those who know them well — wild grape, wild Crab, wild rose and honeysuckle. The odor of the Lindens in bloom brings back to many of us the soaring wail of the treetoads, the first fireflies in the dusk, the banging of June beetles on the window screens, the limpness of the flags at Fourth of July, and all that is a boy's-eye view of those languorous first days of vacation from school.

As a wild tree, this Linden, or Basswood as lumbermen and farmers call it, grows sometimes as much as 130 feet tall, with a trunk 3 or 4 feet thick, forming a broadly round-topped crown with short, often pendulous branches. It flourishes in low woods, in company with White Elm, White Ash, and Cottonwood; formerly it often formed nearly pure groves in some spots. Today, though much reduced within its natural range, it is common in cultivation, as a street and lawn tree. There it has rivals in a number of Lindens of European origin, including many hybrids. Some of these are preferred for their pretty little leaves, and their profusion of flowers. But none of them equals the American Linden in splendid stature — a tree completely benignant and well worthy of planting beside the door, to shade the roof with its lovely crown. The great heart-shaped leaves, though not so prettified as those of some exotic species, cast a deep cool shade. Rather unusually, it is the undersides of the leaves that are shiny, not the upper surface. When the cold wind that just precedes the advance of a summer thunderstorm rushes through the Lindens, the blades are flung over and shine unearthly bright against the black advancing skies.

Bees, when the Lindens bloom, forsake all others and cleave only unto these flowers. The honey that they make of Linden nectar is white in color, with a rather strong flavor, but regarded as of high quality. Though to the shortness of the blooming period, about three weeks, is added the drawback that abundant honeyflows can be depended on only two or three years out of every five, yet when an unusually heavy flow comes, it yields enormous quantities.

As a timber tree, this Basswood belongs to a special class of woods which, though without a beautiful figure, and soft and very light and weak in the position of a beam, have their own sort of value. For the reason that it is so light, Basswood is used for crates and boxes and the core of chair stock that is to be veneered with fine cabinet woods, for toys and drawer sides, window sashes, picture frames, and musical instruments. It is familiar to us all as the wood in which comb honey is framed, as the household or dressmaker's yardstick, and on the backs of picture puzzles. Because it is cheap and still fairly abundant, it is coming to be important in paper-pulp manufacture. Basswood collectively (lumbermen make no distinction between this and other species recognized by foresters) ranks fourteenth in the cut of American woods, just after Hickory and ahead of such a sturdy hardwood as Ash.

The inner bark of Basswood yields some of the longest and toughest fibers in our native flora. It was stripped by the Indians in spring, and thongs prepared from it without further processing. Good rope, however, was made from it by retting — keeping the bark under water for about a month, until the soft tissues should rot away, leaving the somewhat slippery fibrous tissue. Or sometimes the bark was pounded, or simmered in wood ashes, in a kettle. Long strips of rope or string were then twisted to form cordage, which the Indians used to insist was softer on the hands when wet than the white man's hempen fibers, and not so liable to kink. Thread of Basswood bark was used to stitch together the mats made of cat-tail leaves, and the bark, perhaps because of its mucilaginous qualities, was used to bind up the warrior's wounds. Some of the Iroquois' masks were carved in the sapwood on the living tree, and then split off from the trunk and hollowed out from behind.

A closely related, somewhat obscure species, is *Tilia venulosa* Sargent, of the southern Appalachians, which differs in having the leaves hoary-downy when they unfold, the main ribs of the leaves connected by conspicuous cross-veinlets, the free portion of the flower stalk 1 to 1½ inch long, the bract 3 to 6 inches long, the twigs stout and red, not slender and gray.

Tilia neglecta Spach is a little-known species with the foliage distinctly downy (though not densely woolly) all over the underside, even in summer; the blades are 4 to 5½ inches long and 1¼ to 1½ inches broad. It forms a tree 75 to 90 feet tall, with deeply furrowed, scaly, and pale reddish-brown bark. The range is from Montreal to the coast of Massachusetts and the valley of the Potomac, and west to western New York and Missouri, but it appears to be rare or lacking in wide areas within the external boundaries of its distribution.

Tilia alabamensis Ashe reaches our circumscription from the south on the piedmont of Virginia and in the foothills of the southern Appalachians. It is a large tree with leaves 3 to 5 inches long, 2¾ to 4 inches wide, obliquely truncate or cordate at base, hairy when unfolding in spring, but later in the season with abundant light brown hairs only on the lower surface and not in axillary tufts; the bracts are 2 to 5 inches long, ½ to 1 inch wide, the free portion of the flower stalk 1 to 2 inches long.

WHITE BASSWOOD

Tilia heterophylla Ventenat

OTHER NAMES: White Linden. Beetree.

RANGE: White Sulphur Springs, West Virginia, south to Tallahassee, Florida, and Dallas County, Alabama; west through Kentucky to the Ohio River counties of Ohio and Indiana, and southern Illinois. Common in western North Carolina, but lacking in western Kentucky and western Tennessee.

DESCRIPTION: *Bark* deeply furrowed, with broad ridges, dark gray. *Twigs* with slender, reddish or yellowish brown bark. *Winter buds* slightly flattened, egg-shaped, ⅓ inch long. *Leaves* 3 to 5 inches long and 2½ to 2¾ inches wide, dark green above, and below covered with thick, firmly attached, white or brownish woolly hairs. *Flowers* ¼ inch long, on stalks covered with branched hairs, in 10- to 20-flowered clusters; the bract 4 to 6 inches long, 1 to 1½ inches wide; sepals covered with pale hairs; petals ⅓ longer than the sepals, narrow and long-pointed. *Fruit* ⅓ inch long, covered with rusty-brown woolly hairs. *Wood* similar to that of the American Linden.

Josephine, Empress of the French and wife of Napoleon, cut a figure of pathos as a ruler, but as a botanist she was a distinguished student and a truly regal patron of the art and science of floriculture and tree growing. As her professional advisor in her garden at "Malmaison," she employed Etienne Pierre Ventenat, the distinguished systematist, and it was he who discovered this tree as a new species. Not that he found it in the wild, as his countrymen the two Michauxs discovered so many treasures, but as a plant growing in the gardens — a specimen collected in America when, and by whom, he may not have known, any more than we know. It is odd that though this tree must have been abundantly seen by the elder Michaux, and by that early explorer of the southern Appalachians, John Fraser, they never suspected its separate identity. Yet it makes a lofty growth, at its best, sometimes 90 feet high. Its flowers bloom in June or July, after the leaves are fully formed, and are consequently almost out of sight of the observer on the ground. Yet, if you happen to be tramping abroad at that season, the haunting odor may waft down wind to you, or you may hear the roar of the nectar-mad bees at its flowers. One's memory of it is apt to be linked with the perpetual breeze from some waterfall that sets the handsome leaves to twirling restlessly, turning over and again reversing, with all the liveliness of Aspen or Cottonwood, and all the contrast in color between the dull green of the upper surface and the silvery lower face of the wild hydrangea's foliage.

The variety *Michauxii* (Nuttall) Sargent, ranges from southern Pennsylvania and western New York south along the Appalachians to Georgia and through eastern Kentucky and Tennessee to northeastern Mississippi and Dallas County, Alabama; it also grows west through southern parts of Ohio, Indiana, and Illinois, and across Missouri from the northeastern to the southwestern part, and into northwestern Arkansas. It differs in having coarser teeth on the margin, the apex of the blade more abruptly short-pointed, the leafstalks longer (over 1½ inches), the free portion of the flower stalk much longer (1¾ to 2 inches).

Tilia truncata Spach is a closely related species with very oblique leaf bases and long-pointed tips, the upper surface of the blade dark green and shining, the lower coated densely with woolly hairs, the leafstalk up to 3 inches long, the free portion of the flowering and fruiting stalk 1½ inches long, the flowers ½ inch long, with the staminodia as long as the petals, the fruits ¼ to ⅓ inch long, and rusty-downy, and the twigs stout, bright red becoming brown. It grows between 2500 and 3000 feet in the mountains of Tennessee, North Carolina, and southwestern Virginia.

THE HERCULES'–CLUBS
(*Aralia*)

A DISTINGUISHING MARK of the whole genus *Aralia* is the way that the flowers occur in umbrella-like clusters, these in turn often in very large spikes or branched compound clusters. Leaves are twice-compound with an odd number of primary divisions and of leaflets. The tree-sized members of the genus are thorny and aromatic, with fleshy roots and pithy twigs, and leafstalks dilated at base and clasping the stem. Growth, at least in our species, is by a terminal bud. The small but very numerous flowers are bisexual or sometimes unisexual, with the calyx adherent to the ovary. The 5 distinct petals are affixed to the disk by their broad bases, and are incurved at tip. Inserted on the edge of the disk are the 5 stamens. The ovary terminates in 2 to 5 erect, spreading styles that are incurved above the middle. The style remnants crown the fleshy, laterally compressed or 3- to 5-angled berries which contain 2 to 5 light reddish brown, bony, compressed, 1-seeded nutlets. The seeds appear, likewise, compressed, with light brown seed coats.

HERCULES'–CLUB

Aralia spinosa Linnæus

OTHER NAMES: Angelica-tree. Spikenardtree. Prickly Ash. Prickly Elder. Toothache-tree. Shotbush. Pigeontree.

RANGE: From southern New York, Pennsylvania to northern Florida, and west through southern parts of Ohio, Indiana, and Illinois to southeastern Missouri and eastern Texas.

DESCRIPTION: *Bark* dark brown, thin, divided into an irregular broken surface by shallow fissures, with prickles (occurring both on trunk and branches) orange-colored. *Twigs* light orange at first, becoming light brown, lustrous and flecked with pale oblong lenticels, with pale green inner bark and nearly encircled by prominent leaf scars. *Leaves* dark green, pale beneath, twice-compound, the over-all length 3 to 4 feet, the leaflets usually numbering 10 to 12 and a long-stalked terminal one, each 2 to 3 inches long. *Flowers* in many-flowered, loosely branched, umbrella-shaped clusters 3 to 4 feet long; petals white; stalks straw-colored at flowering time but turning purple in autumn. *Fruit* in heavy clusters, growing black as it ripens. *Wood* soft, brittle, close-grained, and weak, very light, with brown summerwood sharply contrasted with yellow springwood, and a very few layers of pale sapwood.

Back in the last century when trees were often cultivated for their very grotesqueness, this strange, clumsy, disproportionate, at once pretentious and yet somehow insignificant little tree or tall shrub was in fashion. With the cast-iron mastiff on the lawn, the wooden gingerbread on the eaves, or — if the mansion were stone — the castellations on the roof, a fine, flourishing, horrendous specimen of Hercules'-club produced an effect which might wake envy in the bosoms of less fortunate neighbors.

To any who can remember this tree thus used as the acme of ostentatious ugliness, it is odd to see it growing innocently in the forest. Even to those with briefer memories, it may look strangely foreign, as though it came from some other flora, or some past geologic age. But it is in truth a North American species belonging to a genus found all around the northern hemisphere except in Europe, and to a family no older than most.

Though this tree of many names and curious appearance may attain 35 feet on the Great Smokies, it is often only a shrub 6 feet high. Its wood, of many poor qualities, does not appear in commercial statistics, though it is said to take a very high polish and "is made into small shop articles, like button boxes, photograph frames, pen racks, stools, and arms for rocking chairs".[1] In our day of ten-cent-store plastic items like the above, one cannot imagine such use to be abundant, nor can one easily find current reference to the medicinal use of berries and bark of the root mentioned by Sargent in his *Silva*. Perhaps no one, any more, relies on this species in case of toothache, but Le Page Du Pratz in his *History of Louisiana* (1758) states that the "inner bark has the property of curing the tooth-ach. The patient rolls it up to the size of a bean, puts it upon the aching tooth, and chews it till the pain ceases. Sailors and other such people powder it, and use it as pepper." This awkward little tree, that in autumn looks bowed with the weight of its own fruits, seems to have had its day, and though it may flourish contentedly in its natural stations, few select it now for the lawn or try to cure toothache or rheumatism with it.

[1] Gibson and Maxwell, *American Forest Trees*.

THE TUPELOS
(*Nyssa*)

Tʜᴇsᴇ ᴀʀᴇ large trees with alternate simple leaves clustered near the end of the twigs and without marginal teeth. The male flowers, found in compound or simple clusters on long stalks arising from the leaf axils, have a disk-shaped calyx and thick erect petals inserted on the edge of the prominent flower disk, and, in 2 series, 5 to 12 stamens. The pistillate flowers occur in 2- or few-flowered clusters on axillary stalks, or they may be solitary and surrounded at base with little scales. The calyx tube is bell-shaped with small spreading lobes. Present in the female flowers are 5 or 10 stamens, giving the appearance of a bisexual flower, but often they are not fertile and always they are short-stalked. Sepals, petals, and stamens all number 4. The ovary terminates in a straight style with a knob-like terminal stigma, while the fruit is a drupe with thin, oily, acidulous flesh surrounding the ribbed stone.

BLACK GUM

Nyssa sylvatica Marshall

OTHER NAMES: Sour Gum. Tupelo. Pepperidge.

RANGE: In typical form from western Maine to northern Florida, west to Lake Champlain, the north shore of Lake Erie, southern Michigan, the south shore of Lake Michigan, northern Missouri, extreme northeastern Texas, and probably adjacent Oklahoma. Most abundant on the coastal plain of the North Atlantic states and in the Ohio valley, rare in the southeastern states and the southern Appalachians. Absent from the Gulf coast, Texas, and the lower Mississippi valley. (Replaced there, and in the South generally, by varieties).

DESCRIPTION: *Bark* thick, rough, dark grayish black, deeply and narrowly furrowed and scored with abundant, irregular cross-checks, resulting in many small, squarish plates. *Twigs* at first light green to orange, becoming the first winter light brown and flecked with pale lenticels and minute crescent-shaped leaf scars. *Winter buds* becoming brilliant red in spring, and marking the twigs with small scars. *Leaves* firm and somewhat leathery, dark green and very lustrous above, the lower surface at maturity hairless, or practically so, the tip short-acute or blunt. *Flowers* appearing in the axils of conspicuous leafy scales, when the leaves are 1/3 grown, the male in many-flowered dense clusters, with thick deciduous petals and a disk-like minute calyx, the stamens 5 to 12 and much

longer than the petals; female flowers in few-flowered clusters with a
stout exserted stigma longer than the petals, and some short or aborted
stamens. *Fruit* a drupe on long drooping stalks, 1 to 3 in each cluster,
⅓ to ⅔ inch long, dark blue with thin acid flesh and a pitted stone.
Wood medium-soft, medium-strong, extremely tough, medium-light (39½
pounds to the cubic foot, dry weight), the heartwood yellowish white
and the very thick sapwood white.

When, to the amusement of Creole society, the tall and emaciated
General Andrew Jackson leaped beside the short and immensely fat
Mrs. Jackson, at a ball held after the battle of New Orleans, it was to
the jig tune of "'Possum Up De Gum Tree." The 'possum, we may
suppose, goes up the Gum tree in fall to get the fruit — or perhaps is
merely treed there by hounds — but that does not make it clear why
this species is called a Gum. Nowhere on the American continent has
anyone ever expressed from this dry and disobliging vegetable one
fluid ounce of any sort of gum. Yet lumbermen and foresters insist on
the name. The title of Pepperidge seems derived, by far-fetched analogy, from an old English word for the barberry bush. As for Tupelo,
applied to this species in New England, it is said to come from the
Creek language, *eto* meaning "tree' and *opelwv* "swamp." Tupelo is
thus our paleface attempt to speak Creek, and bad as that would sound
to General Jackson's proud enemies, the "Red Sticks," it might do
nicely if it were not strongly objected in Dixie that Tupelo should be
reserved for another tree. Perhaps the open-minded bystander will ap-
prove, for once, the Latin binomial. *Nyssa* has a lovely sound, as it
should, since it was the name of a water nymph in classical mythology;
sylvatica, of course, means that it is of the forest.

Growing in swampy woods throughout its wide range, this water
nymph of the forest has, in the full tide of summer, an almost tropical
look about its glossy, leathery leaves. One would think they were
evergreen. But in the fall, the foliage turns a gorgeous deep Burgundy
color. Frequently one half of the leaf retains its lustrous summer green
intact, adding to the effect by contrast. After the leaves have fallen, the
handsome blue drupes swing a while until the robins get them; then
the female trees stand as barren as the male, and the Black Gums are
revealed in all their rigid nakedness. For the ponderous trunk rises
more or less a mast, giving off short, scraggly branches, as stiffly as the
main stem of a Conifer. When spring comes back to the swamp, the
leaf buds very early take on much the same vivid color as the autumnal

foliage, and are more beautiful by far than the inconspicuous flowers that bloom as the young leaves are thrusting out.

The Black Gum grows about 60 feet tall at the most, and frequently never attains over 30 feet. Decay sets in early, as time is measured by tree growth, and death often starts at the top of the tree and works downward. At first these dead tops help to identify the tree, in a not very complimentary fashion, but, when the tops keep breaking off, the tree actually grows shorter as it grows older — perhaps the only case of a tree which commonly does so.

Usually the decay attacks the heartwood first, so that hollow trees are common. When the country folk in the South find such a tree, they cut it down and saw it into short sections. These are then stood up on boxes, with a board laid over the top, for beehives. Hence the time-honored name of bee-gums for hives. Longer sections are often arranged as traps for rabbits and laid in the woods; the hunter calls these rabbit-gums.

To the Black Gum, as a timber tree, the pioneers said anathema with every abhorrence. For its fibers are not only interbraided but cross-woven. It is as easy to split across as lengthwise — that is, it can't be done at all, even with wedge and sledge. As our ancestors were a nation of rail splitters, they left the Black Gum pretty well alone. More, in contact with the soil its wood decays quickly, which is unusual in a swamp tree. Though it yielded to the saw, it warped and shrank so, before the days of dry kilns, that it was considered just too worthless for a self-respecting lumberman to fight into boards.

But precisely because nothing can split it, Black Gum was worked into the handles of heavy-duty tools. It carried the head of the maul, and took up the shock of the blow that split other, nobler timbers into rails. Quarter-sawed and stained it makes a good imitation of Mahogany, but if it will never be a fine cabinet wood in its own right, yet it has borne the tremendous strains of the rollers over which the great cables in mine shafts are dragged by the steam donkeys. It has been used for gunstocks and pistol grips. As a veneer for berry crates it has the advantage over the usual deal of being unbreakable. It is in favor for scaffolding and chopping bowls, for the wooden parts of agricultural machinery, and the floors of factories which receive the hardest usage.

The Yellow Gum or Upland Tupelo is simply a variety of this

species, variety *caroliniana* (Poiret) Fernald. It differs on the technical grounds of having thinner, less glossy leaflets, with rather long tips, the under surface persistently somewhat downy and covered with minute warty excrescences easily seen under an ordinary hand lens. The young twigs are brittle, not limber. Yellow Gum is not a swamp tree, like Black Gum, but an inhabitant of dry land, hills, and the coves of the southern Appalachians which it ascends to 3500 feet. There it grows up to 90 or 100 feet tall, much taller than the Black Gum. The range is not perfectly known but appears to be from Philadelphia to Detroit, south to the mountains of South Carolina and in the Ohio valley; it is widely distributed in Tennessee and Arkansas and reaches eastern Texas and northern Mississippi.

"Pioneers," says Charles C. Deam, state forester of Indiana,[1] "have always insisted that there were two kinds of black gum. They distinguish them by their splitting qualities. The form very difficult to split was known as the black gum, and the form that 'split like poplar' was known as yellow gum. The bark of the variety much resembles that of the tulip tree and the branches are usually ascending." Much Yellow Gum lumber has undoubtedly been sent to market as Yellow Poplar. This variety therefore belongs in the category of genuine timber trees and has none of the disadvantages, yet none of the advantages, of the refractory old Black Gum.

[1] *The Flora of Indiana* (1940).

THE CORNELS

(*Cornus*)

ALTERNATE or opposite simple deciduous leaves, mostly without teeth, round twigs with scaly buds, and perfect or unisexual flowers, characterize the Cornels. The 4- or 5-toothed calyx is minute, with short lobes; there are 4 or 5 separate petals, with the stamens inserted on the margin of the conspicuous disk. The inferior ovary terminates in a short style and broad stigma. The fruit, a drupe, contains one or 2 oblong-egg-shaped seeds with membranous coats. Sometimes the heads of flowers are enclosed in broad petal-like bracts.

FLOWERING DOGWOOD

Cornus florida Linnæus

OTHER NAME: Virginia Dogwood.

RANGE: Extreme southern Maine and southern Vermont across southern New York, the southern tip of Ontario, southern Michigan and northern Illinois to the southeastern half of Missouri, eastern Oklahoma, and Texas south to the Gulf of Mexico.

DESCRIPTION: *Bark* on old trunks nearly black, checked into numberless little squarish or many-sided plates divided by as many deep furrows. *Twigs* at first pale green tinged with red, turning yellow-green or bright red by the first winter, and finally light gray tinged with red. *Terminal buds* conspicuous, pearly or silver-gray, squarish, consisting in 2 opposite, pointed outer scales folded over 2 inner scales. *Leaves* 3 to 6 inches long, 1½ to 2 inches wide, bright yellow-green, paler or almost white below, thick and firm, with impressed nerves on upper surface. *Flowers* inconspicuous, but petal-like bracts white, flecked with parallel green veins and with a handsome spot of green on the notched tips, 4 in number, the whole sometimes 4 to 5 inches across. *Fruit* brilliant scarlet, shiny, 30 or 40 in a head. *Wood* very hard, very heavy (50 pounds to the cubic foot, dry weight), with very small cylinder of chocolate-colored or greenish heartwood and 30 or 40 rings of pinkish sapwood.

Stepping delicately out of the dark woods, the startling loveliness of Dogwood in bloom makes each tree seem a presence, calling forth an exclamation of praise, a moment of worship from our eyes. On the almost naked branches the blossoms shine forth like stars, and these blossoms are borne in long flat sprays of bloom along the boughs, turning their pure faces up toward the sky with a suggestion of the most classical traditions of flower arrangement. It is a botanist's quibble to point out that the four white "petals" are not petals indeed but bracts; by any name, they make a clear and pleasing design, in detail as in mass. And the little tree bears them with a royal grace, tier upon snowy tier, the slim trunk often leaning slightly from the hillside, as though to offer its burden of blossom, princess-like, to the spring world.

But it makes no great demands on its environment. It is well suited to comparatively dry soils; it comes up quickly after fire; it shines through sterile pine woods and troops along the fence rows that divide field and pasture, and along every country roadside, where the birds have voided the seeds. It steals out of the neighboring woods to invade the clearing left by loggers, or the field abandoned by farmers. It goes, too, climbing high in the mountains, and lights up the somber coves; by stream banks its white branches or, in fall, its scarlet berries gleam as brightly as the waters.

Man's hand has widened this wide distribution. The Flowering Dogwood is the state tree of Virginia, and the noblest of Virginians

have cherished it. George Washington was an inveterate planter of Dogwood. On his birthday in 1785, he noted in his diary that he had removed some from the woods to a "Mount Vernon" shrubbery, and speaks on March first of that year of planting "a circle of Dogwood with a red bud in the Middle, close to the old Cherry near the South Garden House." Thomas Jefferson loved it too, and planted it in "the open ground on the west" of his house at "Monticello." An especially prized variety has pink blooms.

Lovely as it is, Dogwood stoops also to be useful. The wood has an extremely high resistance to sudden shock, ahead even of Persimmon and inferior only to Hickory. For that reason Dogwood has long been a favorite for the heads of golf sticks and for the handles of chisels, since they can be hammered on the ends without "brooming," that is, splitting and mushrooming out. The same virtue makes it useful for mauls, mallet heads, and wedges. Small pulleys, and spindles too, of Dogwood are strong and light and serviceable in the textile industry. Knitting needles and sledge runners are made of it because it wears smoother with use, and in the old days its fine properties made it a favorite for distaffs, spindles, hog yokes, hay forks, barrel hoops, hubs of small wheels, machinery bearings, and rake teeth. Still the jeweler prefers Dogwood sticks for cleaning out deep-seated lenses, since they do not scratch the glass.

But fully 90 per cent of the Dogwood cut in the last century has gone to the making of shuttles in the textile industry. When the shuttle was thrown from hand to hand by the weaving woman, almost any wood might do, but with the invention of mechanical looms, where the shuttle is hurled at top speed, carrying the weft thread, the shuttle is in continual contact with the threads of the warp. So a wood must be used which will not crack under continuous strain and will wear smoother, not rougher, with use. Walnut wears smoother, but is too weak. Hickory is stronger, but wears rough with usage. Dogwood is ideal. Yet it did not come into much use while Turkish Boxwood was plentiful. Then, about 1865, the roller-skating craze began to absorb the market for Box, and Dogwood came to the fore. Cut in the South, it was manufactured and used in New England or exported as logs from the southern seaports to Britain, France, Germany, Italy, and Switzerland. Soon it was found cheaper to ship the manufactured article, and most Dogwood shuttles are now made in small but numerous mills in the South.

Dogwood is lumbered where it can be found in the virgin forest because the longest, straightest, knot-free trunks are grown there. It is also felled by the farmers at the time they are cutting their woodlots in winter for fuel, and sold, a few sticks at a time, or traded at the local general store which then piles the wood on sidings for the trip to the mill. Commonly, then, Dogwood is sold by the cord, because of its small dimensions and high prices. At the mill it is seasoned with great care, halved into flitches, quartered, then cut out into rectangular blocks roughly parallel to the annual growth rings. Highly skilled labor is required, for the buyers demand absolutely perfect, defect-free shuttles and unfortunately insist on the pure white sapwood, though the heartwood is no whit inferior, nor is there danger of splitting where heartwood and sapwood meet.

The cut of commercially valuable Dogwood is far in excess of the annual growth rate. Formerly Dogwood was uprooted or bucked down by tractors in the lumbering operations amid the great pineries of the Gulf states. Owing to the high price for the fine kind of Dogwood grown under Yellow Pine, it is now sold off to contractors and removed before logging of the Pines begins. True that Dogwood is on the increase in abandoned fields, among second growth of Virginia Scrub Pine, along fence rows and roadsides; but such open-grown trees retain their lower boughs, and superior though they are in beauty, they are too short and knotty for the block mills. At present the greatest stand of merchantable Dogwood is in Arkansas, and when the virgin timber there is seriously reduced, the future supply has a far from bright outlook.

Certain obsolete uses of Dogwood make picturesque footnotes to our history. The aromatic bark, above all the inner bark of the root, has marked bitter and astringent properties; the alkaloid cornin or cornic acid is the active principle. The Indians used it as a remedy for malaria; the pioneers improved on this by steeping the Dogwood bark in whiskey, and imbibing this when they had "the shakes" and the "ague." When the blockade of the southern ports by the U.S. Navy, from 1861 to 1865, caused a shortage of quinine in the Confederacy, Dogwood bark was used like "Peruvian bark." And farther back in our fading past, certain Indians derived from the roots a scarlet dye for coloring porcupine quills and bald eagle feathers.

Today our modern savages destroy the tree chiefly for the sprays of

its pure white bloom. Around Washington, D.C., the threat to the tree was so merciless that the Wild Flower Preservation Society waged a long battle to save it from local extinction. Their method was simple and immensely effective. They placed posters on the fronts of the city's streetcars, urging the public to save Dogwood by refusing to cut or buy any. As a result, the sales of Dogwood on the streets, where it had been commonly vended, on the roadsides, in florists' shops and markets has fallen off so severely that merchants have stopped buying it. And this prompt and effective conservation has been achieved without the tedious and imperfect method of passing a law; that powerful legislature, public opinion, was called upon to utter the decree.

PIGEONBERRY

Cornus alternifolia Linnæus the Younger

OTHER NAMES: Blue, Pagoda, or Umbrella Dogwood. Blue, Purple, or Alternate-leaved Cornel. Green Osier.

RANGE: Nova Scotia to the northern shore of Lake Superior and Minnesota, Iowa, and eastern and middle Missouri; south to the mountains of Alabama and to western Florida.

DESCRIPTION: *Bark* thin, dark reddish brown, smooth or fissured and cross-checked. *Twigs* light bright green at first, becoming dark green and flecked with pale lenticels and marked by pale crescent-shaped leaf scars. *Leaves* alternate or rarely opposite, clustered at the ends of the twigs, 3 to 5 inches long, 2½ to 3½ inches wide, bright yellow-green above and very pale or whitened below, with the midrib bright orange below. *Flowers* minute, the sepals, petals, and stamens all 4 in number. *Fruits* on bright red stems, in diameter ⅓ inch, the skin dark blue-black, with thin bitter flesh and 1 or 2 many-ribbed, thick-walled stones. *Wood* hard, medium-heavy (41 pounds to the cubic foot, dry weight), with reddish brown heartwood and thick paler sapwood.

Usually only a many-stemmed shrub, the Pigeonberry in the deep forests of the Southern Appalachians forms a flat-topped understory tree 25 feet tall. The horizontal branches are arranged in tiers of

whorls, the higher successively smaller; this produces a pagoda-like tree. Because the leaves are clustered near the ends of the twigs they form an umbrella-like shade. The cream-colored flowers bloom in midspring, but not until the foliage turns yellow or scarlet in the fall, and the handsome blue berries ripen on their bright-red stalks, does the Pigeonberry come into its full beauty.

Even then this modest tree might pass unnoticed by many, appreciated by few. It belongs, something like the warbling vireo which eats the Pigeonberry's fruits, to the class of subtle sylvan things little seen and even quite unheard of, by most people. It is most enjoyed by those who, while not necessarily trained as field botanists, have a gardener's eye, and a plantsman's habits of mind, when they walk abroad in the woods. Those habits include a refusal to be hurried, even by amateur mountaineers or other hyperthyroid fauna, and a resolute lack of other objective than the first fine spot encountered. Such persons are alert not only for the rare, but are forever sweeping the familiar with appreciative eyes. They stop to examine any plant that does not proclaim its identity as a known species. Your true plantsman then explores the new subject with fingers and nose, as well as eyes, and casts about for further specimens that may perhaps represent the other sex of the same species, or a tree in a different stage of its growth or its annual cycle. So the Pigeonberry may come to be known, and by that much is the scene deepened in perspective, and companioned with the secrecy of recognition.

THE VIBURNUMS

(*Viburnum*)

Shrubs or small trees, the Viburnums have simple opposite leaves, tough flexible branches, large winter buds encased, in our species, in a pair of scales, and flower buds large, swollen below the middle, and contracted to a short point. The flowers occur in flat or low dome-shaped, branched clusters, and are bisexual, with minute 5-lobed calyx and small 5-lobed, spreading corolla; the stamens number 5, inserted in the corolla tube. The inferior ovary terminates in a conic style divided into 3 stigma lobes. The fruit takes the form of a drupe, with thin juicy flesh and a tough, sharp-pointed, much flattened stone which contains a bright reddish-brown seed concave on one face.

Several species of Viburnum, such as *V. Lentago* and *V. rufidulum,* which are trees in the South, are only shrubs within the circumscription of this book.

The Viburnums are frequently placed much farther along in some of our botanical manuals, but the relationship of *Viburnum* to *Cornus* is so striking that it has been thought reasonable to place it here, as was done, indeed, by such great systematists as De Candolle, Bentham and Hooker, and, in recent times, by Bessey and Pool.

BLACK HAW

Viburnum prunifolium Linnæus

OTHER NAMES: Stagbush. Sheepberry. Nannyberry. Sweet Haw.

RANGE: Neighborhood of New York City south to the valley of the Savannah River, Georgia, west to central parts of Michigan, to Illinois, Missouri, and Kansas.

DESCRIPTION: *Bark* thin, irregularly broken into red-brown, plate-like scales. *Twigs* slender and spine-like, at first bright red, then green, turning reddish gray and covered with a slight bloom and marked by large crescent-shaped leaf scars and bright orange lenticels; ultimately dark brown tinged with red. *Winter buds* brown. *Leaves* 1 to 3 inches long, ½ to 3 inches wide, with meshed veinlets, dark green above, paler below, thick or almost leathery. *Flowers* white, about ½ inch long, with nearly round petals. *Fruit* in red-stemmed, few-fruited clusters, ½ to ⅔ inch long, dark blue or nearly black and covered with a pale bloom. *Wood* hard, strong, very heavy (52 pounds per cubic foot, dry weight), the heartwood brown tinged with red, the thick sapwood paler.

Roadsides and fence rows, dry rocky hillsides and prairie groves, are the habitats of this bushy understory tree, with its short, crooked, spindling, bandy-legged trunk and its graceless rigid branches like widespread arms. Seldom over 30 feet high, it is not impressive, but it has its beauties. The heads of creamy flowers have much the charm of elder blossoms, the dark green foliage is very cleanly and neat; but it is in the fall that the Black Haw comes into its own. The leaves turn either a brilliant scarlet or a deep Burgundy red, while the blue-black fruits, on their red stalks, make a handsome contrast.

Viburnum prunifolium is still on the official list of plant *materia medica* of the U.S. Pharmacopoeia; the bark of the roots has been used in the treatment of dysmenorrhea and as a nerve tonic, although it is now rarely prescribed. However, the fruits remain popular with gray foxes, white-tailed deer, bobwhites, wood-wandering boys, and botanists.

THE RHODODENDRONS
(*Rhododendron*)

THESE ARE crooked-stemmed understory trees of bushy habit, or usually shrubs, with growth by terminal buds formed during the summer. Commonly the simple, untoothed leaves are clustered at the ends of the twigs. The flowers appear from buds with numerous deciduous scales, in large, compact, terminal clusters. The 5-lobed calyx is small but persistent under the fruit; the corolla has a short tube and flaring limb that is 5-lobed. A slender style, with a knob-like stigma, crowns the ovary, and the fruit takes the form of a woody pod containing many minute seeds.

BIG RHODODENDRON

Rhododendron maximum Linnæus

OTHER NAMES: Late or Summer Rhododendron. Bigleaf, Deertongue, or Great Laurel. Rose Bay.

RANGE: Appalachians from southern Vermont to Georgia, and in Connecticut, southern New York State, and northern New Jersey. Isolated stations in central Maine, New Hampshire, Massachusetts, the neighborhoods of Philadelphia and Washington, central North Carolina, central and southern Ohio, and western Kentucky.

DESCRIPTION: *Bark* of trunk very thin, scaly, light red-brown. *Twigs* at first covered with rusty-red, bristly, sticky hairs, later smooth and dark green, becoming the second year bright red-brown and finally gray and shreddy and marked with the remote conspicuous scars of the bud scales. *Winter buds* large, conic, dark green, covered with many closely overlapping, sticky scales. *Leaves* thick, leathery, dark blue-green, 4 to 12 inches long 1½ to 2 inches broad, with thick, pale midrib which is deeply impressed on the upper surface, but strong on the lower surface which is pale or whitish. *Flowers* appearing from large, cone-shaped buds formed the previous year and covered with leaf-like scales; stalklets of

the compact flower cluster pink and clammy-hairy; each bloom subtended by a papery, resinous, big, downy scale; corollas with a very short
tube and wide flaring limb, the lower pair of petals slightly smaller than
the upper three; stamens 8 to 12 on stalks of various lengths; ovary
terminating in a long style with 5-rayed stigma. *Fruit* a dark red-brown
pod covered with sticky, stiff hairs, splitting to release the oblong flattened seeds with their papery appendages. *Wood* hard, strong, brittle,
medium-light (39 pounds to the cubic foot, dry weight), with clear
light brown heartwood and thin, paler sapwood.

It is only on the southern Appalachians that this species becomes a
tree. At Highlands, North Carolina, which in the opinion of the late
Professor Sargent of the Arnold Arboretum has the finest trees in the
eastern United States, a Rhododendron 23 feet tall was found, a
quarter of a century ago, to have a trunk 9 inches thick at two feet
from the ground.[1] How large that particular specimen might be today
is conjectural, but 40 feet has been recorded as the height of some of
the Big Rhododendrons on the cool, rain-soaked slopes of the Great
Smokies.

The mountain folk of the southern Appalachians and the visitors
from the north will never agree on the proper name for this shrub or
tree. To the mountaineer it is Laurel (with or without adjectives),
while the visitor wishes to call the next species (*Kalmia latifolia*) a
Laurel, or Mountain Laurel. This the mountaineer rejects scornfully;
why, anybody knows that that (*Kalmia*) is "Ivy"! The English horticulturist, who is much interested in both these plants, rejects all these names
with pity for our illiteracy: the classic Laurel and the English ivy are
quite unrelated to the species under discussion here.

But, call it Laurel or Rhododendron, no other tree or shrub of the
southern Appalachians is so famous. Its very name is more closely
associated with their beauty, and their folk, than any ten other plants
of any sort. One thinks of the Blue Ridge or the Great Smokies together with Rhododendron as surely as one associates Scotland and
heather, Maine and the White Pine, California and Sequoia. Big
Rhododendron, as an understory tree or great shrub, covers unmeasured thousands of square (and more or less vertical) mountain miles,
laves its roots in all the mountains' rushing streams, crowds up in
every rocky cove. In winter, its leaves, though evergreen, droop and
roll inwards. Always it is linked in memory with the sound of rushing

[1] Coker and Totten, *Trees of the Southeastern States.*

or tinkling water, with the delicious odor of the peat-like soil beneath its perpetual shade.

Tradition has it that Rhododendron hides the moonshiner and his still, and tradition is frequently right. Rhododendron may even play its part in the excessive isolation of mountain life; too high to see over, yet low enough to form an impenetrable twiggy thicket of crooked stems, it grows so thickly in many places that it cannot be penetrated until a path is cut through it. Nothing is easier than to get lost in the Rhododendron thickets, especially where the terrain is very steep. If a child is lost in them, or an adult who is already exhausted with climbing, hunger, or, above all, cold, the outlook is serious. Commonly one used to see, in the country post offices of the southern mountains, notices of persons lost in the mountains. In most cases their trouble came in the Rhododendron thickets.

If Rhododendron is a somber and even a menacing growth, at its most formidable, it is also one of the loveliest. In spring, when the new leaves first appear at the ends of the twigs, they stand erect, and look something like the pricked-up ears of rabbits, all the more for being woolly and pinkish. At maturity they hang gracefully in umbrella-like clusters at the twigs' ends, gleaming softly, with none of the hard brilliance of the Mountain Laurel.

At precisely that season when the shade grows dense and the breath of the valley is hot, when the thrush sings more and more briefly at dawn and after sunset, and all the other nine species of Rhododendron in the southern Appalachians have long since bloomed themselves out, the Big Rhododendron at last opens its great, cool blossoms from the immense buds. Sometimes pure white, sometimes pink, rarely deep rose, the corollas cluster, usually 16 to 24 together, in an umbrella-shaped head of close flowers. Part of the charm of the flowers is in their slight irregularity. The three upper petals are larger than the lower pair, and the middle of the upper three is always flecked with big green spots, looking almost like pollen dust and by contrast intensifying the immaculate purity of the other petals. The stamens are of various lengths, the upper ones with the shortest filaments, the lowest with long, down-sweeping stalks that turn up abruptly at the tips to bear small anthers. The green ovary is tipped by the long white style which, like the filaments of the stamens, curves downward and hangs out of the flower, then abruptly bends upward and ends in the five-rayed, bright scarlet stigma held up as if in eagerness for the pollen.

In sum, for refinement of detail, in form and color, it would be difficult to discover a lovelier flower in the American flora. Yet in the forest, Big Rhododendron in flower is not gaudy or showy; it is far surpassed in eye-taking splendor by its relative the Catawba Rhododendron that in June clothes the highest peaks of the southern Appalachians in purple.

In the age of the Michauxs, the Bartrams, and the Frasers, our eastern American Rhododendrons were eagerly collected, along with our Magnolias, Stewartias, and Kalmias, as the most garden-worthy of American plants. As early as 1736 the present species is known to have been grown by Peter Collinson, the famous Quaker merchant and plantsman, in his garden near London; probably he received it from his great co-religionist, John Bartram of Philadelphia. But when the Asiatic species began to reach Europe in the early nineteenth century, the American species lapsed out of fashion. Not, however, before much hybridizing had been done, and it is said that the "blood" of *Rhododendron maximum* flows in many a famous European hybrid still.

The nectar of Big Rhododendron makes a distinctly poisonous honey, carefully avoided by the beemasters of the Appalachians. More than two thousand years ago Xenophon mentions that the Greek soldiers in Asia Minor were poisoned by eating honey made from the flowers of *Rhododendron ponticum;* probably the whole genus is suspect on this score, but the honey does not appear to poison the bees.

THE MOUNTAIN LAURELS

(*Kalmia*)

THESE SHRUBS or small trees grow by lateral buds and are characterized by scaly bark and elongated axillary flower buds covered by overlapping scales. Usually evergreen, the foliage has untoothed margins
and very short stalks. The flowers occur in umbrella-like clusters from
the axils of the feathery leaf-like scale leaves; the calyx, persistent
under the fruit, is 5-hearted, the corolla with a short tube, with a wide
saucer-shaped, flaring limb with 5 lobes and 10 pouches just within the
throat, in which are lodged, when the flower first opens, the anthers of
the 10 short stamens; the ovary, which is free from the calyx, terminates
in a slender style crowned with a knob-like stigma. The numerous
minute seeds are contained in a woody capsule (pod) which splits
tardily along 5 valves and is crowned by the persistent remnants of
the styles.

MOUNTAIN LAUREL

Kalmia latifolia Linnæus

OTHER NAMES: Sheep, Poison, or Wood Laurel. Calicotree. Calico-flower. Spoonwood. Mountain, Big-leaved or Poison Ivy. Ivywood.

RANGE: New Brunswick to western Florida, Louisiana, and central Tennessee. Ascending the Appalachians to 4000 feet.

DESCRIPTION: *Bark* very thin, dark brown tinged with red, with long furrows and narrow ridges, flaking into long narrow scales. *Twigs* slender, at first light green tinged with red, becoming shiny by winter and then turning bright red-brown the second year, marked with deeply impressed leaf scars. *Winter buds* in the axils of the leaves just below the flower buds, the inner scales becoming 1 inch long, light green and covered with white glandular hairs in spring, and marking the base of the twigs, after they fall, with broad scars. *Leaves* in pairs or in threes, alternate or opposite, 3 to 4 inches long, 1 to 1½ inches wide, yellow-

green and shining on the upper surface, somewhat paler below with a broad yellow midrib, leathery in texture, evergreen. *Flowers* from big buds from the axils of the leaves, forming a compound, many-flowered, umbrella-shaped mass of bloom 4 or 5 inches across, the individual blossoms 1 inch in diameter on long, slender, sticky-hairy stalks; calyx divided nearly to the base; corolla white or pink. *Fruit* a woody pod,

³⁄₁₆ inch in diameter, covered with sticky hairs, containing the oblong, light brown seeds. *Wood* hard, strong, brittle, medium-heavy (45 pounds to the cubic foot, dry weight), the heartwood brown tinged with red, the sapwood paler.

Peach-blow and Redbud, Apple-blossom time and Dogwood season, each in their turn take over the countryside and make it enchanting, but the crown of all the year is the moment when the Mountain Laurel blooms. No other shrub or tree in the eastern United States is finer when in flower, and rightfully the English, the best gardeners of Europe, envy us this plant; the English climate does not permit them to bring it to perfection, though they grow it on the estates of the most discriminating owners rather than have it not at all.

Even in America it is difficult to raise Mountain Laurel outside its natural range, for it is not tolerant of the limestone soil of the Middle West and coastal California; it is not tolerant of transplantation, since it requires an acid, peat-like soil, rich in certain endophytic fungi; it is not tolerant of the shadeless conditions demanded by so many other garden plants, and will not make a satisfactory roadside or garden hedge. It loves the red clay soils of the Atlantic seaboard, grows happily only in the shade of other trees, preferably the Pines, asks for rainy summers, and is most luxuriant where the winters are mild.

Where such conditions prevail, the best way to have this superb flower in your garden is to buy yourself an Appalachian hill (where the Mountain Laurel may grow 30 feet tall), forget your gardening tools, your bales of peat, your soil injections of silicate of aluminum, and wait for May. The result has no rival; for the moment, all the world is fair and good. The redbird on his bough cries "pretty-pretty-pretty!" The thrush, at day's break and ending, is in full voice; the first fireflies drift through the trees and grass. Then one would not trade the hour when Mountain Laurel blooms, for Japan or California or the Riviera.

So abundant and so popular is this little tree in parts of the South that when it blooms the country folk sell it on the roadside, and they are apt to call it Ivy, for they insist that the name of Laurel should be applied to the Big Rhododendron. No matter what you call it, it is a disappointment to bear away a branch unless it can swiftly be plunged in water, for at the first hint of thirst the exquisite corollas fall and dangle sadly on the stamens and styles.

These dainty corollas, like tiny starched crinoline or calico skirts of some child of long ago, gave this Laurel its alternative name of Calicoflower, or Calicotree. The corolla may be frosty white or pink or rose-colored, but always it is exquisitely marked with that wavy, rose-hued band just inside the throat and delicately penciled above the tiny pouches with purple. The pouches themselves — concave on the outside of the flower — add to the unique charm of the blossoms, and if you will watch the flower when it is just opening you will see how when a bee visits it, she trips the spring-like mechanism of the tense filaments of the stamens, causing the anther to be dragged out of the pouch, the filament to fly erect and the pollen to be shaken out of the anther, like pepper from a pepperpot, upon the bee.

Amongst Southerners there is a well-founded belief that the honey from Laurel nectar is poisonous. As early as 1794, the Philadelphia physician and botanist Benjamin Barton described a case of Laurel-honey poisoning from New Jersey, and since that time numberless cases have been attributed to Laurel. Although the bees are not harmed by it, Laurel honey when sampled by humans has a nauseating odor and pungent taste and causes a burning sensation at the back of the mouth, abdominal cramps and vomiting, coldness of the extremities, feeble heart, pallor, surface coldness of the skin, and frequently syncope. Most apiarists throw away the honey made just after the Laurel is in bloom, and are the more careful to do so especially as the best honey of the year, in the southern Appalachians, is produced immediately afterward by the nectar of the Sourwood, the following species. The leaves of Mountain Laurel are likewise poisonous. They contain andromedotoxin, which produces in browsing animals salivation, weeping, emesis with convulsions, and paralysis of the limbs. Usually it is only young animals, especially lambs, which are so unwary as to eat Laurel leaves in spring when no other browse is afforded in the woodlot pasture.

In one respect only has Mountain Laurel ever attained as a wood any commercial importance; it has long been cut for the making of briar tobacco pipes, along with the burls of the preceding species. A briar pipe, to be properly so called, must be a member of the Heath Family (*bruyère*, in French —hence our word briar) and it must be made of that rare and abnormal type of wood called a burl. By this standard only Mountain Laurel and Big Rhododendron, in our sylva, could furnish a genuine briar. The center of the Laurel briar industry is in the neighborhood of Hendersonville and Brevard, North Carolina. The reason for this is that there, almost uniquely in the southern Appalachians, are found those boggy spots, supersaturated with soil water and deficient in oxygen, which seem to produce on the roots of members of the Heath Family the type of wood known as burl. Appearing externally like a lump or knot, the wood is usually far heavier and harder and denser than normal wood of the species; for that reason it will not readily burn out when the tobacco is lit inside the bowl. The contorted fibers of burl wood also give to pipe bowls the ornamental figures which the true pipe collector appreciates and carefully cherishes.

Objection has been raised against Laurel briar pipes, as "inferior," by merchants who prefer to sell foreign briars because they fetch higher prices for the retailer, and the friends of our native scenery have raised a cry that the pipe industry was destroying a beautiful tree with reckless waste, all for the sake of a small amount of pipe wood. The latter charge was carefully investigated some years ago by P. L. Ricker, president of the Wild Flower Preservation Society, and denied by him. He saw no visible reduction in the quantity of Laurel and Rhododendron and no serious waste was observed.

THE SORRELTREES

(*Oxydendrum*)

T HE MEMBERS of this genus exhibit slender twigs without a terminal
bud and marked by triangular, elevated leaf scars, and numerous dark,
elevated, oblong lenticels. The minute winter buds are axillary and
tightly imbedded in the bark and are covered with dark red scales.
Alternate, simple, and deciduous, the leaves are acid-tasting and have
minute, incurved callous teeth and meshed veinlets. The flowers nod
on long spikes in compound clusters, with the calyx small and divided
nearly to the base, the corolla with a jug-shaped tube and a very short
flaring limb of 5 lobes. The 10 stamens, inserted on the very base of
the corolla, are included within the flower, while the ovary terminates
in a columnar style crowned by a thick stigma which is exserted from
the corolla. Taking the form of a many-seeded, 5-celled capsule, the
fruit is crowned with the remains of the persistent style.

SOURWOOD

Oxydendrum arboreum (Linnæus) A. P. De Candolle

OTHER NAMES: Sorreltree. Sour Gum. Arrowwood. Lily-of-the-valley-tree.

RANGE: Southwestern Pennsylvania to the coast of Virginia and of North Carolina, southward to western Florida and eastern Louisiana, west to southern Ohio, extreme southern parts of Indiana and Illinois, western Kentucky and Tennessee. Ascending the southern Appalachians to 3500 feet.

DESCRIPTION: *Bark* gray tinged with red and divided by deep longitudinal furrows into broad, rounded ridges covered with small scales, and commonly cross-checked, resulting in a blocky appearance. *Twigs* rather stout, often zigzag and sometimes angled, green, orange-brown, or red, dotted with the conspicuous dark lenticels, and marked with the shield-shaped or half-round leaf scars. *Leaves* 5 to 7 inches long, 1 to 3 inches wide, finely toothed, the upper surface shining and bright yellow-green, the lower paler. *Flowers* creamy white, in compound clusters 7 to 8 inches long, the individual flowers small. *Fruits* drooping, 1/3 to 1/2 inch long, containing the pale brown seeds which are about 1/8 inch long. *Wood* hard, medium-heavy (46½ pounds to the cubic foot, dry weight), with red-tinged brown heartwood and very thick layers of paler sapwood.

The glittering leaves of the Sourwood, wondrously fresh-looking and spirited, have completed their growth long before the flowers appear, yet so handsome are the great bouquets of bloom at the ends of the branches that they are not put out of countenance by the splendid foliage but, looking like hundreds of little lilies-of-the-valley, they sway and dance in the warm, friendly wind of late June and early July. In case you have not looked up and seen them, you may soon be made aware of them by the roar of the bees gone nectar-mad at their lips.

When autumn comes, the foliage turns a gorgeous scarlet or orange or crimson, doubly welcome because the Sourwood in general grows outside the range of the Sugar Maple and the Aspen, and takes their place in the South. Then, especially in the southern Appalachians where Sourwood grows 50 and 60 feet tall, is the season to set out afoot, or on horseback, or in your car, to buy Sourwood honey from your country neighbors. Some of them put out little signs along the roadside, but all you have to do is to watch for a row of "bee gums" not far from the farmer's house. For if the Southern farmer has hives at all, he has Sourwood honey for sale. Fortunately the blooming period of Sourwood is just after the fading of Mountain Laurel and Rhododendron whose honeys are poisonous. Their honey the bee-keeper throws away, but he is very careful to store his Sourwood honey, for it is the finest, in the opinion of many epicures, in the southeastern states and is not surpassed even by the most tangy sage honey of California.

Sourwood honey is medium-light in color, of heavy body, and slow to granulate. An average flow of as high as 75 pounds per colony from Sourwood has been recorded. Usually the local demand takes the entire crop at prices above the open market, so that Sourwood is a honey like some of the choicest wines of the vineyards of Europe — that is, it practically does not appear upon the market at all and can be had only by those epicures who will journey far to partake of it. One buys Sourwood honey as one buys any such rare product from its producers — not in a commercial spirit, paying for it and carrying away the wares — but with all the due ceremony observed between a collector and a creative artist. You ride up to the cabin door; a woman appears at the barking of the hounds, with children peeping out from behind her skirts, and mountain courtesy requires that you begin, not by stating your business but by telling where you come from. Then you assure her that she has a "right pretty place"; you praise her portulacas, her turkeys, and so, across the landscape, you arrive at her bee gums. Then you ask if she likes Sourwood honey as much as you do. You tell her that you would go far to obtain a little if only you could find somebody who would give up a few pounds of it. When the honey is produced, as it certainly will be, you accept it before asking the price. This will be shyly stated. You may safely pay it for your haggling was all done, by indirection, in your previous parley. And you are paying no more than a fico for nectar and ambrosia.

The very hard wood scarcely enters into the lumber business but is cut locally by farmers for the handles of tools. Once on a time in the days of home medicine, the leaves were brewed as a tonic, and they still, with their pleasant acid taste, quench the thirst of the hot, perspiring mountain climber.

THE EBONIES

(*Diospyros*)

THE PERSIMMONS display alternate, simple, untoothed leaves and unisexual flowers, commonly all of one sex on a single tree, but sometimes the sexes intermix on the same tree. Growth is by scaly axillary buds; no terminal bud is present. Generally the male flowers are found in 2-flowered, branched clusters while the female are solitary in the axils of the leaves. The 4-lobed calyx is persistent on the fruit. Four-lobed, too, the corolla is generally jug-shaped with a contracted throat and short, recurved lobes. Sixteen stamens, inserted on the bottom of the corolla in 2 rows and in pairs, show the outer row on longer stalks than those of the inner. The ovary is topped by 4 styles, each 2-lobed at the apex and bearing 2-lobed stigmas. The fruit, technically a several-seeded berry, appears somewhat like a plum; spherical or oblong, it is surrounded at base by the enlarged persistent calyx. The oblong, compressed seeds have dark, shining, thick, and bony coats.

PERSIMMON

Diospyros virginiana Linnæus

OTHER NAMES: Possumwood. Date Plum.

RANGE: Southern Florida, north to the neighborhood of New Haven, Connecticut, the central parts of Ohio, Indiana, Illinois, and Missouri, and west to the eastern part of Kansas, Oklahoma, and Texas. Not in the higher Appalachians.

DESCRIPTION: *Bark* thick, dark brown or dark gray tinged with red, and deeply divided into innumerable square plates. *Twigs* zigzag with very thick pith, at first light brown, becoming ashy gray by winter and marked with occasional orange-colored lenticels and elevated leaf scars with deep, horizontal, crescent-shaped depressions. *Winter buds* minute, with thick overlapping dark red-brown or purple shining scales. *Leaves* 4 to 6 inches long, 2 to 3 inches wide, leathery, dark green and shining above, pale below, with broad flat midrib and about 6 pairs of conspicuous primary veins which arch and join near the margin, and meshed veinlets. *Flowers* male in 2- to 3-flowered, stalked clusters, the female solitary on short recurved stalks; corolla of the male flower tubular, ½ inch long, and slightly contracted at the throat; the 8 stamens with short, slightly hairy stalks; female flowers with greenish-yellow or creamy-white corolla nearly ½ inch broad; the ovary conic and terminating in 4 slender, hairy styles. *Fruit* on a short thick stem, depressed-spherical or egg-shaped, rounded or pointed at the apex, ¾ to 3 inches thick, with tough, puckery skin, at first green, then amber, then orange, and finally purple-black, the flesh thick, yellowish, very austere and astringent until dead ripe; seeds oblong, much flattened, straight on one edge and rounded on the other, ½ inch long, ⅓ inch wide, with thick, hard, pale-brown wrinkled coat. *Wood* very strong, extremely hard, very heavy (52 pounds to the cubic foot, dry weight), the heartwood dark brown, the very thick sapwood pale brown.

"If it be not ripe," said doughty Captain John Smith, of the persimmon he first tasted near Jamestown, "it will draw a man's mouth awrie with much torment." And your own first bite into a persimmon fruit, unless you have been brought up in the region where it is a familiar article of diet, may, unluckily, be an unforgettable experience. It will be a day before you can get the puckery taste out of your mouth, and in all probability you will be disposed never to make another trial of the fruit whose name, *Diospyros,* means "fruit of Zeus." But that is because most people attempt persimmons before they are truly ripe. At first green, then amber, then glaucous orange, a persimmon is not ripe until the skin is wrinkled, and unappetizing in appearance, and the pulp is so mushy that one cannot eat it without washing the hands afterwards.

Close relative of the *kaki,* or Japanese persimmon, our native fruit is not usually so large or handsome or firm of flesh. Yet it is esteemed by connoisseurs, who will travel miles to gather the fruit of a particularly fine tree, and they tell you that the art of eating a persimmon consists (in addition to persuading one's self that a fruit may be a perfect mush and yet delicious) in avoiding the skin altogether, for the intensely tannic taste never leaves that part of the fruit. Certain it is that some trees produce large, some small fruit; some fruits are delicious, some never good at any season; some ripen in August, some in December, and others hold their fruit until spring. Obviously, amidst such variation there are strains well worth propagating and breeding.

During the Civil War, when Confederate soldiers boiled persimmon seeds as a substitute for coffee, Professor F. P. Porcher published in Richmond a book, *Resources of the Southern Fields and Forests,* intended to show the way to meet the blockade of Rebel seaports by utilizing the native products, and in this book he gives as a recipe for persimmon syrup the following:

"The persimmons are mixed with wheat bran, baked in pones, next crushed and put in vessels, water poured on, and all allowed to stand twelve hours. Strain and boil to the consistency of molasses." Porcher adds: "A good vinegar very much like and equal to white wine vinegar is made as follows: Three bushels of ripe persimmons, three gallons of whiskey, and twenty-seven gallons of water. To those who can get the persimmons, the vinegar thus produced will be relatively cheap, even at any price which the elastic conscience can ask for the spirits" — a thrust at war profiteers, that. Perhaps some persons, if they had three gallons of whiskey, would not, even for the sake of obtaining vinegar, mix them with persimmons.

Professor Milton Hopkins [1] tells us how to make a persimmon pudding:

"Three eggs, 1/2 teaspoon salt, 2 cups sweet milk, 3 1/2 cups flour, 1 qt. seed persimmon fruits, I pint cold water, 1 teaspoon soda, 1 cup granulated sugar.

"Wash and seed the fruit (to make 1 quart, about 3 quarts of whole fresh fruit required) and soak them in cold water for about an hour. Then run them through a colander. Mix the other ingredients in the order given, stirring thoroughly. Pour the batter into a greased pan and bake at 400° for one hour or until the pudding is a dark brown in color. Serve either hot or cold with whipped cream or hard sauce, and garnish with maraschino cherries. The pudding keeps well in the icebox for several days."

Naturally persimmons were an important article of diet among the Indians. DeSoto was offered loaves made of persimmons by the Indians in the neighborhood of Memphis, and discovered dried persimmons (called prunes in the narrative) in the villages deserted before his warlike advance in Arkansas. The English naturalist John Bradbury,

[1] "Wild Plants Used in Cookery." New York Botanical Garden *Journal*, vol. 43 (1942), pp. 71-76.

while traveling up the Missouri, was received amongst the Osages and offered a bread called *staninca*, made of the pulp of persimmon pounded with maize; he described the taste as like gingerbread.

Le Page Du Pratz in 1758 wrote, in his *History of Louisiana,* of the persimmon or *placminier* of the Creoles that: "When it is quite ripe the natives make bread of it, which they keep from year to year; and the bread has this remarkable property that it will stop the most violent looseness or dysentery; therefore it ought to be used with caution, and only after physic. The natives, in order to make this bread, squeeze the fruit over fine sieves to separate the pulp from the skin and the kernels. Of this pulp, which is like paste or thick pap, they make cakes about a foot and a half long, a foot broad, and a finger's breadth in thickness: these they dry in an oven, upon gridirons, or else in the sun; which last method of drying gives a greater relish to the bread. This is one of their articles of traffick with the French."

But no matter how we humans improve the breed, or cook the fruit, the persimmon will never mean to us what it does in the lives of the wild animals. It is eaten by birds, notably the popular bobwhite, by the half-wild hogs that rule the Ozarks, by flying squirrels and foxes, by raccoons and skunks and white-tailed deer, and above all by the opossum. According to song and story, most 'possum hunts end at the foot of a 'simmon tree, and when Audubon came to paint his great picture of the opossums, he showed them devouring the strange, puckery-looking fruits, high in the branches of this grand old tree.

Anyone can name a Persimmon when it is in fruit; in its winter nakedness or its heavy summer greenery with those dark, gleaming, tropical-looking leaves, it is not so easy to distinguish it; at least it is apt, as to leaves, to be confused with the Black Gum, and both trees have deeply furrowed and cross-checked bark. But Black Gum bark has rather regular narrow ridges cut by remote cross-checks, while the bark of Persimmon is irregularly broken into countless small blocks; it has a distinctly reptilian sort of corky hide. In winter the naked Persimmon is revealed as a not very graceful tree with short crooked branches and fine crooked twigs, and in autumn the leaves, very late in the season, fall without turning the gorgeous colors of the Black Gum. But in the first hot weather of summer the flowers appear, and all that is tropical-seeming about this member of a very tropical family is expressed in the blossoms. True, they do not make a brilliant show; they are too small for that and overtopped by the foliage, but, of a waxy white, they breathe forth from their thick, jug-shaped corollas a heavy perfume that is the very spirit of the southern summer.

The Persimmon often forms dense thickets on dry, eroded slopes. Not only has the tree a deep taproot, but it sends out long stolons or subterranean runners which are both wide-spreading and deeply penetrating. Trees grown from stolons, however, are apt to be shrubby, and are very difficult to eradicate once they have penetrated the soil of an abandoned field. The finest trees, from the point of view of wood production, are, or were, those growing under primeval forest conditions where competition with other trees has forced them to their maximum growth of 100 or even 130 feet in height. Of course the fruit on such a tree is unhandy to pick, and the gatherer of persimmons greatly prefers the dense bushy thickets that spring up on the sides of gullies and in old fields. Although not a fast-growing tree, Persimmon begins sometimes to bear fruit at an early age. It succeeds in the most adverse sites: on the coal lands of Illinois stripped of all the top soil, or in bottom-lands where the water may stand for several months. A more adaptable tree would be hard to find, and the extent to which it is cherished in southern farmyards would make one think it common. Actually it seldom occurs in pure stands, and as soon as the lumberman tries to find specimens suitable for cutting, he discovers that, wide though the range of this species, it is not individually so very numerous.

Persimmon belongs to the same genus as Ebony (*Diospyros Ebenum*) of the Orient, and betrays the relationship in its heartwood, so dark a brown as to be nearly black. This, however, sometimes does not develop until the tree is over a century old; the very thick sapwood is a pale brown. Persimmon belongs in the class of the very strong woods, and is surpassed in our sylva only by Sweet Locust and Black Locust. When green it is not so very hard, but no other wood gains more in hardness when it is well seasoned; it falls in the class of the extremely hard woods, as hard as Mountain Laurel, and surpassed only by Ironwood and Dogwood among the woods of the circumscription of this book. In weight it is in the very heavy class. It shrinks greatly in drying and will crack unless the ends are protected by paint or paraffin. Difficult to glue, it is never used in built-up or ply or fabricated wood, but when once seasoned properly it retains its shape to perfection. The more it is used, the higher and glossier its polish.

Because the trunk is seldom more than a foot in diameter, this tree can never be an article of great commerce, in spite of its valuable properties and the good price it fetches. Its strength as a beam cannot be utilized, because of the rarity of dimension timber; indeed, Persimmon is commonly sold by the cord. Almost all woods of any value find special employment for which their properties fit them uniquely, and so because of the hardness, smoothness, and non-warping qualities of Persimmon its chief use is for the making of shuttles for textile looms. Some woods, valuable in many other ways, cannot endure an hour under the terrific wear of the looms without cracking, splitting, or wearing rough; Persimmon, like Apple and Dogwood, can endure 1000 hours of furious activity in the mills. Because it holds its shape so well, it has been employed in the wooden lasts over which children's shoes are built, but is too expensive for use in shoes of adults whose styles in footwear change often. The heartwood has been used extensively for the heads of golf sticks because it does not crack under a sudden or impact load, and takes such a high polish. It is used for billiard cues, beautiful parquet flooring, and, in the days of spinning wheels, the small sort at which the women took their places seated were made of Persimmon wood in the South.

The name of Persimmon is old; the Lenape Indians, with whom William Penn treated, called it *pasimenan*. But older still is the geologic ancestry of this tree. Fifty-five million years ago, when the ancestors of the horse were small and short-legged as ponies, Persimmons of numerous species were widespread in North America. On what is now the ranch country of western Oregon grew, for instance, an extinct species (*Diospyros oregana*) whose closest living relatives are now in Java. But many changes in altitude and climate have swept the ancient Persimmons from the West, and today this single species, within the circumscription of our sylva, lives on, as much a reminder of a far-off time as the opossum, our only remaining marsupial.

THE SILVERBELLS

(*Halesia*)

Minutely branched hairs, slender pithy twigs without a terminal bud, and alternate, simple, deciduous leaves, are characteristic of the Silverbells. The bell-shaped white corolla, with 4 lobes, surmounts the ovary which is adherent to the very small, 4-lobed calyx, while the 8 to 16 stamens are slightly attached to the base of the corolla or sometimes free from it. The ovary is gradually contracted into an elongate style. The fruit, marked by a hop-like external skin which is flattened with 2 or more broad wings, is tough and readily separable from the bony stone. Within this lies the solitary elongated seed with its shining, light brown, lustrous coat.

COMMON SILVERBELL

Halesia carolina Ellis

OTHER NAMES: Belltree. Bellwood. Opossumwood. Calicowood. Tisswood. Snowdroptree. Wild Olive. Rattlebox.

RANGE: The Virginias, the Carolinas, Georgia, Alabama, Tennessee to eastern Texas; rare in Kentucky and southern Illinois.

DESCRIPTION: *Bark* thin, reddish brown, with close, thin scales. *Twigs* pithy, orange-brown, marked by large, inversely heart-shaped leaf scars, becoming, the second season, dark reddish brown. *Winter buds* with dark red scales, the inner ones in spring elongating and turning bright yellow. *Leaves* dark yellow-green above, paler below, 3 to 4 inches long, 1½ to 2 inches wide, or much larger on sucker shoots, with small and remote callous teeth. *Flowers* ½ inch long, nodding on long stalks, the corolla narrowed below into a short tube, or rarely lobed almost to the base; stamens 10 to 16. *Fruit* 1½ inch long. *Wood* medium-soft, medium-light (32 pounds to the cubic foot, dry weight), the heartwood light brown and the thick sapwood paler.

The silver bells of this charming little understory tree chime with the pale-green, half-grown leaves upon the airs of a southern April. And though they make no sound, every beholder will intone their praises when whole hillsides are clothed with these enchanting blossoms. Sometimes the corolla is blushed with an exquisite pink. No wonder that the Silverbell has been eagerly taken up by horticulturists from early times and is now a favorite garden tree, grown as far north as New England and far into the Middle West. In autumn the foliage turns a soft pleasing gold and the odd fruits a handsome red.

Bellwood, as the lumberman likes to call this tree, has been more studied by the specialist in wood morphology than appreciated by the wood-using industries. Its beautiful figures do not appear when the wood is cut like ordinary lumber, but when the log is turned against the rotary veneer knives a beautiful bird's-eye figure, and sometimes mottled and pitted figures, may emerge.

MOUNTAIN SILVERBELL

Halesia monticola (Rehder) Sargent

RANGE: Mountains of North Carolina and Tennessee, between 2500 and 4500 feet altitude.

DESCRIPTION: *Bark* thin, freely separating into long reddish-brown plates. *Twigs* slender, becoming shiny light orange-brown, then dark red-brown the second year. *Winter buds* much compressed, arched on the back, the outer scales bright red, shining and thick. *Leaves* 8 to 11 inches long, 1½ to 2½ inches wide, thin, dull dark green above, paler below. *Flowers* 2 inches long, 1 inch across, on stalks ½ to 1 inch long. *Fruit* 1¾ to 2 inches long, 1 inch in diameter, 4-winged; stone prominently angled, ½ to 1 inch long.

In the rich cool coves of the southern Appalachians there is a naturally consorting group of trees (an association, in ecological terminology) which live like the kings they are. Ecologists call this the cove climax, and by climax they mean a stage in the normal succession of one association by another which has reached such stability amidst its component members and so perfectly suits the environment that no other can surplant it in the present geologic moment, unless axe or fire violently displace it. The cove climax is made up of such aristocrats as the Tuliptree, the Canada Hemlock, the Mountain

Magnolia, the White Linden, the Cucumbertree, the Sugar Maple, the Chestnut Oak, the Black Walnut and White Ash, the Butternut and the Sweet Buckeye. But loveliest of them all is the Mountain Silverbell, a species separated with some doubt by botanists from the Common Silverbell, but distinct enough in its much larger flowers and leaves. No other tree of the cove climax has such enchanting flowers, swinging in the chill spring airs, 80 or 90 feet above the forest floor. Trees 100 feet high, with trunks clear of branches for 50 feet, and sometimes 4 feet in diameter, have been sighted by the experts who have penetrated the tallest timber. So that the Mountain Silverbell, though never an abundant tree, must be admitted to the society of true forest giants such as we had commonly in the days of virgin abundance. He who has seen this tree in the Great Smoky Mountains

National Park will never forget his first sight of it in bloom, or the grandeur of its columns, and he will say to himself with pride that he once beheld one of the rare and noblest hardwoods of the North American continent.

THE SWEETLEAVES

(*Symplocos*)

S IMPLE ALTERNATE LEAVES, a 5-lobed, bell-shaped calyx adhering to the ovary, and a 5-parted corolla divided nearly to the base characterize these plants. The flowers are bisexual with numerous stamens of an indefinite number in several rows or series inserted on the short corolla tube, while the inferior ovary terminates in a slender style tipped with a small stigma. The fruit takes the form of a nut-like drupe crowned by the persistent remains of the calyx, with a thin, dry outer covering and a bony stone containing a solitary seed.

SWEETLEAF

Symplocos tinctoria (Garden) L'Héritier

OTHER NAMES: Horse-sugar. Yellowwood. Florida Laurel. Dyebush.

RANGE: Northern Florida to Louisiana and southern Arkansas, and north to the Delaware peninsula. Ascends the southern Appalachians to 4000 feet altitude.

DESCRIPTION: *Bark* thin, ashen, roughened with wart-like excrescences, somewhat fissured. *Twigs* stout, pithy, at first light green, becoming ashy gray or reddish brown, later darkening and roughened with horizontal, inversely heart-shaped leaf scars and small elevated lenticels. *Winter buds* at the time of their opening displaying pale-green inner scales. *Leaves* 5 to 6 inches long, 1 to 2 inches wide, dark green and shining above, paler beneath, in our area deciduous. *Flowers* in tight clusters, the calyx cup-shaped and 5-lobed, the petals ¼ inch long, with protruding stamens in 5 clusters and with orange-colored anthers. *Fruit* ¼ inch long, dark orange-colored; seed with a papery chestnut-brown coat. *Wood* soft, medium-light (33 pounds per cubic foot, dry weight), with light brown heartwood and thick, nearly white sapwood.

Sooner or later, as you tramp the woods in an Appalachian spring, you will come on a little tree with dense clusters of honey-yellow flowers seated directly on the naked wood, which breathe forth an intense sweetness — flowers which, in structure, resemble no others. And that for the very good reason that they belong to a genus entirely tropical and subtropical, save for this one species, the Sweetleaf. Horses are said to be very fond of its foliage, and if you will chew a bit of the leaf you will be amazed at the sugary taste.

In Florida the leaves are evergreen and much more leathery; in our climate they drop in winter. If plucked and left to fade, the leaves turn a vivid yellow on account of the dye-stuff within them. In an interesting little pamphlet on vegetable dyes published at Saluda, North Carolina, a recipe is given for dyeing wool yellow with the leaves of Dyebush, as the native craftsmen prefer to call it.

"Mordant 1 lb. wool with ½ oz. Muriate of Tin and 2 oz. Cream of Tartar in a covered vessel for an hour. Have ready a peck of Dye Bush leaves, and 2 gals. of boiling water in the dye pot. Transfer mordanted wool to the dye pot and add thereto the leaves. Boil for three-quarters of an hour. Remove, rinse, and hang in the sun to dry." [1]

Dyeing with Sweetleaf is now a practice several centuries old in the South and never lost as an art, but the use of the bitter aromatic bark of the root as a tonic seems to be forgotten. Sweetleaf was one of the trees first described for science by Mark Catesby, the naturalist whose first visit to Virginia in 1712 produced such a wealth of fine specimens of birds and trees that he was encouraged by the great collector Hans Sloane to revisit this country. Fixing his residence in Charleston in 1722, he explored probably to the foot of the Blue Ridge (then very wild country) and it was at this time that he discovered the Sweetleaf, describing and illustrating it in his splendid *Natural History of Carolina* in 1731. The famous Dr. Alexander Garden of Charleston, correspondent of Linnaeus, described it under the then new Linnaean system in 1764, and it was first grown in England by the distinguished physician Dr. John Fothergill, friend of Benjamin Franklin. Today one might search for it in gardens anywhere in vain.

Sweetleaf is primarily an inhabitant of the borders of Cypress swamps on the coast, but it is an inhabitant, too, of rich forests in the southern Appalachians. Though it is often only a shrub, a tree specimen 30 feet tall with a trunk 8 inches in diameter was measured near Blowing Rock, North Carolina, and who can doubt that many another such might be found in the lonely, high, cool coves of the Blue Ridge?

[1] *The Katherine Petit Book of Vegetable Dyes,* by Wilmer Stone Viner and H. E. Scrope Viner. 1946.

THE FRINGETREES

(*Chionanthus*)

Simple opposite leaves, thick pith in the twigs, buds with numerous opposite scales, flowers in clusters of three, and 1-seeded fleshy drupes for fruits characterize the members of this genus. The minute calyx and the very long-lobed corolla are both deeply 4-parted. Two stamens are inserted on the base of the corolla. The ovary terminates in a short columnar style and thick stigma. The brown-coated seed fills the stone.

FRINGETREE

Chionanthus virginica Linnæus

OTHER NAMES: Flowering Ash. Old-man's-beard.

RANGE: Tampa Bay and the Manatee River in Florida north to Lancaster County, Pennsylvania, west to northeastern Kentucky, northern Arkansas, southeastern Oklahoma, and the valley of the Brazos River in Texas. Ascends the Appalachians to 4000 feet.

DESCRIPTION: *Bark* thin, covered with reddish-brown scales. *Twigs* stout and often much thickened between the nodes, at first light green, becoming light brown or orange and marked by semicircular leaf scars and dark lenticels. *Winter buds* with scales light brown on the outer surface, bright green within. *Leaves* 4 to 8 inches long, ½ to 4 inches wide, firm and thick, dark green above, pale beneath. *Flowers* with strap-shaped petals 1 inch long; some flowers bisexual, others functionally unisexual (organs of one or the other sex aborted or sterile). *Fruit* dark blue or nearly black and often covered with a bloom, 2 inches long, 1 inch thick. *Wood* hard, medium-heavy (40 pounds per cubic foot, dry weight), the heartwood light brown, the sapwood thick and pale.

Only a little tree at best, 30 to 40 feet high, with a very slim-waisted trunk, the Fringetree is as gracile and feminine-seeming as any that grows beside the rushing stream or climbs the warm slopes of the Blue Ridge under the shelter of sturdier growths. Close relatives of the useful and mighty Ashes, kin to the fruitful Olive, the Fringetree is the little sister of the family. If it has no economic importance, it contributes to the higher things of life: it is a raving beauty when in midspring it is loaded from top to bottom with the airest, most ethereal yet showy flowers boasted by any member of our northern sylva. A faint sweet fragrance breathes subtly from the flowers. In autumn the leaves turn a clear bright yellow. Naturally so charming a little tree has been cultivated far beyond its natural range, in New England and the Middle West.

THE ASHES

(*Fraxinus*)

AﾐﾐES have opposite, deciduous, usually pinnately compound leaves, twigs with thick pith, compressed, obtuse terminal buds and unisexual flowers with the sexes on different trees (or perfect flowers sometimes mixed with unisexual), in slender-branched, vernal clusters that develop from large buds covered with 2 scales. The small bell-shaped calyx is free from the ovary; the corolla may be lacking; if present there are 2 to 4 lobes or free petals. Generally the stamens number but 2. The ovary is contracted into a style terminated by a 2-lobed stigma. The fruit takes the form of a mostly 1-winged samara, the body of the fruit containing the compressed seed in its chestnut-brown coat.

BLACK ASH

Fraxinus nigra Marshall

OTHER NAMES: Hoop, Basket, Brown, Swamp or Water Ash.

RANGE: Western Newfoundland, Anticosti Island, and Quebec to Manitoba, North Dakota, and Iowa, south to the Ohio River valley, northern Virginia, northern Delaware, central New Jersey, and western Connecticut. Rare in western New Brunswick, and absent from southeastern New England and Long Island and large areas between Lake Superior and Hudson Bay.

DESCRIPTION: *Bark* thin, gray, divided into large irregular plates with papery scales. *Twigs* stout, round, dark green, soon becoming orange or ashy gray and flecked with large lenticels, darkening the first winter and then displaying a semicircular row of conspicuous scars. *Winter buds* dark brown, with 3 pairs of scales that fall in spring to display the strap-shaped, pinnate, leafy inner scales. *Leaves* in over-all dimensions 12 to 13 inches long, with 7 to 11 leaflets, thin, firm, dark green above, paler below, 4 to 5 inches long, 1 to 2 inches wide. *Flowers* sometimes unisexual, sometimes perfect, covered in bud by black scales, the male flower consisting of 2 large deeply pitted dark-purple anthers attached on broad stalks, the female in an ovary terminating in a long slender style deeply divided into 2 purple stigmas, or the pistillate flower accompanied by 2 small stamens with pink anthers. *Fruit* in long openbranched clusters, each samara 1 to 1½ inches long, ⅓ inch wide, with a thin wing surrounding the short fat body. *Wood* rather soft and not strong, durable, coarse-grained, medium-light (39½ pounds per cubic foot, dry weight), the heartwood dark brown, the thin sapwood nearly white.

There are a number of fairly good reasons why this should be called the Black Ash. The shiny blue-black winter buds, for one, the very dark green of the foliage too, perhaps, and the dark heartwood, which frequently in this species occupies almost the entire woody cylinder of the trunk, even in comparatively young trees.

Deep cold swamps are the favorite site of this most northerly of all Ashes, in the company of Tamarack, Black Spruce, and Arbor-vitæ in the North Woods. On drier soil in the north it keeps company with Hemlock, Balsam, Hard Maple, and Yellow Birch; farther south, it lines the stream banks, with Elm, Soft Maple, and Willow. No fine stands of Black Ash are known south of Pennsylvania and Ohio. Seldom now do we see specimens 90 feet tall with trunks 20 inches through, as in the virgin North Woods, but at all times the Black Ash may be known by its strikingly slim figure. The slender branches are almost upright, and form a narrow head, making a remarkably gracile outline for an Ash. When the odd flowers appear on the naked wood in spring, they are not without their loveliness. Very late, the leaves at last appear. Handsome for their brief season of greenery, they turn at the first hint of the northern fall a rusty brown, with none of the subtlety of White Ash coloration. Then they drop all at once, so that for perhaps eight months, in the Canadian clime, the Black Ash is bare.

This is the tree that George Washington, surveyor of his own land claims on the Kanawha and Ohio Rivers, always called "hoop tree" in his notes. Those were the days when surveyors notched "witness trees," instead of setting up stone or metal boundary markers — two hacks of the hatchet for a corner, three for a line or pointer — and the young surveyor called it hoop tree for the same good reason for which it is called Basket Ash. For the wood of Black Ash, which lacks the proverbial strength and shock-resisting qualities of some of its sister species, has certain properties they do not possess. Among them is its capacity for splitting easily into very thin yet remarkably tough pieces. The springwood — that is, the portion of the annual growth ring that is laid down in the spring months when water and sap are abundant and growth is fast — is made up almost entirely of large pores, with precious little wood fiber between them, so that it is largely air spaces. As a result, billets of Black Ash are easily separated into thin strips, the line of cleavage following the springwood's weakness. The Indians, with some vigorous beating, thus separated long strips of tough summerwood, just as they did with the Arbor-vitæ, and of the splints made fish baskets. The white man turned this property into account for the making of woven chair bottoms and barrel hoops. A dozen minor uses are known for this tree, from washboards to church pews, but though the form of the trunk in a fine old tree is the lumberman's delight, rising straight and thick as a granite column, it has never been a great commercial timber tree.

When a great old Black Ash grows in a swamp, it sends out aggressive roots everywhere. No other tree has a chance in close proximity and prolonged competition with a Black Ash. As a result of long occupation by Black Ashes, however, swamps become shallower, by filling up with decay and muck, and finally become almost dry ground. Time then for ecological succession by another association of trees adapted to low ground, but not standing water; then the short-lived Black Ash has to give way to Elm and Linden and Red Maple.

Trees growing in supersaturated and oxygen-deficient conditions are especially likely to develop burls. Black Ash burls as big as washtubs sometimes develop on the trunks of old swamp-grown trees. They seem to owe their origin to the stifling of adventitious buds inside the wood, buds that are thwarted yet send out shoots that branch like stunted little trees, and though hopelessly bound by the wood, they braid and distort it in every direction, as well as bulging out the trunk in great bark-covered tumescences. Veneers of Black Ash burl look like contour maps of mountainous country, like displays of the aurora borealis, like a dark and riffling tide sweeping over clear white sands. Curly Ash, as lumbermen call the burl grains, is cut as veneer and sold to cabinetmakers who esteem it as perhaps the most beautiful of all American woods.

BLUE ASH

Fraxinus quadrangulata A. Michaux

RANGE: Western Pennsylvania and southwestern Ontario to central Illinois, Missouri, eastern Kansas, northeastern Oklahoma, and rarely in southeastern Wisconsin and central Iowa, south to Tennessee and northern Mississippi.

DESCRIPTION: *Bark* thin, divided irregularly into big plate-like scales, light gray tinged with red. *Twigs* stout, 4-angled, and 4-winged between the nodes, dark orange at first, becoming gray tinged with red in the second year and then marked by large, elevated, inversely heart-shaped leaf scars and a few pale lenticels. *Winter buds* — the terminal ones with 3 pairs of scales, the outer thick and dark reddish brown, the inner strap-shaped, coated with light brown woolly hairs, and becoming an inch or more long in spring. *Leaves* in over-all dimensions 8 to 12 inches long, the leaflets 5 to 11 in number, 3 to 5 inches long, 1 to 2 inches wide, thick, firm, and yellow-green above, paler below. *Flowers* perfect, appearing from small obtuse buds with keeled scales; corolla none; calyx reduced to an obscure ring; stamens 2, with dark purple anthers; ovary narrowed to a short style divided at tip into two light purple stigma lobes. *Fruit* 1 to 2 inches long, ½ inch broad, the wing surrounding the flat body. *Wood* medium-heavy (45 pounds to the cubic foot, dry weight), medium-hard, strong but brittle, the heartwood light yellow streaked with brown, the sapwood very thick and paler.

Of all the Ashes this is the easiest to identify, for it is the only one with square and winged twigs. More, the sap turns blue on exposure to the air. If you stir a twig of this tree in a glass of water, the inner bark soon turns the water blue; the pioneers used to make a blue dye from the bark. Finally, unless you live in the Middle West or the middle reaches of the Mississippi valley in the south, you will not see this tree at all. Which is a pity, because it makes a fine appearance, 60 to 70 feet tall or even as much as 120 feet under exceptional conditions, with a trunk 2 to 3 feet thick, and a slender crown formed by the small spreading branches. The flowers are not without their handsome qualities, though lacking petals and sepals, when they bloom just as the leaves are beginning to burst their big buds. In autumn the foliage is a clear bright yellow.

The Oak and Hickory woods so characteristic of the Middle West and parts of Kentucky and Tennessee are the site of this vigorous, always fresh-looking, and swift-growing tree. The soil in these groves is generally fairly dry, but rich and deep, and overlying limestone. Of all the eastern Ashes, this one is best able to endure dryness. Nowhere very abundant, it reaches its largest size in the valley of the Wabash River.

There are seldom any statistics on the quantity of Blue Ash that is cut, for it is lumped, in most accountings, with and under the name of White Ash. Manufacturers of tool handles, however, often prefer this species because of the thickness, strength, and cleanly appearance of the sapwood. It is a favorite for the D-handles of spades, shovels, and such implements, and for scythe-naths and forks. Blue Ash wood is the heaviest of all the Ash woods in the circumscription of this book; this, however, is no particular recommendation in a tool handle, but the handsome whiteness of the sapwood tickles the fancy of the customer in the hardware store, and his tastes are not disputed by the manufacturers while he is willing to pay for them.

RED ASH

Fraxinus pennsylvanica Marshall

OTHER NAMES: River, Bastard, Black, or Brown Ash.

RANGE: Nova Scotia and the Gaspé peninsula west to Manitoba, eastern Wyoming, central Kansas and northeastern Oklahoma, northern parts of Mississippi, Alabama, and Georgia, and central parts of the Carolinas. Absent from the southern coastal plain and the Appalachians, from northeastern Nova Scotia and Prince Edward Island.

DESCRIPTION: *Bark* thin, brown tinged with red, furrowed into numberless braided ridges. *Twigs* slender, ashy gray or light brown tinged with red and often with a glaucous bloom, flecked with pale lenticels and marked with semicircular leaf scars. *Winter buds* — the terminal small, with 2 pairs of rusty-woolly scales. *Leaves* in over-all dimensions 10 to 12 inches long, with 7 to 9 thin, firm, light yellow-green leaflets which are coated below with silky hairs, each 4 to 6 inches long, 1 to 1½ inches wide. *Flowers* with the sexes on different trees, covered in bud with rusty-woolly scales; petals none; male flowers with a minute, cup-shaped calyx and 2 stamens with pale green, purple-tinged anthers; female flowers with deeply divided, cup-shaped calyx and 2 green stigma lobes. *Fruit* 1 to 2½ inches long, ½ inch wide, the thin wing gradually tapered to the slender body. *Wood* medium-light (39 pounds to the cubic foot, dry weight), hard, rather strong, the heartwood light brown, the sapwood lighter brown streaked with yellow.

The Red Ash could take its name from the cinnamon-colored inner bark, or from the rusty woolliness of the hairs on the bud scales. In form, at least as grown in the open, it makes a good show, with its very handsomely braided ridges on the bole, and ascending branches forming a fine crown, both tall and fairly wide. Under the best conditions, Red Ash may grow 60 feet tall, with a trunk over a foot and a half in diameter. Stream banks and low grounds are the favorite site of this tree. In pioneer times it was split for rail fences, but today it goes to market for prosaic uses — flooring and boxes, butter tubs and interior finish. It is unimportant compared to its close relative:

GREEN ASH, var. *subintegerrima* (Vahl) Fernald. The distinguishing points of this variety are the narrower, shorter, and more sharply toothed leaflets, which are shining on both surfaces, and not hairy beneath except sometimes on the midrib. The twigs are hairless, not downy as in the Red Ash. The range is much wider than in the typical species, from western Maine and the vicinity of the city of Quebec south to northern Florida and Brownsville, Texas, west to Alberta, central Montana, and south through the Rocky Mountain States (but not in the mountains) to southern Arizona and northwestern New Mexico. It is absent from the Appalachians above 2500 feet, and from central and western Texas. Fast-growing in its favorite site of stream banks, shallowly but widely rooting, extremely hardy with respect to climatic conditions — cold or heat, drought or flood — Green Ash is a ubiquitous sort of tree, which, if it will never win a prize in a beauty contest, is, like its close associates the Box Elder and the Cottonwood, an infinite number of times better than no tree at all, once one gets out on the Great Plains. No other Ash is so often planted, in the Western states, as a dooryard and street tree.

The wood of Green Ash is much heavier (44 pounds to the cubic foot, dry weight), than that of Red Ash, and harder and stronger too. It is generally sent to market, though, as White Ash, which it most nearly resembles in the many fine qualities of that species, and as White Ash grows scarcer, Green Ash supplants it in industry. For instance, almost all oars and paddles now are made of Green Ash instead of the costlier White Ash, for Green Ash has the same virtues of toughness, elasticity, straight grain, and great strength. Unfortunately Green Ash weighs more than White; rowing must have been easier in the days of White Ash oars!

Green Ash makes a quick hot fire when used for fuel. Where there is not much Pine, as along the lower Mississippi, it was a favorite for stoking wood-burning engines of all sorts, for it splits easily and has a fuel value 90 per cent that of White Oak taken as a standard of one hundred.

WHITE ASH

Fraxinus americana Linnæus

OTHER NAMES: American, Biltmore, or Cane Ash.

RANGE: Nova Scotia to southern Quebec, south to northern Florida, northern Louisiana, and northeastern Texas, west to Minnesota, and eastern parts of Nebraska, Kansas, and Oklahoma. Absent from the Gaspé peninsula, the north shore of Lake Superior, the higher Appalachians, and usually from the neighborhood of the South Atlantic and Gulf coasts.

DESCRIPTION: *Bark* ash-gray, finely and shallowly furrowed, with innumerable narrow, flat, braiding ridges. *Twigs* stout, round, at first dark green or brown tinged with red, becoming light orange or ashy gray and shiny under a glaucous bloom, and marked by large, pale, semicircular leaf scars and pale lenticels. *Winter buds* — the terminal broad and blunt with 4 pairs of rusty-downy scales, the innermost becoming vivid green and elongating in spring. *Leaves* in over-all dimensions 8 to 12 inches long, with 7 (sometimes 5 or 9) leaflets, these 3 to 5 inches long, 1½ to 3 inches wide, thin but firm, a rich dark green above but whitened below or much paler. *Flowers* with the sexes on separate trees, appearing from buds covered with big scales, the calyx bell-shaped in the male flower, deeply lobed in the female; petals none, stamens 2 or 3, with almost black anthers, and the ovary bearing a deep purple, lobed stigma. *Fruits* 1 to 2½ inches long, ¼ inch wide, the wing gradually tapered to the slender roundish body. *Wood* medium-heavy (41 pounds to the cubic foot, dry weight), strong, tough, hard, pliant, not durable in contact with the soil, the heartwood brown, the sapwood yellowish white.

Every American boy knows a great deal about White Ash wood. He knows the color of its yellowish white sapwood and the pale brown grain of the annual growth layers in it. He knows the weight of White Ash not in terms of pounds per cubic foot but by the more immediate and unforgettable sensation of having lifted and swung a piece of it, of standard size. He even knows its precise resonance and pitch, the ringing *tock* of it when struck. For it is of White Ash, and of White Ash only, that good baseball bats are made. Ash is the commonest wood for the frames of tennis racquets, for swing seats, for hockey sticks, for polo mallets, and playground equipment. The reasons why it is the favorite wood for sporting goods are found in its fundamental properties; it is tough, too tough to break under much strain, but pliant, and just pliant enough, not too much so. It can be bent into desired shapes and worked with comparative ease, yet it is hard. Despite its great strength, Ash is comparatively light. At least, true White Ash is so. A number of other botanical species, the Green Ash, the Blue Ash, for instance, go to market as White Ash; they are not quite the equals of true White Ash in all its virtues, but they are nearer to them than any other woods, and the lumberman may be allowed his broad general classification.

True that White Ash is not as strong as the best Hickory, and so it is not used for the handles of tools that, like hammers, are to be violently struck. But Hickory is a much heavier and more expensive wood. Ash is ideal for the tools of most garden and agricultural implements. It is used in preference to all others for the D-handles of spades and shovels. The list of the uses of White Ash would take up many pages. It goes into both church pews and the floors of bowling alleys, into rods for sucker pumps, and oars and keels of small boats, into butter-tub staves, and garden and porch furniture, into airplanes and farm wagons — everywhere that strength and lightness must be combined. White Ash has occasional fancy grains — the curly figure such as is seen in fiddle-back Maple and the step figure so popular in

Walnut; special beauty in these is brought out by quarter-sawing and is used as veneers in the cabinetmaker's art. But plain-sawed Ash is still a very fine wood, if you can admire the honest, functional beauty of the growth layers of a tree that grows straight and at a regular pace. Ash furniture, especially in modern styles with much plain surface and geometrical and functional lines, if given a light stain or a very thin coat of paint in a gray or almost neutral green color, will cause the most casual observer to exclaim over its beauty and ask what wood that is.

The uses of White Ash are, on the whole, so specialized that when it is cut it is not usually stored in the general hardwood lumber yard but is shipped on to a few companies that buy and sell little else. Actually the amount of White Ash, the country over, is not great. The largest part of it is not found today in virgin forests or in dense stands anywhere; it is mostly growing in the farmer's woodlot, which may be anywhere in an area of a million square miles, in any state east of the Mississippi and several beyond it. Yet normally the quantity of White Ash in the woodlot will not be more than 4 per cent of the total stand of timber. Fortunately very large and ancient trees are not required for most of the uses to which Ash is put. On the contrary, the toughest, strongest, soundest White Ash, with the greatest proportion of the pale sapwood that retail buyers prefer, is cut from the fast-growing, comparatively young trees of second growth, such as commonly constitute most of the woodlots of the eastern states. Fortunately, too, the chief Ash-using industries require quality, not quantity of board feet.

Many of our valuable hardwoods are extremely difficult to propagate or to manage for timber production. In the case of White Oak, for instance, where dimension timbers are required from a very slow-growing tree, one would have to lay plans to harvest a merchantable crop 150 years from now. Not so with White Ash. With a little forest management the present seedling crop could be increased and hurried to a stand that is mature, from a lumberman's viewpoint. For what a White Ash chiefly needs is room and light. Its seedlings may be fairly numerous in the woods, but suppressed by shade from more unbrageous trees; a seedling only a foot high may be fifteen years old and have developed an extensive root system, if growing in deep shade. If the forest crown is thinned, these seedlings, with their highly developed root system, will shoot up with surprising speed, producing more

valuable timber than those White Ashes of the virgin forest that used to live 300 years and grow 175 feet tall, with a trunk 5 feet or more in diameter. Most such are vanished, anyway, and today we call a White Ash with half those dimensions a splendid specimen, as indeed it is. When an old White Ash is felled, it sprouts very freely from the stump, the more so if the stump is cut low. Growth of these sprout trees, too, is very rapid, for the old root system is all there to draw water, while the growth from the long-suppressed buds seems to release a green fountain of refreshed energy.

The chosen site of White Ash is a deep, rich, sweet loam, with abundance of ground water but good drainage. It is at its best in the zone of the broad-leaved deciduous trees of the cool temperate regions, in the company of Beech, Birch, Maple, and Basswood, as in the high coves of the Appalachians. In the prairie groves of Illinois, where the rainfall is lower and the evaporation is higher, White Ash takes to low, but not saturated ground, and associates with White Elm, American Linden, Cottonwood, and Hackberry. In New England and New York it is found on rocky upland soils with Oaks, but is never so tall a tree there as on the deep loams of the Middle West.

When a White Ash is young it has a narrow head. But with age the boughs widen until the crown is broader than long, if the tree is growing in the open without too severe competition, and a great pool of shade results. The foliage tends to cluster on the outside of the tree, so that when you stand beside the bole and look up, you see through easily to the sky, and can observe what business the birds are at — the nuthatches gleaning the bark with soundless thrift, the woodpeckers drilling at the trunks with red heads moving so fast they are a blur, and high overhead the hawks waiting-on in noble style and whistling their shrill war cry. As it is not too umbrageous a tree, so too the shade of White Ash is further lightened by the softly shining, almost silvery undersides of the foliage, so that to stand and look up under it is to see a misty whiteness, while, viewed from outside, the foliage is richly dark and gleaming.

When a White Ash grows old, it is apt to bear great horizontal arms, wondrously strong and springy, from which swings may be safely hung. If it is late in leafing out in spring, yet the flowers, on the naked wood, are (to those who have eyes for such things) very striking, with their clusters of black anthers and purple stigmas. No tree makes less litter beneath it — only those neat little winged fruits on the female trees, that plummet soundlessly down and spear the grass. In fall, White Ash is the most versatile colorist of all our woods. Some trees may stand, like transfixed angels, shining in a light of heavenly gold; others may robe themselves in royal purple. But the bronze and mauve tints that are the rarest in our autumn displays are the specialty of the White Ash.

How many thousand-thousand of untold White Ash trees are the respected companions of our doorways, kindliest trees in the clearing beyond the cabin? No one can say. But this is a tree whose grave and lofty character makes it a lifetime friend. White Ash has no easy, pretty charms like Dogwood and Redbud; it makes no over-dramatic gestures like Weeping Willow and Lombardy Poplar. It has never been seen through sentimental eyes, like the Elm and the White Birch. Strong, tall, cleanly, benignant, the Ash tree with self-respecting surety waits, until you have sufficiently admired all the more obvious beauties of the forest, for you to discover at last its unadorned greatness.

Charles Darwin once wrote to his friend Asa Gray, the great Harvard botanist, asking him what plant might be considered to top the list of the vegetable kingdom in its long story of evolution from a pond scum to a flower. Englishmen are known to have "hearts of oak" and Darwin wondered if the apex of plant evolution might not be an Oak. But Gray replied that the plant kingdom has no single culminating species. Botanists believe that the two great evolutionary lines in the seed plants do culminate in, respectively, the Orchid Family and the Composite Family. Neither of them, however, has anything that could properly be called a tree. Yet this much one may say, that so far as concerns the trees of northeastern North America, the White Ash is Nature's last word.

That is not to say that the Ash is "higher" than other trees, for the whole concept of "higher" and "lower" species is unscientific; there are only older types and more recent types. It is a long way, in pages and species and perhaps in geologic time, from the very old type of the White Pine, with which this book opened, to the newer one of the White Ash. But one is not a finer tree than the other, nor better adapted to its environment. And the same would be true of all the intermediate species. Each has its place; each is, or it was in the days of virgin innocence, adjusted to its environment and held with its neighbors in a precise ecologic balance. All are equal in the sight of an impartial Nature. All are fellow citizens of the grand American sylva.

KEYS TO SPECIES
AND GENERA

GLOSSARY

INDEX OF
SCIENTIFIC NAMES

INDEX OF ENGLISH NAMES

KEYS TO SPECIES AND GENERA

THE SO CALLED KEYS used by botanists and zoologists are devices for finding one's way to the name of an organism without having to compare a specimen with every description and illustration in the book. Keys are most easily employed by those who have had a little classroom training in their use, but there is no reason why the botanically untaught should not use a key, with the following instructions.

A key is something like the game of "twenty questions," where a series of choices is made, beginning with the most general categories and narrowing the choices down to more and more specific cases. It could also be compared to a signpost at a fork in the road, where one sign reads "To Boston," the other "To New York." In the case of the botanical key, however, one may be asked whether the leaves are alternate or opposite on the twig. If they are opposite, then the next question (indented just under the first one) may be: leaves compound, or leaves simple? If they are compound, the next choice (again indented) is between leaflets toothed or leaflets without marginal teeth — and so on, until one is led to the name of the correct species or, if it is a member of a large genus, then the reader is referred to one of the short supplementary keys. The name of the species is followed by the page number in the text, to which the student then turns for a more careful study of the full description there, and the illustration.

Many keys require the student to know about flowers, fruit, and leaves, all at once, though one seldom has a specimen showing all seasons' growths. The present keys are based almost entirely on foliage, and on mature, not early spring, foliage. Only in a few cases, notably the key to Hawthorns, are fruiting characters, of necessity, employed.

General Key

A. Foliage scale-like or needle-like, resinous and, except in Tamarack, evergreen. B.

  B. Leaves in bundles, or solitary and alternate and scattered on the twig, needle-shaped or awl-shaped, erect or spreading, not scale-like nor flattened to and overlapping on the twig. C.

    C. Leaves needle-like, in bundles of 2 or more, not solitary except on sucker shoots. D.

      D. Needles in bundles of 2 to 5, enclosed at base in a deciduous or persistent papery sheath   PINES (see Key A, p. 582)

      D. Needles more than 5 in a bundle, on short, spur-like shoots, each leaf in the axil of a deciduous scale   TAMARACK, p. 33

    C. Leaves solitary, scattered, not in a bundle, nor long and narrow, but flattened or squarish. E.

      E. Leaves on short stalks

        Foliage lying all in one plane on the twig

                    EASTERN HEMLOCK, p. 39

        Foliage bristling all around the twig

                    CAROLINA HEMLOCK, p. 41

      E. Leaves attached to twigs without stalks. F.

        F. Foliage blunt-tipped

          Lower surface of leaf with 8 to 12 rows of stomata (seen under lens as whitish lines)

                    SOUTHERN BALSAM, p. 59

          Lower surface with 4 to 8 rows of stomata

                    NORTHERN BALSAM, p. 57

        F. Foliage with sharp callous tips. G.

          G. Twigs of the first summer's and winter's growth downy; leaves pleasantly scented

            Foliage appearing brushed forward, the needles blue-green and hoary above, shining below   BLACK SPRUCE, p. 47

            Foliage bristling all around the stem, the needles dark yellow-green and very lustrous   RED SPRUCE, p. 50

          G. Twigs without downiness from the first; leaves unpleasantly scented when crushed, blue-green or pale green

                    WHITE SPRUCE, p. 45

  B. Leaves in pairs or whorls of 3, awl-shaped and concave-convex, with prickly tips, or else scale-like and flattened against the twig and much overlapping. H.

    H. Twigs flattened; fruit cone-like, not a berry

      Foliage yellow-green; cones with oblong, dry, brown scales

                    ARBOR–VITÆ, p. 65

Foliage blue-green; cones with button-shaped, semi-fleshy bluish scales SOUTHERN WHITE CEDAR, p. 71

H. Twigs not flattened, either closely beset by overlapping scales (which make the twig appear 4-sided) or with erect, sharp-pointed, concave-convex scales arranged in distinct (not overlapping) whorls of 3; fruit a berry

Buds scaly; flowers axillary; leaves all prickle-pointed, concave-convex, and spreading widely from the stem; seeds usually 3 COMMON JUNIPER, p. 77

Buds naked; flowers terminal; only the leaves on young shoots as above, those of mature shoots closely flattened to the twig and overlapping; seeds usually 1 or 2 EASTERN RED CEDAR, p. 79

A. Foliage broad and leafy, not scale-like or needle-like. J.
  J. Leaves compound. K.
    K. Leaflets all borne at the tip of the leafstalk, spreading finger-like

Leaflets gradually long-pointed; petals nearly equal in length, shorter than the stamens; fruit covered with prickles OHIO BUCKEYE, p. 477

Leaflets abruptly long-pointed at apex; petals unequal in size, longer than the stamens; fruit without prickles SWEET BUCKEYE, p. 479

    K. Leaflets not as above. L.
      L. Leaves opposite on the twig
        Leaflets 3 to 5 BOX ELDER, p. 472
        Leaflets more than 5, at least on most leaves ASHES (see Key L, p. 590)
      L. Leaves alternate (though the leaflets sometimes opposite). M.
        M. Stems or twigs or leafstalks usually thorny. N.
          N. Leaflets of an odd number
            Foliage with translucent dots (seen with a hand lens, when held against the light) TOOTHACHE-TREE, p. 427
            Foliage not as above
              Leaflets toothed HERCULES'-CLUB, p. 493
              Leaflets not toothed
                Leafstalks clammy-hairy ROSE-FLOWERING LOCUST, p. 421
                Leafstalks not clammy-hairy BLACK LOCUST, p. 415
          N. Leaflets of an even number
            Leaflets acute at apex SWEET LOCUST, p. 403
            Leaflets blunt WATER LOCUST, p. 406
        M. Stems, twigs, leafstalks not thorny. O.
          O. Foliage with translucent glands (seen under a hand lens when held to the light) HOPTREE, p. 433
          O. Foliage not as above. P.
            P. Leaflets not toothed
              Foliage lustrous above POISON SUMAC, p. 439

   Foliage dull above
    Leaves twice-compound   COFFEETREE, p. 499
    Leaves once-compound   YELLOWWOOD, p. 410
  P. Leaflets toothed
   Q. Veins of leaves bleeding milky juice when broken; foliage
    covered below with a whitish bloom
             STAGHORN SUMAC, p. 437
   Q. Veins not containing milky juice; foliage seldom with a
    bloom, sometimes silvery-scaly below
    Flowers perfect, in open clusters, with white petals; fruit a
    small red pome with acid flesh
              ROWANTREE, p. 331
    Flowers unisexual, in catkins, not petal-bearing; fruit a nut
    with heavy husk
    Pith of the twigs solid
           HICKORIES (see Key D, p. 584)
    Pith of the twigs (when split lengthwise) in plates
    Leaflets 11 to 17 in number, each 2 to 3 inches long
              BUTTERNUT, p. 119
    Leaflets 15 to 23 in number, each 3 to 5 inches long
           BLACK WALNUT, p. 121
J. Leaves simple. R.
 R. Leaves opposite
   Margins toothed, with at least a few large or small teeth or tooth-like
    lobes   MAPLES (see Key J, p. 589)
   Margins not toothed or lobed
   Primary veins arising only from the lower ⅔ of the midrib and
    then strongly curving toward the tip
           FLOWERING DOGWOOD, p. 503
   Veins not as above
    Blades 4 to 8 inches long at maturity   FRINGETREE, p. 555

    Blades at most 2 to 3 inches long   BLACK HAW, p. 513
 R. Leaves alternate. S.
  S. Foliage evergreen, more or less hard or leathery
   Texture hard; margins spiny-toothed
           CHRISTMAS HOLLY, p. 447
   Texture leathery; margins not spiny
   Twigs stout; blades 4 to 12 inches long
         BIG RHODODENDRON, p. 517
   Twigs slender; blades ½ to 4 inches long
         MOUNTAIN LAUREL, p. 523
  S. Foliage deciduous, more or less soft and thin or only somewhat leath-
   ery. T.
  T. Blades more or less deeply lobed or with earlobe-like appendages at
   the base. U.
   U. Tip of the leaf with a very wide shallow notch
           TULIPTREE, p. 267

U. Tip of the leaf acute or blunt but not as above. **V.**

  V. Base of the leaf with 2 earlobe-like appendages

    Blades 20 to 30 inches long, 9 to 10 inches wide

        LARGE–LEAVED MAGNOLIA, p. 279

    Blades 10 to 12 inches long, 6 to 7 inches wide

        MOUNTAIN MAGNOLIA, p. 281

  V. Base of leaf not as above

    W. Leaves palmately lobed

      Blades mitten-shaped or with three forward-pointing lobes at the apex

        Foliage light green and glossy; sap mucilaginous

          SASSAFRAS, p. 291

        Foliage dull dark green above; sap milky

          RED MULBERRY, p. 261

      Blades not mitten-shaped, lobed all the way around

        Foliage aromatic; lobes with deep acute sinuses between them; stalks slender; old twigs corky-winged; bark of trunk furrowed, not scaling off

          SWEET GUM, p. 307

        Foliage not aromatic; blades irregularly lobed, with broad shallow sinuses between the lobes; twigs never winged; bark smooth, scaling off in thin plates

          SYCAMORE, p. 315

    W. Leaves pinnately lobed. **X.**

      X. Lobes shallow, broad, with many small teeth; small, often bushy trees often with spiny branches; fruit a pome

        Petals not clawed at base; seeds contained in bony nutlets; spines when present borne below or opposite the leaf   HAWTHORNS (see Key H, p. 586)

        Petals clawed at base; seeds contained in tough, papery, parchment-like carpels (the apple core); spines when present terminating short-shoots

          APPLES (see Key G, p. 586)

      X. Lobes usually deep and narrow, with only a few teeth; tall forest trees, in our species; fruit an acorn; twigs never spiny   OAKS (see Key F, p. 585)

T. Blades not, or not essentially, lobed. **Y.**

  Y. Margins not toothed nor regularly and deeply wavy, nor bristly-spiny (though the midrib running out beyond the tip of the blade as a single bristle-like tooth in a few species). **Z.**

    Z. Blades as broad as long or broader and more or less heart-shaped

        REDBUD, p. 393

    Z. Blades not as broad as long **a.**

      a. Leaves 10 to 20 inches long

        Leaves unpleasantly scented, scattered on the twig, 10 to 12 inches long   PAWPAW, p. 287

        Leaves not malodorous, clustered at the ends of the twigs

          UMBRELLATREE, p. 277

a. Leaves less than 10 inches long. b.
  b. Stipules or their scars present
     Stipules encircling the twig
                        CUCUMBERTREE, p. 275
     Stipules or their scars 2, one on each side of the twig
       Midrib of the leaf usually off-center, base of the
       leaf unsymmetrical; fruit a berry
                        SUGARBERRY, p. 257
       Midrib of leaf central, base not markedly unsym-
       metrical; fruit an acorn
                        OAKS (see Key F, p. 585)
  b. Stipules or their scars none. c.
    c. Terminal bud present
       Twigs green, aromatic; leaves aromatic when crushed
       and mucilaginous to the taste; blades sometimes
       lobed   SASSAFRAS, p. 291
       Twigs variously colored, but not aromatic; leaves not
       lobed
        Blades yellow-green, not shining above; veins not
        recurving; veinlets not meshed
                        PIGEONBERRY, p. 508
        Blades dark green and shining above; veins recurv-
        ing; veinlets more or less meshed
         Bark with narrow, rather regular, ridges and
         rather remote cross-checks
                        BLACK GUM, p. 497
         Bark irregularly broken by numerous cross-checks
         into many small blocks
                        PERSIMMON, p. 535

Y. Margins toothed or regularly wavy. d.
  d. Stipules or their scars present. e.
    e. Sap milky, oozing from veins and leafstalks when they are
       broken   RED MULBERRY, p. 261
    e. Sap not milky. f.
      f. Winter buds resinous   POPLARS (see Key B, p. 583)
      f. Winter buds not resinous. g.
        g. Blades fully 3 or more times as long as broad
                      WILLOWS (see Key C, p. 583)
        g. Blades not so long in proportion to their breadth. h.
          h. Blades wavy-margined, with blunt, scallop-like teeth,
            not sharply toothed
             Winter buds naked of scales; scallops only on the
             upper (outer) half of the blade
                        WITCH HAZEL, p. 301
            Winter buds with several pairs of overlapping scales;
             scallops all around the margin of the blade
            Veins extending beyond the bristly teeth
                        CHINQUAPIN, p. 190

Veins not extending beyond the margins as bristly
teeth   OAKS (see Key F, p. 585)
h. Blades sharply toothed; if wavy-scalloped then also
     sharp-pointed or bristle-tipped.   j.
   j. Teeth few, large, low, and broad, but with incurved,
      almost bristle-like tips   BEECH, p. 179
   j. Teeth numerous, fine, often gland-tipped.   k.
     k. Blades usually heart-shaped or truncate at base.   l.
       l. Blades twice as long as broad or nearly so; stalk
          of the flowers or fruits not adherent to a
          leaf-like bract
          Leaves densely white-woolly above when
            young; flowers appearing with or be-
            fore the leaves; fruit dry and tasteless
              SHADBLOW, p. 335
          Leaves only slightly downy when young;
            flowers appearing after the leaves; fruit
            sweet and juicy
              SARVISSTREE, p. 336
       l. Blades as broad as long, or less than twice as long
          as broad; main stalk of flowers and fruits
          adherent for part of its length to a leaf-like
          bract   LINDENS (see Key K, p. 589)
     k. Blades usually rounded or narrowed at base.   m.
     m. Foliage and twigs mucilaginous
              SLIPPERY ELM, p. 250
     m. Foliage and twigs not mucilaginous.   n.
       n. Twigs, at least some of them, corky-winged
         Leaves shining above, oblong-oval
             CORK ELM, p. 246
         Leaves dull above, oblong-elliptic
             WAHOO, p. 248
       n. Twigs not corky-winged.   o.
         o. Blades 3-nerved from the base
            HACKBERRY, p. 255
         o. Blades not 3-nerved from the base
           p. Margins of leaves toothed near the tip
            only   SUGARBERRY, p. 257
           p. Margins toothed all around or nearly so.
            q.
            q. Fruit a pome; ovary inferior or es-
              sentially so
              Petals clawed; nutlets seed-like and
               soft
                APPLES (see Key G, p. 586)
              Petals not clawed; nutlets bony
             HAWTHORNS (see Key H, p. 586)

q. Fruit not a pome; ovary usually superior. r.

r. Fruit a drupe or berry-like

Flowers bisexual; fruit a drupe containing a single stone; leafstalks often bearing 1 or more glands PLUMS AND CHERRIES (see Key I, p. 588)

Flowers unisexual; fruit a berry-like drupe containing several nutlets; leafstalks never glandular MOUNTAIN HOLLY, p. 449

r. Fruit not a drupe or berry. s.

s. Fruit a samara; bark of trunk with long, vertical, scaly ridges, not papery-scaly nor smooth

WHITE ELM, p. 237

s. Fruit a 1-seeded nut or nutlet, often inclosed in papery bracts; bark papery-scaly or smooth, not with long vertical scaly ridges

t. Bark not papery or scurfy but smooth, the limbs fluted and with twisted and rounded ridges

HORNBEAM, p. 155

t. Bark not smooth, or if so then peeling in papery layers; limbs not or but little fluted

Bark rough-scurfy; fruit a cluster of hop-like bracts

IRONWOOD, p. 161

Bark falling away in papery layers or if close then white, gray or red; fruit thin, winged BIRCHES (see Key E, p. 584)

d. Stipules or their scars none. u.

u. Leaves sweet to the taste SWEETLEAF, p. 551

u. Leaves not sweet to the taste

v. Leaves acid to the taste; twigs zigzag, greenish-red

SOURWOOD, p. 529

> v. Leaves not acidulous; twigs straight, light brown to dark
> brown or dark gray
>> Teeth of the leaf-margins fine and numerous; flowers
>> ½ inch long; fruit 1 to ½ inch long
>>> COMMON SILVERBELL, p. 545
>> Teeth remote and coarse; flowers and fruit 2 inches long
>>> MOUNTAIN SILVERBELL, p. 546

Key A (To Pines)

Foliage in bundles of 5 (rarely 4), soft, slender, 3 to 5 inches long, bluish green,
whitened on the lower surface by bands of stomata; sheaths around the
base of the bundle early deciduous   WHITE PINE, p. 3
Foliage in bundles of 2 or 3 (rarely 4), more or less rigid and thick, not whitened
beneath; sheaths persistent
  Needles 3 (rarely 4) in a bundle
  Leaves 3 to 5 inches long
    Needles supple, slender, less than $\frac{1}{16}$ inch in diameter
      SHORTLEAF PINE, p. 26
    Needles rigid, stout, a little more than $\frac{1}{16}$ inch in diameter
      PITCH PINE, p. 20
  Leaves 6 to 10 inches long
    Needles stiff, pale green, and somewhat glaucous
      LOBLOLLY PINE, p. 24
    Needles supple, dark yellow-green, not glaucous
      POCOSIN PINE, p. 24
  Needles 2 in a bundle
  Needles 3 to 6 inches long, slender, supple
    Leaves 5 to 6 inches long, lustrous   RED PINE, p. 15
    Leaves 3 to 5 inches long, not lustrous
      SHORTLEAF PINE, p. 26
  Needles 3 inches long or less, thick and rigid except in Scrub Pine
    Foliage crowded; needles rigid, twisted, dark blue-green, 1¼ to 2½
    inches long   BUR PINE, p. 29
    Foliage sparse and scrubby
      Leaves short (¾ to 1¼ inches long) and at maturity dark green
        JACK PINE, p. 17
      Leaves longer (1½ to 2 inches long) and gray-green
        VIRGINIA SCRUB PINE, p. 27

Key B (To Poplars)

Leafstalks laterally compressed
  Buds slightly resinous
    Winter buds without pubescence; leaf-margins finely toothed
                              TREMBLING ASPEN, p. 87
    Winter buds pubescent or hairy; leaf-margins coarsely toothed
                              BIGTOOTH ASPEN, p. 90
  Buds very resinous
    Twigs light yellow, winter buds minutely downy; leaf-margins very coarsely toothed   GREAT PLAINS COTTONWOOD, p. 95
    Twigs gray or reddish brown; winter buds hairless; leaf-margins less coarsely serrate   EASTERN COTTONWOOD, p. 92
Leafstalks round in cross-section
  Blades distinctly heart-shaped at base   BALM–OF–GILEAD, p. 100
  Blades rounded or truncate or but lightly heart-shaped at base
    Buds very resinous; bark smooth; tree of Canada and the northernmost United States   BALSAM POPLAR, p. 98
    Buds somewhat resinous; bark of trunks rough; tree of southern swamps and river flood plains   SWAMP COTTONWOOD, p. 96

Key C (To Willows)

Leaves green on both surfaces, the lower face often paler but not glaucous or silvery or bluish; blade very long and narrow (16 to 24 times as long as broad)
  Teeth of the margins close, not glandular   BLACK WILLOW, p. 105
  Teeth of the margins remote, glandular   SANDBAR WILLOW, p. 110
Leaves much paler beneath, usually whitish, silvery, glaucous, or bluish; blades only 3 to 6 times as long as broad
  Twigs easily and neatly snapped off at the articulated base
                              PEACH WILLOW, p. 107
  Twigs not easily snapped off at the tough base
    Tips coming abruptly to a short acute point   BEBB WILLOW, p. 113
    Tips gradually drawn out to a point
      Twigs dark purple in their first year's growth; flowers appearing before the leaves   PUSSY WILLOW, p. 111
      Twigs not dark purple; flowers appearing with or after the leaves
        Blades 4 to 6 inches long; twigs light green in the first year
                            MISSOURI WILLOW, p. 114
        Blades 2 to 4 inches long; twigs red-brown or gray-brown
                            WARD WILLOW, p. 108

Key D (To Hickories)

A. Foliage silvery-scaly beneath   SAND HICKORY, p. 132
A. Foliage not silvery-scaly beneath. B.
  B. Leaflets 3 to 7 in number and generally the terminal one broadest above the middle. C.
    C. Twigs stout
      Bark usually shaggy
        Twigs light red-brown   SHAGBARK HICKORY, p. 133
        Twigs orange   BIG SHELLBARK HICKORY, p. 138
      Bark not shaggy; twigs bright brown   WHITE HICKORY, p. 143
    C. Twigs slender
      Winter buds rusty-pubescent
        Terminal leaflet 3 to 4 inches long, 1 to 1½ inches wide
                     BLACK HICKORY, p. 145
        Terminal leaflet 4 to 6 inches long, 2 to 2½ inches wide
                     ARKANSAS HICKORY, p. 146
      Winter buds variously pubescent or hairless, but not rusty
        Terminal leaflet 6 to 7 inches long   RED HICKORY, p. 141
        Terminal leaflet 4 to 5 inches long   BROOM HICKORY, p. 129
  B. Leaflets 7 to 17 in number, broadest at or below the middle
    Bud scales bright yellow; nut with bitter kernel; tree of wide distribution
                     BITTERNUT HICKORY, p. 146
    Bud scales not bright yellow; kernel very sweet; tree confined, within our circumscriptions, to the Mississippi bottom-lands   PECAN, p. 148

Key E (To Birches)

(ADAPTED FROM *Gray's Manual of Botany*, 8TH ED.)

Leaves of fruiting branches with 8 or more pairs of nerves impressed on upper surface
  Bark of twigs sweet-aromatic
    Bark of trees dark brown, close   CHERRY BIRCH, p. 172
    Bark yellowish or silvery gray, loosely exfoliating
                     YELLOW BIRCH, p. 180
  Bark of twigs not aromatic, tree bark pinkish white to terra-cotta, shaggily exfoliating   RIVER BIRCH, p. 175
Leaves of fruiting branches with 7 or fewer pairs of prominent nerves
  Leaves hairless or soon becoming so
    Bark opaque, chalky or ashy white, close, not regularly exfoliating
                     GRAY BIRCH, p. 168
    Bark lustrous, creamy to pinkish white, freely exfoliating
                     BLUE BIRCH, p. 169
  Leaves downy beneath at least when young, bark of young trunks warm brown, soon exfoliating and exposing the creamy white, thick, soft bark, freely exfoliating bark of mature trees   PAPER BIRCH, p. 175

Key F (To Oaks)

A. Veins of the leaves not running out beyond the margins in bristly tips. B.
  B. Blades coarsely sinuate-toothed or shallowly but not deeply lobed
     Foliage only slightly paler, not silvery or whitish, on the lower surface
                             CHESTNUT OAK, p. 206
       Foliage whitish or silvery below or very pale
       Leaves light yellow-green above, broadest near the middle
                             CHINQUAPIN OAK, p. 211
       Leaves dark green above, broadest above the middle
         Lobe-like, broad, rounded points of the leaves less than 12 to a side
                         SWAMP WHITE OAK, p. 204
         Lobe-like points of the margin more than 12 to a side
                             BASKET OAK, p. 209
  B. Blades deeply lobed half way, or nearly so, to the midrib
     Lower surface hairless at maturity   WHITE OAK, p. 195
     Lower surface more or less downy, hairy or woolly below even at maturity
       Blade deeply lobed only in the lower half of the leaf, the broad upper
         half merely deeply wavy-toothed   BUR OAK, p. 213
       Blade deeply lobed in upper as well as lower half
         Lobes rather narrow and pointed   OVERCUP OAK, p. 203
         Lobes rather broad and rounded   POST OAK, p. 202
A. Veins of the leaves running beyond the margins as bristly teeth. C.
  C. Blades narrowly oblong, not lobed, sometimes slightly angled
     Lower surface hairless   WILLOW OAK, p. 231
     Lower surface downy or woolly   SHINGLE OAK, p. 230
  C. Blades broader, deeply lobed or broadly angled. D.
    D. Leaves broadest above the middle, the lobes low and very wide and
       scarcely toothed, or no more than angled
                             BLACK JACK OAK, p. 233
    D. Leaves broadest at or below the middle
       Foliage dull above   NORTHERN RED OAK, p. 218
       Foliage shining above
         Foliage whitish or grayish below   SPANISH OAK, p. 220
         Foliage green on both sides
           Leaves of 2 sorts, those on lower branches short and broad with
             about 5 lobes, the sinuses between them going less than half
             way to the midrib, those on upper branches longer, with
             about 7 narrow lobes, and deep sinuses
                             SHUMARD OAK, p. 224
          Leaves alike on upper and lower branches
           Inner bark of branches yellow or orange
            Blades lobed only half way to the midrib
                            BLACK OAK, p. 225
          Blades lobed more than half way to the midrib

NORTHERN JACK OAK, p. 229
Inner bark not yellow or orange; blades lobed more than half
way to the midrib
Axils of the veins on the lower surface furnished with large
tufts of pale hairs PIN OAK, p. 227
Axils of veins below with only small tufts of rusty hairs, or
none SCARLET OAK, p. 222

Key G (To Apples)

Foliage at maturity hairy or downy IOWA CRAB, p. 325
Foliage at maturity hairless except some tufts in the veins
Blades 3 times as long as wide *Malus lancifolia*, p. 325
Blades broader
Leaves of flowering shoots distinctly heart-shaped at base
Malus glabrata, p. 325
Leaves of flowering branches narrowed or rounded at base, only those on
vigorous sterile shoots sometimes heart-shaped at base
Leaves at the ends of vigorous sterile shoots distinctly lobed
Leaves thin, light green beneath without a bloom
WILD SWEET CRAB, p. 323
Leaves thick, the lower surface with a bloom
Malus glaucescens, p. 325
Leaves at the ends of vigorous sterile shoots not, or scarcely, lobed
Foliage dull green above SOUTHERN CRAB, p. 327
Foliage lustrous above *Malus platycarpa*, p. 325

Key H (To Hawthorns)

A. Veins of the leaves extending both to the points of the lobes and to the sinuses
between them WASHINGTON THORN, p. 358
A: Veins of the leaves extending to the points of the lobes only. B.
B. Leafstalks very short, thick, usually more or less heavily wing-margined
above the middle; flowers appearing after the leaves. C.
C: Leaves leathery or thickish, dark green and shining above and usually
toothed only above the middle, with thin or deeply impressed veins,
or veins quite concealed within the tissue of the leaf
Leaves downy or hairy beneath even at maturity
ENGELMANN HAWTHORN, p. 365
Leaves hairless at maturity
Veins sunken within the tissues of the very thick leaves
COCKSPUR HAWTHORN, p. 364
Veins not as above; leaves only semi-leathery
Cratægus algens, p. 365

C. Leaves thin or thinnish, with prominent veins
> Stalks of the fruit clusters densely woolly
>> SANDHILL HAWTHORN, p. 363
> Stalks of the fruit clusters hairless
>> FLAT–TOPPED HAWTHORN, p. 360

B. Leafstalks more or less elongated, at any rate not or but slightly wing-margined. D.

D. Blades at base heart-shaped, rounded, truncate, or abruptly narrowed to a broadly wedge-shaped base. E.

E. Fruit ½ to ⅝ inch thick
> Fruit erect   GROVE HAWTHORN, p. 349
> Fruit drooping
>> Fruit distinctly angled, at first green and frosty, becoming dark purple-red late in the season; leaves oval, not more than 1 to 2 inches long   FROSTED HAWTHORN, p. 351
>> Fruit not or only slightly angled, not frosted though sometimes with a bloom early in the season
>>> Fruit ellipse-shaped, oval, or pear-shaped
>>>> VARIABLE HAWTHORN, p. 348
>>> Fruit compressed-spherical or nearly spherical
>>>> ALDER HAWTHORN, p. 349

E. Fruit ⅝ to ⅞ inch thick. F.

F. Fruit erect
> Leaves concave   *Cratægus Pringlei*, p. 346
> Leaves plane
>> Blades 2½ to 3 inches long   EGGERT HAWTHORN, p. 347
>> Blades 1½ to 2 inches long   *Cratægus filipes*, p. 352

F. Fruit drooping
> Fruit with a frosty bloom, borne on short stalks
>> NEW LONDON HAWTHORN, p. 348
> Fruit not with a frosty bloom, borne on slender stalks
>> Leafstalk and primary veins slender
>>> Leaves at maturity rough to the touch on the upper surface
>>>> SCARLET HAWTHORN, p. 345
>>> Leaves at maturity smooth above
>>>> HOLMES HAWTHORN, p. 346
>> Leafstalk and primary veins thick
>>> Blades rounded, truncate or heart-shaped at base
>>>> RED HAW, p. 341
>>> Blades broadly wedge-shaped at base
>>>> Leafstalks 1 to 2 inches long, bright red, winged near the apex   PILGRIMS' WHITETHORN, p. 344
>>>> Leafstalks ¾ to 1 inch long with dark red glands along the upper side   *Cratægus anomala*, p. 345

D. Blades at base narrowly wedge-shaped, that is, gradually acute to the leafstalk. G.

G. Upper surface of foliage harsh to the touch, the lower surface hairless
>> BRAINERD HAWTHORN, p. 367

G. Upper surface at maturity smooth or, if harsh, then the lower surface downy. H.

H. Foliage at maturity downy beneath, at least in the axils of the veins

Fruit erect　　　　　　　　　　　PEAR HAWTHORN, p. 365

Fruit drooping

Fruit juicy, nearly spherical; anthers 10 to 20, rose-colored

Leaves leathery, the midrib deeply impressed above

Cratægus succulenta, p. 367

Leaves thin; midrib but slightly impressed above

CHAPMAN HAWTHORN, p. 366

Fruit dry and mealy; anthers 20, pale yellow

GREENTHORN, p. 352

H. Foliage at maturity hairless on both sides

Leaves yellow-green and dull above

BOYNTON HAWTHORN, p. 357

Leaves dark green and shining above

Fruit covered with a frosty bloom

SHINING HAWTHORN, p. 354

Fruit not frosty

Fruit nearly spherical, dark crimson

ROUNDLEAF HAWTHORN, p. 356

Fruit longer than broad (short-oblong)

Fruit bright carmine red　　　*Cratægus Jonesæ*, p. 357

Fruit dull dark red, or rusty orange-red or yellow

MARGARET HAWTHORN, p. 355

Key I (To Plums and Cherries)

A. Leaves mostly gradually long-pointed to the tip. B.

B. Leaves flat-extended. C.

C. Blades with large lobe-like teeth, these again finely cut with gland-tipped teeth

Leafstalk bearing numerous scattered dark glands

GARDEN WILD PLUM, p. 376

Leafstalk glandless　　　　WILD BLACK CHERRY, p. 385

C. Blades simply toothed

Teeth glandless　　　　　　　FIRE CHERRY, p. 381

Teeth glandular

Leaves thick, firm, dark green and dull above

PURPLE SLOE, p. 375

Leaves thin, light green, shining on the upper surface

WILD GOOSE PLUM, p. 379

B. Leaves half folded trough-wise　　WILD RED PLUM, p. 373

A. Leaves shortly or abruptly pointed or rather obtuse

Teeth spreading, not glandular　　CHOKE CHERRY, p. 383

Teeth incurved, glandular　　　　CANADA PLUM, p. 371

Key J (To Maples)

Twigs after their second or third year of growth striped, like the bark of the trunk, with broad pale lines, and leaves with 3 terminal lobes all more or less forward-pointing   STRIPED MAPLE, p. 469
Twigs not striped, the 2 lateral of the terminal lobes more or less spreading
  Foliage silvery or heavily glaucous beneath
    Blades deeply palmately 5-lobed with many fine teeth
                                  SILVER MAPLE, p. 462
    Blades 3-lobed above the middle, with few teeth
                              CAROLINA MAPLE, p. 468
  Foliage paier beneath but not silvery and only rarely glaucous
    Teeth coarse and few
      Blades plane   SUGAR MAPLE, p. 453
      Blades with drooping sides   BLACK MAPLE, p. 460
    Teeth fine and numerous
      Blades rather longer than broad, coarsely and doubly toothed, stiff and thickish   RED MAPLE, p. 465
      Blades as broad as long, simply and glandular-toothed, rather soft and filmy   MOUNTAIN MAPLE, p. 470

Key K (To Lindens)

A. Lower surface of mature leaves hairless or nearly so. B.
  B. Twigs of summer shoots hairless
      Spring leaves practically hairless when unfolding, except for the axillary tufts of hairs; summer leaves sparsely hairy beneath, coarsely toothed; apex of bract rounded   AMERICAN LINDEN, p. 485
      Spring leaves hairy when unfolding but soon hairless; leaves of summer shoots with abundant light brown hairs on the lower surface, coarsely or finely toothed; apex of bract often pointed
                            Tilia alabamensis, p. 488
  B. Twigs of summer shoots downy or woolly; leaves averaging more than 3 inches wide, generally glaucous beneath   *Tilia venulosa*, p. 487
A. Lower surface of mature leaves woolly, downy, or felted. C.
  C. Leafstalks short, mostly under 1½ inches long; lower surface of sun leaves brownish white with an abundance of close clustered hairs; lower surface of bract with numerous clustered hairs; flowers small (¼ inch long) in clusters of 10 to 25   WHITE BASSWOOD, p. 488
  C. Leafstalks over 1½ inches long. D.
    D. Blades mostly finely toothed; lower surface of sun leaves white or nearly so, with thick branched hairs; axillary tufts almost none

Foliage thick; flowers about ⅓ inch long
>*Tilia heterophylla* var. *Michauxii*, p. 490

Foliage thin; flowers about ½ inch long   *Tilia truncata*, p. 490
D. Blades mostly coarsely toothed; under surfaces of leaves with rather thin
    downiness, and axillary tufts present and conspicuous; blades thick;
    flowers ⅛ inch long   *Tilia neglecta*, p. 488

Key L (To Ashes)

(Contributed by Norman C. Fassett)

A. Twigs round in cross-section
   B. Lateral leaflets stalked; rachis of leaf either evenly velvety or else smooth or
       with only a few white hairs at the base of the leaflets; body of fruit
       roundish, not winged to the base. C.
      C. Base of lateral leaflets with the two sides ending unevenly, usually rounded
          or making an angle of more than 45 degrees; the leaf scars near the
          middle of last year's twig crescent-shaped and rarely more than ⅓ as
          wide as long; body of mature fruit with more than 4 ridges which
          are usually indistinct   WHITE ASH, p. 566
      C. Base of lateral leaflets with the two sides ending evenly, usually making an
          angle of less than 45 degrees; leaf scars usually more than ½ as wide as
          long; body of mature fruit with 2 to 4 distinct ridges on each side. D.
         D. Twigs, leafstalks and leaflets velvety   RED ASH, p. 564
         D. Twigs, etc., hairless or with a few scattered hairs
                                                   GREEN ASH, p. 565
   B. Lateral leaflets not stalked; rachis of leaf with a dense tuft of reddish hairs at
       the base of each leaflet, otherwise hairless; fruit winged to the base, the
       body scarcely thickened   BLACK ASH, p. 559
A. Twigs 4-angled   BLUE ASH, p. 562

GLOSSARY

Aborted. Incompletely developed, defective in form.

Acidulous. Having acid properties and taste.

Akene. A dry, often seed-like fruit not opening or splitting on any natural sutures.

Alternate. Growing singly at the nodes (*q.v.*) on the stem or axis or rachis; not opposite (*q.v.*) nor in whorls (*q.v.*).

Anther. The part of a stamen which contains the pollen. Anthers consist in 1 or more pollen sacks opening variously by pores or slits. If there is no stalk or filament, then the anther of itself constitutes the entire stamen (*q.v.*) and is exactly synonymous with it.

Apetalous. Without petals.

Apex. The tip; the upper or outer end, farthest removed from the stalk, axis, or stem.

Appressed. Closely and flatly pressed against.

Aril. An appendage or outer covering of a seed, an outgrowth of the hilum (*q.v.*), sometimes appearing pulpy. Example: the Yew fruit.

Awl-shaped. Sharp-pointed and narrow.

Axil. The inner (upper) angle of a leaf with the stem, or of a scale with the axis.

Axillary. In the position of an axil.

Axis. The central shoot of a compound leaf, cone, inflorescence, or root, etc.

Bark. The outermost, often more or less corky or leathery cell layers on stems, branches, twigs, and roots, formed by the cambium cells. The bark of trees usually has two layers, the outer and the inner, more or less distinct in structure, texture, color, etc.

Base. The lower end of an organ, that is, the part nearest the stalk, stem, or axis of an organ.

Bast. The soft tissue of the fibers of wood, especially of the inner bark; often employed in making thread and rope.

Beard. Long bristle-like hairs, especially upon petals or styles.

Bearded. Having a beard (*q.v.*).

Berry. As defined by botanists (only) a fleshy fruit proceeding from the ripening of a single pistil but with more than one seed, the seeds not enclosed in a "stone." Example: tomatoes. Practically all fruits called berry by berry growers, as strawberry, blackberry, raspberry, blueberry, cranberry, are excluded by botanists from their definition of the word. The berries of the Juniper are really cones whose scales have become fused and pulpy but are in effect, if not in origin, berries.

Bisexual. Having the parts or organs of both sexes simultaneously, as a flower which contains both pollen and ovules.

Blade. The leaf, apart from its stalk.

Board foot. A unit of lumber measurement 1 foot long, 1 foot wide, and 1 inch thick, or an equivalent volume.

Bole. A tree trunk, especially that of a large tree.

Bract. A more or less modified leaf, generally subtending a flower, fruit, stalk, or flowering or fruit cluster, or head, or spike.

Bud. An incipient shoot bearing embryonic leaves or flowers or both.

Bushy. Having the growth form of a bush; that is, with numerous branches or shoots from the base but little or no central trunk.

Calyx. The outer series of envelopes of a

flower, generally green and more or less leaf-like but, in the absence of petals, sometimes petal-like. Usually the word calyx is used to denote all the component sepals (*q.v.*) especially when the sepals are united. See also *Tube, Limb, Lobe, Throat.*

Cambium. In trees, the thin layer of tissue just under the inner bark and just outside the wood, which by cell division increases the tree in diameter, giving off bark cells on the outside and wood cells on the inside.

Capsule. A compound pod; a dry, thin-walled, few- or many-seeded fruit splitting at maturity. Example: Rhododendron.

Carpel. A solitary pistil, or one of the units of a compound pistil.

Cartilaginous. Parchment-like, hard and tough.

Catkin. A more or less compact spike of mostly unisexual flowers. A term used generally of the peculiar inflorescences of certain trees, such as the Willows, Poplars, Walnuts, Hickories, Oaks, and more loosely, of the Conifers, having few or very reduced floral envelopes and those often consisting of bracts and scales rather than sepals and petals, while the flowers or florets are often reduced to the organs of the one sex or the other.

Checked. Said of bark, when it is marked by horizontal cracks or grooves.

Claw. The narrowed or stalk-like base of the petals or sepals of certain flowers.

Compound. Said of any organ composed of two or more similar parts. A compound leaf is one composed of 2 or more leaflets, as in the case of Walnuts and Locusts (see *Simple* for contrast). A leaf is once-compound when the leaflets are arranged on a single, unbranched axis or rachis. They are twice-compound when the axis or rachis is branched. A compound leaf may be known from a twig bearing simple leaves by the fact that there is a bud in the axil of a leaf but not of a leaflet.

Cone. A dense and more or less conical mass of flowers or fruits, or (more strictly) of seed-bearing scales, on a central axis. Loosely used for the fruits of Magnolias, Alders, etc.; but more specifically for the female inflorescence of the Pine Family. The cones of Pines and their relatives consist in the more or less woody, leathery, papery, or fleshy seed-bearing scales of the female catkins after fertilization, these arranged on a central axis forming a homogeneous fruit which generally detaches as a unit.

Conelet. A small, or immature, or ungrown cone. Commonly said of the female catkin of the Pine family.

Conifer. A member of the Pine family.

Coniferous. Of or pertaining to the Conifers.

Corolla. The inner series (petals, *q.v.*) of floral envelopes; used especially where the petals are fused at base into a common tube. See also *Tube, Throat, Limb, Lobe.*

Cortex. Surface, as of bark, or the bark-like rind of stems.

Deciduous. Naturally falling; said especially of the foliage of trees that become naked during the unfavorable seasons.

Declined. Bent downward.

Deflexed. Abruptly turned down.

Disc, disk. A more or less fleshy development of the receptacle (*q.v.*) of a flower around the pistil.

Dorsal. On the upper ("back") or outer face of an organ or part. (See *Ventral.*)

Drupe. A fleshy, 1-seeded fruit which contains a single stone which in turn contains the seed; a stone fruit. Examples: Plum, Cherry, Almond, Peach, Sassafras, Dogwood, etc.

Drupelet. A little drupe; more particularly one of a number of similar fruitlets in a compound fruit. Example: Mulberry.

Duct. A pit, chamber or gland, usually filled with sap, resin, or other secretion.

Ecological. Of or pertaining to ecology.

Ecologist. One who studies ecology.

Ecology. The life habits and interrelations of plants and animals with each other and with environmental influences. Botanical ecology has been picturesquely characterized as "the sociology of plants."

Endophytic. Within the tissues of a plant. Said particularly of certain fungi living symbiotically in the root and other tissues of trees.

Evergreen. Remaining green through the seasons; never naked of foliage. All "evergreens" eventually shed their leaves but not as do deciduous trees — all at once or before new growth appears.

Exfoliating. Peeling away in papery

plates or strips, as the bark of Syca-more, Birch, Eucalyptus, etc.

Exserted. Projecting beyond, as stamens which stand out beyond the corolla.

Female. Said of the flowers having ovules and (except in the conifers) ovaries, but not male organs (stamens, pollen). Said of inflorescences or of trees having only female flowers. See also *Male, Fertile, Perfect, Unisexual, Bisexual.*

Fertile. Capable of producing fruit. Sometimes used to denote flowers wholly female, or a pollen-bearing anther, as contrasted with a sterile one or staminodium. Also seed-bearing fruits.

Fertilization. Impregnation within the ovule of the egg cells by union with the sperm cells.

Filament. The stalk of an anther.

Flesh. The pulpy part of a fruit.

Flora. The plant population (or more strictly the flowering plants) of an area. Also a book dealing with their enumeration and identities.

Floral. Of or pertaining to flowers or inflorescences.

Floret. A little flower, especially when it is a part of a compact and specialized type of inflorescence such as a catkin, *q.v.*

Flower. There are two definitions of a flower: The older and more popular conceives the flower as consisting in the organs of one or both the sexes enveloped in sepals and, commonly, also in petals. This, however, could not include the Pines, Oaks, and fully one-third of our trees which yet have stamens and pistils, pollen and ovules, and bear fruits. The more scientific and inclusive definition depicts the flower as consisting primarily in reproductive organs (stamens and pistils, or pollen-bearing and ovule-bearing bracts and scales, as in the Pine Family). This definition does not, however, entirely exclude some of the fern-allies which are considered flowerless. There is, therefore, no perfect definition of this highly evolutionary and variable group of organs, the flower, but the second definition is much the better.

Follicle. A free pod-like fruit opening only on the front suture.

Free. Not joined to other organs; said, for instance, of stamens free from the petals or any ovary free from the calyx.

Frond. Used sometimes for a compound leaf or for a spray of foliage.

Fruit. The seed-bearing organ; the ovary or pistil and sometimes adjacent and cohering parts.

Fruitlet. A little fruit when it is a part of a compound fruit.

Furrowed. Marked with longitudinal grooves.

Genus. A group of species (*q.v.*) which resemble each other more than they differ, or an isolated species showing marked differentiation from any other. The first of the two Latin names of a plant.

Gland. A secreting pore or part or prominence often exuding resinous, sticky, oily, or sweet substances; said also of hairs terminating in a knob-like tip, especially when exuding clammy substances, and of the teeth of leaves when gland-like in appearance (thickened and colored), and of any colored prominences of gland-like appearance — as those on the leafstalks of Plums and Cherries.

Glandular. Of or pertaining to a gland or of gland-like appearance.

Glaucous. With a bloom or cast of a bluish white appearance.

Habit. The growth form of a plant.

Habitat. The situation, with regard to soil, light, temperature, and associated species, in which a plant grows.

Head. A compact cluster; a very short dense spike.

Heartwood. The hard, inner cylinder of a woody stem, consisting of dead and heavy and more or less dense wood elements, usually darker, from the deposition of tannin, gums, resins, and pigments, than the sapwood (*q.v.*).

Horizontal. At right angles to the (normally) up-and-down axis of growth.

Husk. The outermost covering of a fruit, usually of a heavy character — woody as in the case of the Walnut husk, leathery in the Locust pod, leafy in the hazelnut, and papery in the Hop Hornbeam's fruits.

Inferior. In a lower position. Said especially of ovaries which are adherent to, or surmounted by, the calyx.

Inflexed. Bent inwards.

Inflorescence. The reproductive shoot composed of shorter shoots bearing flowers.

Involucre. A whorl (*q.v.*) of small leaves or bracts subtending a flower or an inflorescence or fruit-cluster.

Irregular. Said of a flower when the parts or members of any one of the sets or series (particularly the petals) are unlike the others or eccentrically placed, or when the flower is bilaterally symmetrical.

Keel. A ridge like the keel of a boat, especially on a fruit or seed. Also the keel-shaped pair of united petals on the lower side of a flower of the pea family.

Lateral. On or at the side; not terminal.

Leaf. The lateral outgrowth of a stem or shoot, appearing from a bud, and usually flattened, veinous and, at maturity, green from the presence of chlorophyll; the principal photosynthetic organ of a tree. A leaf may consist in two parts, the stalk (when present) and the blade or leaf proper. Dimensions of leaves are usually given to include only the blade.

Leaflet. A single division of a compound leaf.

Legume. A pod opening by two sutures. Example: the pod of a pea.

Lenticel. A pore in the bark.

Limb. The flat or expanded part of an organ; in particular the flaring and lobed part of a corolla or calyx as distinct from its throat or tube. "Limb" in the sense of a branch of a tree is not usually employed in formal botanical descriptions.

Lip. One of the parts in an irregular corolla or calyx; usually the lower (or apparently lower) one.

Lobe. A segment of an organ usually separated from similar parts by a regular space or sinus, as in the lobed leaves of Oaks, or the lobed corolla of Rhododendron.

Male. Said of flowers which bear pollen and, except in the Pine Family, stamens. Said of a tree that bears only male flowers and never fruit.

Medullary. Relating to the pith. Medullary rays, seen in cross-sections and quartered cuts of woods, radiate from the pith.

Membranous. Thin and wide, membranelike.

Midrib. The central or main and heaviest rib or nerve or vein of a leaf or leaflet.

Needle. The peculiar, very long and narrow leaf, commonly triangular or plano-convex in cross-section, of Pines and (more loosely) of some of the relatives of Pines.

Nerve. A principal vein or slender rib, of a leaf, especially when it is one of several arising from the base of the blade.

Node. The point on a shoot, at which a branch, bud, leaf, or flower or other organ appears.

Nut. A hard, non-splitting fruit, usually 1-seeded even though sometimes the product of more than 1 carpel, the seed most often being a starchy kernel.

Nutlet. A small nut-like part, usually one of several, within a fruit.

Opposite. Said of leaves when they appear in pairs at the same node (*q.v.*) of the stem but on opposite sides of it; not alternate (*q.v.*) nor whorled (*q.v.*).

Ovary. The part of the pistil enclosing and bearing the ovules.

Ovule. The minute body, borne within the ovary and containing the female cells (eggs), which after fertilization becomes the seed.

Palmate. Veined, lobed, or divided as the fingers of the hand or like the leaf of a fan Palm.

Perfect. Said of flowers when they are bisexual (*q.v.*).

Persistent. Remaining attached, not falling off.

Petal. A member of the inner series of floral envelopes, standing between the sepals and the stamens, and usually thin and colored (not green). See also *Corolla.*

Pinna. The primary division of a compound leaf.

Pinnate. Said of a compound leaf with leaflets arranged along a common axis.

Pinnule. The secondary division or pinna of a leaf twice or more compound.

Pistil. The ovule-bearing and seed-bearing organ of a flower, consisting in the ovary (*q.v.*), the stigma (*q.v.*), and when present, the style (*q.v.*); the whole female organ. See also *Carpel.*

Pith. The soft, spongy, loosely cellular tissue found within the woody cylinder of a stem, most characteristic of twigs and seedlings.

Pod. A dry fruit, splitting or otherwise opening at maturity; as differentiated from a capsule, a pod is usually larger and thick-walled.

Pollen. The spores or grains containing

the male element and borne, except in the Conifers, in an anther (*q.v.*).

Pollination. The transfer of pollen from the anther to the stigma.

Polygamous. Bearing both perfect (*q.v.*) and unisexual flowers.

Pome. Fruit with papery inner wall and fleshy outer tissue, of which the apple is a type; also pear, quince, sarvisberry, and the fruits of Hawthorn, Mountain Ash, etc.

Polypetalous. Having separate, not united, petals.

Precocious. Coming to flower or fruit early in the year, or in the life of a plant.

Pubescence. Soft short hairs.

Pubescent. Covered with short soft hair.

Punctate. Having translucent dots or pits.

Rachis. Axis shoot of a compound leaf or inflorescence; the central stalk or mid-rib.

Receptacle. The elongated or enlarged end of a shoot or flower axis on which some or all of the flower parts are borne.

Regular. Said of a flower when the parts or members in each series (as sepals, petals, stamens, pistils) are like each other and symmetrically disposed on 3 or more radii.

Resin. Secretions, usually formed in special passages or chambers, either hard or liquid, usually aromatic, insoluble in water, soluble in alcohol, ether, or carbon disulphide, and burning with a sooty flame.

Resinous. Containing, bearing, or impregnated with resin (*q.v.*).

Ribs. Principal nerves, usually parallel or all arising from the base, of a leaf; sometimes, also, the ridges between furrows, on fruits, seeds, etc.

Ribbed. Having ribs (*q.v.*).

Root. The usually underground part of a plant distinguished from a stem by its origin at the opposite end of the embryo, and by its generally downward growth. Roots give rise to rootlets but never to buds or stems.

Sack (sac). A pouch or receptacle or cavity in an organ, as the pollen sacks of an anther.

Samara. A winged fruit not naturally splitting even at maturity. Examples: the fruits of Maples, Elms, Ashes.

Sapwood. The woody cylinder between the bark and the heartwood, usually paler than the heartwood, less heavy and dense, and more permeable.

Scale. A term used variously for different organs and appendages; often employed in connection with much reduced stem leaves and, in Conifers, with the small leaf-like appendages of the cone, between the woody bracts.

Scurfy. Flaky.

Seed. The ovule (*q.v.*) after fertilization, containing the embryonic plant, within one or more coats, and often accompanied by a store of starch — the endosperm or "meat."

Sepal. One of the leaves or lobes of the calyx (*q.v.*); usually said when the parts are not united at base.

Sheath. Any tubular structure surrounding an organ or part; the sheaths of Pines are short, papery tubes enclosing the base of the bundle of needles.

Shoot. Any growing axis of a stem, or a new plant or branch growing from an old one.

Short-shoot. A shortened and condensed and usually thickened branch or twig usually bearing flowers, or a tuft of foliage, or spines.

Simple. Said of leaves that are not compound, that have a single unbranched midrib engaged continuously with the blade.

Sinus. The space or bay between two lobes of an organ.

Species. The unit of classification, composed, as a rule, of individuals which resemble each other more than they differ, are inter-fertile, are frequently sterile to other species and breed true, reproducing their own kind.

Spike. A simple elongated cluster.

Spine. A sharp-pointed, strong, woody shoot.

Spore. A simple reproductive body, usually consisting in a detached cell.

Stalk. The stem of any organ as of a leaf, flower, inflorescence, anther, etc.

Stamen. The pollen-bearing or male organ. A single stamen, with or without floral envelopes, may, in the case of certain unisexual flowers, constitute a male flower. In bisexual flowers, the stamens usually stand outside the female organs but within or upon the floral envelopes.

Staminodium. (pl. *staminodia*). A sterile or aborted stamen, without anthers or pollen, usually more or less modified in form (club-shaped, flattened, etc.) or even petal-like.

Stem. The main axis of growth above ground, bearing the buds, leaves, and flowers, as contrasted with the root-bearing axis.

Stigma. The part of the pistil that receives the pollen. Generally it is somewhat sticky and of a definite form, but it may occupy only an indefinite or stigmatic area on the style (*q.v.*).

Stigmatic. Of or pertaining to the stigma; often said of that portion of a style functioning as, but not clearly separated as, a stigma (*q.v.*).

Stipule. Generally a little appendage-like part of a leaf, growing one on each side of the base of the leaf stalk and sometimes fused with it, sometimes deciduous.

Stoma (pl.: *stomata*). A breathing pore of a leaf.

Style. The stalk-like or columnar part of the pistil surmounting the ovary and upholding the stigma (*q.v.*). Frequently the style is branched, thus representing a union of styles. Sometimes the styles are separate to the base, representing a union of carpels (*q.v.*). Sometimes no stigma is present, and the styles merely exhibit a stigmatic surface on one or more sides.

Superior. Placed above; said of an ovary that is free from, and not surmounted by, the calyx.

Suture. A natural groove or line along which splitting takes place, especially in fruits.

Sylva. The forest trees of a region, collectively considered. A book dealing with the trees of an area.

Taproot. A vertical, strong, central root that continues growth, in line with the axis of the stem, straight down.

Terminal. At the end of a branch, shoot, style, etc.

Throat. The opening or orifice in a flower with united petals or united sepals at the point where the tube expands into the limb (*q.v.*).

Tortuous. Twisted, sinuous.

Transverse. Crosswise, across.

Tridentate. 3-toothed, especially at the apex of a part or organ.

Truncate. Cut off along a straight or essentially straight margin.

Tube. The unexpanded, more or less cylindrical and basal portion of a calyx (*q.v.*) or corolla (*q.v.*). See also *Throat* and *Limb.*

Turgid. Distended by pressure from within.

Twig. A branchlet; the ultimate division of a woody shoot.

Unarmed. Without thorns, prickles or spines.

Unisexual. Composed of one sex only; said of a flower having pollen *or* ovules, but not both.

Valve. The separable part of a pod or capsule; the walls of such fruits, between the sutures (*q.v.*).

Variety. A fraction of the unit of classification (species, *q.v.*); a group of individuals within a species set aside from others by their exclusive resemblances in minor ways.

Vein. A branch of the sap-conducting tissue, of a leaf, petal, scale, bract, seed coat, etc. See also *Veinlet, Midrib, Nerve.*

Veinlet. A secondary vein.

Veiny. With the veins heavily or darkly or intricately marked.

Venation. The system (variously patterned) of midribs, nerves, and veins in a leaf, petal, etc.

Venous. Of or pertaining to the veins or system of veins.

Ventral. On the under ("belly") or inner face of an organ or part. (See *Dorsal.*)

Vesicle. A chamber, blister, hollow, pit or duct, usually filled with sap, resin or other secretion.

Whorl. Three or more leaves or other organs arising in a circle from one node (*q.v.*) of a shoot.

Wing. A flat, thin expansion of an organ, as the corky wings of Sweet Gum twigs, the papery wings of Elm and Maple fruits, the winged leaf stalks of certain Hawthorns, or the winged seeds of Pines. The word is also used to denote the lateral petals of a flower of the pea family.

Winter Bud. A dormant, much condensed shoot formed during the previous season.

INDEX OF SCIENTIFIC NAMES

T HE WORDS in bold-face represent valid specific names; those in italics are synonyms referred to valid names. These synonyms, however, will not be found in the text of the book itself.

Abies americana Mill., see Tsuga canadensis
Abies balsamea (L.) Mill., 57
Abies canadensis Michx., see Tsuga canadensis
Abies canadensis Mill., see Picea glauca
Abies denticulata Michx., see Picea mariana
Abies Fraseri (Pursh) Poir., 59
Abies intermedia Fulling, see Abies balsamea
Abies mariana Mill., see Picea mariana
Acer barbatum Michx., see Acer saccharum
Acer carolinianum Walt., see Acer rubrum
Acer dasycarpum Ehrh., see Acer saccharinum
Acer eriocarpum Michx., see Acer saccharinum
Acer montanum Ait., see Acer spicatum
Acer Negundo L., 472
Acer nigrum Michx., f., 460
Acer pensylvanicum L., 469
Acer rubrum L., 465
  Var. **tridens** Wood, 468
Acer saccharinum L., 462
Acer saccharinum Wang., see Acer saccharum
Acer saccharophorum K. Koch, see Acer saccharum
Acer saccharum Marsh., 453
Acer spicatum Lamk., 470
Acer striatum Du Roi, see Acer pensylvanicum
Æsculus flava Ait., see Æsculus octandra
Æsculus glabra Willd., 477
Æsculus hybrida DC., see Æsculus octandra
Æsculus lutea Wang., see Æsculus octandra
Æsculus octandra Marsh., 479

Amelanchier arborea (Michx. f.) Fern., 335
Amelanchier Botryapium DC., see Amelanchier arborea
Amelanchier canadensis of Auths., not L., see Amelanchier arborea
Amelanchier lævis Wieg., 336
Andromeda arborea L., see Oxydendron arboreum
Anona triloba L., see Asimina triloba
Aralia spinosa L., 493
Argentacer saccharinum Small, see Acer saccharinum
Asimina triloba (L.) Dunal, 287

Betula alba var. *papyrifera* Spach, see Betula papyrifera
Betula alleghaniensis Britt., see Betula lutea
Betula cærulea-grandis Blanch., 169
Betula lenta L., 172
Betula lutea Michx. f., 170
Betula nigra L., 175
Betula papyrifera Marsh., 165
Betula populifolia Marsh., 168
Betula rubra Michx. f., see Betula nigra

Carpinus americana Michx., see Carpinus caroliniana
Carpinus caroliniana Walt. 155
Carpinus virginiana Mill., see Ostrya virginiana
Carya alba (L.) Nutt., see Carya tomentosa
Carya amara Nutt., see Carya cordiformis
Carya arkansana Sarg., see Carya texana var. arkansana
Carya cordiformis (Wang.) K. Koch, 146

Carya glabra (Mill.) Sweet, 129
Carya illinoënsis (Wang.) K. Koch, 148
Carya laciniosa (Michx. f.) Loud., 138
Carya megacarpa Sarg., see Carya ovalis
Carya microcarpa Nutt., see Carya ovalis
Carya ovalis (Wang.) Sarg., 141
Carya ovata (Mill.) K. Koch, 133
Carya pallida (Ashe) Engelm. & Graebn., 132
Carya Pecan Engelm. & Graebn., see Carya illinoënsis
Carya texana Buckl. var. arkansana (Sarg.) Little, 145
   Var. villosa (Sarg.) Little, 145
Carya tomentosa Nutt., 143
Carya villosa Schneid., see Carya texana var. villosa
Castanea dentata (Marsh.) Borkh., 189
Castanea pumila (L.) Mill., 190
Celtis lævigata Willd., 257
Celtis mississippiensis Bosc, see Celtis lævigata
Celtis occidentalis L., 255
   Var. canina (Raf.) Sarg., 257
   Var. crassifolia A. Gray, 257
Cerasus borealis Michx., see Prunus pensylvanica
Cerasus virginiana Michx., see Prunus serotina
Cercis canadensis L., 393
Chamæcyparis thyoides (L.) B.S.P., 71
Chionanthus virginica L., 555
Cladrastis fragrans Raf., see Cladrastis lutea
Cladrastis lutea (Michx. f.) K. Koch, 410
Cladrastis tinctoria Raf., see Cladrastis lutea
Cornus alternifolia L.f., 508
Cornus florida L., 503
Cratægus albicans Ashe, see Cratægus pedicellata
Cratægus algens Beadle, 365
Cratægus alnorum Sarg., see Cratægus basilica
Cratægus anomala Sarg., 345
Cratægus apiomorpha Sarg., see Cratægus macrosperma
Cratægus arborescens Ell., see Cratægus viridis
Cratægus arduennæ Sarg., see Cratægus Crus-galli
Cratægus arkansana Sarg., see Cratægus mollis
Cratægus basilica Beadle, 349
Cratægus Boyntonii Beadle, 357
Cratægus Brainerdi Sarg., 367
Cratægus callicarpa Sarg., see Cratægus coccinoides
Cratægus Calpodendron (Ehrhr.) Medic., 365

Cratægus campestris Britt., see Cratægus succulenta
Cratægus champlainensis Sarg., see Cratægus submollis
Cratægus Chapmani (Beadle) Ashe, 366
Cratægus chrysocarpa Ashe, 356
Cratægus coccinea L., see Cratægus pedicellata
Cratægus coccinoides Ashe, 347
Cratægus collina Chapm., 363
Cratægus corusca Sarg., see Cratægus pedicellata
Cratægus Crus-galli L., 364
Cratægus delecta Sarg., see Cratægus pedicellata
Cratægus deltoides Ashe, see Cratægus rugosa
Cratægus diffusa Sarg., see Cratægus filipes
Cratægus dilatata Sarg., 348
Cratægus Ellwangeriana Sarg., see Cratægus pedicellata
Cratægus Engelmannii Sarg., 365
Cratægus filipes Ashe, 352
Cratægus Gaultii Sarg., see Cratægus succulenta
Cratægus gemmosa Sarg., see Cratægus succulenta
Cratægus Holmesiana Ashe, 346
Cratægus illinoënsis Sarg., see Cratægus succulenta
Cratægus ingens Beadle, see Crat æguscollina
Cratægus Jonesæ Sarg., 357
Cratægus lobulata Sarg., see Cratægus Pringlei
Cratægus lucorum Sarg., 349
Cratægus macracantha Lodd., see Cratægus succulenta
Cratægus macrosperma Ashe, 348
Cratægus Margaretta Ashe, 355
Cratægus mollis (T. & G.) Scheele, 341
Cratægus neofluvialis Ashe, see Cratægus succulenta
Cratægus neolondinensis Sarg., see Cratægus dilatata
Cratægus nitida (Engelm.) Sarg., 354
Cratægus pausaica Ashe, see Cratægus punctata
Cratægus pedicellata Sarg., 345
Cratægus penita Beadle, see Cratægus collina
Cratægus pentandra Sarg., see Cratægus macrosperma
Cratægus Phænopyrum (L. f.) Medic., 358
Cratægus Pringlei Sarg., 346
Cratægus pruinosa (Wendl.) K. Koch, 351
Cratægus punctata Jacq., 360
Cratægus roanensis Ashe, see Cratægus macrosperma

Cratægus Robesoniana Sarg., see Cratægus pedicellata

Cratægus rotundifolia Moench, see Cratægus chrysocarpa

Cratægus rugosa Ashe, 351

Cratægus scabrida Sarg., see Cratægus Brainerdi

Cratægus sera Sarg., see Cratægus mollis

Cratægus sertata Sarg., see Cratægus pedicellata

Cratægus sordida Sarg., see Cratægus collina

Cratægus submollis Sarg., 344

Cratægus succulenta Schrad., 367

Cratægus tardipes Sarg., see Cratægus Holmesiana

Cratægus tenuifolia Britt., see Cratægus Holmesiana

Cratægus tomentosa L., see Cratægus Calpodendron

Cratægus viridis L., 352

Cratægus virilis Sarg., see Cratægus succulenta

Cupressus thyoides L., see Chamæcyparis thyoides

Cynoxylon floridum Raf., see Cornus florida

Diospyros virginiana L., 535

Fagus americana Sweet., see Fagus grandifolia

Fagus ferruginea Ait., see Fagus grandifolia

Fagus grandifolia Ehrh., 179

Fagus latifolia (Muench.) Sudw., see Fagus grandifolia

Fagus sylvatica var. *atropunicea* Marsh., see Fagus grandifolia

Fraxinus alba Marsh., see Fraxinus americana

Fraxinus americana L., 566

Fraxinus biltmoreana Beadle, see Fraxinus americana

Fraxinus campestris Britt., see Fraxinus pennsylvanica var. lanceolata

Fraxinus Darlingtonii Britt., see Fraxinus pennsylvanica

Fraxinus epiptera Michx, see Fraxinus americana

Fraxinus nigra Marsh., 559

Fraxinus pennsylvanica Marsh., 564
    Var. *lanceolata* (Borkh.) Sarg., see var. subintegerrima
    Var. **subintegerrima** (Vahl) Fern., 565

Fraxinus quadrangulata Michx., 562

Fraxinus sambucifolia Lamk., see Fraxinus nigra

Fraxinus viridis Michx. f., see Fraxinus pennsylvanica var. subintegerrima

Gleditsia aquatica Marsh., 406

Gleditsia monosperma Walt., see Gleditsia aquatica

Gleditsia spinosa Marsh., see Gleditsia triacanthos

Gleditsia triacanthos L., 403

Guilandina dioica L. see Gymnocladus dioica

Gymnocladus canadensis Lamk., see Gymnocladus dioica

Gymnocladus dioica (L.) K. Koch, 399

Halesia carolina Ellis, 545

Halesia monticola (Rehd.) Sarg., 546

Halesia tetraptera L., see Halesia carolina

Hamamelis virginiana L., 301

Hicoria alba Britt., see Carya tomentosa

Hicoria Buckleyi var. *arkansana* Ashe, see Carya texana var. arkansana

Hicoria Buckleyi var. *villosa* Ashe, see Carya texana var. villosa

Hicoria cordiformis Britt., see Carya cordiformis

Hicoria glabra Britt., see Carya glabra

Hicoria laciniosa Sarg., see Carya laciniosa

Hicoria microcarpa Britt., see Carya ovalis

Hicoria minima (Marsh.) Britt., see Carya cordiformis

Hicoria ovalis Ashe, see Carya ovalis

Hicoria ovata Britt., see Carya ovata

Hicoria pallida Ashe, see Carya pallida

Hicoria Pecan Britt., see Carya illinoënsis

Hicorius amara Raf., see Carya cordiformis

Hopea tinctoria Gard. see Symplocos tinctoria

Ilex ambigua Torr., see Ilex montana

Ilex canadensis Marsh., see Ilex opaca

Ilex montana T. & G., 449

Ilex monticola A. Gray, see Ilex montana

Ilex opaca Ait., 447

Juglans alba L., see Carya tomentosa

Juglans amara Michx. f., see Carya cordiformis

Juglans cathartica Cutler, see Juglans cinerea

Juglans cinerea L., 119

Juglans cordiformis Wang., see Carya cordiformis

Juglans glabra Mill., see Carya glabra

Juglans illinoënsis Wang., see Carya illinoënsis

Juglans laciniosa Michx., see Carya laciniosa

Juglans nigra L., 121

Juglans olivæformis Michx., see Carya illinoënsis

Juglans ovata Mill., see Carya ovata

Juglans Pecan Marsh., see Carya illinoënsis

Juglans porcina Michx. f., see Carya glabra
Juglans tomentosa Lamk., see Carya tomentosa
Juniperus canadensis Burgsd. see Juniperus communis
Juniperus caroliniana Mill., see Juniperus virginiana
Juniperus communis L., 77
Juniperus Sabina Hook., see Juniperus virginiana
Juniperus sibirica Burgsd., see Juniperus communis
Juniperus virginiana L., 79
  Var. **crebra** Fernald & Griscom, 80

Kalmia latifolia L., 523

Larix americana Michx., see Larix laricina
Larix laricina (Du Roi) K. Koch, 33
Laurus Sassafras L., see Sassafras albidum.
Liquidambar Styraciflua L., 307
Liriodendron Tulipifera L., 267

Magnolia acuminata L., 275
Magnolia auriculata Lamk., see Magnolia Fraseri
Magnolia Fraseri Walt., 281
Magnolia macrophylla Michx., 279
Magnolia tripetala L., 277
Magnolia umbrella Lamk., see Magnolia tripetala
Malus angustifolia (Ait.) Michx., 327
Malus coronaria (L.) Mill., 323
Malus fragrans, Rehder, see Malus coronaria
Malus glabrata Rehd., 325
Malus glaucescens Rehd., 325
Malus ioënsis (Wood) Britt., 325
Malus lancifolia Rehd., 325
Malus platycarpa Rehd., 325
Mohrodendron carolinum Britt., see Halesia carolina
Morus rubra L., 261

Negundo aceroides Moench, see Acer Negundo
Negundo Negundo Karst., see Acer Negundo
Nyssa biflora Walt., see Nyssa sylvatica
Nyssa multiflora Wang., see Nyssa sylvatica
Nyssa sylvatica Marsh., 497
  Var. **caroliniana** (Poir.) Fern., 500

Ostrya virginiana (Mill.) K. Koch, 161
Ostrya virginica Willd., see Ostrya virginiana
Oxydendrum arboreum (L.) DC., 529

Padus nana Borkh., see Prunus virginiana

Padus virginiana Mill., see Prunus serotina and Prunus virginiana
Pavia lutea Poir., see Æsculus octandra
Pavia ohioensis Michx. f., see Æsculus glabra
Picea alba Link, see Picea glauca
Picea australis Small, see Picea rubens
Picea balsamea Loud., see Abies balsamea
Picea canadensis Link., see Tsuga canadensis
Picea canadensis (Mill.) B.S.P., see Picea glauca
Picea Fraseri Emerson, see Abies balsamea
Picea glauca (Moench) Voss, 45
Picea mariana (Mill.) B.S.P., 47
Picea nigra Link, see Picea mariana
Picea rubens Sarg., 50
Picea rubra (Du Roi) Link, see Picea rubens
Pinus alba Michx., see Picea glauca
Pinus americana Du Roi, see Tsuga canadensis
Pinus americana Gaertn., see Picea mariana
Pinus balsamea L., see Abies balsamea
Pinus Banksiana Lamb., 17
Pinus canadensis L., see Picea glauca
Pinus divaricata (Ait.) Du Mont, see Pinus Banksiana
Pinus echinata Mill., 26
Pinus Fraseri Lodd., see Pinus rigida
Pinus hudsonia Poir., see Pinus Banksiana
Pinus inops Ait., see Pinus virginiana
Pinus laricina Du Roi, see Larix laricina
Pinus mitis Michx., see Pinus echinata
Pinus nigra Ait., see Picea mariana
Pinus pungens Lamb., 29
Pinus resinosa Ait., 15
Pinus rigida Mill., 20
Pinus rubra Lamb., see Picea rubens
Pinus rubra Michx. f., see Pinus resinosa
Pinus rupestris Michx. f., see Pinus Banksiana
Pinus serotina Michx., 24
Pinus squarrosa Walt., see Pinus echinata
Pinus Strobus L., 3
Pinus Tæda L., 24
Pinus variabilis Lamb., see Pinus echinata
Pinus virginiana Mill., 27
Platanus glabrata Fern., see Platanus occidentalis
Platanus occidentalis L., 315
Populus angulata Ait., see Populus deltoides
Populus angulata var. *missouriensis* Henry, see Populus deltoides
Populus aurea Tidestr., see Populus tremuloides
Populus balsamifera L., 98
  Var. **candicans** (Ait.) A. Gray, 100

Populus canadensis Moench, see Populus balsamifera

Populus candicans Ait., see Populus balsamifera var. candicans

Populus carolinensis Moench, see Populus balsamifera

Populus cercidiphylla Britt., see Populus tremuloides

Populus deltoides Bartr., 92

Populus grandidentata Michx., 90

Populus heterophylla L., 96

Populus Michauxii Dode, see Populus balsamifera var. candicans

Populus monilifera Ait., see Populus balsamifera

Populus Sargentii Dode, 95

Populus tacamahacca Mill., see Populus balsamifera

Populus tremuliformis Emerson, see Populus tremuloides

Populus tremuloides Michx., 87

Populus trepida Pursh, see Populus tremuloides

Populus virginiana Foug., see Populus deltoides

Porcelia triloba (L.) Pers., see Asimina triloba

Prinos ambigua Michx., see Ilex montana

Prunus alleghaniensis Port., 375

Prunus americana Marsh., 373

Var. **lanata** (Sudw.) Mack. & Bush, 375

Prunus demissa Dietrich, see Prunus virginiana var. demissa

Prunus eximia Small, see Prunus serotina

Prunus hortulana Bailey, 376

Prunus lanata Mack. & Bush, see Prunus americana var. lanata

Prunus Munsoniana Wight & Hedr., 379

Prunus nana Du Roi, see Prunus virginiana

Prunus nigra Ait., 371

Prunus pensylvanica L. f., 381

Prunus serotina Ehrh., 385

Prunus virginiana L., 383

Var. **demissa** (Nutt.) Torr., 385

Ptelea angustifolia Benth., see Ptelea trifoliata

Ptelea Baldwinii T. & G., see Ptelea trifoliata

Ptelea coahuilensis Greene, see Ptelea trifoliata

Ptelea crenulata Greene, see Ptelea trifoliata

Ptelea jucunda Greene, see Ptelea trifoliata

Ptelea microcarpa Small, see Ptelea trifoliata

Ptelea pentandra Moç. & Sessé, see Ptelea trifoliata

Ptelea rhombifolia Heller, see Ptelea trifoliata

Ptelea serrata Small, see Ptelea trifoliata

Ptelea tomentosa Raf., see Ptelea trifoliata

Ptelea trifoliata L., 433

Ptelea verrucosa Greene, see Ptelea trifoliata

Pyrus americana DC., see Sorbus americana

Pyrus bracteata Bailey, see Malus bracteata

Pyrus coronaria L., see Malus coronaria

Pyrus glabrata Bailey, see Malus glabrata

Pyrus ioënsis Bailey, see Malus ioënsis

Pyrus lancifolia Bailey, see Malus lancifolia

Pyrus platycarpa Bailey, see Malus platycarpa

Quercus acuminata Sarg., see Quercus Muehlenbergii

Quercus alba L., 195

Quercus Alexanderi Britt., see Quercus Muehlenbergii

Quercus ambigua Michx. f., see Quercus borealis

Quercus bicolor Willd., 204

Quercus borealis Michx. f., 218

Quercus Castanea Mühl., see Quercus Muehlenbergii

Quercus coccinea Muenchh., 222

Quercus digitata (Marsh.) Sudw., see Quercus falcata

Quercus ellipsoidalis Hill, 229

Quercus falcata Michx., 220

Quercus ferruginea Michx. f., see Quercus marilandica

Quercus imbricaria Michx., 230

Quercus lyrata Walt., 203

Quercus macrocarpa Michx., 213

Quercus marilandica Muenchh., 233

Quercus Michauxii, see Quercus Prinus

Quercus minor (Marsh.) Sarg., see Quercus stellata

Quercus montana Willd., 206

Quercus Muehlenbergii Engelm., 211

Quercus obtusiloba Michx., see Quercus stellata

Quercus olivæformis Michx. f., see Quercus macrocarpa

Quercus pagoda Raf., see Quercus falcata var. pagodæfolia

Quercus palustris Muenchh., 227

Quercus Phellos L., 231

Quercus platanoides (Lamk.) Sudw., see Quercus bicolor

Quercus Prinus L., 209

Var. **acuminata** Michx. f., see Quercus Muehlenbergii

Var. **discolor** Michx. f., see Quercus bicolor

Var. **monticola** Michx. f., see Quercus montana

Var. **palustris** Michx. f., see Quercus bicolor

Quercus rubra L., 218
Quercus Shumardii Buckl., 224
Quercus stellata Wang., 202
Quercus tinctoria Bartr., see Quercus velutina
Quercus triloba Michx., see Quercus falcata
Quercus velutina Lamk., 225

Rhododendron maximum L., 517
Rhush hirta Sudw., see Rhus typhina
Rhus typhina L., 437
Rhus venenata DC., see Rhus Vernix
Rhus Vernix L., 439
Robinia Pseudo-Acacia L., 415
    Var. rectissima Raber, 419
Robinia viscosa Vent., 421
Rufacer carolinianum Small, see Acer rubrum var. tridens
Rufacer rubrum Small, see Acer rubrum
Rulac Negundo Hitch., see Acer Negundo

Sabina virginiana Antoine, see Juniperus virginiana
Saccharodendron barbatum (Michx.) Nieuwl., see Acer saccharum
Saccharodendron nigrum Small, see Acer nigrum
Salix amygdaloides Anderss., 107
Salix Bebbiana Sarg., 113
Salix caroliniana Michx., 108
Salix discolor Muhl., 111
Salix fluviatilis Nutt., see Salix interior
Salix interior Rowlee, 110
Salix longifolia Muhl., see Salix interior
Salix ligustrina Michx. f., see Salix nigra
Salix missouriensis Bebb, 114
Salix nigra Marsh., 105
Salix Wardii (Bebb) Schneid., see Salix caroliniana
Sassafras albidum (Nutt.) Nees, 291
Sassafras officinale Nees & Eberm., see Sassafras albidum
Sassafras Sassafras (L.) Karst., see Sassafras albidum
Sassafras variifolium Ktze., see Sassafras albidum
Sorbus americana Marsh., 331
Sorbus decora (Sarg.) Schneid., see Sorbus americana
Strobus Strobus Small, see Pinus Strobus
Strobus Weymouthiana Opiz, see Pinus Strobus
Svida alternifolia Small, see Cornus alternifolia
Symplocos tinctoria (Gard.) L'Hér., 551

Thuja occidentalis L., 65
Tilia alba Michx. f., see Tilia heterophylla var. Michauxii
Tilia alabamensis Ashe, 488
Tilia americana L., 485
Tilia americana Marsh., see Tilia neglecta
Tilia canadensis Michx., see Tilia americana
Tilia cinerea Spach, see Tilia truncata
Tilia eburnea Ashe, see Tilia heterophylla var. Michauxii
Tilia glabra Vent., see Tilia americana
Tilia heterophylla Vent., 488
    Var. Michauxii (Nutt.) Sarg., 490
Tilia Michauxii Nutt., see Tilia heterophylla var. Michauxii
Tilia Michauxii Sarg., see Tilia neglecta
Tilia monticola Sarg., see Tilia truncata
Tilia neglecta Spach, 488
Tilia nigra Borkh., see Tilia americana
Tilia tenera Ashe, see Tilia heterophylla
Tilia truncata Spach, 490
Tilia venulosa Sarg., 487
Toxicodendron pinnatum Mill., see Rhus Vernix
Toxicodendron Vernix Ktze., see Rhus Vernix
Tsuga canadensis (L.) Carr., 39
Tsuga caroliniana Engelm., 41
Tulipastrum acuminatum Small, see Magnolia acuminata

Ulmus alata Michx., 248
Ulmus americana L., 237
Ulmus fulva Michx., 250
Ulmus pubescens Walt., see Ulmus fulva
Ulmus racemosa Thomas, see Ulmus Thomasii
Ulmus rubra (Ait.) Michx. f., see Ulmus fulva
Ulmus Thomasii Sarg., 246
Ulmus viscosa Michx., see Ulmus fulva

Viburnum prunifolium L., 513
Virgilia lutea Michx. f., see Cladrastis lutea

Wallia cinerea Alef., see Juglans cinerea
Wallia nigra Alef., see Juglans nigra

Xanthoxylum americanum, see Zanthoxylum americanum

Zanthoxylum americanum Mill., 427

INDEX OF ENGLISH NAMES

Acacia, Bastard, 415
  False, 415
  Three-thorned, 403
  Thorny, 403
Aguebark, 433
Aguetree, 291
Alligatorwood, 307
Angelicatree, 427, 493
Anise, Pickaway, 433
Apple, 321
  American Crab, 323
  Custard, 287
  Iowa Crab, 325
  Southern Crab, 327
  Thorn, 341
Arbor-Vitae, 63, 65
Arrowwood, 529
Ash, 557
  American, 566
  Basket, 559
  Bastard, 564
  Biltmore, 556
  Black, 559, 564
  Blue, 562
  Brown, 559, 564
  Flowering, 555
  Green, 565
  Hoop, 255, 559
  Mountain, 331
  Poison, 437
  Prickly, 425, 427, 493
  Red, 564
  River, 564
  Swamp, 559
  Wafer, 433
  Water, 559
  White, 566
  Yellow, 410
Aspen, Bigtooth, 90
  Quaking, 87
  Trembling, 87
Balm-of-Gilead, 98, 100

Balsam, 57
  He-, 50
  Northern, 56
  She-, 57
  Southern, 57
Bam, 98
Banana, Wild, 287
Bass, 485
Basswood
  Common, 485
  White, 488
Bay, Rose, 517
Beech, 177
  American, 179
  Blue, 155
  Water, 155, 315
Beetree, 488
Belltree, 545
Bellwood, 545
Birch, 163
  Bitter, 170
  Black, 172, 175
  Blue, 169
  Canoe, 165
  Cherry, 172
  Gray, 168, 170
  Mahogany, 172
  Paper, 165
  Poplar-leaved, 168
  Poverty, 168
  Red, 175
  River, 175
  Silver, 165, 170
  Sweet, 172
  White, 165
  Wire, 168
  Yellow, 170
Black Haw, 513
Box Elder, 472
Buckeye
  Big, 479
  Fetid, 477

Ohio, 477
  Stinking, 477
  Sweet, 479
Butternut, 119
Buttonballtree, 315
Buttonwood, 315

Calicoflower, 523
Calicotree, 523
Calicowood, 545
Canoewood, 267
Cedar, 65
  Eastern Red, 79
  Northern White, 65
  Pencil, 79
  Post, 71
  Southern White, 71
  Swamp, 71
Cherry, 369
  Bird, 381
  Choke, 383
  Fire, 381
  Pigeon, 381
  Pin, 381
  Red, 381
  Rum, 385
  Whiskey, 385
  Wild Black, 385
  Wild Red, 381
Chestnut, 187
  American, 189
  Horse, 475
Chinkapin, 190
Chinquapin, 190
Coffeebean, 399
Coffeenut, 399
Coffeetree, 397
  Kentucky, 399
Confederate Pintree, 404
Cornel, 501, (see also Dog-
  wood)
  Alternate-leaved, 508

Pagoda, 508
Umbrella, 508
Cottontree, 92, 96
Cottonwood, Big, 92
Black, 96
Eastern, 92
Great Plains, 95
River, 96
Swamp, 96
Western, 95
Yellow, 92
Crab, American, 323
Bechtel, 325
Fragrant, 323
Iowa, 325
Narrow-leaved, 327
Southern, 327
Sweet-scented, 323
Wild Sweet, 323
Cucumbertree, 275
Ear-leaved, 281
Custard Apple, 287
Cypress, False, 69

Date Plum, 535
Dogwood, (see also Cornel)
Alternate-leaved, 508
Blue, 508
Flowering, 503
Poison, 439
Purple, 508
Striped, 469
Swamp, 433
Virginian, 503
Dyebush, 551

Ebony, 533
Elder, Box, 472
Poison, 439
Prickly, 493
Elkwood, 277
Elm, 235
American, 237
Cliff, 246
Cork, 246
Cork bark, 246
Hickory, 246
Mountain, 248
Red, 248, 250
River, 237
Rock, 246
Slippery, 250
Small-leaved, 248
Soft, 237
Water, 237
White, 237
Winged, 248
Witch, 248

Fairy-circle, 77
Fetidshrub, 287
Fir, 55
Balm-of-Gilead, 57
Balsam, 57
Fraser, 57
Flowering Ash, 555
Fringetree, 553, 555

Garlandtree, 323
Gopherwood, 410
Gorst, 77
Greenthorn, 352
Gum, Black, 497
Red, 307
Sap, 310
Sour, 497, 529
Star-leaved, 307
Sweet, 307
Yellow, 499
Gumtree, 307

Hackberry, 253, 255
Mississippi, 257
Sugar, 257
Hackmatack, 31, 77
Haw (see also Hawthorn), 339
Black, 513
Dotted, 360
Red, 341
Sugar, 365
Sweet, 513
Tree, 352
Hawthorn, 339
(see also Haw and Thorn)
Alder, 349
Boynton, 357
Brainerd, 367
Chapman's, 366
Downy, 341
Eggert, 347
Engelmann, 365
Flat-topped, 360
Frosted, 351
Grove, 349
Maple-leaved, 358
Margaret, 355
New London, 348
Pear, 365
Roundleaf, 356
Scarlet, 345
Shining, 354
Variable, 348
Virginia, 358
Hazel, Snapping, 301
Winter, 301
Witch, 301

He-Balsam, 50
Hemlock, 37
Canadian, 39
Carolina, 41
Eastern, 39
Hercules'-club, 427, 491, 493
Hickory, 127
Arkansas, 145
Big bud, 143
Big Shellbark, 138
Bitternut, 146
Black, 129, 145
Broom, 129
Brown, 129
Pig, 146
Red, 141
Sand, 132
Scalybark, 133
Shagbark, 133
Shellbark, 133
Swamp, 146
White, 143
Whiteheart, 143
Holly, 445
American, 447
Christmas, 447
Evergreen, 447
Mountain, 449
Prickly, 447
Honeyshucks, 403
Hoop Ash, 255, 559
Hop Hornbeam, 159
American, 161
Hoptree, 431, 433
Hornbeam, 153
American, 155
Hop, 159
Horse Chestnut, 475
Horse-sugar, 551

Indian-bitter, 275
Ironwood
Eastern, 161
Rough-barked, 161
Smooth-barked, 155
Ivy, Bigleaf, 523
Mountain, 523
Poison, 523

Judastree, 393
Juneberry, 335, 336
Juniper, 75
Common, 77
Dwarf, 77
Ground, 77
Virginia, 79

Kingnut, 138

Larch, 31
  American, 31
  Black, 31
  Red, 31
Laurel, Big, 517
  Bigleaf, 517
  Deertongue, 517
  Florida, 551
  Great, 517
  Mountain, 521
  Poison, 523
  Sheep, 523
Lily-of-the-Valley-tree, 529
Lime, 485
Limetree, 485
Lin, 485
Linden, 483
  American, 485
  White, 488
Liquid-amber, 307
Locust, 413
  Black, 403, 415
  Clammy, 421
  Green, 415
  Honey, 403, 415
  Old-fashioned, 420
  Post, 415
  Red, 415
  Rose-flowering, 421
  Shipmast, 419
  Sweet, 401, 403
  Thorny, 403
  Water, 406
  White, 415
  Yellow, 410, 415

Magnolia, 273
  Fraser, 281
  Large-leaved, 279
  Mountain, 281
Mahogany, Mountain, 174
Maple, 451
  Ash-leaved, 472
  Black, 460
  Carolina, 468
  Creek, 462
  Goosefoot, 469
  Hard, 453
  Low, 470
  Manitoba, 472
  Moose, 470
  Mountain, 470
  Northern, 469
  Red, 465
  River, 462
  Rock, 453
  Scarlet, 465
  Silver, 462
  Soft, 462

Striped, 469
Sugar, 453
Swamp, 462, 465
Virginia, 315
Water, 462, 470
White, 462
Mockernut, 143
Moosewood, 469
Mountain Ash, 331
Mountain Laurel, 521
Mountain Mahogany, 174
Mulberry, 259
  Red, 261

Nannyberry, 513
Nettletree, 255
Nickertree, 399

Oak, 193
  Basket, 209
  Black, 225, 229
  Black Jack, 233
  Brash, 202
  Box, 202
  Bur, 213
  Chestnut, 206, 211
  Chinkapin, 211
  Chinquapin, 211
  Cow, 209
  Dyer's, 225
  Eastern White, 195
  Gray, 218
  Hill's, 229
  Iron, 202
  Jack (see also Black, and
    Northern Jack)
  Mossycup, 213
  Mountain, 206
  Northern Jack, 229
  Northern Laurel, 230
  Northern Red, 218
  Overcup, 203
  Pin, 227
  Post (see also Swamp
    Post), 202
  Red (see also Northern,
    and Southern and
    Swamp Red)
  Rock, 206, 211
  Scarlet, 222
  Scrub, 233
  Shingle, 230
  Shumard, 224
  Southern Red, 220
  Spanish (see also Swamp
    Spanish), 220
  Swamp Post, 203
  Swamp Red, 224
  Swamp Spanish, 222

Swamp White, 204
Tanbark, 225
Willow, 231
Yellow, 211, 225, 229
Old-man's-beard, 555
Olive, Wild, 545
Opossumwood, 545

Pawpaw, 285, 287
Pecan, 148
Pepperidge, 497
Persimmon, 535
Peruve, 332
Pigeonberry, 508
Pigeontree, 493
Pignut, 129
  Oval, 141
Pine, 1
  Banksian, 17
  Black, 17, 20
  Blister, 57
  Bull, 24
  Bur, 29
  Fir, 57
  Gray, 17
  Hard, 15
  Hemlock, 39
  Hickory, 29
  Jack, 17
  Jersey, 27
  Loblolly, 24
  Longstraw, 24
  Marsh, 24
  Meadow, 24
  Nigger, 27
  North Carolina, 26
  Norway, 15
  Old-field, 24
  Pitch, 20
  Pocosin, 24
  Pond, 24
  Prickly, 29
  Princess, 17
  Pumpkin, 3
  Red, 15
  River, 27
  Rosemary, 24
  Sap, 20
  Sapling, 3
  Scrub (see Virginia), 17
  Shortleaf, 26
  Silver, 57
  Soft, 3
  Southern
    Mountain, 29
  Spruce, 39
  Table Mountain, 29
  Torch, 20
  Virginia Scrub, 27

Weymouth, 3
White, 3
Yellow (see Shortleaf)
Plane, 315
Planetree, 315
Plum, 369
  Canada, 371
  Date, 535
  "Chickasaw Chief," 378
  Garden Wild, 376
  "General Jackson," 378
  "Golden Beauty," 379
  "Goose Egg," 380
  Goose, Wild, 379
  "Hinckley," 378
  Horse, 371
  Hortulan, 376
  "Isbell," 378
  "King of Plums," 380
  "Late Yellow Chicka-
    saw," 379
  "Miner," 377, 378
  Munson, 379
  "Nolan," 380
  "Old Hickory," 378
  Porter's, 375
  "Tennessee," 380
  "Townsend," 378
  Thorn, 364
  Wild Goose, 379
  Wild Red, 373
  "William Dodd," 378
  Woolly-leaf, 375
Poisontree, 439
Poisonwood, 439
Poplar, 85
  Aspen, 87
  Balm-of-Gilead, 98, 100
  Balsam, 98
  Bigtooth, 90
  Carolina, 92
  Necklace, 92
  Quaking, 87
  Rough-barked, 98
  Sargent, 95
  Tulip, 267
  White, 90, 267
  Yellow, 267
Popple, 87, 90, 267
Possumwood, 535
Prickly Ash, 425, 427, 493

Quininetree, 433

Rattlebox, 545
Redbud, 391, 393
Rhododendron, Big, 517
  Late, 517
  Summer, 517

Rose Bay, 517
Rowanberry, 331
Rowantree, 329
  American, 331

Sarvissberry, 336
Sarvisstree, 336
Sassafac, 291
Sassafras, 289, 291
Savin, Horse, 77
Saxifraxtree, 291
Serviceberry, 335, 336
Servicetree, 336
Shadblow, 333, 335
Shadbush, 335, 336
She-Balsam, 57
Sheepberry, 513
Shellbark, Big, 138
  Bottom, 138
  Thick, 138
  Western, 138
Shotbush, 493
Shumack (see Sumac),
  435
Silverbell, 543
  Common, 545
  Mountain, 546
Sloe, Allegheny, 375
  Purple, 375
  Snowdroptree, 545
Sorreltree, 527, 529
Sourwood, 529
Spikenardtree, 493
Spitberry, 427
Spoonwood, 523
Spruce, 43
  Black, 48
  Bog, 48
  Cat, 45
  Double, 48
  Hemlock, 39
  Red, 50
  Single, 45
  Skunk, 45
  White, 45
  Yellow, 50
Stagbush, 513
Sting-Tongue, 427
Stumptree, 399
Suga, 39
Sugarberry, 257
Sugartree, 453
Sumac, 435
  American, 437
  Mountain, 331
  Poison, 439
  Staghorn, 437
  Velvet, 437
  Virginia, 437

Sumach, see Sumac
Suterberry, 427
Sweet Gum, 305, 307
Sweetleaf, 549, 551
Sycamore, 313, 315

Tacamahac, 98
Tamarack, 33, 98
Thorn, 341
  Cockspur, 364
  Foothill, 363
  Green, 352
  Newcastle, 364
  Pear, 365
  Plum, 364
  Washington, 358
  White, 344
Thunderwood, 439
Tisswood, 545
Toothache-tree, 427, 493
Trefoil, Shrubby, 433
Tuliptree, 265, 267
Tupelo, 495, 497, 499

Umbrellatree, 277

Viburnum, 513
Vinegartree, 437
Virgilia, 410

Wahoo, 248
Wait-a-bit, 427
Walnut, 117
  Bitter, 146
  Black, 121
  Pig, 146
  White, 119
Whistlewood, 469
Whitethorn, Pilgrims', 344
Whitewood, 92, 267, 315,
  485
Willow, 103
  Almond, 107
  Beak, 113
  Bebb, 113
  Black, 105
  Glaucous, 111
  Missouri, 114
  Peach, 107
  Pussy, 111
  Sandbar, 110
  Swamp, 105
  Ward, 108
Winetree, 331
Wingseed, 433
Winterbloom, 301
Witch Hazel, 299, 301

Yellowwood, 409, 410, 551